P9-DTD-272

THE SPIRIT SOLDIERS

A Historical Narrative of the Boxer Rebellion

Other books by RICHARD O'CONNOR

IRON WHEELS AND BROKEN MEN

THE IRISH: *Portrait of a People*

O. HENRY:
The Legendary Life of William S. Porter

THE CACTUS THRONE

THE FIRST HURRAH

PACIFIC DESTINY

THE GERMAN-AMERICANS

AMBROSE BIERCE: *A Biography*

BRET HARTE: *A Biography*

JACK LONDON: *A Biography*

GOULD'S MILLIONS

BLACKJACK PERSHING

Richard O'Connor

The Spirit Soldiers

A HISTORICAL NARRATIVE

OF THE BOXER REBELLION

G. P. PUTNAM'S SONS   *New York*

Copyright © 1973 by Richard O'Connor

*All rights reserved. This book, or parts thereof, must not
be reproduced in any form without permission.
Published on the same day in Canada
by Longman Canada Limited, Toronto.*

SBN: 399–11216–2

Library of Congress Catalog Card Number: 73–81401

PRINTED IN THE UNITED STATES OF AMERICA

Contents

6   Contents

Illustrations appear after page 190

The reconstruction of China's thought is not to be accomplished by the wholesale transplantation of the thoughts of another society; it must follow the natural development and must begin with the proper retention of elements of the old social order.

—L. T. CHEN, *History of Chinese Political Thought*

Prelude

For decades the Western powers, more recently joined by czarist Russia and imperial Japan, had been dismembering the Chinese Empire, dividing it into what they called spheres of influence. During the past sixty years China had suffered a series of defeats and humiliations, each seemingly worse than the previous one, each increasing the Chinese bewilderment at the inability of their own superior civilization to fend off the "outside barbarians." Foreign expeditionary forces of regimental size had time and again easily defeated the Manchu imperial armies.

China was being "zoned" out of existence as an independent power. From 1839 to 1842 there had been the Opium War, in which the British forced the Chinese to allow the importation of opium and to open certain ports to trade with the West. In 1858 Russia seized the territory north of the Amur River. In 1860 France and Britain, charging that China had violated the Treaty of Tientsin, landed forces at Tientsin, marched on Peking, destroyed the Summer Palace, and forced China to grant Britain a ninety-nine-year lease on Kowloon. The Manchu seat, the Forbidden City, was sacked, and the French General Charles Cousin-Montauban, subsequently dubbed the Comte de Palikao for his services as a looter, sent back a splendid matched set of black pearls to the Empress Eugénie. Two years later Portugal assumed squatter's rights over the island of Macao, France occupied a large part of Annam, and the British annexed Lower Burma—a banner year for colonialism. In 1867 the French colonial army in Indochina seized three more provinces and took control of the Mekong River basin. Four years later Russia gnawed off a large piece of Chinese Turkestan, part of which was returned to China in exchange for a sizable indemnity. In 1879 Japan, feeling the stir of expansionist ambitions, occupied the Liu-ch'iu Islands. In 1886 Britain took over Upper Burma, and a year later France completed its conquest of Indochina and acquired 18,000,000 more colonial subjects. There was a lull of eight or nine years during which the various powers digested their new territories. Then in 1894 Japan recovered its appetite, forced a war on China, soundly beat it, and by the Treaty of Shimonoseki obtained the independence of Korea, soon to be violated by its protector, and was ceded Formosa and the Pescadores.

That outrage was compounded soon afterward by the blunt demands of Kaiser Wilhelm's Germany, which had come late to the feasting table but with a ravenous appetite for distant possessions from which the German flag could flaunt the Prussian double eagle as an equal of the French tricolor and the Union Jack.

There was no single cause of that uprising known as the Boxer Rebellion but an interweaving of many strands: the festering resentment of a people who had always believed that theirs was the Celestial Kingdom, whose peace had been disturbed by nations thousands of miles away, who had come to hate the presence of foreign missionaries and their unsought ministrations, who believed they were being oppressed by inferior races. But one strand of that tangle of motives, impulses, and resentments has been tagged as the crucial one. A French historian, naturally enough and rightly in this case, blamed the blowup on the Germans; Henri Cordier identified German clumsiness as "not the sole but the principal cause" of the Boxer Rebellion.

Germany indeed had behaved with something less than the imperial grace of the French and British in falling upon a large morsel of the Chinese carcass. In 1895 it had demanded the right to establish a coaling station on the coast, which the Chinese refused. The following year two German priests in Shantung, the rich peninsular province jutting into the Yellow Sea, were murdered. Using this as a pretext, Berlin ordered its warships to Kiaochow, seized the port, and also occupied Tsingtao. Germany in addition obtained mining and railway concessions in Shantung, which became a German sphere of influence.

Shantung was rapidly converted into a sort of Oriental Prussia, with *verboten* signs all over the place, engineers swarming, and missionaries proselytizing everywhere. Within a few years Tsing-tao was converted into a Far Eastern Düsseldorf, the most orderly, the neatest, cleanest and least Chinese, the best-fortified city in China. "The area," as the deposed Chancellor Prince Bismarck dourly observed, "is large enough for us to commit plenty of follies." Kaiser Wilhelm, who had a gift for vivid but unfortunate phrase-making, sent his brother Prince Heinrich to the China Station with a number of warships and the admonition "If anyone at all should try encroaching on our rights, go at him with a mailed fist!"

The harshness of the German policy only compelled the admiration of the rival powers. Russia, by way of emulation, demanded and obtained a lease on Port Arthur and Darien, along with the right to build a railroad connecting them with the Trans-Siberian rail system. The *Times* of London commented on November 16, 1897, that Germany, "instead of wasting time making remonstrances at Peking, which would assuredly have been met as usual with the innumerable dilatory devices of Chinese diplomacy," had acted with admirable dispatch. Taking that semiofficial organ's suggestion at its face value, the French seized the important anchorage of Kwangchowwan on the South China coast. The British secured a twenty-five-year lease on Weihaiwei. Even the Italians put forth a claim, demanding cession of a naval station on Sanmen Bay in Chekiang Province.

Just before the turn of the century China felt itself to be in the position of a corpse laid out on the international dissecting table. In six decades it had become a patchwork of spheres. Germany had claimed Shantung for its area of influence, the British had staked out the whole Yangtze Valley, Russia dominated Manchuria, Japan was taking over Fukien Province opposite Formosa, and France had earmarked the provinces of Yunnan, Kweichow, and Kwangsi in addition to Indochina. In all those regions the foreign powers claimed the right to trade, develop mining concessions, and build railroads. There was virtually nothing left to China and its 350,000,000 people but the privilege of serving their foreign masters, directly or indirectly.

By the last year of the century, however, the imperial government was beginning to take a more resistant attitude. Peking firmly informed Italy that if it set foot in Chekiang Province, it would be met by all the available imperial military force. And on November 21, 1899, an imperial edict was issued to the viceroys and governors of all the provinces, reading:

> The present situation is becoming daily difficult. The various Powers cast upon us looks of tiger-like voracity, hustling each other in their endeavors to be the first to sieze upon our innermost territories. In view of China's present financial and military strength, we surely would not start any war on our part. But there may occur incidents in which we are forced to face the situation. Should the strong enemies become aggressive and press us to consent to certain things which we can never accept, we have no alternative but to rely upon the justice of our cause, the knowledge of which will strengthen our resolve and steel us to a united front against our aggressors. . . . With such a country as ours, with her vast area, stretching out for several tens of thousands of *li*, her immense natural resources and her hundreds of millions of inhabitants, if all would prove their loyalty to the Emperor and love of their country, what indeed is there to fear from any strong invader? Let us not think of making peace, nor rely solely upon diplomatic maneuvers.

The growing spirit of resistance flamed highest in the province of Shantung. The people of that province were noted for their tough-minded independence, their sturdy sense of individuality. If there was one province where the "mailed fist" which Kaiser Wilhelm urged his emissaries to exhibit was not likely to make the hoped-for impression, it was Shantung. The idea of being converted into Teutonic Asians was resisted with spirit and resourcefulness by the Shantungese. They protested against the extension of the German railroads, which were throwing thousands of boatmen out of work, and with equal vehemence against the German missionaries who interfered with native courts when Chinese Christians were involved. Whenever the Chinese resistance became too daunting, German punitive expeditions were sent into the interior to destroy whole villages.

That was the genesis of the Boxer movement. A secret society, or underground movement, called in Chinese the Fists of Righteous Harmony, which was translated into the Boxers by the foreigners, sprang up in Shantung and spread to the neighboring province of Chihli.

The exact origins of the Boxers are still somewhat dim and mysterious, subject to the disputation of various China scholars. It seems clear, however, that they antedated their appearance in Shantung at the end of the nineteenth century.

Secret societies had been embedded in Chinese culture since before Christ. The various Triad groups have been examined in detail by Dennis Bloodworth (*The Chinese Looking Glass*), who finds that their activities threaded through every phase of Chinese history. Often their purpose was patriotic, such as when the Triad societies dedicated themselves to restoring the Ming dynasty and throwing out the Manchus, who came down from the north in 1644 and maintained their supremacy until 1911. Always they were surrounded by elaborate ritual, a belief in magic, a reliance on incantations and exotic ceremony to prevail against physical force. Bloodworth noted:

> Within their lodges, secret-society office-bearers don the elaborate paraphernalia laid down for their hierarchy, and a headman is a phantasmagoric figure solemnly clothed in what appears to be the ceremonial regalia of a slightly absent-minded high priest. He wears a red headband with five loops in it and a red robe inscribed with the mystic symbols of Chinese cosmology. His left fist is laid across his breast, the middle and little fingers extended in the secret sign that indicates his rank. . . .
> The Triads have a complicated system of hieratical tattoo marks, and a multitude of slogans and test phrases, secret finger and hand signals, recondite ways of holding everyday objects like teacups and umbrellas and chopsticks. . . .

One of the more powerful secret societies was the White Lotus, which was credited with having helped drive out the Mongols and which later revolted against the Ming dynasty when it became corrupt. Various authorities have decided that the Boxers were an offshoot of the White Lotus, as well as having affiliations with the Eight Diagram Sect, the Red Fists, and the Big Knives.

Even before the Boxers sprang up in Shantung, the Big Sword

Society was reported active in the province. Li Ping-heng, the provincial governor, sent a memorial to Peking labeling the Big Swords a "heretical sect" which was stirring up trouble. "The riots now stirred up by the secret societies," he reported in July, 1896, "have origin in the conflicts between the people and the Christians. . . . The reason they could not live together peacefully is that the Christians, with the support and protection of the missionaries, bullied and oppressed the common people."

It was not until almost two years later, according to Professor Chester C. Tan (whose work *The Boxer Catastrophe* is the definitive authority on the origins of the Boxer Rebellion), that the Boxers were first mentioned in the dispatches of the Shantung and Chihli authorities. The Fists of Righteous Harmony, who had been suppressed by imperial edict in 1808, sprang back to life in the spring of 1898. In September, 1899, a rural magistrate and scholar named Lao Nai-hsuan published a treatise titled *Study of the Origins of the Boxer Sect* which identified them as an offshoot of the Eight Diagram Sect, which had been active in Shantung, Chihli, and Kiangnan early in the nineteenth century, then slumbered underground until the spring of 1898. By then they had attracted the unfavorable attention of the imperial governors, not so much because they were circulating handbills in Shantung and Chihli advocating the slaughter of Christians as because they were regarded as enemies of the Manchu overlords.

The provincial government, not to mention the German occupation forces in Shantung, had every reason to be wary of the growing popular appeal of the Boxer society. In October, 1898, the Boxers managed to assemble a thousand followers to attack the house of a Chinese Christian in Kuanhsien and drive him and his family away. A short time later they killed two Christians and wounded a third, also in Kuanhsien, and burned down a chapel and twenty houses in Weihsien.

The sources of the Boxers' growing appeal for the Chinese masses are easily determined. They were also plentiful. First they appealed to the anti-Christian sentiment of much of the populace. The unconverted majority was repelled by Christian fervor, which indeed is difficult to comprehend seven decades later when Christianity has lost its militancy. As Pat Barr put it in a book recently published in Britain (*To China with Love*), "Exactly why the Taylors of Barnsley were so feverishly determined to convert the Wangs of Ningpo to their own deep, narrow brand of Christianity remains a mystery to the lay mind." The Chinese could no more understand the missionaries' determination to "save" them than the missionaries could grasp why the benighted Chinese, inhabiting a country which (as one said) "stank in its every part," should resist their efforts.

Inevitably, too, the Chinese had come to resist the inordinate influence of a mere 2,000 missionaries, Catholic and Protestant, embedded in their hundreds of millions. Nathaniel Peffer has observed:

> Given the fundamental elements in the situation—the West impinging by force on the East—and given the nature of human beings as well, the difficulties were inherent and inescapable. Indeed, had it not been for the discrepancy in power between the two races, they would have been greater, would have caused more upheavals and more bloodshed. . . . The meeting of peoples of different color, tradition, and habits is always precarious at best. . . . And when the one that imposes himself on the other seeks to force his conception of God and the universe on the other, when he strikes at that which is deepest in the other, the intervention of providence alone can prevent an explosion. Such an imposition the missionaries made or attempted to make in China. . . .

It was also true that most missionaries were poorly prepared for the task of proselytizing among people of an ancient and sophisticated culture, that many of them were unaware that the Chinese even had a religion or philosophy of their own. Many of them, educated in some cornfield seminary, went forth in a spirit of arrogance which the early Christian Fathers would have found abhorrent. The missionaries, Peffer wrote, "publicly ridiculed the most sacred of Chinese beliefs—ancestor worship, the Confucian precepts, and religious rites in temples. . . . In many places they were known to charge into temples while Chinese were worshipping and denounce them for bowing to idols. When they made converts they compelled them to break with all the practices of the community, the clan and the family."

In exercising an often muscular brand of Christianity the missionaries were protected by the doctrine of extraterritoriality, under which no foreigner could be punished by a Chinese court. "If a missionary made himself unbearably offensive and the wrath of the community mounted," Peffer continued, "the local mandarin sought to calm it down. . . . What was worse, he soon extended his immunity to his Chinese converts. . . . An alien irritant had been injected into the Chinese social body and it was bound to fester."

Another source of the Boxers' appeal was their extraordinary claims, which only confirmed the missionaries' conviction that all Chinese were ignorant and superstitious. They guaranteed the invulnerability of their followers to the foreign devils' weapons. And they promised a tremendous victory over the forces which had been oppressing them, declaring that "eight million spirit soldiers will descend from heaven and sweep the empire clean of all foreigners." In the Boxers' lexicon the foreigners were "first-class devils," Chinese converts to Christianity were "second-class devils," and those who worked for or collaborated with foreigners were "third-class devils."

To the Chinese mind, with its fascination with theatrics, there was also the considerable attraction of the ritual surrounding the Boxers' program to drive out the foreigners through the superiority of the Chinese spirit and its affinity with an unseen world ruled by demigods and the heroes of a legendary past. The Boxers wore red ribbons around their wrists, yellow sashes, and yellow talismans. Their shamans conducted demonstrations in which a musket (loaded with a blank cartridge) was fired at a follower and the presumed bullet had no effect on him. They murmured incantations which induced a trancelike state, and they had all sorts of secret recognition signals and passwords. Westerners inclined to sneer at "mumbo jumbo" might have recalled that back in their own countries there were lodges and secret societies with equally outlandish pretensions and gaudier regalia.

But it was the claim of invulnerability, coupled with the promised protection of ancient gods, which was the most appealing of all the Boxers' propaganda. One incantation summoned up all sorts of invisible powers to the side of the Harmonious Fists:

The instructions from the God Mi T'o to his Disciples—proclaiming upon every mountain by the Ancient Teachers—reverently inviting the Gods from the central southern mountains, from the central eight caves—your Disciple is studying the Boxer art, to preserve China and destroy Foreigners. The Iron Lo Han, if cut with knife or chopped with axe, there will be no trace. Cannon cannot injure, water cannot drown. If I urgently invite the Gods they will quickly come, if I tardily invite them they will tardily come, from their seats in every mountain cave. Ancient Teachers, Venerable Mother, do swiftly as I command. . . .

In addition to gathering followers by the thousands, the Boxer propagandists were adept at stirring up hatred of the foreigners and their religion. They claimed that the Catholic Church sheltered fugitives from Chinese justice, that Chinese children were mutilated in Christian orphanages, that Chinese women were lured into Christian churches to be raped. The old China hands among the Americans may have been away from their native land too long to realize it, but much of the Boxer doctrine resembled that of the Ghost Dancers, many of whom were massacred at Wounded Knee in 1890; the Ghost Dancers, using a similar ritual to induce trances, to obtain invulnerability against the whites' guns, believed they could drive their own "foreign devils" away and bring the buffalo back to the Great Plains. The Chinese, however, were more sophisticated than the Sioux and other Ghost Dancers, and operated clandestine printing presses to circulate thousands of handbills and proclamations among the people of Shantung and Chihli. One such handbill, issued by the "Lord of Wealth and Happiness," promised to bring back the life-giving rains, as well as to drive out the foreign troops:

The Catholic and Protestant religions being insolent to the gods, and extinguishing sanctity, rendering no obedience to Buddha, and enraging Heaven and Earth, the rain clouds no longer visit us; but eight million Spirit Soldiers will descend from Heaven and sweep the Empire clean of all foreigners. Then will the gentle showers once more water our lands; and when the tread of soldiers and the clash of steel are heard heralding woes to all our people, then the Buddhist Patriotic League of Boxers will be able to protect the Empire and to bring peace to all its people. Hasten, then, to spread this doctrine far and wide, for if you gain one adherent to the faith your own person will be

absolved from all future misfortunes. If you gain five adherents
your whole family will be absolved from all future misfortunes,
and if you gain ten adherents your whole village will be absolved
from all calamities. Those who gain no adherents to the cause
shall be decapitated, for until all foreigners have been exterminated the rain can never visit us.

Disregarding the fact that the Boxers were originally anti-Man-
chu as well as antiforeigner and constituted a sketchy under-
ground revolutionary movement, many Westerners then living in
China believed they had been secretly organized by the authorities
in Peking. This was the view of Sir Robert Hart, the chief of the
Chinese Customs Service, in his memoir *These from the Land of
Sinim.* They regarded it as incredible that such a sizable movement could spring up without encouragement from the Forbidden
City. This theory of the Boxers as a shadowy extension of the
Manchu grandees was adopted by Professor George N. Steiger of
Yale, whose *China and the Occident* was the leading scholarly
work on the subject until Professor Chester C. Tan published his
book based on an exhaustive study of all the available Chinese
sources. "It is impossible to believe," Steiger wrote, "that a secret
society, holding heretical doctrines and known to have revolutionary aims, would deliberately go out of its way to institute a
campaign of bitter hostility against Christian missions, and thus
stir up against itself the activities of the officials and the
complaints of the foreign diplomats. Such procedure would have
been contrary to all that is known of the history of secret societies in China, and is without precedence in the history of the
country."

Many secret societies, in both the near and far distant past, had
set themselves up as an underground opposition to the ruling
dynasty. They had organized against the Mongols and the Mings
just as they now opposed the Manchus as a corrupt regime which
had failed to protect China from repeated foreign invasions. That
the Manchus later succeeded in diverting the Boxers from their
opposition to the throne, in amalgamating with the Boxers for the
common fight against the foreigners, does not prove they sponsored such a potentially dangerous sect. In dismantling Steiger's
theory, Professor Tan pointed out that if the Boxers were a form
of militia organized by the Manchu authorities, "it is necessary to

explain why they took such miraculous formulae as were characteristic of the secret and heretical societies. Their charms and
incantations, their intricate ritual, and their belief in certain
supernatural powers which would render them invulnerable and
invincible, all savored heavily of heresy."

There were too many punitive campaigns undertaken against
the Boxers to indicate a conspiracy between them and the imperial
government, and besides, late in 1898, the dowager empress issued
an edict calling for the organization of a militia in provinces where
foreign pressure and intervention were the greatest:

> As to the militia, they only require to undergo regular training
> for a sufficient period to know the military tactics; they then
> could be relied upon in case of emergency. We therefore decree
> that these matters be started first in Chihli, Mukden, and
> Shantung and then in other provinces. Generals, viceroys, and
> governors of the various provinces must advise the gentry and
> common people, so that these measures may be carried out with
> the utmost energy.

The Boxers and the newly raised militia at first were uneasy
bedfellows. The former must have suspected that the latter had
been organized to wipe out the Boxer movement. In March, 1899,
however, Chang Ju-mei was replaced as governor of Shantung by
Yu Hsien, who was violently antiforeign and apparently let it be
known that he looked upon the Boxer societies with favor. The
Boxers became increasingly active in the Pingyuan district, where
they took over whole villages and openly flourished their swords,
spears, and rifles. In October about 300 Boxers went on a rampage
and looted the homes of Chinese Christians in that district. The
regional magistrate, Chiang Kai, apparently unaware that his
superior favored the Boxers, sent provincial troops against the
Boxers, and twenty-seven of them were killed in a pitched battle.
Governor Yu Hsien removed Chiang Kai from office and
cashiered the commander of the provincial troops.

For the rest of 1899 the Boxers operated with impunity under
the patronage of the provincial governor. They felt so encouraged,
in fact, that on December 30, 1899, the first *white* Christian was
killed by a Boxer band. The victim was the Reverend S. M.
Brooks, an English missionary in Shantung, who was cut down

when he tried to escape from his Boxer captors. There was a series of sharp protests, particularly from the German and English legations in Peking, over the way things were going in Shantung.

Two Boxers were executed and another was sentenced to life imprisonment for the killing of the Reverend Mr. Brooks. Yu Hsien was replaced as governor of Shantung by Yuan Shih-kai, a strong law-and-order man. But the dowager empress' edict of January 11, 1900, only further aroused the apprehensions of foreigners; she appeared to be viewing the situation with a benign approval and to be cautioning regional officials against acting too harshly against the dissidents:

> Recently in all the provinces brigandage has become daily more prevalent, and missionary cases have recurred with frequency. Most critics point to seditious societies as the cause, and ask for rigorous suppression and punishment of them. But societies are of different kinds. When worthless vagabonds form themselves into bands and sworn confederacies, and relying on their numbers create disturbances, the law can show absolutely no leniency to them. On the other hand, when peaceful and law-abiding people practice their skill in mechanical arts for the self-preservation of themselves and their families, or when they combine in village communities for the mutual protection of the rural population, this is only a matter of mutual help and mutual defense. Some local authorities, when a case arises, do not pay attention to this distinction, but listening to false and idle rumors, regard all alike as bandit societies, and involve all in one indiscriminate slaughter. The result is that, no distinction being made between the good and the evil, men's minds are thrown into doubt and fear. . . .

Obviously the dowager empress was slyly encouraging the employment of "mechanical arts"—such as sword swinging?—against the foreigners whenever it was deemed necessary for "self-preservation." Or so it seemed to many of the diplomats in Peking. The British, German, American, French, and Italian ministers joined in protesting the edict but were ignored by the dowager empress and the Manchu court. They were further dismayed when she issued three edicts warning Governor Yuan

Shih-kai against "relying solely on military force" to put down the disorders in his province and to be "extremely careful" in dealing with dissidents. Members of her court, as it was later learned, were already urging that the Boxers be incorporated into the provincial militia.

If he had not been reined in by orders from Peking, Yuan Shih-kai undoubtedly could have suppressed the Boxers early in 1900. Then, suddenly, it was too late. In the spring of 1900 anarchy spread throughout North China. Both natural and economic causes, as well as the underlying resentment of the people, contributed to the flash-point condition. The opening of the Peking-Tientsin railroad, followed by the construction of the Peking-Paoting section of the line which was to connect the imperial capital with Hankow, threw thousands of carters and boatmen out of employment. The newly built telegraph was regarded as an affront to the spirits of the air and water.

Worst of all had been the natural disasters which struck Shantung and Chihli provinces with particular force and which the Chinese peasantry blamed on the foreign presence as an intolerable affront to their ancestral gods, various sprites, and demons.

Two successive harvests having failed, there was widespread famine in the two most affected provinces. A plague of locusts only added to the general misery. On top of that the Yellow River had flooded its banks and washed over hundreds of villages.

Throughout the provinces of Shantung and Chihli there was an increase in rioting and disorder, burning out of Chinese Christians, destruction of churches and chapels. Behind most of those incidents could be discerned the agitation of the Boxers, now directed more at foreigners and Chinese converts than at the Manchu throne. The magistrates charged with maintaining order in the outlying districts were so concerned about the growing anarchy that five of them called a conference in Chihli, but their recommendation for immediate action against the Boxers got lost in the channels of a waffling bureaucracy, the like of which had not been seen since the fall of the last Byzantine emperor. The disintegration was allowed to continue, it was almost becoming a part of imperial policy.

In mid-March, 1900, a *North China Herald* correspondent wrote contemptuously of the "droll drill of the Boxers" and the "flummery and rigamarole" of their rituals. People in the Peking foreign colony found it amusing. It was just about the last time the foreigners in China found anything laughable about the Boxers.

I. THE HOUR OF THE DOG

The East bowed low before the blast
In patient, deep disdain;
She let the legions thunder past
And plunged in thought again.

—MATTHEW ARNOLD

1. *Foreign Devils First Class*

A small Japanese steamship plying the Yellow Sea between Japan and the Chinese coast, the SS *Nagato*, lay off the port of Chefoo the morning of April 1, 1900. An impenetrable fog covered the barren coastline of Shantung Province. Along with a number of other ships beating their way up the North China coast, the *Nagato* had dropped her anchor hours before rather than risk running aground. Among the more impatient passengers were Mrs. Edwin H. Conger, her daughter Laura, and four ladies from the States who were to be the Conger family's guests. Mrs. Conger, the former Sarah Pike, was the wife of the United States minister to Peking and was eager to prove to her Stateside friends what a marvelous Christian work was being done in China by the Americans and other enlightened Westerners.

Mrs. Conger was a determined woman, a devout Christian Scientist, with an inquiring and reflective mind, as her letters from China (later published in her memoir) amply demonstrate. Early in 1898 her husband had been appointed to the Brazilian legation, but when William McKinley assumed the Presidency, Conger was promoted to Peking. Like President McKinley, Conger was a Civil War veteran, and the two men became friends while serving together in the Congress. The Congers were transferred to Peking late in 1898. In the autumn of the following year Mrs. Conger and her daughter had gone home to Iowa for a visit while her husband, using the cruiser *Princeton* for transport, inspected the American consulates strung along the China coast.

Now Mrs. Conger was anxious for a reunion with her husband, who was supposed to meet her with a steam launch this day in the anchorage off the Taku Bar and escort her in style to Tientsin and home. They had been becalmed for a day and a half. It was irritating that she could not advise the captain as she would her husband under such circumstances; she was one of those strong-willed American women, what Thomas Beer would call Tita-nesses, newly conscious of their prerogatives.

She had to remind herself that a Japanese was commanding the *Nagato* and that he wouldn't be impressed by a mere female's unsought suggestions. "The Captain is running this ship according to sea rules and I must 'hands off,'" she wrote in her diary that day. "The ship is clean; the cabins are roomy; there is good service; we are comfortable . . . but we do want to go on."

It was two more days before the fog-dispelling wind came up and the *Nagato* was able to proceed toward the Taku anchorage. The captain's caution had been justified. On the way up the coast they came across lifeboats filled with passengers from a ship which had run aground. The lifeboats were picked up; the *Nagato* steamed on to Tientsin.

Mrs. Conger faced the future without trepidation. Before she had left China, she had heard reports of the Boxer activities but did not take them seriously enough to prevent her from bringing her four friends, as well as her young daughter, for a carefree summer in Peking.

Yet she was aware that "a spirit of discontent" was running high throughout North China. She wrote her sister:

> The anti-foreign thought has been openly growing for many months, and for the past few months it has presented itself in organized and organizing bands called Boxers. These are com-posed of the coolie class. As there has been no rain for many months, and as famine threatens this great mass of people, they say there is a cause for the gods of rain not answering their prayers. They believe that the "foreign devils" have bewitched their gods, poisoned their wells, brought sickness upon their children, and are striving to ruin them completely. The Boxers

come together and go through all sorts of strange rites and incantations to win back the good spirits . . .

Such concerns were forgotten, however, in the excitement of landing at Tientsin. "Happy, happy day!" as she later wrote in her diary.

Her stolid, bearded husband came out to the *Nagato* in a launch commandeered from the U.S. Navy which, like those of other Western nations, maintained a watchful presence off Taku.

Handkerchiefs and parasols waved. Mrs. Conger and her ladies were helped into the launch by the sailors, followed by their luggage. Immediately on landing they were swathed in diplomatic prerogatives which the Congers, homespun and down-to-earth Middle Westerners though they might be, were learning to accept with an unembarrassed air.

A special train was waiting to whisk Mrs. Conger and her Stateside friends off to Peking, with breakfast laid on in the dining car. Shortly before noon they steamed into Machiapu station just outside the walls of the imperial capital. Immediately they were enveloped by the special bouquet of the Peking air, the pungent ingredients of which were the sesame oil used in Chinese cooking, garlic, manure (or night soil, as polite Westerners called it), beetroot, and an extra something, indefinable and penetrating, which the explorer Sir Ernest Shackleton called the "smell of the moth-eaten centuries."

Sedan chairs were waiting—it was regarded as undignified for Western ladies to be seen on foot, rubbing shoulders with coolies—and the luggage followed in a string of carts. They entered the city through the YungTing Gate, passed through the thronging outer city with its busy shops and crowded outdoor markets, then came to another massive wall surrounding the Tatar City, inside which lay the Legation Quarter. Beyond the Tatar Wall were the well-guarded mysteries of the Imperial City, tightly enclosed from the importunities of a world the Manchu aristocracy viewed with disdain, and inside that the Forbidden City, where the dowager empress lived and conspired at the dynastic heart of the empire. As foreigners always said, Peking was like a Chinese nest of boxes, with always one more mystery to be penetrated.

Mrs. Conger's homecoming was as ceremonial and picturesque as she had promised her guests it would be. Their sedan chairs were borne through the streets of the Legation Quarter. In Legation Street they stopped in front of the American compound and parted the side curtains of their sedan chairs to find the servants lined up and kowtowing just inside the gates. A fireworks display was set off to celebrate the return of the minister's lady.

"I go from room to room rejoicing," as Mrs. Conger wrote in her diary, "and our beautiful Chinese things speak to me."

She soon settled into the diplomatic routine, picnics out on the Western Hills, tea parties, formal calls, staid dinners at the British legation and livelier ones at the French, lawn parties given by the gallant old bachelor Sir Robert Hart, chief inspector of the Imperial Chinese Customs. Mrs. Conger herself presided over homely "Wednesday afternoons," at which sophisticates from the European sector of the foreign colony tried to adjust themselves to the Iowa concept of hospitality.

Yet almost from the day she returned it seemed that things were not and might never be the same. Worrisome rumors from the interior. Dinner parties given over to the latest rumors of Boxer activity instead of gossip about the latest flirtations.

Soon Mrs. Conger was beginning to wonder whether she had made a mistake in bringing her daughter and her guests from the States, though everyone assured her that the Chinese wouldn't dare endanger the foreign diplomats with all that naval power only ninety miles away off Tientsin.

The Congers were not the most popular members of the Peking diplomatic corps, and certainly not the most admired. They were regarded as rather dull and stodgy, and Minister Conger's diplomatic abilities were rated accordingly.

Even if Conger had been another Talleyrand, however, he could not have expected to be treated with the respect of the European ministers. The British were top dogs, followed by the French, the Germans, the Italians, and the Russians. The Japanese were tolerated oddities. This rating system, of course, was based on the vigor of their colonial endeavors, as well as the glossier social finish of men who had been educated at Oxford, Cambridge, the Sorbonne, and Heidelberg.

The United States itself, like the inelegant Congers, was a

country cousin among the imperialist powers. In China its competitors regarded Americans as hypocritically sharing in the spoils while dodging responsibility and maintaining a lofty moral attitude. America had refrained from establishing its own sphere of influence, thereby escaping the necessity of sending in troops to protect its holdings, but now it was insisting that China be converted into an open marketplace. Recently Secretary of State John Hay had proclaimed the Open Door Policy and was determined to cajole the other powers into agreeing to equal trading rights for all.

Even that policy, however, bore a made-in-Britain benchmark. As one Far Eastern historian has traced the process by which the Open Door Policy came into being, Britain feared that Russian encroachments in China would lead to "eventual collision of the Powers and a Balkanization of China." This fear was shared by Japan, which had its own large-scale ambitions in that area. The British had a sizable stake in the China trade, with two-thirds of China's foreign commerce conducted with Britain and four-fifths of it carried in British ships. While John Hay was U.S. ambassador to London, he was carefully coached in the Foreign Office view that something must be done to offset the growing Russian influence in the Far East. When Hay became Secretary of State, he brought with him to Washington the design imprinted on his mind by the British. "While it is too much to say that gentle British persuasions in London had already converted him to the idea of diplomatic intervention in China to secure guarantees of free competition in all alienated territories," Nathaniel Peffer has written, "they had at least prepared him for conversion." Although the United States would claim the Open Door as its own conception, it had been subtly foisted on our Secretary of State during his service as ambassador to Great Britain. "The inception of the Open Door was British. . . . The initiative in propounding it as an international policy and even in formulating it was British."

Aside from the matter of its sponsorship, however, the policy fitted in nicely with American aspirations to widen and deepen its penetration of the Eastern Asia marketplace. Even while uttering equivocal slogans, the United States had recently joined the competition for colonial possessions by falling upon the moribund Spanish Empire, snatching away Cuba and Puerto Rico, then occupying the Philippines over the violent opposition of the Filipinos. Senator Henry Cabot Lodge had rejoiced in the capture of Manila because it was the "thing which will give us the Eastern trade," but American forces were now fighting a brutal colonial war against *insurrectos* on Luzon and the outlying islands.

With some scorn and much amusement the European nations listened to the self-justification offered by American politicians and publicists. They were harking, it seemed, to voices of destiny inaudible to less perceptive mortals. People of Nordic blood, Americans were told, were destined to rule the world for its own good. The Anglo-American "race," together with the Germans, Professor John W. Davis proclaimed, were "particularly endowed with the capacity for establishing nation states, and are especially called to that work; and therefore they are entrusted, in the general economy of history, with the mission of conducting the political civilization of the modern world."

There was a curious division of opinion among Americans on this subject, with liberals to be found where conservatives ought to have been. The Socialist novelist Jack London, for instance, warned that the "Yellow Peril" was real and "the menace to the western world lies, not in the little brown man, but in the four hundred millions of yellow men should the little brown men [the Japanese, that is] undertake their management." Socialism, he added, was for the more "advanced" nations. On the other hand, there was the fiercely conservative, often reactionary Ambrose Bierce, who bitterly opposed the Cuban and Philippine adventures. He wrote that the United States could defeat Spain with barely a twitch of its sword arm because "we belong to the race of gluttons and drunkards to whom dominion is given over the abstemious. We can thrash them consummately and every day of the week, but we cannot understand them; and is it not a great golden truth, shining like a star, that what one does not understand one knows to be bad?"

One of the spokesmen for the cause of American imperialism, odd as it may seem now, was the *Atlantic Monthly*, one of whose writers urged early in 1900:

> It would be difficult to do a greater wrong to the people of China than to leave the nation to itself. Here is the substance of the matter: China needs protection and guidance even to the

point of wise compulsion. . . . There are many signs of the times which assure us that the day is not distant when China will be delivered from its effete civilization and will come under the power of those motives which have their source in the vital truths of the Christian revelation.

Senator Albert Beveridge of Indiana, the handsome and utterly self-assured spokesman of the imperialists in Congress, was even more forceful in presenting the case for commercial and military ventures in China. Not greatly concerned about "Christian revelation," Beveridge was attracted by "China's illimitable markets," from which "we will not retreat." It was the American duty to force its rude philosophy on the lesser breeds, he declaimed to the Senate. "God has not been preparing the English-speaking and Teutonic peoples for a thousand years for nothing but vain and idle self-contemplation and self-admiration. No! He has made us the master organizers of the world to establish system where chaos reigned. He has made us adepts in government that we may administer government among savages and senile peoples." By "senile peoples," he meant the Chinese. The echoes of his arrogant address had hardly died down before the Boxer-inspired Chinese masses were proving that senility should not have been the Senator's main concern.

America by then had acquired a sizable stake in the Chinese market. Its chosen sphere of interest, if not influence, was Manchuria, which brought its ambitions in conflict with those of Russia and Japan. For more than half a century the United States had been developing the Manchurian market. Thus the American Chinese Development Company, in which Standard Oil and the American Sugar Refining Company were the leading participants, was among those entering bids for construction of the central trunk of the Peking-Hankow-Canton railroad. A Belgian concern won the right to build the northern section, but the American company bid successfully for the southern section. It had built about thirty miles of the line north from Canton when the moving spirit of the corporate enterprise died and work was suspended. That venture ended badly from the investors' viewpoint, but the Rockefellers and Standard Oil continued to be keenly interested in the Chinese market. The Rockefellers not only dotted the countryside with Baptist missions but also vigorously promoted the sale of Standard Oil kerosene in China. Too vigorously, perhaps, for the sake of Sino-American relations. To encourage the use of kerosene, they gave away 8,000,000 Mei Foo (good luck) lamps which, presumably, brought good luck only when they burned Standard Oil kerosene. This promotional essay brought them the ill favor of the mandarin merchants as well as the village priests, both of whom advocated the burning of the traditional peanut oil. It was a stroke of commercial genius, but it was accomplished at the cost of offending two powerful classes of Chinese society. Soon caravans carrying drums of kerosene were to be seen in the most remote parts of China.

Thus the corporate interests, not only the Rockefellers but J. P. Morgan and other financial titans, were greatly interested in extending American influence to the Asian mainland. They saw China as the greatest market yet to be fully exploited, and they believed the United States had a right to shoulder its way in by virtue of its conquest of the Philippines. Trade righteously, by nineteenth-century standards, followed the flag. They could only cheer when the business-oriented McKinley administration saw things the same way and Hay enunciated his Open Door Policy, which provided that the various powers "Will in no way interfere with any treaty port or any vested interests within any socalled 'sphere of influence' or leased territory in China. . . . That the Chinese treaty tariff of the time being shall apply to all merchandise landed or shipped to all such ports as are within said 'sphere of influence.' . . . That it [any of the participating powers] will levy no higher harbor dues on vessels of another nationality, and no higher railroad charges over lines built, controlled or operated within its 'sphere' on merchandise belonging to citizens or subjects of other nationalities transported through such 'sphere' than shall be levied on similar merchandise belonging to its own nationals transported over equal distances." The doctrine was formally accepted by the other powers, and parvenu America became a more or less silent partner in the exploitation of China just in time to share the responsibilities of confronting the Boxer Rebellion.

The American minister's lady had little interest in diplomatic matters, *démarches,* protest notes, policy statements, protocol, and all the other trivia of international discourse. She was fascinated by the social structure of the Legation Quarter, by its feuds and alliances, by its hallowed and solidified pecking order, and even more by the often lurid and always intricate relationships of those who lived in the Forbidden City, with its eunuchs, carefully graded concubines, and Manchu princelings.

The legations behind their compound walls, their screen of native watchmen, chair bearers and servants, were isolated completely from the Chinese swarming around them in a city like a broken anthill. At times it seemed like living in a prairie village, with one main street, one industry (diplomacy), and one obsessive recreation (gossip). The intelligent and perceptive Mrs. Conger could take the word of Bertram Lenox Simpson, a slightly raffish Englishman who was employed by the Chinese Customs and who would write the scandalous *Indiscreet Letters from Peking* under the pseudonym of B. L. Putnam Weale, that Peking society had become much less lighthearted in the several years following the Sino-Japanese War. In those gayer, happier days, Simpson wrote:

> We were all something of a happy family. There were merely the eleven Legations, the Inspectorate of Chinese Customs, with the aged Sir Robert Hart at its head, and perhaps a few favoured globetrotters or nondescripts looking for rich concessions. Picnics and dinners, races and excursions, were the order of the day, and politics and political situations were not burning. Ministers Plenipotentiary and Ministers Extraordinary wore Terai hats, very old clothes, and had an affable air—something like Teheran must still be.

But the Japanese aggression in 1894–95 changed all that, Simpson explained, and intrigue took the place of affability. Everyone had begun to scramble for the spoils. The Germans were overly anxious to wring the last bit of profit out of Shantung. There was constant bickering over carving up Manchuria, especially after one Baron de Pokotilov of the Russo-Chinese Bank appeared on the scene with a sinister black beard and a mysterious black briefcase and was constantly observed in conspiratorial huddles at the Hôtel de Pekin and elsewhere. The international jockeying for position and favor were bad enough, but the tension increased when there were upheavals in the Forbidden City; those Manchu grandees who wanted modernization and Western help contended with the reactionaries, and the dowager empress imprisoned the emperor to keep power in her own hands. The tension was heightened when the bloodthirsty General Tung Fu-hsiang marched in with his Moslem warriors from the remote and savage province of Kansu; he was still encamped with his aggressive soldiery just beyond the city walls.

The old easygoing Peking society had vanished, Simpson related:

> In its place are highly suspicious and hostile Legations—Legations petty in their conceptions of men and things—Legations bitterly disliking one another—in fact, Legations richly deserving all they get, some of the cynics say. [The atmosphere is] highly electrical and unpleasant in these hot spring days. Squabbling and cantankerous, rather absurd and petty, the Legations are spinning their little threads, each one hedged in by high walls in its own compound. . . . Outside and around us roars the noise of the Tartar City. At night the noise ceases, for the inner and outer cities are closed to one another by great gates; but at midnight the gates are opened by sleepy Manchu guards for a brief ten minutes, so that gorgeous red and blue-trapped carts, drawn by sleek mules, may speed into the Imperial City for the daybreak audience with the Throne. These conveyances contain the high officials of the Empire. It has been noticed by a Legation stroller on the Wall—the Tartar Wall—that the number of carts passing in at midnight is far greater than usual; that the guards of the city gates now and again stop and question the driver. It is nothing. . . .

To Sarah Pike Conger, however, the rumors of political intrigue, the elbowing of financial interests, the interplay between the nations as reflected in the *corps diplomatique,* were only part of the droning gossip over teacups and dinner tables.

What fascinated her was the controversial figure of the Dowager Empress Tzu Hsi. Mrs. Conger was something of a feminist, and the lady who sat on the Manchu throne, it appeared to her, was a veritable standard-bearer of the cause of women's rights. Even after all that happened in Peking the summer of 1900, her admiration of the dowager empress was undiminished, and nine years later she would still proclaim Tzu Hsi a "great woman" in whose person existed "much of the concealed force and value of

China's women," that "ignorance of these qualities had brought a pronounced misrepresentation of China's womanhood."

To her continuing wonder and delight Mrs. Conger had been one of seven wives of the foreign envoys in Peking to be granted an audience with the dowager empress on December 13, 1898, which was Tzu Hsi's sixty-fourth birthday. Until that day the dowager empress had never admitted a "female barbarian" to her presence. The curiosity on both sides, undoubtedly, was intense. The dowager empress had heard all sorts of reports on the brazen and indelicate conduct of Western women, a secondhand impression immediately dissipated when seven tremulously sedate ladies of the diplomatic corps were ushered into her presence. On their part the diplomatic wives had listened for years to gossip about the dowager empress' hyperactive sex life, her method of disposing of rivals by having them dropped down one of the palace's many convenient wells, her murderous tempers, and the lethal fickleness of her disposition. They expected to confront an old she-dragon but found instead, on that occasion at least, an Oriental version of Queen Victoria, with whom, in fact, the dowager empress liked to be compared.

Mrs. Conger, along with the wives of the British, Dutch, French, German, Russian, and Japanese ministers, were transported in sedan chairs to the Forbidden City. Lady Macdonald, as wife of the dean of the diplomatic colony, was appointed bellwether of the nervous little flock.

The confrontation between Eastern and Western femininity was arranged with considerable ceremony. Each lady was attended by five chair bearers and two mounted soldiers. On the way to the Winter Palace they were joined by Sir Claude Macdonald, four interpreters, and sixty mounted servants. Mrs. Conger wrote:

> When we reached the first gate of the Winter Palace we had to leave our chairs. . . . Inside the gate were seven red-upholstered court chairs in a line, with six eunuch chair-bearers each, and many escorts. We were taken to another gate inside of which was standing a fine railroad coach presented to China by France. We entered this car, and eunuchs dressed in black pushed and hauled it to another stopping place, where we were received by many officials and served with tea. This railroad passed through a beautiful city, clean and imperial. After a little rest and

tea-sipping, we were escorted by high officials to the throne-room.

They were presented first to Prince Ching, then to the dowager empress and Emperor Kuang Hsü, who was alive and well enough to confute rumors that he had been not only deposed but mistreated as well. Cynics in the diplomatic colony, in fact, had alleged that the dowager empress was granting the unprecedented audience mainly to prove she hadn't chopped her nephew's head off and to still the apprehensions recently voiced by the British minister.

After short speeches by Sir Claude and Lady Macdonald, the Western ladies each approached the throne, bowed, shook hands with the emperor. Then, with understandable trepidation, they approached the Motherly and Auspicious ruler of all China, or all that was left of its sovereignty, on the Dragon Throne. To their eyes she was a figure of barbaric splendor. With a jewel-encrusted screen as her backdrop, she wore the heavy brocaded ceremonial robes, the Manchu headdress covered with pearls, jade, and diamonds, her famous necklace of 300 perfectly matched, thumb-sized pearls, a jewel-studded belt, and satin bootees with high platform heels. She was a tiny lacquered figure whose claws were sheathed with gold nail protectors.

With guileless curiosity she studied her guests, each of them dressed in the latest from Paris fashion houses, or copies thereof: picture hats with ostrich feathers, ribbons, and flowers; ankle-length gowns of lace and velvet with leg-of-mutton sleeves, and their waists cinched in by whalebone so their busts—enormous to the Chinese eye—seemed about to burst through their bodices. Later the dowager empress, whose little black-currant eyes missed very little, commented on the coarseness of the Western complexions.

"We then stepped before Her Majesty," Mrs. Conger recalled, "and bowed with a low curtsey. She offered both her hands and we stepped forward to her. With a few words of greeting, Her Majesty clasped our hands in hers, and placed on the finger of each lady a heavy, chased gold ring, set with a large pearl. After thanking Her Majesty, we backed from the throne and took our places as before."

From start to finish the audience was a great success. The

dowager empress had expected to be entertaining a band of harlots, brazen and defiant, and was pleasantly surprised to be presented with a covey of awestruck middle-aged women whose femininity was so far below the delicate Chinese standard. She was so pleased by the comparison between those coarse-featured Westerners and the fragile beauty of the ladies of her court that she kept the visitors in the Winter Palace for five hours, repeatedly summoning them back into her presence as if determined to verify her first impressions. The Western visitors, who had heard so many shocking stories about Tzu Hsi, were enchanted by her.

"One family," she kept murmuring, "all one family."

That phrase would be repeated in the Legation Quarter, almost as a talisman, during the dangerous months ahead. It seemed to indicate that the ruler of China regarded the whole human race as one family. Actually it was polite hyperbole, confusing though it was to literal Westerners who could not conceive of words used to convey a passing mood.

Mrs. Conger and her bedazzled companions were escorted from the audience chamber to a banqueting hall over which Prince and Princess Ching, along with five other princesses, presided. After that feast they were led into another hall for tea. They had not expected to see the dowager empress again, but there she was, smiling maternally and beckoning them closer to her imperial chair of yellow satin. "She was bright and happy," Mrs. Conger wrote, "and her face glowed with good will. There was no trace of cruelty to be seen. . . . Her Majesty arose and wished us well. . . . 'One family; all one family.' "

The audience continued. Again the dowager empress took leave of them. They were escorted to a theater where the court interpreters explained the dynamics of Chinese drama. Then they were taken to another banqueting hall and served tea, upon which there was another imperial visitation. It almost seemed that the Dragon Lady could not bear to part with them. "When tea was passed to us she stepped forward and tipped each cup of tea to her own lips and took a sip, then lifted the cup, on the other side, to our lips and said again, 'One family, all one family.' She then presented more beautiful gifts; alike to each lady."

Mrs. Conger returned home in her sedan chair "intoxicated with the novelty and beauty" of the imperial audience, and wrote in her diary, "Think of this! English was the first language spoken at Court to Their Majesties by foreign women. English, modified, is the commercial language of China and its purity has been carried to the very throne of China by a woman."

Despite the benign, "Motherly and Auspicious" aspect the dowager empress had displayed on that occasion—even the cautious Sir Claude Macdonald agreed that she had "made a most favourable impression, both by the personal interest she took in all her guests and by her courteous amiability," as he reported to his Foreign Minister—that imperious lady had several other sides to her character, which at times would resemble that of Lady Macbeth rather than Florence Nightingale: "A passionate old woman," as Bertram Simpson described her, largely from whatever gossip filtered through the layers of silence and fear which insulated her from the world, "a veritable Catherine of Russia in her younger days they say, with her hot Manchu blood and her lust for ruling men."

That may have been a trifle too harsh, as Mrs. Conger's view was perhaps too bedazzled, but there were certain interludes in the imperial career which smelled more of musk and blood than lavender and old lace.

Beauty, intelligence, and a strong will had raised her from rather lowly beginnings to the Dragon Throne. She was born in the household of a captain in the Banner Corps, the Manchu dynasty's equivalent of a palace guard. At birth she was given the name of Yehonala, later the "flower name" Orchid, and indeed her physical development was orchidaceous. At sixteen, because of her beauty and ability to charm, she was designated a third-grade concubine to the Emperor Hsien Feng. Along with other candidates for the imperial bed she was presented to the young but weak and sickly emperor and attracted his attention immediately. Not the least of her fascinations was what Sir Robert Hart would describe as a "velvet" voice, low-pitched and insinuating.

One night she was wrapped in a red robe and borne to the emperor's bedchamber. From that night on, she was the imperial favorite; her son Tung Chih was designated as his successor, and thenceforth her life was dedicated to attaining and maintaining a position of supreme power. The imperial palace was a labyrinth of intrigue, a hotbed of conspiracy both political and sexual, an arena of dynastic ambitions in which losing players often were put to death. One of her biographers observed that she survived the murderous intrigues of the Forbidden City, with its swarm of warlords, courtiers, bureaucrats, viceroys, first secretaries of this-and-that, first of all by the exercise of a fascinating and complex personality. She had such high-voltage charm, such magnetism that:

> she could irresistibly impose her will on nearly everyone else. Her intelligence was undoubtedly exceptional, but her will-power was outstanding, outstripped only by her most unusual characteristic of all—boundless ambition. This was indeed remarkable in the daughter of an ineffectual smalltime Manchu official and a mother who although admittedly charming and cultured was not in any other respect outstanding. There was definitely something enigmatic in Yehonala's personality that she did not inherit from either parent, a unique quality that was to set her apart from and above all other women in the world.

Undoubtedly some of her unique quality was traceable to an element of cunning, knowing whom to wheedle for a favor, seeking out flaws and weaknesses, sensing the outcome of power plays. For a third-grade concubine to become in effect, if not in rank and title, the consort of the emperor required more than the firmness of character so evident to her biographer. Emperor Hsien Feng being a weakling, she knew that the uphill path to overriding influence lay through the chambers of the then dowager empress. Calculating every step, she became the favorite not only of the pallid and debilitated emperor, who had not long to live, but, more important, of his mother.

Undoubtedly she also sought the favor of that unofficial power center, the corps of eunuchs. A whole regiment of *castrati,* 3,000, headed by a chief eunuch who was almost a co-emperor, swarmed through the corridors and courtyards of the Forbidden City. The corruptive power of the eunuchs was believed to have sped the downfall of the Ming dynasty, and at first their Manchu successors kept them in line. Later and weaker rulers, however, allowed the eunuchs to regain control of palace affairs. They not only ran the household but formed a barrier around the throne which could be penetrated only by the payment of squeeze. The official of an outlying province with an important message or a crucial change in policy to recommend had to cajole, scheme, and bribe his way through successive grades of the eunuchs, and if they did not approve of him or his politics, he might wait forever in a remote antechamber.

The eunuchs, as sly and grasping as they were ubiquitous, were grand masters of the squeeze system, variously known in other parts of the world as baksheesh, la mordita or the little bite. As a highly observant concubine, Yehonala must have known all about their methods, yet when she was designated the dowager empress, she tolerated their thievery. They charged her the equivalent of about eight U.S. dollars for her favorite dish, eggs poached in chicken broth, which could be purchased for a few coppers in any market stall outside the Imperial City. They also submitted accounts totaling $700 a day for feeding her small personal entourage.

Her tolerance of those practices indicated that she owed much to their support when she was conniving her way up from the ranks of concubinage. Their services were also required when someone in serious disfavor, too well connected to be brought before the Clansmen's Court, had to be dropped down a palace well. And the corps of eunuchs was essential to maintaining the sybaritic style of the Manchu court. It took twenty-six eunuchs, two amahs, and four servant girls, for instance, to convey the dowager empress from her private chambers to the audience chamber, a distance covered at a stately pace in two minutes, with Tzu Hsi ensconced in a sedan chair. One of her ladies-in-waiting described the procession:

> The chair is carried by eight eunuchs all dressed in official robes. . . . The head eunuch walked on her left side and the second eunuch on her right side, each with a steadying hand on the chair pole. Four eunuchs of the fifth rank walked in front and twelve eunuchs of the sixth rank walked behind. Each eunuch carried something in his hand, such as Her Majesty's clothes, shoes, handkerchiefs, combs, brushes, powder boxes, looking glasses of different sizes, perfumes, pins, black and red ink, yellow paper, cigarettes, water pipes, and the last one carried her yellow satin-covered stool. Besides this there were two amahs [old women servants] and four servant girls all carrying some-

thing. This procession was most interesting to see and made one think of a lady's dressing room on legs.

The lady-in-waiting, Princess Der Ling, who had been educated in the West, was also astonished at the variety of the imperial menu. Before the evening meal was done, 150 different dishes had been offered the dowager empress and her companions. The empress herself was content with a special serving of lotus flower seeds cooked with sugar, watermelon seeds, walnuts prepared in various fashions, sweetmeats, and sliced fruits. When it came to tea, her tastes were more elaborate. She drank from a cup carved from pure white jade on a solid-gold saucer. Honeysuckle and rose petals were floated on the infusion with a pair of gold chopsticks.

Getting the old lady to bed was an elaborate ceremony in itself. She slept in a huge canopied bed with bags of scent suspended from the top of the frame. There were three thick mattresses covered with yellow brocade. Her sheets were of varicolored silk embroidered with gold dragons and blue clouds. She slept on a special pillow, designed to quiet the fears which queens were heir to. It was stuffed with dried flowers and had a square hole in the middle. Supposedly when she placed her head on the pillow, with her ear in the hole, she could hear the slightest sound made by anyone approaching her bed.

Her jewelry was kept in a treasure vault covered with shelves from floor to ceiling. On each shelf was a row of ebony boxes, 3,000 in all, which contained what she called her "everyday jewels." The collection was so large that even Tzu Hsi didn't know what all the boxes contained, but she opened several for Princess Der Ling's inspection. Among the more fanciful creations she displayed for her young protégée were a peony fashioned from coral and jade, the petals of which trembled like those of a real flower; a jade butterfly with workable wings; and chains of pearls which seemed long enough to tow a barge up the Pei Ho.

The amatory and political intrigues which marked her ascent to the Dragon Throne were numerous and intricate. They silhouette the psychological profile of a woman who dedicated herself to ruthless opportunism, was sometimes deflected from her objectives by circumstance, but never lost her driving force.

She did not become regent until 1861, when the Emperor Hsien-Feng died and left her an ambitious widow of twenty-seven. Immediately after that sketchily mourned event, she began disposing of her enemies with an efficiency which would have done credit to one of the later Roman emperors. She had already secured the backing of the eunuchs and, as the daughter of an officer of the Banner Corps, the palace guard. There was an inimical clique headed by Su Shun, who never held any government title but functioned as a sort of grand vizier, opposed to her regency. Once she laid hands on the Seal of Legally Transmitted Authority, she disposed of Su Shun, briskly noting that two of his henchmen had been graciously permitted to commit suicide and two others sentenced to life imprisonment. "As to Su Shun," she dictated, "his treasonable guilt far exceeds that of his accomplices and he fully deserves the punishment of dismemberment and the slicing process. But we connot make up our mind to impose this extreme penalty and therefore, in our clemency, we sentence him to immediate decapitation."

When she assumed the regency on behalf of her son Tung Chih, her taste for power only sharpened, and any vestige of maternal love in her makeup was replaced by resentment of the fact that she would one day have to hand over power to her son. The regency lasted until 1872, when her son was declared of age.

Whatever the actual reasons which hastened Tung Chih's departure so soon after he assumed power, there was much evidence that the Dowager Empress Tzu Hsi, who was also dignified as the Orthodox, the Heaven-Blessed, the Illustrious, Prosperous, All-Nourishing, Brightly Manifest, Calm, Sedate, Perfect, Long-Lived, Reverent and Worshipful (not all the honorifics to be taken literally), was greatly perturbed. Power meant everything to her, and she was determined to regain it. She believed that only she had the strength of character to save the Manchu empire from disintegration. Her son, like his father, was a weakling. So, it was said, she encouraged him in his debaucheries and brought about his early death. He ruled for only three years. Tung Chih's pregnant widow died in what were charitably described as mysterious circumstances a short time later.

Once again Tzu Hsi gladly assumed the regency, this time for her nephew Kuang Hsü. It was a troubled period for China, with chunks of the empire broken off and falling into barbarian hands.

The dowager empress listened to endless debates in her Grand Council between the progressives, who wanted to westernize China sufficiently to make it capable of defending itself from the circling pack of foreign aggressors, and the reactionaries, who believed that China's strength was rooted in tradition and proper respect for the ancient gods. She was inclined to favor the case of the reactionaries: Tradition, coupled with her own abilities, had placed her on the Dragon Throne; who knew what changes modern technology, a westernized army, and educational system might bring?

In 1889 the dowager empress again had to yield the executive power when Kuang Hsü took the throne at the age of seventeen. Her clique in the palace diligently spread the word that Kuang Hsü was a near-moron, that he was sexually undeveloped (a serious slander in a country where alchemists searched endlessly for the perfect aphrodisiac), that he was more interested in playing with his Swiss toys and the miniature railway which ran along the banks of the palace lakes than in ruling the nation. She was no longer officially the regent, but the dowager empress continued to dominate the Imperial City and the government.

During the years between 1889 and 1898, however, Emperor Kuang Hsü began listening to the counsels of his former tutor, Weng Tung-ho, the leader of a group of Peking intellectuals who advocated westernization. Weng Tung-ho, who was appointed to the Grand Council, succeeded in persuading the emperor to issue a number of reform decrees which brought on the internal crisis of 1898. One of them read, in part:

> The bases of education will continue to rest on the canons of the Sages, but at the same time there must be careful investigation of every branch of European learning so that there may be an end to empty fallacies. . . . Parrot-like plagiarisms of shallow theories are to be avoided and catchwords eschewed. . . . The Peking University is to be made a model for the Empire, and all officials of the rank of Board Secretaries, officers of the bodyguard, future magistrates, sons of high officials and Manchus of hereditary rank, are to be entitled to enter upon a college course in order that their talents may be trained to meet the needs of these critical times. No proscrastination or favoritism will be tolerated, nor any disregard of these, the Throne's admonitions.

Other decrees, which struck even deeper into embedded tradition, provided for permission for junior officials to petition the throne directly, the promotion of the railroad system, the abandonment of superfluous temples and monasteries, and the abolition of a number of governorships. The army and navy were to be modernized along western lines, and they were to be supplied with the newest weapons, as well as the most efficient tactics.

The dowager empress gave ground to the extent that the decrees were allowed to be issued, but she insisted that the dynastic affairs of the empire, the assurance that the Manchu clans would retain all their hereditary powers and privileges, remain intact. Then, during the summer of 1898, Tzu Hsi began her counterattack on her nephew and the men influencing him. Her favorite militarist, Jung Lu, was appointed viceroy of the troubled province of Chihli and commander in chief of the northern armies. Furthermore, she dictated the dismissal of the emperor's chief adviser, Weng Tung-ho, from the Grand Council. One day the latter was summoned to the Summer Palace and handed a Vermilion Rescript, a directive that could have been personally issued only by the dowager empress; it read in part that Grand Secretary Weng Tung-ho "has frequently been impeached, and when questioned by Ourselves has allowed his manner to betray his feelings, even daring to express approval or displeasure in Our presence. His conduct has gradually revealed a wild ambition and a tendency to usurp Our authority: it is no longer possible to retain him on the Grand Council."

For what was known as the Hundred Days, Emperor Kuang Hsü was permitted to issue decrees and dismiss hundreds of reactionaries from their posts in the government. The dowager empress shrewdly waited for pressure among the reactionaries to build until daily delegations appeared at audiences in the Summer Palace imploring her to strike down the emperor. She learned that the reformers had collected 7,000 troops to support the emperor, but the commander of those troops was an old comrade of Jung Lu and disclosed to him the reformers' plan to bolster Kuang Hsü and reduce the powers of the dowager empress.

That was enough—too much—for the dowager empress. Jung Lu's troops were brought to the Forbidden City to replace the emperor's palace guard. The emperor then realized that he had been checkmated and wrote one of his advisers:

> In view of the present difficult situation, I have found that only reforms can save China, and that reforms can be achieved only through the discharge of the conservative and ignorant ministers and the appointment of the intelligent and brave scholars. Her Graceful Majesty the Empress, however, did not agree. I have tried again and again to persuade her, only to find Her Majesty more angry. . . .

Late in September, 1898, the empress deposed her nephew and imprisoned him in the Ying Tai Palace in the Winter Palace Lake. All his servants were either executed or banished. His only companions were four guards who treated him insolently and, occasionally, his empress, who was the dowager empress' protégée and spy. Undoubtedly she would have preferred to have Kuang Hsü put to death, and in fact, a few days after he was deposed, a palace bulletin announced that he was very ill and "all medical treatments have proved ineffective." That condign solution was deemed unwise, however, when the British minister in Peking delivered a note to the Tsungli Yamen, the Chinese Foreign Office, stating the "firm conviction that should the Emperor die at this juncture of affairs, the effect produced among Western nations would be most disastrous to China."

The sad young emperor effected a remarkable recovery and thus was spared the fate of so many of the dowager empress' rivals, which was, in the poetic language of her court, to "ascend the fairy chariot for the distant journey." He was to be trotted out on ceremonial occasions, such as his aunt's reception for the foreign envoys' wives, a visible symbol of her wayward sense of mercy.

Though her power as regent was now absolute, Tzu Hsi was increasingly vexed and frustrated. Her military forces were unable to contend with foreign incursions or deal effectively with the Boxers. More and more she was listening to the Boxers' claims that they could summon 8,000,000 "spirit soldiers."

Aside from their numbers, they had another magical attraction. Those ghostly brigades would not have to be fed, clothed, or armed from the treasury's depleted resources. She began to convince herself that the Boxers and their invisible allies might prevail against Western armies and navies. In that conviction, with the blind willfulness that had always marked her character, she spent the funds allotted for constructing new naval squadrons on rebuilding her beloved Summer Palace. Perhaps she hoped there might be phantom warships manned by Spirit Sailors among the heavenly host the Boxers had promised to summon.

The Boxers' accomplices await them in Peking;
they mean to attack the churches first, then the
Legations. For us, in our cathedral, the date has
actually been fixed. Everybody knows it, it is the
talk of the town.

—Bishop Favier *to the Council of Ministers*

2. *The Dangerous Month of May*

If there was a sense of impending disaster among the 500 or so residents of the Legation Quarter of Peking in May, 1900, they generally concealed it with the practiced urbanity of professional cosmopolites.

It was true that the observant remarked upon houseboys, gardeners, and amahs disappearing without a word to their employers, that even the coolies in the streets tended to eye Westerners with a new insolence and even mutter "foreign devil" in passing. In the marketplaces of the native city, too, there was a sudden sprouting of signs reading SWORDS MADE HERE, and they were businesslike weapons rather than ceremonial sidearms.

Westerners able to decipher Chinese ideograms could read posters which overnight appeared on the walls of buildings. "The will of Heaven," they proclaimed, "is that the telegraph wires be first cut, then the railways torn up, and then shall the foreign devils be decapitated."

If there was something ominous in the air, the Westerners were inclined to blame it on the weather. Coming from nations which enjoyed four clearly defined seasons, they were more sensitive than others to the climate; their superstitions were meteorological. May was a hot dry month, with winds that reminded the French of the sirocco, and the searing dust-laden winds that blew all the way from the furnace of the Gobi Desert were depressing, sometimes maddening. The dust clogged everything. It made tempers rise with little cause. *Cafard* was the expressive word the French had for the condition, made all the more discomfiting for the effect it had on the sensitive French liver.

Sir Claude Macdonald, the *doyen* of the diplomatic corps, was convinced that the political troubles, the threat of violence made more than credible by reports from surrounding provinces, could be ameliorated by a change in the weather forecast. On May 21 he wrote his Foreign Office: "I am now convinced that a few days' heavy rainfall, to terminate the long-continued drought which has helped largely to excite unrest in the country districts, would do more to restore tranquillity than any measures which either the Chinese Government or foreign Governments can take."

The Americans and the French, however, were inclined to take a more alarmist view. As early as March, Conger had advised Washington there was likely to be serious trouble, possibly endangering the legations in Peking. M. Stéphen Pichon, the French envoy, was also considerably alarmed, and he had what other diplomats somewhat pejoratively called the "best intelligence corps in the world," the Catholic priests of China. The French, in fact, were already clamoring for a recall of the legation guards which had been stationed in Peking during the internal crisis of 1898 but had since been returned to the warships off Tientsin. M. Pichon was suspected of having leaked the contents of a letter from Bishop Favier, who not only presided over the Peitang Cathedral in Peking but was the vicar apostolic of the hundreds of thousands of Chinese Catholics, addressed to the Council of Ministers on May 19.

The bishop had urged that guards be furnished for his cathedral and "gave his grounds for making such a demand logically and calmly—depicted the damage already done by an anti-foreign and revolutionary movement in the districts not a thousand miles from Peking, and solemnly forecasted what was soon to come." And there were other portents. In the middle of May Dr. Robert Colter, an American physician who had practiced in the capital for eighteen years, reported to the United States legation that a grateful Chinese patient had passed along a warning that the Boxers intended to annihilate all foreigners.

The Council of Ministers, mainly influenced by Sir Claude, with so much of his nation's prestige behind him, so much of the famous British phlegm sustaining him, had turned down the proposal to summon back the legation guards. Sir Claude had served with the British forces in Egypt before taking up a diplomatic career, and in his opinion the Worthy Oriental Gentlemen were good at stirring up unpleasant rumors but not much good at carrying out their threats. It would all blow over, as soon as the rains came. . . .

The foreign colony in Peking was not, as events would prove, a particularly cohesive community. It was divided by national rivalries and antagonisms, most of them reflecting European wars of the past several centuries. Most of the French and Germans were certain they would go to war again within a generation to settle the unfinished business of the Franco-Prussian War. The Americans and the British were not enamored of each other, the British convinced that the Americans were riding their coattails and sharing in the commercial rewards of dismembering China without assuming their part of the military burden. Russians were regarded by the others as semibarbaric figures out of *Boris Godunov.* Italians were garlic-scented and clownish in their volubility. Nobody knew what to make of the Japanese, except that they seemed overly ambitious for such a doll-like race. Even people of the same nationality were not necessarily on chummy terms. About half of the foreigners living in Peking were literally beyond the pale; they were missionaries and teachers attached to the cathedrals and churches and chapels, the schools and hospitals and orphanages scattered around the Tatar City. They were seldom, if ever, invited to the more or less elegant social functions of the legations—the gulf between do-gooders and diplomats was as unbridgeable as the difference in their outlooks. There was a third social sector which included various foreign merchants who catered to the Westerners, a number of transient businessmen, concession hunters, and bankers, plus assorted adventurers and adventuresses, social butterflies, and world travelers who happened to be passing through.

Even among the laborers in God's vineyard, especially among them, there was a bitter rivalry between the Roman Catholics and the Protestants, each faction engaged in a contest, as much statistical as it was spiritual, in gathering adherents among the Chinese. Each side claimed that the other gathered in "rice Christians" rather than true believers, natives who came to their missions only for food, medical care, or educational advantages.

In the soul-saving enterprise the Catholics had long been dominant, having established missions in China even before the Manchus invaded from the north. They had built an ecclesiastical empire. As latecomers to China, the Protestant missionaries naturally were envious of the Catholic success in gathering the larger flocks. They especially resented a document called the "Memorial as to Official Intercourse Between Chinese Local Authorities and Roman Catholic Missionaries," which the French legation as official representative of the Vatican imposed on the Chinese imperial government in 1899. This provided, much to the disgust of plain-living Protestants, for Catholic bishops to be granted the public graces of the Manchu aristocracy, to be allowed to wear the mandarin's button on their robes, to be sheltered by the "umbrella of honor," to go abroad with a retinue of outriders, chair bearers, and footmen. All this reeked of Mother Rome's obsession with the trappings of religion rather than its substance. A gaunt Baptist missionary from Indiana watching a French or Italian churchman making his regal progress down a Chinese street in his sedan chair, surrounded by gaudily uniformed linkboys and bodyguards, was a study in ecclesiastical shock.

Yet in those days when the antiforeign agitation was cresting, when the missionaries in the provinces and their converts were being harassed and threatened with massacre, the Protestants and Catholics could not find common cause. Ecumenism was unthinkable. The heathen were swarming outside their compounds, but they were still bemused by ancient doctrinal quarrels.

The kernel of Western influence, the Legation Quarter, was a rectangular section of the Tatar City divided by the noisome canal that flowed from the Imperial City, which ran north and south. Its southern boundary was the Tatar Wall, forty feet high and forty feet thick, beyond which lay the Native City. On the north it was bounded by the equally imposing wall of the Imperial City, its flanks colored pink with yellow tiles along the top. To the east was the Great Eastern Street which led to the Tsungli Yamen, the Chinese Foreign Office. At the western end there was a Chinese residential quarter.

On Legation Street were located the Dutch, United States, German, Russian, Japanese, French, and Italian legations, with the British and Austrians quartered to the north. Clustered around the legations were various enterprises, commercial and financial, which catered to the foreign colony, the Hong Kong and Shanghai Bank, the Russo-Chinese Bank, the offices of Jardine Matheson, the great trading combine, Imbeck's and Kierulff's shops, Watson's drugstore, the Hôtel de Pekin, and the Peking Club. The racecourse upon which much of the social activity was centered was located three miles outside the city walls. And beyond the diplomatic enclave, with its walled compounds and its strictly maintained isolation, living more dangerously amid the native masses, were the Peitang Cathedral and the East and South cathedrals, the American Presbyterian mission, the Anglican mission, the London mission, the American Methodist mission and their various dependencies, schools, hospitals, and orphanages.

There must have been a few men with military experience among the 500 foreigners in Peking who occasionally brooded over how all those diverse elements of the foreign presence, with all their political differences and religious prejudices, could be defended if the Chinese masses rose against them. If so, their confidence in the military and naval strength no farther than Tientsin was sufficient to calm their fears.

On May 24, as unperturbed by reports from the hinterland as Wellington's officers dancing at the ball on the eve of Waterloo, the British legation celebrated Queen Victoria's eighty-first birthday, festivities which could have been canceled only by a major catastrophe. The elect, some sixty members of the British community in Peking, were borne to the legation in sedan chairs. The state dinner was hosted by Sir Claude Macdonald, a tall bony Highlander with a mustache whose waxed points extended several inches beyond his cheekbones. He was a man of impressive stolidity and impenetrable reticence, and only with a visible effort could he manage a festive air for the occasion.

Undoubtedly it was the premier social event of the diplomatic year. Only Britons were invited to the dinner to join in the ritual toast to the queen. Afterward the party expanded, with guests invited from the other legations, and overflowed into the princely gardens, the lawn, and the tennis court, on which there was dancing. A purplish light was provided by paper lanterns strung over the scene, music by the forty-piece Chinese brass band sponsored by Sir Robert Hart and conducted by a Portuguese. An Irish bachelor, Sir Robert had lived in China for forty-six years and prided himself on his knowledge of the Chinese mentality. He was the most impressive figure among those present, next to Sir Claude himself. He assured everyone that the Boxers meant no real harm, presented no physical danger; they could count on the goodwill of the moderates among the ruling circle at the Manchu court. Sir Robert was the most enchanted of Sinophiles and continued to be until his death.

Despite Sir Robert's eupeptic optimism and Sir Claude's imposing calm, there were more excitable souls present who wondered aloud if there wasn't something a trifle frivolous about guzzling champagne cups on the manicured lawn of the British compound when the Boxer disturbances were coming closer to the capital every day. Bertram Simpson later avowed that he was struck by the incongruity of it all. As a member of Sir Robert's customshouse staff with its own sources of intelligence he knew there wasn't much to be cheerful about and was willing to salute the French minister for contributing a touch of Gallic realism. M. Pichon attracted Simpson's attention by his vehement manner. Simpson drifted over to eavesdrop on M. Pichon's conversation, which the Britons among his auditors found amusing because of his droll pronunciation. Every sentence, as Simpson could hear, was punctuated by references to *"Les Boxeurs . . . Les Boxeurs. . . ."*

With what seemed to his hosts like Gallic perversity, M. Pichon could not be diverted from airing his views of the situation, disregarding his diplomatic duty to be gay and congratulatory on the occasion of the queen's birthday. M. Pichon was still irked by the Council of Ministers' refusal to agree that marine guards be summoned for the legations and other foreign property in Peking. He kept quoting the premonitory letter from the vicar apostolic, particularly Bishop Favier's warning that there was an alarming resemblance between the present crisis and that preceding the Tientsin massacres of forty years before. "The same placards, the same threats, the same warnings, the same blindness. I implore you, M. le Ministre, to believe me; I am well informed and do not speak idly. This religious persecution is only a façade; the ultimate aim is the extermination of all Europeans. . . . The Boxers' accomplices await them in Peking; they mean to attack the churches first, then the Legations. For us, in our Cathedral, the date has actually been fixed. Everybody knows it, it is the talk of the town." Bishop Favier cited the fact that on May 17 three villages had been burned and sixty-one native Christians massacred ninety miles from Peking. A day later, only forty miles from the capital, a London mission chapel had been destroyed. Thousands of native refugees from the Boxer terror were moving aimlessly over the countryside in Shantung and Chihli. He had ended his appeal to M. Pichon with the suggestion that forty or fifty French sailors be brought in to protect the Peitang Cathedral.

Repeating all this, M. Pichon was "irate," and when he had finished his unseemly harangue, taking leave of his equally annoyed hosts, he "slipped quietly away—possibly to send more telegrams."

Well after midnight the champagne fountain stopped flowing, and the Chinese band packed up their instruments to the dismay of the dancers on the tennis court. "So," recorded the cynical and iconoclastic Simpson in his diary, "yawning and somewhat tired from the evening's convivialities, we go our separate ways home, in our Peking carts and our official chairs, and are soon lost in sleep—dreaming, perhaps, that we have been too long in this dry Northern climate, and that it is really affecting one's nerves."

Only a few blocks from the British compound the guests returning home from the party might have noticed, if they hadn't imbibed too many champagne cups, a poster newly plastered on a wall and headed "An admirable way to destroy foreign buildings," followed by precise instructions for the ambitious incendiary.

Within just four days of that legation party the situation darkened with alarming rapidity, and the British no longer snickered at Gallic apprehensions. Suddenly large numbers of refugees, many of them Europeans employed by the railways and mining concessions, began flooding into Peking, Tientsin, and the treaty ports. Among them were a young American mining engineer named Herbert Hoover and his wife, who headed for the safety of the Foreign Settlement in Tientsin.

Alarming reports appeared in the columns of the Shanghai *Mercury*:

> A foreigner in Shanghai has telegraphed to the Governor of Shansi offering 5,000 pounds sterling reward for the safe escort of Mr. Pigott, his wife, son and a friend from Taiyüan to Shanghai. . . . A party of thirty missionaries from Langchow and Chinchow are on their way through Szechuan to Hankow. A telegram has been sent to the Viceroy Wei asking him to order the magistrates of his viceroyalties to escort them safely through the regions ruled by them, and to send men to conduct them through Szechuan to Hankow. . . . A telegram has also been sent to Governor Yu of Shansi stating that he will be held personally responsible for the safety of more than sixty missionaries in his province.

Among the hundreds of missionary families fleeing the interior for the presumed safety of the foreign enclaves on the China coast was that of a boy named Henry Luce, born in a Presbyterian mission, whose experiences on that nightmarish journey, it was said, contributed greatly toward his influential position on China when he became a dominant figure in magazine publishing.

A flood of reports came in from the countryside telling of burned villages, slaughtered Christians, destruction of foreign-owned property, masses of Boxer partisans on the move toward the capital. "There is much uneasiness among the foreigners; threatening words have come to us," wrote Mrs. Conger in her diary.

Many now recalled the premonitions of Bishop Favier and M. Pichon as well as a letter which had appeared in the Peking and Tientsin *Times* two weeks earlier. It was written by a Chinese resident, a minor official in the government who was well disposed toward foreigners and on friendly terms with many of them. "I write in all seriousness and sincerity," he warned, "to inform you that there is a great secret scheme, having for its aim to crush all foreigners in China, and wrest back the territories 'leased' to them. . . . All Chinese of the upper class know this, and those who count foreigners among their friends have warned them, but have to my knowledge been rather laughed at for their pains than thanked." The dowager empress herself, he added, had become a patroness of the Boxer societies.

In that febrile atmosphere, with one atrocity tale tumbling in after another, with Peking's communications to the interior being cut tendril by tendril, every whispered rumor of the Imperial City's attitude was studied minutely. A notorious figure with a finger in every plot, Pihsiao-li, who was known as the "false eunuch" because he was said to have obtained entry into the inner councils of the court by having falsely pretended to be emasculated, but who had a wife and children living in the Native City, was reported to have been appointed the go-between for the dowager empress and the Boxers. Another rumor, later verified, had it that four known reactionaries had been appointed to the Tsungli Yamen, with the amiable Prince Ching replaced as president of the Foreign Office by the bitterly antiforeign Prince Tuan.

The temper of the streets, always important in an Asian city, where moods are reflected instantly and a quiet thoroughfare can burst into anarchic violence within a few minutes, had also become ominous. Bertram Simpson noted in his diary that the distributors of the Peking *Gazette*, the official organ of the government, no longer strolled along the streets but ran about with woodblock-printed edicts wet from the press, shouting, "Aside, our business is important!"—the Oriental equivalent of newsboys hawking extras. The growing rudeness of the natives toward foreigners, Simpson thought, was one of the "little things that are always precursors of the coming storm in the East. . . ."

Before that day (May 28) was out, the foreign colony in the capital knew that the Boxers would soon be more than a scare story from the hinterland or something to enliven a chat over drinks at the Peking Club.

Early that afternoon a messenger stirred up a dust cloud as he rode into the capital from the west. He still had enough breath when he reached Legation Street to shout the news that the Boxers were burning Fengtai station, the junction of the Peking-Tientsin line with the branch which eventually would link Peking and Hankow but which now ran only as far as Paoting.* But there was worse news than that the rebels were within striking distance of the capital: They had also besieged the compound at Changhsintien, sixteen miles from Peking, where the railway staff and the construction engineers, mostly Belgians, had taken refuge. Several

* The dowager empress' private car was among the property burned at Fengtai station.

foreigners who had been in Fengtai when the Boxers attacked had escaped on a train, but those at Changhsintien were unable to escape in similar fashion because the line ran through Fengtai. The telegraph lines had been cut. It was feared that the engineers and railroad men, few of whom were known to be armed, would be massacred before nightfall.

The Council of Ministers was hastily summoned into an emergency session, with Sir Claude looking less like a Highland chieftain now and more like a debt-ridden crofter, and M. Pichon trying to suppress an I-told-you-so gleam in his little black eyes. There was only one item on the agenda: Should a telegram be dispatched immediately to Tientsin for legation guards? The ministers unanimously agreed they should. M. Pichon, with a shy smile, disclosed to his confreres that he had already telegraphed the French naval commander for a detachment. A delegation was then appointed to visit the Tsungli Yamen and ask—or demand, rather—that permission be given for the entry of foreign troops. The officials at the Tsungli Yamen cited "loss of face" as a reason for objecting to bringing in the legation guards, but their objections were brusquely turned aside. Danger, as Mrs. Conger observed, had suddenly united the foreign colony. "The foreigners are all closely united and stand by one another," she wrote in her diary that afternoon. "Telegrams, letters, messages and people are constantly coming to Mr. Conger. All foreigners are anxious. The Boxers are cruel, frenzied!"

Among those who watched the burning of Fengtai station was a party of Americans on the Western Hills. They were among the diplomatic families who customarily rented summer homes in the upland coolness. It was a small, unprotected party, including Mrs. Herbert Squiers, the wife of the first secretary of the American legation, and Miss Polly Condit Smith, a lively, young, and attractive visitor from the States. The Squierses were the most popular of the Americans with other members of the diplomatic colony. While the Congers were regarded as somewhat stuffy, reserved and old-fashioned, the Squierses were young, fashionable, and gregarious. Squiers was a professional diplomat (while Conger was a political appointee), a handsome, energetic, and decisive fellow whom his fellow professionals believed more suitable for the post of United States minister.

With the pretty and vivacious Mrs. Squiers, in addition to her houseguest, were her three small children, a German governess, a French governess, and several very nervous Chinese servants. They had arrived on the Western Hills a few days before to occupy the old temple which had been converted into a villa. The previous day a squad of spear-carrying Chinese militia had been sent to the Squiers villa by the local authorities for their protection. During the night the soldiers had disappeared without a word.

Now Mrs. Squiers and Miss Smith (who as "Mary Hooker" wrote an illuminating and perceptive account of her unfortunate stay in Peking) stood on the balcony of the remodeled temple and watched a column of smoke and flame rise from Fengtai on the vast dusty plain below. They could also see the houses of the foreign engineers being set afire. The steel bridge near the station was blown up. It now seemed desperately unwise for Mrs. Squiers to have left for the Western Hills without an armed protector, but her husband, like the British whose unflappable style he sought to emulate, believed in business as usual and showing the natives they were not impressed by the Boxers' threats.

They were fifteen miles from Peking and didn't dare try to return to the capital without an escort. Worrisome hours passed, with Mrs. Squiers and Miss Smith trying to calm the fears of the children, the governesses, and the house servants. Finally, late in the afternoon, they saw on the road below a "dusty figure ambling along on a dusty Chinese pony," at a distance more a Sancho Panza than a Sir Lancelot.

The man approaching them was a venturesome Australian journalist, Dr. George Ernest Morrison, correspondent for the *Times* of London, whose subsequent dispatches won him a permanent place of honor in journalistic history. He was now thirty-eight years old. He had exposed the traffic in slave labor between the South Sea Islands and the Queensland sugar plantations. Later he qualified as a physician, served as a doctor in the Spanish copper mines and as personal medical attendant to the sultan of Wazir; but as he said, he was an "incurable wanderer," and before resuming his journalistic career as a *Times* correspondent, he had walked across China—as he had once made it on foot across the Australian continent, unarmed and alone—from Shanghai to the Burmese border.

Earlier that day, on hearing that the railway junction was being attacked, he had mounted his pony and rode out to Fengtai, verified the reports and started back to Peking. It was his duty to get to the telegraph office as quickly as possible and dispatch a cable to the *Times*. Then he remembered that Mrs. Squiers had gone to the villa in the Western Hills earlier than the rest of the foreign colony and decided it was more important to check on her safety than file a story to London.

An hour after Dr. Morrison was gratefully welcomed by Mrs. Squiers and her companions, Squiers himself made a dash to the family retreat. He had borrowed one of the seven Cossacks stationed at the Russian legation, with which the Americans were on close neighborly and diplomatic terms, and hurried to the villa.

That night the party watched the flames over Fengtai slowly die down. Nobody except the children could sleep. In the morning they left for the capital in Peking carts which took five hours to cover the fifteen miles. It looked very much as though the Squierses and their houseguest would have to spend the summer in the suffocating heat of the city.

There were still the beleaguered Westerners in Changhsintien to be rescued. During the night of May 28–29, a number of people in the capital wondered whether the Belgian engineers, some of them with wives and children, could have survived. Obviously none of the legations was going to do anything about it. At the Hôtel de Pekin, however, there were several people willing to risk their lives on a rescue mission to Changhsintien. They included the proprietor of the hotel, the thirty-three-year-old Auguste Chamot, a Swiss, and his adventurous young American wife.

The Chamots insisted that the Belgians couldn't be abandoned without an effort to save them and enlisted four Frenchmen and a young Australian to join them in a sortie through the hostile countryside. Shortly after dawn the rescue party rode off on ponies. They dashed into the smoking outskirts of Changhsintien to the foreign compound. There they found twenty-nine Europeans, including nine women and seven children, waiting for the Boxers to massacre them.

The Chamot party, armed with rifles and revolvers, escorted the Europeans out of the charred city only an hour before their houses were looted and burned by the imperial troops which had been sent to protect the city.

Anxiety threaded every hour of the next several days. The legations had wired Tientsin and the naval commanders to send a guard force, but the Tsungli Yamen kept stalling over granting official permission for the guards to enter the city. On May 29 representatives of the various legations were given equivocal replies to their petition. The next day, according to Mrs. Conger, they presented an ultimatum to the yamen: "We give you until six o'clock tomorrow morning for a favorable answer, and if it does not come, we will bring the guards anyway." The officials at the yamen replied, "We cannot give an answer under three days. It would take one day to send the request to the Summer Palace; one day for the Court to reply; another to send Their Majesties' reply to the Foreign Ministers."

At two o'clock the following morning Conger and the other ministers were awakened by messengers from the Yamen. The reply was favorable, its swiftness unexplained. A collective sigh of relief went up from breakfast tables in the Legation Quarter.

By then the allied naval forces off Tientsin had begun moving. Signals were exchanged; solemn admirals conferred in each others' cabins; guns and ammunition were broken out. To the senior commander, Admiral Sir Edward Seymour, the flotilla was reminiscent of 1860, when an Anglo-French expedition to Peking had been mounted with disastrous results for the Summer Palace. There were seventeen warships, including the U.S. light cruiser *Newark*, British, French, German, Japanese, Italian, and Russian vessels off the Taku Bar.

At dawn on May 29, 50 U.S. marines in khaki battle dress, with high-crowned campaign hats and loaded rifles, began climbing into barges from the side ports of the *Newark*. Nearby other marines and sailors were being loaded into gunboats, barges, and lighters to be ferried ashore. In all 337 officers and men were included in the contingent which was to entrain for Peking. Four days later they would be joined by 52 German and 37 Austrian sailors.

The American marines and their comrades from the allied

warships were ferried past the three Taku forts guarding the mouth of the Pei Mo (North) River, where they would board a train at the river port of Tangku for the Tientsin station, then the eighty-mile rail journey to Peking. The marines crouched low as possible behind the steel flanks of their barges, expecting at any moment the Taku forts to open up and blow them out of the water. But the Chinese guns stayed silent.

Among the officers were Captain Jack Myers and Captain Newt Hall, both of whom would be garlanded with journalistic fame. But a bantam-sized private, Daniel Joseph Daly, who once sold newspapers at New York's City Hall, was the one whom military history would single out. He was only five feet five and weighed 125 pounds, but he had studied the art of combat against the Manhattan street gangs. Daly, who would become a legend in the Marine Corps, calmly honed his bayonet with a whetstone while his comrades worried about the Taku guns.

May 31 was an anxious day in Peking. Around the hot dusty streets on which the foreign compounds were located buzzed the question: Will the legation guards be allowed to march in without interference either from the imperial troops or Boxer-led street mobs? It seemed distinctly ominous that 6,000 troops, the fierce Moslem warriors from Kansu behind their black and blue velvet banners, had been deployed between the railroad terminus at Machiapu outside the city walls and the Yung Ting Mien, the southern gate through the outer wall by which the allied force would enter. All day the tension seemed to heighten. Mobs formed in the streets and listened to menacing speeches. Some Europeans tried on native dress—the ladies disguising themselves as Manchus because Manchu women did not bind their feet—and planned to escape from Peking in native carts if the guards did not arrive.

At the American legation Minister Conger late in the afternoon dispatched several members of his staff to await the train from Tientsin at Machiapu station. They spent hours at the station five miles beyond the city walls staring up the track.

Everyone stayed behind the walls of his compound as the afternoon hours passed.

At dusk there was still no word from Machiapu, and rumors sped around the foreign compounds that the Kansu troops were planning to attack the legation guards as soon as they detrained.

Some tried to keep up appearances. At the French compound the fat and pessimistic M. Pichon and his lady had invited eighteen guests to dinner. Among them was the sardonic Bertram Simpson, whose published recollection of those days would infuriate so many of his companions in duress. The food and wine at M. Pichon's table were predictably excellent, as Simpson observed, but the host kept harping on the increasing danger from the Boxers. At a British dinner party, under such circumstances, there would be a lively discussion of the latest cricket scores. But at the Frenchman's table "we had Boxers for soup, Boxers with the entrees, and Boxers to the end . . . the Boxers surrounded us in a constant vapour of words so formidable that one might well have reason to be alarmed. . . . But we became more and more valiant as we ate and drank. . . ."

When the emboldening effects of the wine wore off, and the evening hours passed without the tread of military boots, depression again settled over M. Pichon's guests and the "wives were sighing in unison," because it weighed on everyone's mind that "although the Guardian of the Nine Gates—a species of Manchu warden or grand constable of Peking—has been officially warned that foreign guards, whose arrival has been duly authorized by the Tsungli Yamen, may be a little late, and that consequently the Chien Men, or the Middle Gate, should be kept open a couple of hours longer, the chief guardian may become nervous and irate and incontinently shut the gates. This alone might provoke an outbreak. . . ."

It was close to ten o'clock before M. Pichon and his guests could relax. A strip of red-lined Chinese writing paper was brought in, a bulletin notifying the French minister that the guards were marching toward the Legation Quarter. Simpson was consoled by the thought that, in allowing the guards' entry, the "Chinese Government, in spite of its enormous capacity for mischief, could not yet make up its mind how to act."

The dinner party broke up, with everyone eager to watch the troops arrive.

Without interference from the Kansu infantry, the 337 officers and men of the various national detachments, bayoneted rifles on their shoulders, stores and supplies left behind in case they would have to fight their way into the walled city (the Russians had forgotten their field gun in their haste), marched into the Legation Quarter.

Before each compound the foreign civilians had gathered to welcome their protectors with cheers and waving handkerchiefs. The Americans, as Polly Condit Smith pridefully observed, led the march. They filed into the Russian compound across Legation Street, their own compound being too small to accommodate them.

"All right, now! Close ranks. Raise that flag," shouted Captain Jack Myers, USMC, as his small column passed his legation.

"Thank God you've come," Minister Conger told him. "Now we're safe."

Private Dan Daly, who heard the minister's greeting, would recall those words one night a month and a half later as he crouched behind the barricades on the Tatar Wall. Captain Myers, too, was taken aback by the minister's cheeriness; he was certain the worst was still to come. On the march through the city he had considered the "dense mass of Chinese which thronged either side of the roadway more ominous than a demonstration of hostility would have been."

Nor was Bertram Simpson, maintaining his air of cynical detachment, inclined to throw his hat into the air that night. He found the exuberance in the Legation Quarter rather depressing, and recorded in his diary: "By one or two in the morning everybody was very gay, walking about and having drinks with one another, and saying that it was all right now." Simpson, however, reminded himself that June was the historic month for Chinese crises to begin.

He strolled around the various compounds to have a look at the troops as they bivouacked for the night:

> The men of the various detachments were brushing each other down and exchanging congratulations that they had been picked for Peking service. It was, perhaps, only because they were so glad to be allotted shore duty after interminable service afloat off China's muddy coasts that they congratulated one another; but it might be also because they had heard tell throughout the fleets that the men who had come in 1898 after the *coup d'état,* had had the finest time which could be imagined—all loafing and no duties. . . .

That night the foreigners in Peking slept soundly for the first time in several weeks.

The city had grown very quiet after the fleet landing force arrived. Even the usual nocturnal hum of an Oriental city was absent. The native residents had barricaded themselves in their houses, the way they did at the onset of a Mongolian dust storm. Even the all-night restaurants and food stalls in the marketplaces were closed.

All was quiet in the Legation Quarter as armed men patrolled the various compounds. Most people dropped off to sleep without asking themselves how 337 men could protect them if thousands of Boxers and their sympathizers decided to attack.

We are told that the Chinese generally, if not always, fight in daylight.

—*Diary of* MRS. SARAH CONGER

3. *The Baron Brandishes a Mailed Fist*

For the next several days there was a deceptive inactivity in the unquiet city. No more mobs formed; the Boxer agitation seemed to have stopped; the missionaries and other Westerners who had run to the legation compounds for shelter in the past several days returned to their own homes.

The British minister telegraphed the allied fleet commander, Admiral Seymour, that it didn't seem likely naval reinforcements would be required off Tientsin. Sir Claude was one of those who put faith in a "show of force" and other contemporary catchphrases like "send a gunboat" or "run up the flag." To the pessimists, including M. Pichon of the French legation, it seemed more probable that the Boxers were merely regrouping, infiltrating more partisans from the provinces, while the dowager empress and her Grand Council decided what to do about the affront offered by the legations when they rammed through the train from Tientsin; certainly the xenophobic and reactionary voices now closest to the Motherly and Auspicious ear were demanding some sort of reprisal.

Just at that moment, in the first few days of June, the Westerners in Peking could have spared themselves a considerable ordeal. They could have run down their several flags and evacuated the capital, moved to Tientsin or some other coastal enclave until the turmoil subsided. At the very least they could have sent out the women, children, and elderly, all but the able-bodied men. But such a solution was unthinkable, or anyway unvoiced, even though it was apparent that the dowager empress would have provided a safe-conduct, even have laid on the transport to send them on their way. But they regarded themselves as the frontline troops of diplomacy, and in 1900 one didn't show one's heels to the "wogs" or concede for a moment that moral superiority might not be on the side of the colonizing and Christianizing powers.

Even if the situation disintegrated, if the Manchus were overthrown and the central government crumbled, the foreign colony "would be the last place attacked," Sir Claude Macdonald cabled the British Foreign Office. He couldn't afford to betray the least flicker of apprehension in his dispatches, it was whispered in the other legations, because the Secretary for Foreign Affairs, Lord Salisbury, reputedly had stated that he had heard enough of the Boxers at a time when Britain was still trying to find a reasonable ending to hostilities in South Africa.

For a few days an appearance of normality returned to the diplomatic hive. The British adjourned at sundown to the Peking Club for their whiskey and sodas and gin slings to grumble about Count von Soden, the German military attaché, "a gentleman who wears bracelets and is somewhat effeminate" and worse yet was openly anti-British.

Yet within two days after the legation guards arrived it had become apparent that the calm surface of Peking was an illusion. The Boxers had not been daunted; the situation in the provinces in which missionary outposts were located was becoming more desperate daily.

At the American legation Mr. Conger was suffering through an agony of indecision. To his subordinates and many other Americans he appeared to be paralyzed. Americans were being killed. The Boxers seized the American Baptist mission at Taiyüan, where Mrs. Arnold Lovitt pleaded with her captors, "We have done you no harm, but only tried to help you. Why do you treat us so?" A Boxer executioner carefully removed her glasses before chopping her head off. At Paoting-fu two American missionaries, the Reverend Horace Tracy Pitkin and the Reverend Herbert Dixon, were surrounded in their compound, along with thirty others. Each of the men confronted the situation in his own way. Pitkin fired at the Boxers until all his ammunition was used up.

Dixon refused to defend himself, and the last entry in his diary read, "Thank heaven we drove them off without killing any." All were massacred.

An urgent plea came to the U.S. legation from the American Board mission at nearby Tungchow, where the populace was especially enraged because the city had been an entry port for rice brought from the interior until the canal was replaced by the railroad and thousands of boatmen were thrown out of work. A military escort was requested to bring out the beleaguered missionaries and their converts. Conger replied that he could not risk any part of the Marine force guarding the legation, which to many Americans seemed a trifle pusillanimous. The Reverend W. S. Ament, a missionary then posted in Peking, took on the job single-handed. Unarmed, he went into turbulent Tungchow and guided the people to Peking.

While Mr. Conger dithered in his study, confronted daily by telegrams from the interior pleading for rescue missions and appeals from the American community in North China to *do* something, Mrs. Conger brooded in the drawing room she loved so much, with its Ming vases standing next to Morris chairs and Tiffany lamps, and wrote defensively in her diary. The missionaries, she noted, "urge Mr. Conger to make the Chinese officials act more quickly and protect them and the native converts. In their distress they forget that they have been here for many years and know that the Chinese mode of thought and action is not easily or rapidly changed. And, too, our Government cannot say what the Chinese Government shall or shall not do with its own people. The Chinese converts to Christianity are Chinese subjects, and the Chinese Government has the right to protect or punish them according to its law. . . ."

A few days later she was writing that her husband visited the Tsungli Yamen at least once a day to test the temperature. The attitude of the officials there seemed to be all-important. If they were polite, it was an indication that the court was becoming less hostile. It was her husband's belief, she said, that the Chinese government was divided and its actions were dictated by increasing or decreasing fears of the Boxers.

The other powers were no more successful in their efforts to protect their nationals or impress upon the Chinese foreign ministry the urgency of restoring order in the northern provinces.

The British legation received reports that two English missionaries, Harry Norman and Charles Robinson, had been captured by the Boxers and beheaded at a village forty miles south of Peking.

When Sir Claude stomped over to the shabby building housing the Tsungli Yamen—its decrepitude, as some foreigners saw it, a subtle Chinese insult to the diplomatic corps—one of the four members of the yamen who heard his protest over the killing of Norman and Robinson fell asleep and gently snored through Sir Claude's peroration.

During those early June days the mood of the foreigners in Peking was mercurial. One moment hopes soared on rumors that the imperial troops were about to crack down on the Boxers; the next came word that the rail line to Tientsin had been cut by the partisans. The Westerners lived from one rumor to the next. In the uncertainty of their situation, many began taking a close look at their hitherto-faceless Chinese servants and wondering just how much household loyalty could be expected of them. Practically all the servants working in the Legation Quarter compounds were, as Bertram Simpson noted, members of the Eight Banners, meaning they were direct descendants of the Manchu conquerors; some were even Red Girdles, lineal descendants of the collateral branches of the imperial house. Most of them were also Catholic converts.

Their attitude, like that of their employers, was one of anticipation. The question was whether they anticipated with joy or dread. Many Westerners recalled the direst of Chinese maledictions: "May you live in interesting times." Certainly this promised to be an interesting time. During those critical early June days, Simpson observed, the Chinese servant "does not move a muscle nor show any passing indignation, as he would were the ordinary rules and regulations of life still in evidence. He, like every one of the hundreds of thousands in Peking and the millions in North China, is waiting—waiting more patiently than impatient westerners, but waiting just as anxiously . . . to know whether the storm is going to break or go away. There is something disconcerting, startling, unseemly in being waited on by those who, you know, are in turn waiting on battle, murder, and sudden death."

The Westerners depended on their servants to bring the latest rumors, as well as fresh vegetables, from the Peking marketplaces.

Back with their straw baskets they conveyed a mixture of impressions more puzzling than enlightening to their eager auditors. "Sometimes the balance swings this way, sometimes that; sometimes it is ominously black, sometimes only cloudy. . . . Who passes in and who passes out of the Palace now streaks like wildfire round the whole city." Many of the younger male servants were reservists in the Peking Field Force. Naturally their employers wondered where their loyalty would lie if they were called up and imperial troops supported the Boxers.

One bellwether of government sentiment, closely watched by old China hands because of his influence in the dowager empress' councils, was the "false eunuch," Pihsiao-li, who was running back and forth between his business interests in the city and the Summer Palace on the Wan-shou-shan, "the hills of ten thousand ages." Pihsiao-li reportedly owned half the banks and pawnshops in Peking and boasted a fortune of 30,000,000 taels. "The eunuch has a mighty fortune at stake," Simpson noted, "and all natives believe he will betray himself." To avoid making a wrong move, and hoping not to get caught in the crossfire of contending factions, the "false eunuch" in his gilded cart drawn by four splendid black mules was constantly trafficking between Prince Tuan, now the dowager empress' chief adviser, and the Boxer leaders.

On the night of June 4, Simpson's houseboy, a reservist in the Peking Field Force, came back from the Native City shouting, "Master, I have seen myself this time. Three long carts full of swords and spears have passed in from the outer city through the Ha Ta Gate. The city guards stopped and questioned the drivers—then let them go. They had a pass from the Governor of Peking, and the people all say it is now coming!"

The official attitude that the dowager empress would oppose the Boxer movement, held most strongly in the British legation, crumbled suddenly during the first days of June. On June 5 Sir Claude Macdonald sought an interview with Prince Ching, and though he did not report the exact details, he was now convinced, he said, that the dowager empress had landed on the side of the Boxers.

Meanwhile, it seemed that the Boxers were almost as invincible as they asserted, through overpowering numbers if not the magical protection they claimed to receive from their incantations. A party of French and Belgian railway engineers trying to escape from Paoting to Tientsin had been cut off by the Boxers. Four had been killed and three wounded. The Russian command in Tientsin agreed to send a troop of twenty-five Cossacks to their rescue. Before they could reach the surviving engineers, they ran into a night ambush and were forced to retreat to Tientsin. A few days later the engineers fought their way to the coastal enclave with seven of their party missing and presumably beheaded.

Even more alarming than such incidents, news of which arrived several times daily at the various legations, was the cutting of the rail communications between Peking and Tientsin, the lifeline for all the foreigners in North China. On June 4 a large force of Boxers attacked and set fire to the Hwangtsun station on the Tientsin-Peking line. The regional imperial troops, under the command of General Nieh Shih-cheng, possibly the bravest and most skillful of the Manchu commanders, obeyed a recent imperial edict and ordered that "the railway be protected." Perhaps General Nieh had not been advised of the true sentiment of the central government, but in any case he was opposed to the Boxers. His troops fired on the Boxers and killed several hundred.

At first General Nieh's action was regarded as a good omen by the Westerners, but within a few days it became apparent that slaughtering Boxers was not what the Imperial City expected of its field commanders. General Nieh was rebuked, and his troops were marched off to their camp at Lutai for reindoctrination. Two days later the trains between Tientsin and Peking again stopped running, the Kaopeitien station had been seized by the Boxers, and the Pei Ho bridge had been destroyed.

"General Nieh's men let their rifles crash off," a Westerner cynically observed in regard to the Boxer slaughter, "not because their sympathies were against the Boxers, but probably because every living man armed with a rifle loves to fire it at another living man when he can do so without harm to himself." Yet that clash between imperial troops and Boxers at Hwangtsun was a strange episode in Chinese military history. "On such occasions it is always understood that you fire a little in the air, warhoop a great deal, and then come quietly back to camp with captured flags and banners as undeniable evidence of your victory. This has been the old method of making domestic war in China—the only one."

Aside from the omens to be read into the use of live

ammunition in a purely Chinese fracas, it seemed even more ominous that rail service was not restored on the line between the capital and the coast. Gloom among the increasingly isolated Westerners only coagulated that same day (June 6) when an imperial edict clarified the throne's attitude toward the Boxers. It seemed to place the blame for massacres and other atrocities in the northern provinces on the Chinese Christians, their invariable victims, rather than the perpetrators.

"Recently," the edict read, "many churches have been established in the various provinces. As the converts become numerous, there are bad elements mingling with them. . . . These bandits, under the name of Christians, oppress the common people and domineer in the villages." As for the Boxers themselves, "because they practice the art of self-defense for the protection of their rural communities and have not created any trouble, the local officials are ordered by Imperial decrees to control the situation in a proper way. They are not to care whether people join the Society or not, but only to consider if they are bandits. Any one who stirs up riots should be severely punished. . . . If there are seditious elements who stir up disturbances, the societies should surrender the ringleaders to be punished in accordance with law. . . . It is important, however, to distinguish between the leaders and the followers."

The dowager empress seemed to be saying that the Christians were all troublemakers but that for the time being the throne considered that there were good Boxers and bad Boxers. She appeared to be sitting on the fence but leaning toward the Boxer side. Obviously there would be a full-dress review of the situation by the dowager empress, the Grand Council, and her military and other advisers before they decided whether to throw the prestige and resources of the Manchu dynasty behind the Boxer movement. Many of the southern viceroys were known to be anti-Boxer, and in their provinces there had been little or no Boxer activity. There was serious doubt whether the partisans could command any decisive support anywhere but in the North.

So Peking, a thousand years older than Paris, a treasure house of antiquity, continued for several more days to be ridden with doubt, indecision on all sides, and agonizing apprehension. Threatened as they were by massacre at any hour, daily surprised to wake in the morning and find the city still quiet, the Westerners were unable to pull together. At the American legation Mr. Conger was refusing to divide his marine force into small ineffectual squads and scatter them in the defense of various other U.S. installations in the city.

Mrs. Conger meanwhile busied herself making room for ten refugees bearing U.S. passports and preparing for a further influx. "I have had our storeroom filled with extras," she wrote on June 8, "much flour, cornmeal, beans, rice and sugar, besides chickens and other supplies. We may need all with our increasing family. We filled our coal bin and bought large *kangs* holding great quantities of water." As the daughter of pioneers she understood the necessities of "forting up," this time against Chinese spears instead of Indian arrows.

Anglo-Saxon solidarity did not seem to be working out as well under pressure as in the theories expressed by various literary and political proponents back in the home islands and in the States. The English diplomats, down to the last consular student, viewed Mr. Conger as a bumbling amateur with even less style than intellect. First Secretary Squiers of the U.S. legation was heard to refer to the "stoical, skeptical, ill-informed British Legation." The Americans were on better official terms with the Russians, Germans, and French, but there was little sense of a united front among any of the diplomatic groupings, too long involved in bickering over territory, privileges, and concessions. The compound walls that isolated each legation were symbolic, as well as physical; it would take the most nightmarish dangers to bring them all together.

June 7 and 8 passed without alarming incident, though the residents of the Legation Quarter noticed that the Chinese, except for their servants, were avoiding the neighborhood as though it had been quarantined. There was a sudden stir of apprehension over the report that the dowager empress unprecedentedly had moved back to the Forbidden City from her Summer Palace with the fierce General Tung Fu-hsiang and his Moslem cavalry trotting behind her conveyance. Undoubtedly something was stirring behind the pink walls of the Imperial City, and rumors leaked out about a grand imperial conference at which it would be decided whether to encourage the uprising against the foreigners.

On June 9 the situation worsened considerably. No trains were reaching the capital from Tientsin, though the telegraph was still operating. That day the Boxer menace approached to within three miles of the city's walls. The Boxers destroyed the racecourse, the bastion of Western privilege, and burned one of the caretakers in the embers of the grandstand. For the British, in particular, this was a punishing blow. The racecourse was the chief local instrument of the British class system; you didn't see low-church missionaries, low-ranking bureaucrats, "other ranks" of the military in its paddock, or trading company clerks in its grandstand— only the socially qualified and their guests. No Chinese. No muckers or social climbers from other nations. The British consciousness about social class, in fact, was matched only by the Chinese with their equally careful gradation of everyone from coolie to mandarin.

Immediately after the racecourse went up in flames, a party of young Englishmen, consular students spending a summer's internship at the legation, were assaulted by a spear-carrying mob of Boxers. This happened even closer to the Legation Quarter. The students were out riding on the sands below the Tatar Wall when they were attacked. They escaped by firing their pistols and riding like hell for their compound.

A council of the ministers was summoned immediately, but several envoys acted on their own before that convocation took place. Conger wired the State Department that more marine guards were definitely required. M. de Giers, the Russian minister, telegraphed St. Petersburg: "In my judgment, the role of the diplomats has come to an end and the admirals must take charge of the situation. Only the prompt arrival of a strong detachment can save the foreigners at Peking." Sir Claude Macdonald, deeply shocked by the racecourse incident, had telegraphed Admiral Seymour in Tientsin for reinforcements and advised the Foreign Office that in his opinion the situation was rapidly disintegrating. His evaluation, he said, was based on a curious interview with Lien Fang, one of the interpreters at the Tsungli Yamen. What impressed him, he explained, was *what Lien Fang did not say.* Evidently he meant that the Chinese interpreter failed to give him personal assurances that the foreign colony in Peking was safe from attack. Even so, that message must have puzzled and dismayed his superiors, who were not accustomed to receiving information based on the mood of a minor official or their representative's interpretation of his silence.

The foreign envoys meeting that afternoon again were unable to agree among themselves. The Americans, the Russians, and the British had already wired for reinforcements from Tientsin. Yet the perverse and unpredictable M. Pichon, who had hitherto been the chief alarmist, now counseled delay. It was too drastic a step, the French minister argued. They should await further developments. Somehow M. Pichon persuaded his colleagues to his view. Sir Claude countermanded his telegram of a few hours earlier. Then, later in the day, he received a report that the railway bridge at Yangtsun on the Tientsin-Peking line had been destroyed, and he canceled his countermand, informing Admiral Seymour that the situation was "hourly becoming more serious" and asking that a strong force, equipped to repair the railroad as it came, be dispatched at once.

The dithering of the ministers did little to calm the fears of the various nationals. One of them wrote in his diary that evening:

> Here we are, the Legations of all Europe, with five hundred sailors and marines cleaning their rifles and marking out distances in the capital of a so-called friendly Power, with our *pro forma* despatches still being despatched while our real messages are frightened; attempting to weather a storm which the Chinese Government is powerless to arrest. . . . For the Chinese Colossus, lumbering and lazy, sluggish and ill-equipped, has raised himself on his elbow, and with sheep-like and calculating eyes is looking down on us—a pigmy-like collection of foreigners and their guards—and soon will risk a kick—perhaps even will trample us quickly to pieces. How bitterly everyone is regretting our false confidence, and how our chiefs are being cursed!

An attack was generally expected that night. When it didn't come, Mrs. Conger found an explanation, possibly relayed by her husband. "We are told that the Chinese generally, if not always, fight in the daylight." And that was just another Western misconception to be shattered in the near future.

Hopes rose on June 10 that a strong relief force from Tientsin, perhaps 2,000 or more men, was on its way and would arrive that evening or early the next morning at the latest.

Though they knew Admiral Seymour and his expeditionary force were heading for Peking, the Tsungli Yamen having been duly notified, the Chinese seemed oddly indifferent that day despite the hourly expected arrival of the reinforcements. Simpson observed in his diary:

> No longer are we mere *yang kuei-tzu,* foreign devils; we have risen to the proud estate of *ta mao-tzu,* or long-haired ones of the first class. *Mao-tzu* is a term of some contemptuous strength, since *mao* is the hair of animals and our barbarian heads are not even shaved. The *ta*—great or first class—is also significant, because behind our own detested class press two others deserving of almost equal contempt at the hands of all believers in divine Boxerism. These are *erh-mao-tzu* and *san mao-tzu,* second and third class coarsed-haired ones. All good converts belong to the second class, and death awaits them, our servants say; whilst as to the third category, all having any sort of connection, direct or indirect, with the foreigner and his works, are lumped indiscriminately together in this one, and should be equally detested. The small talk of the teashops now even says that officials having a few sticks of European furniture in their houses are *san mao-tzu.*

That day, too, the moderate and generally amiable Prince Ching, it was learned, had been replaced in the presidency of the Tsungli Yamen by Prince Tuan, who was notoriously antiforeigner. Eternally optimistic, almost Dickensian in his cheeriness, Sir Robert Hart assured everyone that this, somehow, was a good omen.

Several hours before dawn on the morning of June 11 a long procession of carts, escorted by the legation guards, proceeded through the sleeping streets to the Machiapu railroad station to await the arrival of Admiral Seymour's trains. No trains arrived, though carts and escort waited until midmorning in the oppressive heat and dust. Nor did any word come from the relief force. The telegraph lines to the coast had just been cut, and Peking's isolation from the international fleet, and farther back to the world's chancellories, was now complete.

The carts and their escort, along with a number of Europeans who rode out to Machiapu on horseback to constitute a welcoming committee for Admiral Seymour, had to return through jeering clusters of the Kansu troops who were now occupying the open spaces around the temples of Heaven and of Agriculture.

The attitude of the Moslem warriors was openly taunting and belligerent, but they still eyed the weapons carried by the Westerners with some respect.

The hot anxious day passed slowly, quickened only by the rumors brought into the foreign compounds by the Chinese servants.

Around noon two members of the Tsungli Yamen appeared at the American legation and sought an interview with Minister Conger, perhaps because the Americans were regarded by Chinese officialdom as the least arrogant among the diplomatic corps and America had not joined in partitioning China, at least not directly.

The Chinese appealed to Conger to persuade his fellow envoys to stop the expeditionary force before it reached the capital.

"No," Conger replied, "we cannot turn them back. They must come to protect our people. You fail to do that. We are your friends, and are going to help you to protect your people. We ask nothing but protection."

"Other nations," one of the Chinese said, "do not allow troops thus to enter their domains."

Late in the afternoon a message was circulated among the legations suggesting that somebody ought to go to the Machiapu station for further word on Admiral Seymour's expedition. No one in the Western legations, conscious that the Kansu soldiers were swarming along the route to the station, spoke up to volunteer for the mission. In the Japanese legation, however, there was a swift upsurge of the bushido spirit. Several of the attachés almost came to blows demanding the privilege of undertaking the assignment. A brave civilian named Sugiyama, the chancellor of the legation, insisted on his superior diplomatic rank and won the argument. Unarmed except for an umbrella, dressed in a bowler and tailcoat, severely proper in dress and deportment, he set out in a cart for the station outside the city walls. No one bothered him on the way out. At the Machiapu station he was advised that no troop trains had arrived, nor was there any word they were on the way. All rail traffic, in fact, had been suspended.

Darkness had just fallen when his driver, covered with dust and blood, stumbled down Legation Street crying the tragic news. Sugiyama had been killed by General Fu-hsiang's Kansu soldiers. As he and his passenger were returning through the Yung Ting Gate, the Chinese soldiers dragged Sugiyama off the cart and hacked him to death with their swords while a crowd of onlookers cheered. The Japanese chancellor was then decapitated, his heart was cut out and sent to their commander by the murderers, and what remained of his corpse was left lying in the gutter. "May my tongue be torn out," the cart driver swore, "if I scatter false-hoods." Several hundred Westerners milled around in Legation Street lamenting the ghastly event, but none volunteered to recover Sugiyama's corpse.

That night many foreigners fled to the legation compounds, the three cathedrals, or the American Methodist mission. By then all missionaries within reach of the capital had sought asylum within the city walls; others were making for the treaty ports on the Yangtze. The French were guarding the Peitang Cathedral; the Americans the Methodist mission, which would soon be aban-doned as untenable. Captain Myers, the commander of the fifty-man American Marine detachment, walked the streets all night and kept checking on his guard details posted not only around the U.S. compound and the Methodist mission but on the Tatar Wall to give warning of any organized assault.

Despite all the ominous portents, including much hubbub in the Native City and an unexplained firing of Chinese cannon, that night and the following day (June 12) passed without serious incident. An unverified report, utterly false as it turned out to be, stirred hopeful expectations in the American compound. "Good news from our coming troops," as Mrs. Conger wrote in her diary; "they are safe, sixteen hundred strong and are 'coming as fast as they can repair the railroad.'"

The next morning, however, the Legation Quarter was aroused and alarmed by the daunting spectacle of a Boxer parading himself boldly in their midst.

The insolent fellow deliberately drove a Peking cart down Legation Street. He was flaunting all the regalia of his society, with his hair tied up in a red ribbon, red ribbons around his wrists and ankles, and a red girdle fastened around the waist of his white robe. Literally and tauntingly, he was dressed to kill.

Of course, he was a Chinese driving down a Chinese street, regardless of the menacing aspect of his costume, but Westerners were strong for their extraterritorial rights. Some passersby blanched and averted their eyes. Others watched from the legation compounds, and one or two ladies undoubtedly called for smelling salts.

As luck would have it—and it was bad luck—the German minister just happened to strut into the street when the Boxer, with a significant glance at all who might be watching, whipped out a large knife and began stropping its blade on the sole of his boot. The German minister was Baron Klemens von Ketteler, a *"beau garçon,"* as Bertram Simpson described him, "with blue eyes and a handsome moustache, the one really brave man among our chiefs." Fifteen years before, the baron had served at the Peking legation as military attaché and was regarded as the colony's leading lady-killer. Since then, he had donned the striped pants of the diplomatic corps and had served for a time in Washington, during which he married Maud Ledyard, the rather plain and quiet daughter of the president of the Michigan Central Railroad. On acquiring an heiress wife and one of the Kaiser's more important diplomatic appointments, the baron had settled down.*

His Prussian blood boiled at the Boxer's knife-sharpening act, and with an oath which had once sent the Teutonic Knights storming across the Masurian Lakes, Baron von Ketteler hauled the man off his cart and began flailing away with his walking stick. The Boxer, forgetting he was armed with a knife, bolted up an alley with the baron in hot pursuit. The Boxer disappeared after vaulting over the wall surrounding Prince Su's palace, which was located between the Hôtel de Pekin and the walls of the Imperial City.

The baron then returned to the abandoned cart and found another, more youthful Boxer cowering in the bottom of the vehicle. He thrashed the youth with his cane and then turned him over to the guards from his legation, who hauled him into the German compound. He was kept prisoner there, despite demands from the city government that he be released.

The baron's forthright action was applauded by many in the Legation Quarter, those who clung to the belief, undeterred by the Boer outbreak in South Africa and concurrently the American difficulty in subduing the Philippine insurrection, that the natives

---

* Ten days before the incident Sir Claude Macdonald, writing Admiral Seymour about the baron's impetuous nature, commented that "had we allowed the German Minister his head, the partition of China would now be a *fait accompli.*"

could be cowed by a judicious thrashing or two. The baron's caning of the Boxer was as unwise as it was reckless. A few hours later in Customs Street three sword-waving Boxers appeared. They ran past the Customs Inspectorate and the post office, dashed into a temple a few hundred feet away and barricaded themselves in. A number of outraged Westerners besieged them, deciding to attack "only with riding whips, so as to avoid drawing first blood," as Bertram Simpson tactfully put it. When they bashed down the doors, however, they found the trio had escaped through a back window.

A few hours later the city was engulfed in riot and arson.

In 1898 the eclipse of the sun on the Chinese New Year's Day foreboded calamity. . . .

—Sir Robert Hart, *These from the Land of Sinim*

4. *The Other Side of the Wall*

In the Legation Quarter below the pink walls of the Imperial City the main topic of conversation during those critical mid-June days was when the Palace, meaning the dowager empress because she had the ultimate power of decision, would drop the other shoe. Would she favor the Boxer cause? Would the lady on the Dragon Throne permit the Boxers to attack the legations? Would she encourage them in further attacks on Christians, native and foreign, in return for their support among the masses?

No one could say, not even the highest officials in the Forbidden City, because even while the first Boxer outbreaks were occurring and large sections of the capital were being destroyed, it had not been decided whether to shoot the Boxers or pat their heads.

The anxious diplomats could only cross-examine the equally bewildered officials at the Tsungli Yamen, whom they consulted (or badgered) two or three times a day, and read the contradictory communiqués issued by the imperial government. On June 13 the imperial court issued a decree reading:

> We have received a report from Yu Lu [Yu Lu was the viceroy of Chihli Province] saying that more than one thousand foreign troops will come to Peking by train. [Seymour's expeditionary force actually numbered a little more than twice that.] Now that the bandits have stirred up disturbances around the metropolitan

area, we are handling a difficult situation. The legation guards that have arrived at Peking numbered more than a thousand [*sic*] and should be sufficient for protection. If the foreign detachments still come one after another, the consequences would be unthinkable. Let Yu Lu order the whole army under Nieh Shih-cheng back to the railway area near Tientsin to guard the strategical points there. If again there are foreign troops attempting to go north by train, it is Yu Lu's responsibility to stop them. Let Nieh Shih-cheng prepare his troops for any emergency. As for the defense of the Taku forts, let Lo Jung-kuang be on the alert for any surprise. If foreign troops enter the metropolitan area, Yu Lu, Nieh Shih-cheng, and Lo Jung-kuang will certainly be held responsible.

Four days later another decree published in the Peking *Gazette* indicated that the imperial government seemed to be trying to avoid any major hostilities with the Western powers which would result if the Peking legations were attacked. It read:

Lately the people and the Christians have sought means to stir up enmity, and bad language has arisen on every side. Vagabonds have taken occasion repeatedly to burn and rob. All foreign ministers ought to be really protected. Jung Lu is ordered to detail his soldiers at once and energetically to use his authority and go immediately to East Legation Street and vicinity and with all his power protect those ministers. He must not be in the least careless. If the ministers and their families wish to go for a time to Tientsin, they must be protected on the way; but the railroad is not now in working order. If they go by cart road, it will be difficult, and there is fear that perfect protection cannot be afforded. They would better, therefore, abide in peace as hitherto, and wait till the railroad is repaired and then act as circumstances render expedient.

Since that edict was undoubtedly composed at the dowager empress' dictation, it seemed apparent that she did not want the diplomatic community evacuated. There were several possible reasons. "Loss of face" would be incurred if the Westerners trekked by cart to Tientsin and let the world know the Chinese government was unable to protect them against its own people.

There was also the predictable military action of the Western powers to be considered and, if possible, avoided. Another possible motive was that the legations' personnel, if kept in Peking, could be used as hostages.

It all depended, it seemed, on the Manchu court's estimate of just how representative the Boxer movement had become; whether it was wiser to contain it or, if it symbolized a mighty upsurge of Chinese resistance to foreign influences, to ride the tiger. The latter possibility, of course, was qualified by the fact that Boxer activity thus far had been confined mostly to the northern provinces.

The lack of a clear policy toward the Boxers was causing a dangerous amount of confusion just beyond the palace walls. On June 10 General Yau, a native of Anhwei brought to the capital with orders to maintain discipline among the regular troops and the Boxers, learned how little respect the insurgents had for rank or position. He came across a mob of Boxers wearing their red sashes, waving swords, and obviously bent on destruction of some sort. They told the general they were "going out to kill the devils," meaning foreigners and their native collaborators. "You will kill the demons, will you?" General Yau roared at them. "You should bear in mind that the demons may kill you." The Boxers accused him of being a Christian (a "hairy one," as the Boxers called foreigners and native Christians). According to the Peking *Gazette*, "The rebels would not hear him. They took his horse and made him dismount. They then burned incense and a slip of paper containing a written request to know from the oracle if he was a 'hairy one' or not." General Yau failed the test and was cut down by Boxer swords. Another officer rode up and tried to intercede for the general. "Hearing this," the *Gazette* account continued, "the robbers wished to kill him too. He spurred his horse and escaped. He was carrying 200 ounces of silver and two gold bracelets. They fell and the robbers secured them. One officer of the camp embraced the body of the slain man, loudly weeping. He also was killed."

Fatal misunderstandings of that sort would have to be prevented in the future. The Boxers had to be defined either as "robbers" or patriots. If the latter, the army would have to be clearly instructed to treat them as allies instead of criminals.

Momentous decisions faced the Dowager Empress Tzu Hsi,

decisions which could no longer be delayed while her advisers kept testing the depths of the nationalistic impulse. On her return to the Forbidden City from the Summer Palace, she summoned a Grand Council to determine how to proceed. It was to be attended by all the Manchu princes, dukes, and other nobility, by her chief military advisers, by the highest-ranking officials of the Tsungli Yamen and other ministries and government boards—more a convention than a conference.

The Grand Council met for two days, by the end of which it was apparent that the dowager empress had begun to favor the Boxers a long time before that conclave was summoned and that she was more interested in confirmation of her prejudice than arguments against it. On the evidence of various Chinese works and the memoirs of the Princess Der Ling, she had sided with the court's most virulent xenophobes. These included Prince Tuan, the father of the heir apparent and the leader of the pro-Boxer faction at the court. The northern commander in chief, Jung Lu, as his subsequent actions and statements demonstrated, was opposed to unleashing the Boxers because he knew, better than anyone, how poorly China was prepared to meet a national emergency and simultaneously confront the invading forces of the Western powers; but Jung Lu was not only a loyal soldier, but a personal intimate of the dowager empress, and therefore unlikely to directly oppose her wishes.

Unfortunately absent from the Grand Council was the sixty-seven-year-old Li Hung-chang, the wisest and most progressive statesman China had produced in the last quarter of the nineteenth century. After the suppression of the Taiping Rebellion which (though rooted in Christian theology, with native adaptations, rather than the belief in ancestral gods) threatened to inundate the Manchu empire, Li Hung-chang had pressed for railway construction, the opening of the mines and other exploitation of the natural resources, and modernizing the army and navy as a means of confronting the Western inroads. He had sent young men to Europe to study the military arts and the science of weaponry and had supervised the construction of three naval squadrons. Through adroit but eventually frustrated diplomatic efforts, he had tried to avert the disastrous war with Japan in 1894–95. Li Hung-chang was now viceroy of Liang-kwang Province, an aged and weary man who wanted to live in peace with no more responsibilities than those which devolved upon an elder statesman. More than any of her subjects, because she respected him and because he was an objective patriot, Li Hung-chang was needed at the dowager empress' side.

It would have taken a whole corps of Li Hung-changs, however, to reverse the quickening collapse of the Manchus. Like all dynasties of past and present, from the Ptolemys and Caesars to the Ottomans, Hapsburgs, and Romanovs, they were suffering from the terminal disease of decadence. The exercise of despotic power for centuries had not entirely sapped their will to survive, but it had paralyzed their ability to act wisely and decisively.

They were more interested in personal intrigue than wise government. Generations of inbreeding had left many of them all but witless. At times the preservation of their mandarin-length fingernails seemed to be of greater concern than saving their dynastic power over China or governing it effectively; they were debilitated by the excesses of the harem, the resort to drugs and aphrodisiacs; and those with any native intellectual capacity were stifled by the hothouse atmosphere of the palaces, in which the wayward impulses of the queen bee of that hive were more important than any concept of how to save China from a continuing dismemberment.

All those gorgeously brocaded members of the ruling house and the Manchu hierarchy assembled in a great, dark, high-vaulted council chamber on June 16 for the first of the two days of the Grand Council.

From her throne the dowager empress, in that rich contralto which thrilled and charmed so many Westerners, opened the proceedings by stating that the Grand Council must decide two questions:

What was to be done about the Boxers who had now infiltrated the capital in considerable numbers?

What was to be done about the foreign force (Seymour's expedition) advancing from Tientsin to Peking?

One of the ministers present immediately suggested that the Boxers be rounded up and driven from the city. He was shouted down by Prince Tuan. Everyone watched the face of the dowager empress for her reaction to Prince Tuan's tirade. She smiled benignly. Those present, particularly ones of lesser rank and little personal influence over the old lady, knew that their lives depended on what they said. Bad advice, indiscreetly expressed opinions, even a flicker of disrespect had been and would be punished on the chopping block.

Yet Yuan Chang, a minister in the Tsungli Yamen, found the courage to defy Prince Tuan, so obviously the reigning favorite, and suggest that the Boxers were "unreliable," that they were not patriots but rebels.

Prince Tuan was outraged. He had long dabbled in the affairs of the secret societies. According to Princess Der Ling, the devoted lady-in-waiting to the dowager empress and later a tireless producer of memoirs, Prince Tuan, his brother Duke Lan, several of the imperial princes, and a number of high-ranking army officers and civilian officials had long held membership in the White Lotus Society, of which the Boxers were believed to have been an extremist offshoot. Prince Tuan, according to Princess Der Ling, had a taste for low life and often slipped out of the Forbidden City to consort with strolling players, conjurors, swordsmen, and other raffish elements in the Native City and had even taken part in their performances.

Thus he had come into contact with the Boxers and their conspiratorial meetings in the old city. He saw them as an instrument by which the foreigners could be driven out of China. To convince the dowager empress of the Boxers' magical powers, he brought a troupe of the ruffians, sort of a drill team, to perform for her. Two of them, armed with spears, attacked a third, who warded off all their attacks without a weapon in his hands. The dowager empress was excited and impressed by the demonstration, though Jung Lu, a sobersided military man, who also witnessed the performance, "wrung his hands in anguish inside his long sleeves."

The Old Buddha, as she was affectionately known, was not immune to the superstitions which dated back centuries and millennia. "In 1898," as Sir Robert Hart observed in *These from the Land of Sinim*, "the eclipse of the sun on the Chinese New Year's Day foreboded calamity—especially to the Emperor [whom the dowager empress would depose that year, thus fulfilling the prophecy] . . . then, as chance would have it, this year, 1900, is one in which the intercalary month for the Chinese year is the eighth, and an eighth intercalary month always means misfortune. When such a month last occurred the Emperor Tung

Chih died, and accordingly the popular mind was on the lookout for catastrophe in 1900, and perhaps the people were morbidly willing to assist folklore to fulfill its own prophecy." By that calculation the Boxer crisis should have come in September, 1900, but as Sir Robert confessed, "Our calculations were wrong."

In any case the dowager empress was utterly devoted to the ancient beliefs, like most of her subjects, and frequently consulted the Court of Astrologers, an integral part of the palace bureaucracy, for guidance on planetary influences. She had also started practicing the Boxer ritual with its incantations for the destruction of the foreigners, the diary of one of her courtiers testified. Ching Shan wrote:

> The Boxers possess a secret Talisman, consisting of a small piece of yellow paper, which they carry on their persons when going into battle. On it is drawn, in vermilion paint, a figure which is neither that of man nor devil, demon nor saint. It has a head, but no feet; its face is sharp-pointed, with eyes and eyebrows and four halos. From the monster's heart to its lower extremities runs a mystic inscription, which reads: "I am Buddha of the cold cloud; before lies the black deity of fire; behind is Laotzu himself." On the creature's body are also borne the characters for Buddha, Tiger, and Dragon. On the top left-hand corner are the words "invoke first the Guardian of Heaven," and on the right-hand corner, "invoke next the black gods of pestilence."
>
> The Dowager Empress had learned this incantation by heart and repeats it seventy times daily, and every time that she repeats it the chief eunuch [Li Lien-ying] shouts: "There goes one more foreign devil!"

Thus the dowager empress' question to the Grand Council, which she posed shortly after Prince Tuan subsided, was perfectly understandable. "If we cannot rely upon the supernatural formulas," she asked, "can we rely upon the heart of the people? If we lost it, how can we maintain our country?" Those anguished words, as one of her biographers remarked, were crucial to "assessing Old Buddha's personal attitude toward the Boxers." They expressed her rather uncertain hope that the old, pious and obedient China still existed; the China of the Manchu dominance, of the millions toiling in the paddies and sending their rice-tribute to the Imperial Treasury.

The first day of the Grand Council was indecisive. It was somewhat vaguely resolved that the Boxers must be "pacified." Whether that meant making concessions to their avowed program of destroying the foreign influence or persuading them, by means short of military force, to abandon their terrorism, was not made clear. Other resolves indicated that the decision would fall on the side of Prince Tuan and the Boxers' supporters. It was ordered, for instance, that "young and strong" Boxers be recruited for the imperial army. Of greater significance, perhaps, were the orders issued to Generals Nieh and Lo to prevent any reinforcement of the legation guards, which meant resistance would be offered Admiral Seymour's column on its march to Peking.

That night in the honeycomb of the Winter Palace the plotting must have been feverish. Prince Tuan and his fellow conspirators must have been dismayed at their failure to sweep all before them at the first day's council; stronger medicine would have to be administered on the morrow. That night, or perhaps earlier, an "ultimatum" supposedly issued by the Western powers was fabricated. It was designed to convince the dowager empress that she had no choice but to support the Boxers in their attacks on all forms of foreign influence and those Chinese who, either because they had been converted to Christianity or were profiting from associating with Western trading firms, had succumbed to that influence.

The Grand Council was reconvened the afternoon of June 17, at which time Prince Tuan, determined to end the palaver, presented the forged document which he said the foreign envoys had presented to the Tsungli Yamen the day before. The terms of that *démarche*, which were no more arrogant than other demands made by the Western powers in the past, and therefore credible to Prince Tuan's audience, included the following points:

1. The deposed emperor was to be freed from his island prison (although he was often trotted out on ceremonial occasions, and indeed was a participant in the Grand Council) and placed in a residence where he would be accessible to the foreign powers.

2. The supervision of collecting all internal revenues was to be placed in the hands of the Western and Japanese ministers.

3. All military operations were to be controlled by the foreign ministers.

4. The emperor was to be restored to the throne.

As she listened, her majesty's face was congested with rage. Nothing could have been more skillfully concocted to arouse her always testy temper. She was being ordered not only to surrender China's sovereignty but to step down for her detested nephew. No doubt she was determined to follow an antiforeign course in any event, but the forgery served as detonator to the powder keg and was a key factor in plunging China deeper into turmoil.

No one, under the circumstances, immediately questioned the authenticity of the false document which Prince Tuan presented with insolent self-confidence.

The dowager empress, "speaking with great vehemence," a member of the court recorded in his diary, "declared that until yesterday, until in fact she had read the dispatch addressed to the Tsungli Yamen by the Diplomatic Body, it had been her intention to suppress the Boxers; but in the face of their insolent proposal that she should hand over the reins of government to the emperor, who had already proved himself unfitted to rule, no peaceful solution was possible."

With firm and vehement emphasis she then told the Grand Council: "Now they have started the aggression, and the extinction of our nation is imminent. If we just fold our arms and yield to them, I would have no face to see our ancestors after death. If we must perish, why not fight to the death?"

She then elaborated on the great benefits the Manchu dynasty had conferred upon China and predicted that the grateful Chinese would flock to her banners by the millions. "I have always been of the opinion," she added, "that the allied armies had been permitted to escape too easily in 1860. Only a united effort was then necessary to have given China the victory. Today, at last, the opportunity for revenge has come."

Tzu Hsi had brooded for forty years over the sacking of her beloved Summer Palace by the Anglo-French expeditionary force. Her mood now was sulfurous. Yet there were two men present who dared to question the advisability of hazarding the dynasty by calling for war against the foreign powers.

Justifiably frightened as he was of his aunt, the Emperor Kuang

Hsü, though realizing he was present only on sufferance and as a matter of formality, spoke up with dangerous candor when she asked his opinion. "His Majesty, after a long pause and with evident hesitation," according to the diarist quoted above, "urged her to follow Yung Lu's advice, to refrain from attacking the Legations, and to have the Foreign Ministers escorted in safety to the coast. But, he added, it must be for her to decide. He could not dare to assume any responsibility in the matter."

Even more courageously, considering the fact that his position was more exposed to the imperial wrath, Minister Yuan Chang literally risked his neck to the headsman's ax by informing her majesty that he "did not believe in the authenticity of the dispatch demanding her abdication, which Prince Tuan professed to have received from the Diplomatic Body. In his opinion it was impossible that the Ministers should have dared to suggest any such interference with China's internal affairs."

Unexpectedly finding his forgery challenged, Prince Tuan, according to the diarist, "arose and angrily asked the Empress whether she proposed to listen to the words of a Chinese traitor. Her Majesty rebuked him for his loud and violent manner of speaking, but ordered Yuan Chang to leave the audience hall. No one else dared to say anything."

The account quoted above, "The Diary of His Excellency Ching Shan," has sometimes been challenged by historians as a falsification designed to justify the moderate stance of General Jung Lu. Yet the officials of the Tsungli Yamen, such as Yuan Chang, must have known that the "ultimatum" produced by Prince Tuan was a forgery; they simply didn't know how to expose it as such, once Yuan Chang was ordered out of the imperial presence. The day after the conclusion of the Grand Council, June 18, three ministers of the Tsungli Yamen sought an interview with the British minister, evidently in an attempt to verify or discredit the four-point "ultimatum." Sir Claude Macdonald wrote in a dispatch to the Foreign Office: "Li Shan, who made a very favorable impression on me, asked several questions as to the object of our reinforcements and kept calling his colleagues' attention to the reasonableness of my attitude. I said that so far from our troops coming up with any hostile intentions towards the Chinese Government, their presence would be a material assistance in preserving order, and so preventing incidents which would have serious consequences for the Government and for the Dynasty itself, in whose interests therefore their arrival should be welcomed." Professor Tan commented on that interview: "The manner in which the Chinese tried to find out the real situation was subtle, but they were apparently satisfied with the answer of the British Minister, who did not mention any 'four points.' The refusal of the British Minister to stop the international force did not, however, help the Chinese ministers who were inclined to peaceful settlement."

The Grand Council was adjourned after a brief discussion of military matters. To join that discussion, Grand Secretary Hsü Tang, the tutor of the heir apparent, who was violently antiforeign, was summoned. His presence was regarded as significant, since he was not a soldier or a military expert. His hatred of everything foreign was so virulent that he refused to use the Legation Street entrance to his residence, which was in a section adjoining the Legation Quarter. As a result of those final deliberations, an imperial decree was issued to all the provincial governors urging them to forward troops to Peking. It was generally ignored; there was no enthusiasm in the South for joining the Boxer crusade at a time when militant actions seemed certain to bring down the combined wrath of the Western powers and Japan.

There was other resistance to the Manchu court's warlike behavior. The dowager empress ordered the three ministers of the Tsungli Yamen to inform the foreign envoys in Peking that "if they really wanted to start hostilities they could haul down their flags and leave China." When those ministers interviewed Sir Claude, however, they did not transmit the matriarch's belligerent advice.

For several days after the Grand Council that lady herself seemed to be having second thoughts about the advisability of turning the Boxers loose, supporting them with imperial troops, and bringing on an all-out conflict with the West. Certainly she was aware of the trepidations felt by General Jung Lu, her most trusted commander, her friend since childhood, and (some said) her former lover.

Jung Lu wrote his old friend the viceroy of Fukien, who was a Cantonese and, like most of the southern Chinese, strongly opposed to the Boxers, that the Boxers' claim to magical powers was absurd and that "if we imagine for a moment that we shall thus be able to rid ourselves of the accursed presence of the foreigners, we are very much mistaken, and the attempt is foredoomed. . . . You should, of course, act with great discretion, but the main thing is to prevent the Throne's decree from becoming an excuse for the banding together of disorderly characters."

The dowager empress was too shrewd, presided over too omniscient a network of spies, not to realize there was a strong current of resistance running among her closest and most valued advisers, even though they had not dared to speak out in the Grand Council. She must also have known something of the character of the Boxer leaders, most of whom had surfaced from the Chinese underworld. One of the more notorious leaders grandly styled herself Yellow Lotus Holy Mother. Formerly a prostitute in Tientsin, she now claimed extraordinary powers to predict the future. Yu Lu, the viceroy of Chihli, had received her with high honors and, while wearing official dress, had even kowtowed to her—something like a four-star general saluting a private. Yellow Lotus Holy Mother assured the viceroy that she had personally made arrangements for "an angelic host to destroy the foreign devils with fire from heaven." The prophetess did not neglect her earthly opportunities. She presided over a Boxer court in which the eldest son of the elder statesman Li Hung-chang was tried and sentenced to death as a suspected collaborator with the foreign powers. He was freed only after his father paid a large sum of squeeze.

Beset by doubts despite her fiery orations before the Grand Council, the dowager empress on the day after it adjourned telegraphed Li Hung-chang to join her for urgent consultations. The old man never appeared at the palace, having warily decided to stay away from intrigues he could not control. Instead, he fended off the dowager empress' repeated invitations with complaints about his failing health.

It is apparent that Tzu Hsi was badly served by those she should have been able to count on for objective and sensible counsel. And that was mostly her own fault. She had created the atmosphere of silent terror in the corridors of the Forbidden City so that honest men, even her friends and associates of the longest duration, did not dare to speak their minds. Li Hung-chang avoided her company; Jung Lu could not summon the courage to tell her what he told his friends; the imprisoned emperor was told to shut his mouth whenever he dared to volunteer an opinion; the experts on foreign affairs at the Tsungli Yamen were likewise terrified into silence.

The bold gambler Prince Tuan was allowed to gain the upper hand. Within a week of the Grand Council the dowager empress issued an imperial edict praising Viceroy Yu Lu and the Boxers for launching attacks on Seymour's expeditionary force and the foreign quarter of Tientsin. She now made her attitude as plain as could be:

> . . . The Boxers who helped the troops so much in these actions are men of the people; with them, the State need not use a soldier nor spend a dollar. Even the little children wielded arms in defense of their altars and fields. In all their dangers, the spirits of their ancestors, of the gods, and the sages, protected them. The myriads of the people are actuated by one ideal.
>
> We hasten to publish this Edict in praise of the patriotic Boxers, and to assure them that those of their number who are in distress will be cared for. When these troubles are over we intend to bestow on them special marks of our favor. Let these people's soldiers only still continue, with united hearts and utmost efforts, to repel aggression and prove their loyalty, without failing, to the end. This is our earnest desire.

Soon those "people's soldiers" would provide a nightly entertainment for the dowager empress and her court—the spectacle of her capital going up in flames.

I merely obeyed the orders of my superior officers. Otherwise why should a small person like myself take the life of so exalted a personage as the German minister?

—CORPORAL EN HAI

5. *A Rush for Sanctuary*

From the moment Baron von Ketteler thrashed the two Boxers who ventured into the Legation Quarter on the morning of June 13, the plight of the foreigners trapped, as it now seemed, within the walls of Peking grew more desperate hourly.

That afternoon a screaming horde of Boxers brandishing their long swords burst into the Tatar City just to the east of the Legation Quarter. They ran through the streets, breaking into shops, looting, slashing at everyone in their path. Terrified Chinese were fleeing westward past the legations. "Never have I seen such fast galloping and driving in the Peking streets," wrote Bertram Simpson, "never would I have believed that small-footed [Chinese] women, of whom there are a goodly number even in the large-footed Manchu city, could get so nimbly over the ground. Everybody was panic-stricken and distraught, and we could do nothing but look on." The Boxer rampages had brushed close to a picket of Italian legation guards, who were "nearly mad with excitement . . . crimson and shouting at one another." When the night of June 13 fell, there were fires burning all over the city.

A broad belt of flames began licking closer to the eastern end of the Legation Quarter with a sudden shift in the wind. Then, down Customs Street, about a thousand yards from the Chinese Customs Inspectorate and the Austrian legation across the way, the torches of the Boxers could be seen coming closer. The gates to the Austrian compound suddenly swung open, and a squad hauling a machine gun on wheels appeared and began spraying 300 rounds a minute down the street. Simpson found that the crackle of machine-gun fire had a galvanic effect on the bystander; "it stimulates the brain as nothing else can do." The Austrians had opened up on the Boxers at a range of 150 yards but fired too high to kill any of them, as a reconnaissance the next morning determined. It was the most alarming of all the June nights thus far in the foreign colony.

Critical though the situation had become several days before, the various ministers and the commanders of the guard detachments had not yet decided, or even considered, how a mutual defense of the foreign compounds should be arranged. Each legation guarded its own territory. When Boxer attacks threatened the northern and northeastern sides of the quarter that night, the American marines maintained a static defense of their compound. It was left to Mr. Conger and one of his attachés to seek out the officer of a picket of Chinese imperial troops at the end of Legation Street and implore him to keep the Boxers away from the quarter.

Later that night, however, ten U.S. marines joined a platoon of twenty Russian soldiers to venture into the blazing section around the Nantang (South) Cathedral, from which the French had withdrawn their guards to concentrate all their available forces at the Peitang Cathedral. Other volunteer groups joined the rescue effort as the South Cathedral, built in 1600, began bursting into a mass of flame. Simpson and some of his colleagues from the Customs Inspectorate ventured within 300 yards before the heat turned them back. Mocking voices called to them from the shadows of surrounding buildings. One of the party stumbled over something on the road, a native woman, bound with ropes, reeking of kerosene and half-charred, who was still barely alive. Instead of trying to save her, Simpson and his companions pursued the lurking Boxers and fired a hundred rounds without visible effect, then hastily retreated from the scene.

Another and more effective rescue team had also been active in that sector. The Swiss hotelkeeper M. Chamot, his young wife, a McCarthy from San Francisco, and several of their friends had made a dash to the South Cathedral and rescued a priest and twenty-five nuns.

After midnight another group of volunteers from the French

legation and the Customs Inspectorate gathered in the latter's compound while the French minister and Sir Robert Hart conferred. No longer believing in a peaceful outcome, "looking terribly old," Sir Robert had strapped two large Colt .45 revolvers around his waist. The group made another sortie to the South Cathedral, which had now collapsed into a pile of burning rubble. Only a few converts were found alive and taken to the French compound for shelter. The streets were much quieter as the morning hours advanced.

When dawn came up, however, it was apparent that the Boxers had accomplished much in their divine mission of destruction. Their main target had been the district surrounding the South Cathedral, the residents of which were mostly Roman Catholic converts. A large patrol made up of American, Russian, German, and French marines marched to the South Cathedral, rounded up any native Christians they found in hiding, and shot at anyone they suspected of being a Boxer. The burned and looted area around the cathedral was an appalling sight. Hundreds of Christians had been butchered or driven into the flames of their dwellings. The London *Times* correspondent George Morrison, who accompanied the patrol, later described in one of his dispatches (published long after the event) the "women and children hacked to pieces, men trussed like fowls with noses and ears cut off and eyes gouged out." The East Cathedral had also been destroyed, with surviving witnesses telling of the elderly French priest in charge dying in the flames with many of his converts.

One or two survivors of the night's horrors told of seeing dignitaries from the court riding in their gilded carts and watching the slaughter with evident approval. From a greater distance, the dowager empress watched the holocaust, which may have encouraged her to support the Boxers. From the viewpoint of the Forbidden City, as the diary of Ching Shan made clear, it was a glorious spectacle. He wrote:

> Throughout the night flames burst in every quarter of the city; a grand sight! Kang I [a Manchu nobleman] has sent me a message to say that he and Duke Lan went to the Shun Chih Gate to encourage and direct the Boxers who were burning the French Church. Hundreds of converts were burnt to death, men,

women, and children, and so great was the stench of burning flesh that Duke Lan and Kang I were compelled to hold their noses. At dawn Kang I went to the palace to attend the Grand Council.

Major Domo Li Lien-yeng [the chief eunuch] told me that the Dowager Empress had watched the conflagrations from the hillock to the west of the Southern Lake, and had plainly seen the destruction of the French Church. Li Lien-yeng had told her that the foreigners had first fired on the crowd inside the Ha Ta Gate, and that this had enraged the patriotic braves who had retaliated by slaughtering the converts. . . . She is amazed at the Boxers' courage, and Kang I believes that she is about to give her consent to a general attack upon the Legations. Nevertheless, Li Lien-yeng has warned him that exaggerated praise of the Boxers arouses her suspicions and that, with the exception of Jung Lu, all the Grand Councillors are afraid to advise her. Her majesty is moving into the Palace of Peaceful Longevity in the Forbidden City, as all these alarms and excursions disturb her sleep at the Lake Palace. . . .

Guard details from the various legations ventured into the charred streets that morning to bring out the surviving "secondary devils," or Chinese Christians. Mrs. Conger noted in her diary:

Four of our men brought over four hundred refugees past this Legation. As these people of all ages and conditions in life— many hungry, burned, wounded, and slashed—marched by, it was a pitiful sight. The strongest among them were carrying the aged and helpless. They were taken to a large compound within our guarded quarters and are cared for by the Legations. . . . Such fortitude I never beheld as these people manifested during the dressing of their wounds. No shrinking, nor cry of suffering was expressed. . . .

For the next several days and nights, it was much the same. The legations were not yet under siege, but no one ventured beyond the Legation Quarter without armed companions. At night the Boxers renewed their sporadic attacks. It was during this period that the empress dowager was meeting with her Grand Council. The foreign colony took it as a good sign that Chinese imperial troops had not yet joined the Boxers in their depredations, but took the part of interested bystanders.

At night the guerrilla activity continued. The night of June 16 Watson's drugstore was fired and went up with a fireworks display of exploding chemicals. The legation guards potted Boxers whenever the opportunity arose during this period of undeclared war. Minister Conger estimated that "nearly 100 Boxers" had been killed by various members of the guard force. On June 16 a patrol of British, American, and Japanese troops went out looking for Christian refugees. They came across a small Chinese temple and caught a large band of Boxers performing human sacrifices on the blood-drenched altar. Outraged, the troopers surrounded the temple and within ten minutes slaughtered forty-six of the Boxers—no quarter given. Correspondent Morrison, always in the thick of the action, had accompanied the patrol and boasted in his diary that he himself had killed six of the partisans.

That same night the commercial quarter of Peking, including the expensive shops that Westerners patronized, the stores selling pearls and jewelry, silks, furs and tapestries, the lacquered cabinets and bric-a-brac with which Westerners decorated their homes in what they hoped was Chinese style, went up in smoke and flame while imperial troops stood by and made no effort to put out the flames or stop the arsonists. Young Nigel Oliphant and his brother watched with some amusement as the Chinese fire brigade made its noisy appearance on the scene. The fire engines were equipped to intimidate rather than extinguish the flames; they blared into action with a curious paraphernalia of gongs, horns, and whipping banners. Nevertheless, the flames only spread farther, beyond the shops detested because they catered to foreigners.

The fire engulfed one of the most celebrated of the Peking landmarks, the Chien Men, the ceremonial gate facing the Imperial Palace and used only by the emperor on such occasions as his visits to the Temple of Heaven. The front gate tower and the pagoda which topped it were destroyed. "David and I," Oliphant wrote in his diary, "watched the scene for a long time; it was pitiful to see poor wretches hurrying along the street with what little they had managed to save and camping out in the wasteland which stretches away under the wall of the Tartar City. We saw a few Boxers, too, swaggering along the streets, sword in hand, but we never got a chance of shooting at them." Also visible to the young Scotsman and his brother from the top of what remained of the Chien Men were "200 or 300 acres of ruined houses, which once used to be the most prosperous and well-stocked shops in the city." Later he learned at the Peking Club that the fire had spread through miscalculation on the part of the Boxer leaders. According to intelligence gleaned from native sources, the Boxers hadn't intended to burn out the whole section which served as Peking's Rue de la Paix or Bond Street. They wanted to destroy only the shops dispensing patent medicines, which the Boxers regarded as rivals in the miracle-producing business. When he ordered the fires set, the Boxer leader in charge of the operation assured his followers that by employing certain charms and incantations, he would prevent the fire from spreading beyond his control. Somehow it hadn't worked out that way.

To the foreigners China seemed to be bent on an orgy of self-destruction. "Why," Mrs. Conger asked herself, "did the flames devour so many innocent people, render so many homeless, moneyless, and cut off the daily supplies of the poor coolie class?" She noted that her servants told her that "any misfortune befalling the imperial gateway between the Tartar City and the Native City" was regarded as "a very bad omen, 'some great misfortune is coming to the throne.' But it was the work of their own hands." It was also a reflection of the Chinese mood, an almost suicidal despair over the hopelessness of ridding themselves of the quickening encroachments of the foreign powers and halting the destruction of the old Chinese ways. The Boxers were partly composed of underworld elements, but they expressed the prevailing despair of North China.

At that point, with the Grand Council in session a mile or so away, the aggressive attitude of the Germans did not seem helpful to most Westerners. Baron von Ketteler evidently believed that he and his spike-helmeted cohorts were a recrudescence of the Teutonic Knights with the Chinese substituting for the ancient Slavic enemy. On June 17 the energetic baron received a report that a group of fifty to a hundred Boxers were drilling on the sands below the Tatar Wall. The Baron grabbed his pistol, shouted for a squad of his marines, and led them to the top of the wall. The Boxers were about 200 yards away, perfect targets for the Germans' heavy and deadly accurate Mauser rifles. As

Morrison of the *Times* approvingly watched, he wrote, "Ketteler and his merry men" opened fire and dropped seven of the Boxers in their tracks, wounded many others, and sent the whole band fleeing for safety beyond the range of the Mausers.

Baron von Ketteler's essay in sharpshooting brought an immediate protest from many of his ministerial colleagues. Bertram Simpson, who had watched the exhibition of German marksmanship with approval, observed in his diary: "The timid Ministers unhesitatingly condemned the action; all those who understand that you must prick an ulcer with a lancet instead of pegging it with despatch-pens, as nearly all our chiefs have been doing, approved and began to follow the example set. This is the only way to act when the time for action comes in the East. . . ."

Unperturbed by what he regarded as the unmanly queasiness of his colleagues, Baron von Ketteler late that day ordered his marines to open fire on a detachment of General Tung Fu-hsiang's Kansu cavalry. The Moslems had thrown some stones at the Germans; the latter replied with rifle fire. The British minister had not joined in reproving the baron over the Tatar Wall incident earlier in the day, but now he sent a note over to the German legation suggesting it would be more sensible to avoid provoking the natives, adding that "When our own troops arrive we may with safety assume a different tone, but it is hardly wise now."

The foreign colony, in fact, was sharply divided on a number of issues. Many of the younger Westerners agreed with Baron von Ketteler that the other ministers were too timid, too intent on maintaining the cultivated tenor of diplomatic discourse, that they were fatally hesitant to risk their legation guards to save as many Chinese Christians as possible. Not only the venturesome Bertram Simpson but Nigel Oliphant, a young former officer in the Scots Grey, who now worked for the Imperial Chinese Bank, recorded his impression in a diary later published (*A Diary of the Siege of the Legations in Peking*) that only the strong-minded Morrison, as representative of the *Times*, then the organ of the British establishment and almost the mouthpiece of the government, influenced Sir Claude and other ministers to send rescue expeditions after the Chinese Christians. (The ministers, of course, had their own responsibility. They feared their compounds would be overcrowded, that Boxers would be infiltrated among the refugees, that their guests might cause a panic.) The officers of the various detachments also felt that they weren't receiving enough forceful guidance from the ministers, under whose orders they acted. They took it upon themselves, finally, to commandeer carts and tear up paving stones to erect three-foot-thick barricades blocking off the streets leading into the Legation Quarter in hopes of holding off any massed attacks on their positions.

Buckoes like Simpson, to the annoyance of their superiors (his own, Sir Robert Hart, being especially wary of offending the Chinese), went out on nightly expeditions into the native quarters looking for confrontations with the Boxers. Killing a Boxer or a Chinese suspected of being one, often on the most hasty judgment, was regarded as a sporting proposition. Simpson described one such midnight encounter in the offhand way of a hunter recapping the day's grouse hunt on the moors.

A mile and a half from the Legation Quarter, deep in the shuttered streets of the Tatar City, Simpson and his comrades suddenly came across a roving band of twenty or thirty Boxers and gleefully set upon their prey:

> I marked down one man and drove an old sword at his chest. The fellow howled frightfully, and just as I was about to despatch him a French sailor saved me the trouble by stretching him out with a resounding thump on the head with his Lebel rifle. The Boxer curled up like a sick worm and expired. There was not much time, however, to take stock of such minor incidents as the slaying of individual men, even when one was the principal actor, for everywhere men were running frantically in and out of houses, shouting and screaming, and the confusion was such that no one knew what to do. . . . As they caught sight of us, many of the marauders tore off their red sashes and fell howling on the ground in the hope that they would be passed by.

The chase led into a district where the Boxers had just slaughtered a number of the inhabitants, with most of their victims slashed from ear to ear.

> A young French sailor who did not look more than seventeen, and was splashed all over with blood from having fallen in one of the worst places, kept striking them two and three at a time, and

cursing them in fluent Breton. . . . The blood was rising to our
men's heads badly now, and I saw several who could stand it no
longer stabbing at the few dead Boxers we had secured.

Few, if any, Americans joined those unofficial punitive expeditions, taking as their example the ameliatory attitude of Minister
Conger, who still expressed the belief that the Seymour expedition
would fight its way through to Peking and save the situation. Yet
another delegation arrived from the Tsungli Yamen to plead that
any reinforcements be bivouacked outside the city walls. No,
Conger replied, the fresh troops would enter the Legation Quarter
because the Chinese government could no longer be relied upon
for protection. "We know," the Chinese officials wistfully told
him, "the foreign soldiers are better than ours."

Such placatory visits to the sympathetic American compound
ended abruptly on June 19. That was the day the Imperial Palace,
its deliberations having ended two days earlier, dropped the other
shoe, with a thud heard around the world. The crisis arrived that
afternoon when messengers from the Tsungli Yamen appeared at
each of the eleven legations with eleven red envelopes. Each
contained an identical note, which the ministers read with
apprehension. The preamble was menacing enough: "We learn
that foreign troops are about to fire upon our forts near Tientsin,
hence we break off all diplomatic relations with your Government."

The note from the Chinese Foreign Office provided little
consolation for those who hoped for peace. "The receipt of this
news," it continued, "has caused us the greatest astonishment. It
shows on the part of the Powers a deliberate intention to break the
peace and to commit an act of hostility. The Boxer movement is
now active in the capital and there is much popular excitement.
While Your Excellency and the members of your family, etc.,
reside here the Legations are in danger, and the Chinese Government is really in a difficult position as regards affording efficient
protection. The Yamen must, therefore, request that within
twenty-four hours Your Excellency will start, accompanied by the
Legation guards, who must be kept under proper control, and
proceed to Tientsin in order to prevent any unforeseen calamity."
The note added that Chinese imperial troops would form an
escort for the journey to the coast.

The notes were received with unconcealed alarm verging on panic. The hot-blooded Simpson, having no wife or children to worry about, viewed that consternation with a deep contempt and was inclined to blame the evaporation of his fellow Caucasians' fighting spirit on American influence on the world. It made him realize, he wrote in his diary, that the French aristocrats riding in tumbrils to the guillotine with a haughty contempt for the sans-culottes shrieking for their blood, were an exceptional breed. "Things have changed since then," Simpson mourned, "and the so-called Americanization of the world has not been conducive to gallantry. Fortunate are we that there is no white man's audience to watch us impassively, and to witness the effects of this bombshell of an ultimatum."

The ministers of the various legations, having gathered at the Spanish legation, met at four o'clock that afternoon. As counterpoint to those anxious, often recriminatory deliberations there was a series of explosions from a fireworks shop not far from the Spanish legation. A number of proposals on how to reply to the Chinese demand that the entire diplomatic corps evacuate the capital under the questionable protection of imperial troops was discussed; all were found wanting. Baron von Ketteler's Prussian temper had not been quieted by the note received from the Tsungli Yamen. He insisted that all the ministers, in top hats and tailcoats, march over to the yamen in a body and somehow "force" the Chinese government to grant an armistice. Everybody else voted against the proposal. After three hours of hand wringing and disputation, the ministers composed a joint message saying in effect that they accepted the terms of the Chinese note but pleading that twenty-four hours, three of them already exhausted by debate, were not enough for them to pack their belongings. That decision of course involved abandoning several thousand Chinese Christians to the Boxers—almost certain torture and death—but both the French and American ministers were especially vigorous in urging it.

Outside that council opinion among the foreigners was much firmer for defying the Chinese. Many agreed with Baron von Ketteler that to "stay meant *probable* massacre, to go promised *certain* destruction" by the Boxer bands swarming all along the route to Tientsin. When they heard the decision of the Council of Ministers, many of the nondiplomatic residents of Peking vehemently protested and were on the verge of rebelling against the dictates of the envoys. One of them expressed this dissenting opinion: "All of us would have a fair fight behind the barricades, but no massacre of a long, unending convoy. For picture to yourself that this convoy would be crawling out of giant Peking in carts, on ponies and afoot, if it were forced to go; we would be a thousand white people with a vast trail of native Christians following us, and calling on us not to abandon them and their children."

Some busied themselves in a desultory and distracted way for the flight from Peking. Trunks were hauled out of legation storerooms. Servants were sent out to round up carters, who, they reported back to their masters, were demanding a hundred silver taels for the three-day journey to Tientsin. Even so, the carters weren't willing to promise they would show up the next day; it all depended on how the situation looked by daylight.

Others in the Legation Quarter were unable to believe that when the time came, the fainthearted ministers would actually order the evacuation to proceed. They pointed out to each other that the procession of evacuees would be at least a mile long and that it could not be protected by a mere 337 legation guards, nor could they depend on any imperial troops assigned to their convoy actually to fire on their compatriots. Others raged at what Simpson called "mere diplomatic make-beliefs full of wind," by which he meant the diplomatic corps, the aggressive Baron von Ketteler excepted. They were particularly bitter at U.S. Minister Conger.

A feverish concentration on flight certainly seemed to have gripped the American compound. Conger, "to his everlasting dishonor," as Morrison of the *Times* put it, was ordering that a hundred carts be assembled to evacuate all his compatriots and their luggage. Polly Condit Smith, the pretty young houseguest of the first secretary of the legation, was puzzling over how to pack all she would need on the journey into the "tiny amount of hand-luggage we were to be allowed to take, wondering whether to fill the small bag with a warm coat, to protect us on the indefinite journey to the coast, or to take six fresh blouses. . . . It looked very much as if we were all to start out on our deaths the next morning."

Others without the blessed green passport but also relying on the U.S. minister for protection were facing more desperate decisions.

The American Methodist compound a mile to the east of the U.S. legation faced a grim choice. The missionaries could join the evacuation under protection of the American flag, of course, but what about the 700 converts? They did not look upon their Chinese flock, many of them young girls who had been attending various mission schools, as so many "rice Christians," the contemptuous term of many diplomats and concessionaires, but as souls which had been saved and now must be preserved.

They composed a letter to Minister Conger and sent it over to the legation in the early hours of June 20. "For the sake of these, your fellow Christians, we ask you to delay your departure by every pretext possible. We appeal to you in the name of Humanity and Christianity not to abandon them."

Conger was unmoved. He felt that he had larger responsibilities to weigh against 700 Chinese lives. He ordered the collection of carts to continue and all preparations to be made for flight before the Chinese ultimatum expired.

The Methodist missionaries assembled their followers, told them the American legation could not protect them, distributed money to each person, and warned them to be ready to scatter into the city, try to hide themselves among their own people, and escape to the countryside if they could.

The spectacle of her husband turning his back on the people at the Methodist compound evidently so shamed Mrs. Conger, a woman of considerable spirit, that she did not mention it in her account. The Reverend Frank Gamewell was not so charitable. He was a brave and determined man, one of the heroes of the coming days, and had spent much of his adult life persuading the Chinese to become Christians. Now he wondered aloud if abandoning them, as the U.S. legation ordered, could be reconciled with any of his teachings, whether this one long night might prove to be something Western Christianity could never live down.

Hardly anyone in the Legation Quarter slept that night. Everything depended on the Tsungli Yamen's reply to the note the Council of Ministers had dispatched that evening. "The foreign ministers," they advised the Chinese Foreign Office, "can only accept the declaration and they are ready to leave Peking. It is, however, physically impossible to organize their departure within the short space of twenty-four hours." The corps asked for further information on the kind of protection to be given them en route and for a delegation from the Tsungli Yamen to accompany them on the journey to Tientsin. A conference with Princess Tuan and Ching was requested for nine o'clock that morning.

The weary diplomats assembled at the French legation at 9 A.M. to await a reply from the Tsungli Yamen. In seven hours, at 4 P.M., the Chinese ultimatum would expire. Everyone's nerves were taut after a sleepless night, after hours of debate in each of the legations, of receiving and considering protests and suggestions from their various nationals. At 9:30 no reply to the joint note had been received, and several of the ministers were becoming restive. Most, however, thought they should wait a while longer.

The inactivity, the willingness to dither was too much for the German minister, as Sir Claude Macdonald later wrote in an account for the Permanent Undersecretary of State in his Foreign Office.

Baron von Ketteler pounded his fist on the table and declared, "I will go and sit there till they [the ministers of the Tsungli Yamen] do come, if I have to sit there all day."

The Russian minister suggested that it would be more correct if they all proceeded to the Tsungli Yamen under armed escort, since the streets around the Chinese Foreign Office were beyond the barricades of the Legation Quarter.

"There is no danger," the baron replied. "Yesterday and the day before I sent my dragoman [Heinrich Cordes, a Chinese-speaking secretary of the German legation], and he was in no way molested."

"Then," said M. de Giers, the Russian minister, "why not send *him* now?"

The German minister nodded in agreement, but a short time later changed his mind and decided to accompany his interpreter.

The devastated streets lying between the legations and the Tsungli Yamen, about a mile distant, were quiet when Ketteler and Cordes set out in two sedan chairs with scarlet and green trappings indicating their diplomatic status. They were accompanied only by two outriders in livery. Five armed sailors were assembled outside the German legation to act as an escort, but the baron waved them off. Superb in his Prussian arrogance, considering the possible dangers confronting him, Ketteler had armed himself only with a howitzer-sized Havana cigar, on which he calmly puffed, and a book to while away the time in case he was kept waiting in an antechamber.

Off they went, with a patter of the chair bearers' sandals and a puff of cigar smoke from the baron's hooded litter.

Within fifteen minutes the Legation Quarter learned of the bloody end of the baron's mission. He and his companion had been attacked just as they passed through the Arch of Honor on Hata Men Street. Their two outriders, flailing their ponies' hides with Manchu riding sticks, galloped up to the barricades shouting that the German minister had just been assassinated.

People swarmed in the streets of the Legation Quarter and tried to assess the significance of the news. Many believed that the baron was a marked man, who because of his belligerence was cordially hated by the Chinese. Bertram Simpson considered him "our one man of character and decision" and thought his death was a crushing blow, because of not only the personal tragedy but what it portended. It seemed plain enough that somebody high in the councils of the Imperial Palace was reluctant to see the foreigners go in peace. "A quarter of an hour after this," Simpson wrote in his diary, "half the German detachment was marching rapidly down Customs Street, with fixed bayonets and an air of desperation on their harsh Teutonic faces. They were determined to try and at least save the body."

Shortly after the German marines marched out—only to find that the baron's corpse had disappeared, along with the sedan chairs, the chair bearers, and every trace of the killing—Heinrich Cordes stumbled into the American Methodist compound, where the missionaries were preparing to send their converts out into the dangerous streets with little more than their blessings and a few silver coins. Cordes had been shot through both thighs, but somehow managed to make his way to the mission. He collapsed from loss of blood a moment later.

Months later Morrison of the *Times* published Cordes' account of what had happened when their sedan chairs approached the police station on Hata Men Street:

> I was watching a cart with some lance-bearers passing before the Minister's chair, when suddenly I saw a sight that made my

heart stand still. The Minister's chair was three paces in front of me. I saw a Banner soldier, apparently a Manchu, in full uniform with a mandarin's hat and a button and blue feather, step forward, present his rifle within a yard of the chair window, level it at the Minister's head and fire. I shouted in terror "Halt!"

At the same moment the shot rang out, the chairs were thrown down. I sprang to my feet. A shot struck me in the lower part of my body. Others were fired at me. I saw the Minister's chair standing, but there was no movement. . . .

I affirm that the assassination of the German Minister was a deliberately planned, premeditated murder, done in obedience to the orders of high Government officials by an Imperial Banner-man.

The murder-plot charge, of course, was farfetched. No one could have known that Ketteler's sedan chair would be passing down Hata Men Street at that moment. He had changed his mind at the last minute, it will be recalled, and announced his determination to visit the Tsungli Yamen instead of sending Cordes alone as on previous occasions. Yet it is also true that his murderer, Corporal En Hai of the Peking Field Force (one of the armies under the command of the moderate General Jung Lu), confessed he had been ordered by his superiors to murder Ketteler. En Hai was captured by German troops six months after the assassination and decapitated on the spot where he had slain the German Minister, with all the metronomic precision of Prussian justice. Before the ax fell, En Hai proclaimed, "I merely obeyed the orders of my superior officers. Otherwise why should a small person like myself take the life of so exalted a personage as the German minister? My officers offered a reward of seventy taels and promotion to anyone who would shoot the Minister." The luckless corporal had been in German custody long enough before his execution, however, to have been induced to make that confession. Certainly it served the purposes of German policy, intent as it was on exacting merciless reparations from the Chinese.

The baron's death served another and more immediate purpose. It convinced the ministers that flight would be more hazardous than staying and making a stand. Mrs. Conger, as a fellow American, was detailed to go over to the German compound and inform the former Maud Ledyard that her husband had been shot through the head. The British minister's wife then "took her in charge."

The orders went out from the various legations for everyone (Chinese not included) to gather in the British legation and face the prospects of a siege.

The foreigners in Peking now prepared to take their place beside the participants in such horrendous events—set pieces of Western history in confrontation with the problems of colonialism—as the Black Hole of Calcutta, Custer's Last Stand, the Siege of Mafeking, the Siege of Khartoum, the Siege of Querétaro. . . .

Meanwhile, what of Seymour's expeditionary force? Every night for a week people in the Legation Quarter had strained their eyes for the signal rockets of Admiral Seymour's force advancing from Tientsin.

It turned out to be one of those wretchedly mismanaged expeditions which had marked the course of colonial history in the nineteenth century. Overconfidence in confronting the "rabble" of native soldiery was always a principal ingredient in the failure of such ventures.

After a spirited squabble over who should command the relief force, it entrained on June 10 at the Tientsin station under Sir Edward Seymour's leadership and was composed of 2,129 officers and men of various nations. The largest contingent was British, 915; the Germans contributed 512; the Russians, 312; the French, 157; the Americans, 111; the Japanese, 54; the Italians, 42; and the Austrians, 26. They set out in five trains with seven pieces of field artillery and ten machine guns. Among the members of Admiral Seymour's personal staff were two future naval leaders, Captain John Jellicoe and Commander David Beatty, who would fight the Battle of Jutland against the German battle fleet fifteen years later.

Several times the trains had to be halted while damage to the Tientsin-Peking line was repaired, but by June 14 the expedition had reached Langfang, more than half the way to the capital. That day they piled off their trains to meet an attack from several hundred natives, apparently neither Boxers nor militia but peasants armed with spears, swords, and muskets determined to drive off the invaders. Seymour and his officers were taken aback by the determination of the Chinese attack, which was not broken off until sixty natives lay dead in the fields.

Soon the strung-out rail convoy was being attacked up and down the line, even though the vanguard had reached within thirty-two miles of Peking. The last train, shuttling supplies between the base at Tientsin and the spearhead, was blocked at Yangtsun, where the steel bridge over the Pei Ho River was held by well-armed Boxer bands, with General Nieh Shih-cheng's relatively efficient and foreign-trained army also in the vicinity.

Admiral Seymour felt that he could not push on from Langfang with his communications cut off at Yangtsun. He had no pack mules for an advance on foot, though a more determined commander might have given more consideration to the idea of fighting his way forward and bashing his way into Peking. Instead, he decided to fall back on Yangtsun, then move north up the Pei Ho River, the route taken by the 1860 Anglo-French expedition. By following the river, he could haul his guns, ammunition, other supplies, and the wounded (which were a prime factor, perhaps, in his refusal to drive straight for Peking) on junks. The main force retreated to Yangtsun on June 17, when artillery fire could be heard echoing from Tientsin. Apparently its base was under attack. Furthermore the rear guard at Langfang, which was composed of the German contingent, came under a heavy attack by 4,000 Chinese imperial troops and had to make a fighting retreat in which 6 Germans were killed and nearly 50 wounded. The pursuit was conducted by General Tung Fu-hsiang's Moslem cavalry from Kansu Province. The fact that Seymour's rear guard had been attacked both by General Nieh's infantry and General Tung's cavalry indicated to Admiral Seymour that he was now confronted not only by Boxer partisans and an armed peasantry but by the regular troops under direct orders from the Forbidden City. His only choice, he felt, was to pull all his forces back to Tientsin.

By then the potential of seapower, as exhilaratingly expounded by the American naval prophet Captain Alfred Thayer Mahan, seemed much less omnipotent to the commanders of the international fleet anchored off Tientsin. They found themselves cut off from the landing parties so confidently dispatched inland. Admiral Seymour's force was bottled up at Yangtsun. There was a thirty-mile stretch of railroad separating the mouth of the Pei Ho, which was guarded by the Taku forts, and Tientsin, where 2,400 troops were protecting the Foreign Settlement. Thus Chinese forces were interposed at Taku, around Tientsin, around Yangtsun, between the warships and their auxiliaries ashore. A linkage had to be arranged with desperate haste. The allied forces ashore now resembled a gravely wounded snake, all but cut into three segments.

A conference was held on the Russian flagship on June 16 with all the allied commanders except the American participating, to decide whether to seize the Taku forts. One of the warships anchored off the Taku Bar was the USS *Monocacy*, a side-wheeler gunboat built during the Civil War and resembling a Staten Island ferry. The ranking U.S. officer on the scene was Rear Admiral Louis Kempff, whose hands were tied by a Washington directive stating that he was not authorized to engage in any hostile acts against China. Several days earlier his superior, Admiral George C. Remey, commander of the Asiatic Station then aboard his flagship off Manila, had criticized Kempff for cooperating with the allied commanders at Tientsin to "an extent incompatible with the interests of the American government." Under those circumstances Kempff had to stay out of what promised to be a glorious fight. His colleagues, without his moral support, decided to present the Chinese authorities with an ultimatum demanding the surrender of the Taku forts.

Such an assault as was proposed by the fleet captains would be a hazardous affair. They had a mixed bag of nine shallow-draft warships with which to undertake the operation: the British sloop *Algerine*, the modern British destroyers *Fame* and *Whiting*, the German sloop *Iltis*, the Russian gunboats *Gilyak*, *Bobre* and *Koreetz*, the French gunboat *Lion*, and the Japanese ironclad *Atago*. They would be going in against the four Taku forts, low-profiled and flat-topped against the tidal flats, two on each bank of the mouth of the Pei Ho. Foreign engineers had supervised their reconstruction in recent years, and they had been outfitted with new rapid-firing Krupp cannon of heavy caliber. Most of their ships were lightly armored and equipped with obsolete guns, but they were the only elements of the fleet capable of approaching that close to the Taku forts; the heavier warships simply couldn't negotiate the Taku Bar.

When the allied ultimatum was ignored, the nine-ship flotilla moved in for the assault at fifty minutes after midnight on June 17. About six hours of desultory bombardment followed. The allied flotilla opened the proceedings rather unpromisingly when the Russian gunboat *Gilyak* switched on her new searchlight and made herself a splendid target for the shore batteries. The Chinese gunners, however, had been inadequately trained, and they did little damage to the warships, which by 3 A.M. had been able to steam in close enough to put landing parties ashore. Sailors from the various nations, with fixed bayonets, started across the mud flats to assault the forts while their ships pounded away offshore. Dawn's first light helped the allied marksmanship, and the powder magazines in two of the forts were blown up. Two forts were stormed and taken, the other two ran up the white flag, and by breakfast time the fleet had secured a resounding victory at the relatively minor cost of 172 casualties. The Taku forts were the key to the strategic situation. They had to be eliminated before the large-scale operations required to rescue the foreign colonies of Tientsin and Peking could be undertaken.

Not only did the international fleet now have the necessary beachhead over which reinforcements and supplies, coming from all quarters of the globe, could be pumped in, but operations to lift the siege of Tientsin could proceed. That enclave, defended by a 2,400-man force including a recent addition of 1,600 Russian soldiers, was suffering through a foretaste of Peking's coming ordeal.

The defenders of the Foreign Settlement were holding the barricades along a five-mile perimeter against an estimated 10,000 Chinese who were being reinforced daily. Among those endangered by the siege of the Foreign Settlement was a future President of the United States. Herbert Hoover was a mining engineer recently graduated from Stanford, then just short of his twenty-sixth birthday. He had brought his wife to Tientsin for medical treatment. On June 10, a week before the allied assault on the Taku forts, the Hoovers and other foreigners in Tientsin came under fire from artillery fired by Chinese imperial troops who had joined the Boxer cause.

If the bombardment had been followed up by infantry attacks, Hoover later believed, the Foreign Settlement would have been overwhelmed that first Sunday of the siege. The all-out attack was delayed, however, by quarrels among the Chinese over who was in command.

Thus the foreigners in Tientsin were granted just enough time to pull themselves together and organize their defense. A Russian colonel named Wogack, who had the largest contingent under his command, was accepted as the man in charge of those defenses by all, as Hoover noted, "except the British under command of a naval bully named Captain Bailey, who was his own law."

The future President's engineering experience was immediately enlisted, as Hoover recalled many years later in his memoirs:

> Wogack sent word to us to organize the Christian Chinese who had fled to the settlement for safety to build barricades. The settlement was about a quarter-mile wide and a mile long, protected by the river on one side. In hunting material for barricades, we lit upon the great godowns [warehouses] filled with sacked sugar, peanuts, rice and other grain. Soon we and other foreigners whom I enlisted had a thousand terrified Christian Chinese carrying and piling up walls of sacked grain and sugar along the exposed sides of the town and at cross streets. The big attack came the second day, but the marines and sailors repulsed it from behind our bags. . . .

Even as the allied flotilla was taking the Taku forts on the morning of June 17, the Tientsin garrison was under increasing pressure from the numerically superior forces surrounding it. It seemed touch and go; a really determined attack could have swamped the barricades. On June 20 an English civilian accompanied by three Cossacks made a desperate ride down to Taku to inform the naval commanders that the Foreign Settlement couldn't hold out much longer without relief.

Through the infallible instrument of hindsight we can see that the victories of various Chinese forces around Peking and Tientsin in mid-June contributed to an illusion which was fatal to the Chinese imperial government. For it was thus persuaded to encourage the Boxer uprising. In effect, China declared war on the rest of the world because its forces seemed to be winning during the two crucial days of the Grand Council. On June 16, the day the Grand Council was convened, Admiral Seymour's relief

convoy had been sent reeling back to Yangtsun; the Foreign
Settlement of Tientsin was under heavy attack and seemed likely
to be overwhelmed; the whole countryside of North China was
rising against the foreigners with whatever weapons could be
found. Peking could imagine it was catching the rise of a popular
tide. Information that the Taku forts had fallen, since bad news
was always slow to reach the inmost councils of the dowager
empress, was not received before the Grand Council adjourned.
All those victories against inferior allied forces were read as signs
that the foreign powers might not be able to prevail over the
Chinese masses despite their technological superiority.

The next critical day was June 20, when the ultimatum to the
ministers in Peking expired a few hours after the German envoy
was killed by a Manchu soldier. Protection could have been
afforded the legations and the attacks on the foreign quarter of
Tientsin called off, at least those in which imperial troops
participated, if the empress and her closest advisers had not been
determined to continue on their tragic course.

On that same day it should have been apparent to the Manchu
court that China would not rise en masse to join the antiforeign
cause. The viceroys of the various provinces outside of Shantung
and Chihli had not been consulted, but most of them were
opposed to the rebellion, both when it was really a rebellion
against the Manchus and when it became a war against foreign
intervention. From reading hundreds of documents in the Chinese
archives, Professor Tan has concluded that "the viceroys believed
that war with all the Powers was utterly futile, and that to save the
situation it was necessary that the Boxers be suppressed, the
foreign ministers saved, and diplomatic relations be maintained."
The collaboration of the viceroys was needed if South China was
to join the North, if troops and supplies were to be forwarded.
Instead, they grouped themselves around the supremely respected
figure of elder statesman Li Hung-chang and formed a polite but
stubborn resistance movement.

Certainly they made their attitude clear enough from the
beginning. Long before the Boxer movement had spread from the
remote country districts of Shantung and Chihli, they were
warning Peking that it had to be stopped as a danger to the throne
as well as the rest of China. They considered themselves as
patriotic as any red-sashed fanatic, and were as antiforeign, as

hopeful that China could rid itself of outside influences, as any of the empress' hotheaded advisers, but they believed that their country could not undertake such a task until it was much stronger. Meanwhile, it must maintain an amiable façade toward its Western "helpers" and learn everything it could from them before throwing them out.

On June 20 eight viceroys and governors of the Yangtze provinces telegraphed a memorial to the throne proposing the suppression of the Boxers because "no government since the beginning of history can rule a country with rebels who violate laws and kill people, nor can a country preserve itself when it fights six or seven powers at a time and for no good reason." They further suggested that Viceroy Li Hung-chang be appointed to negotiate with the foreign powers. Five days later several of the provincial satraps sent another message to Peking pointing out that China could not possibly hope for a military victory over the invading powers. They did not bother to assert their patriotism but hammered away at the realities of the situation: "From the military point of view, it is impossible for one country to fight all the Powers; the result for China will inevitably be defeat. From the political point of view, the Powers can never yield to one country; they will fight on until they are victorious."

Without consulting Peking, acting on his own hook, Li Hung-chang cabled Chinese ministers abroad to maintain diplomatic relations, if at all possible, and be available to work out a peaceful settlement. A short time later an imperial edict ordered the viceroys to stop payment on foreign loans. Twelve viceroys and governors promptly joined in protesting the measure because it would only increase the pressure abroad for stronger military action against China. "Then war would be spread everywhere," the memorial pointed out, "and the seditious elements in the interior would take the opportunity to stir up disturbances. With aggression from outside and disturbances within, the whole country would be in turmoil. . . . " On that point the central government yielded and countermanded the previous order stopping the loan payments.

As news reached the southern provinces of what was happening in Peking, the viceroys, led by Li Hung-chang, also joined in memorializing the throne to warn that if the foreign diplomats were harmed, China would be regarded as an outlaw nation and "the calamities would be unthinkable." They urged that the most disciplined troops available be assigned to protect the legations.

The viceroys and governors continued to act to the best of their ability as a restraining force. Their combined foot dragging prevented the mobilization of the country's human and material resources behind the uprising in North China, but their influence could no longer prevail against the violent course of events in the sleevelike corridor between Tientsin and Peking.

On the afternoon of June 20, the foreign colony in Peking realized that diplomatic status would no longer protect them. For an incalculable time they would be on their own, beyond reach of the international fleet off Tientsin. There was nothing to do but prepare for a defense; everything had changed within one-quarter of an hour that morning, between the time the German minister left for the Tsungli Yamen and the arrival of news that he had been killed en route.

It was quickly decided to shrink the defensive perimeter and concentrate on holding the British compound, which not only was the largest but was not overlooked by the Tatar Wall and was surrounded by open space. About 900 people poured into the British compound with their portable possessions, the whole foreign colony except for M. and Mme. Chamot, who insisted on clinging to occupancy of the Hôtel de Pekin nearby, plus the missionaries and other refugees from the interior.

A hurried ministerial council, after deciding on turning the British compound into the central redoubt, took up the question of the outlying religious communities. Bishop Favier was determined to hold out with his Catholic converts behind the fortress-like walls of the Peitang Cathedral, but the American Methodists were pleading for sanctuary not only for themselves but for their Chinese followers. The American minister proposed that the white missionaries be invited to the British compound but that their Chinese charges simply be abandoned. Nobody asked for the opinion of Dr. Morrison of the *Times*, but the outspoken Australian gave it anyway. "I would be ashamed to call myself a white man if I could not make a place for these Chinese Christians."

The ministers could not be shamed into sheltering the Chinese converts, so Morrison and a likeminded friend, Professor Huberty

James, a member of the Imperial University faculty, investigated the possibility of using Prince Su's spacious palace and its grounds, which adjoined the British compound and could therefore be included in the defense system, as a sanctuary for the Chinese.

Spared the unseemly predicament of having to live at close quarters with the natives, reassured by the fact that their fellow Christians (but of the wrong pigmentation) would be segregated, the ministers agreed upon a rescue mission to the Methodist compound. Conger dispatched a platoon of twenty U.S. marines, which some believed he had regarded as part of a personal bodyguard, along with a note to the missionaries: "Come at once within the Legation lines. And bring your Chinese with you."

The missionaries at the Methodist compound were given twenty minutes to pack; then a straggling crocodile of refugees, herded by marines, started moving through charred streets toward the Legation Quarter. Among them were 71 missionaries, their wives and children, 124 demure little Chinese schoolgirls, and 700 other Christian converts. Four men carried the stretcher bearing Heinrich Cordes, who had been wounded only a few hours earlier. The whole procession reached the legations without being attacked along the way, and then, as though some unseen shepherd were separating the sheep from the goats, the whites split off and turned into the British territory and the Chinese padded off to Prince Su's palace, where they were joined by 2,000 Catholic Chinese. Thus those within the pale included about three Chinese to every white person.

The refugees gathered in the three-acre British compound. With only a few hours until the expiration of the 4 P.M. deadline, they poured into the walled section and its outbuildings like Western pioneers heading for the nearest stockade under the threat of an Indian attack. Dr. Arthur Smith, the scholarly missionary whose *Chinese Characteristics* was regarded by Westerners (if not Chinese) as the masterwork in the field of explaining China and its people to the outside world, described the scene in his two-volume memoir:

> Uncounted carts loaded with every variety of household furniture continually arrived. Swarms of coolies struggled through the broad passages, the stream of those endeavoring to

enter becoming constantly entangled with the equally strong stream of those trying to get out again in order to go back and reload.

The whole legation had been turned inside out, recharted, and its separate buildings assigned to different nationalities. This was the Russian house, that the French, and a third was devoted to the use of the staff of the Imperial Customs. The spacious front pavilions began to be covered with the most miscellaneous baggage, especially cases of provisions and wines, as this was the headquarters of the numerous Belgian, French and others in the employ of the ruined Le-Han railway. The stable-house was full of Norwegians.

The rear pavilion was "Reserved" and was divided into several messes. In one corner two men represented what was left of the Hongkong & Shanghai Banking Corporation, and in another corner several military officers had such headquarters as were possible, while the *Times* correspondent was content with a mattress on the floor-tiles, near which was stacked up his library, happily rescued just before his house was destroyed.

Even under the threat of imminent attack Sir Claude Macdonald as the host of this involuntary ingathering of the nations had to consider the various sensibilities and national prejudices. The French and Russians were on bad terms and had to be given separate houses. The Germans and Japanese, however, were on amiable footing and shared the consular students' quarters. The royal marines were quartered in the fives court, while the American missionaries were jammed into the chapel, some of them being forced to occupy the choir loft among miscellaneous junk stored there. The former guests of the Hôtel de Pekin were allotted a pavilion.

The legation guards, meanwhile, were being posted on various walls and impromptu ramparts, manning the street barricades and waiting to open fire if the quarter came under a mass attack from the Boxers. No one doubted the attack would come. Otherwise word would have arrived from the Tsungli Yamen notifying them that the 4 P.M. deadline of the ultimatum had been extended.

So frenzied and disorganized were the preparations that it wasn't until the last hour that anyone thought of collecting all the available food supplies before the quarter was cut off from the shops, warehouses, and other sources. Here American practicality at last asserted itself, though it had not hitherto been a quality much admired by the swells and fashion plates of the *Corps Diplomatique.* "There is no denying," observed Bertram Simpson, not ordinarily a warm admirer of all things American, "that on this 20th the Americans showed more energy than anybody else, and pushed everybody to sending out their carts and bringing in tons upon tons of food."

The leader in the last-minute effort was First Secretary Herbert Squiers, whose square-jawed profile might have made him a model for the Gibson Man so popular in American magazine illustrations. With the assistance of his fifteen-year-old son Fargo, he requisitioned everything in sight. Fortunately American credit was good. He scribbled chits for Chinese shopkeepers who had unaccountably stayed open and were smilingly ready to do business. Sheep grazing near the British compound were confiscated. Eight thousand bushels of wheat were carted from the Broad Prosperity Grain Shop in a street near the Legation Quarter. He also found tons of rice in a godown near the Imperial Drainage Canal which cut through the quarter. All the supplies were transported to the British compound and poured into bins or stored in sheds.

Well before four o'clock everyone had taken cover or was standing by his assigned post. On the lawn in front of the British legation a solemn group of Englishmen, having synchronized their watches in the approved military style, were watching the minute hands edging toward the zero hour.

For once the Chinese, ordinarily so contemptuous of the Western obsession with time, were punctual. At the stroke of four Chinese rifles began a fusillade to the northeast just beyond the French legation. From the Tatar Wall the legation guards stationed there could observe maneuvering masses of the black-turbaned Kansu cavalry, the Imperial Bannermen, Prince Tuan's private legion of Glorified Tigers, troops of General Jung Lu's Peking Field Force—and hordes of Boxers joining in the deployment for jump-off positions from which to overwhelm the heathen from the West and their Japanese allies.

Suddenly there was a bassoonlike blare from the long Chinese trumpets, a bull-like roar of challenge almost as frightening as the masses of troops deploying beyond the Tatar Wall.

A French soldier fell with a bullet in his head, the first casualty of the siege of the Peking legations.

It was what the Chinese called the Hour of the Dog.

The dangerous summer had begun.

II. THE ORDEAL BY FIRE

*In any civilized country it would be possible for
us to surrender and so save our lives . . .*

—U.S. MINISTER EDWIN H. CONGER

6. *On the Barricades*

It took hours for the foreigners besieged at Peking to come to
grips with the reality of their situation. The oldest of the old China
hands, particularly, found it difficult to believe that the Chinese
would actually attack them with live bullets and shells and
showers of spears. They were firmly convinced that even if the
Chinese carried out the threats contained in their ultimatum, it
would all be a form of military playacting. There would be
fireworks, a clanging of gongs, a display of martial intentions.
Even the deaths of the past days could not persuade many of the
foreigners with longest residence in China that the Manchu
government meant business. It was even more incredible that the
diplomatic status of the Legation Quarter would be violated.

Even the military had not taken the most necessary step toward
a successful defense of the quarter, that of deciding on an overall
commander. Their efforts were still haphazard and uncoordinated.
Each unit fought for its own territory and provided a capsule
preview of allied operations in the Great War fourteen years later.

Shortly after the first exchange of volleys the small Austrian
contingent (seven officers, thirty men), which had been defending
the barricades around their legation in the northeast corner of the
rectangular perimeter, suddenly abandoned their position. A
glimpse of the Moslem cavalry maneuvering in the distance had
sent the Austrians into a panic along with a number of civilian
volunteers who had reinforced them. The whole lot fled to the

positions around the French legation on Customs Street to the south, where angry recriminations were exchanged by the French officers and Captain von Thomann of the Austrian Navy. Bertram Simpson, who had joined the Austrian contingent, was disgusted by the fact that the diplomats had holed up in the British legation and were too busy making themselves comfortable to give any direction to the defense. He and his fellow fighting men, he would recall, were fuming with indignation. "A number of young Englishmen belonging to the Customs volunteers began telling the French and Austrian sailors that we had been *trahis* [betrayed], in order to make them swear louder. I know that it was becoming funny, because it was so absurd when . . . bang-ping, bang-ping, came three or four shots from far down the street beyond the Austrian legation. That stopped the talking. . . ."

It simply seemed impossible, at first, for many of the foreigners to take the situation seriously. Toward dusk, with shots still flying and rockets searing the gloom, the Italian minister, Marchese di Selvago Raggi, was seen walking about Legation Street in evening dress. Sir Claude Macdonald was strolling around the British compound, also dressed for dinner and puffing on a cigarette. Among all the nationalities there was a disposition that night to maintain the outward aspects of a normal civilized life and wait until tomorrow to worry about the problems of living under siege conditions.

Among the elder members of the foreign colony there was a marked inability to comprehend what was happening, to adjust themselves to the idea of the Chinese as deadly enemies. A tragic instance of this incomprehension was the English professor, Huberty James, who had been a member of the Imperial University faculty as long as anyone could remember, a Sinophile almost as fervent as Sir Robert Hart. James, an "eccentric of the pronounced type," as one of his fellow Britons described him, had worked hard alongside Dr. Morrison of the *Times* to find shelter for the Chinese refugees in the palace and ornamental park recently abandoned by Prince Su. The palace lay to the east, just across the Imperial Drainage Canal from the British compound.

Toward dusk he had checked on the condition of his charges; then, as riflemen on the British barricades watched, he strolled to the north bridge across the canal, which was unguarded and temporarily in the hands of the Chinese. A Chinese rifleman fired on him, and he appeared to have been wounded. Other Chinese suddenly appeared and dragged James away. That night he was tortured, then decapitated. Two days later his head was displayed in a cage placed over the Tung Hua Gate, the face frozen into what a Chinese later described as a "most horrible expression."

The capture of Professor James was disheartening enough. He had what his friend Morrison called a "blind faith in the Chinese." If that could happen to a man with so many Chinese friends, what would be the fate of the rest of the foreigners?

While the British and Italian ministers swanked about in their dinner jackets and proposed that the amenities be preserved, no matter that their defenders were under fire a few hundred yards away, U.S. Minister Conger was still brooding over his lost hope of throwing himself on the mercy of the enemy. An American missionary heard him say that "in any civilized country it would be possible for us to surrender and so save our lives, but to surrender here meant certain death. . . ."

Among the civilians in the British compound that night of June 20 there was stark fear and unaccustomed privation. No lamps could be lit for fear of attracting the attention of a sniper. Great difficulty was experienced by mothers and amahs trying to settle the hitherto-pampered children on mats and other makeshift bedding; the air was stifling, and the children kept crying out for water. It was worse out in the courtyard, where Chinese bullets clipped the branches off the trees overhead. Some of the British, according to one of their countrymen, kept the others awake by holding a boozeup, the theory being that they might as well be dead drunk when the Chinese swarmed over the barricades.

One of the sober and more alert members of the British contingent, out inspecting the compound's defenses, came across a striking example of British phlegm. "Sleeping peacefully in his nice pyjamas under a mosquito net," he would recall, "was found a sleek official of the London Board of Works, who wanted to know what was meant by waking him up in the middle of the night."

The impish Polly Condit Smith joined her hostess, Mrs. Herbert Squiers, in trying to quiet the youngest children of the American legation's first secretary. Somewhat more difficult was the task of keeping the peace between the Squierses' French and German governesses, who had become embroiled in an argument, each haranguing the other in her native tongue. "Mademoiselle is a large woman of formidable proportions in the wrong places, and she had her bosom filled with recommendation papers, which she fingered nervously—they were all she was saving in the way of valuables. Clara, the German governess, had forgotten what her valuables were, and looked quite distraught with fear. She had a French clock in each hand, and was telling me in broken English, German and Chinese how afraid and terrified she was. I said to her, '*Gehen Sie mit mir*,' and she clutched my arm most painfully for the next half-hour." Finally the Squiers children were persuaded to sleep in their cribs, and the German governess was placed at one end of the room, the French governess at the other, with instructions to ignore each other.

The lurid dawn of June 21 rose on a day of confusion and divided counsel. The optimists among the foreign colony pointed out that Admiral Seymour would arrive at any hour, the pessimists that they were all doomed and could only await their fate with Christian grace. Those in between, who hoped to defend themselves to the last bullet, waited for orders from the diplomatic and military seniors. All day, however, the senior officers—"colonial colonels, gentlemen strategists and obstructive veterans of the American Civil War," as one historian has described them—argued among themselves over seniority, questions of command, which sectors to strengthen, which could be abandoned if the pressure became too intense.

Sir Claude, as the leader of the diplomatic corps, finally began pulling himself together at midday and making some sensible arrangements for the defense and victualing of the Legation Quarter. In the best British fashion he acted through a committee system. First he appointed a Fortification Staff. This was to be headed by one of the American missionaries, Dr. Frank Dunlop Gamewell, who, as Sir Claude had been told, built the barricades around the Methodist mission before it was abandoned. Gamewell was the son of the man who invented the first fire-alarm system and had been educated at Rensselaer Polytechnic and the Cornell Engineering School before deciding to become a missionary. He was to supervise the construction of a system of barricades, trenches, and redoubts without which the defenders of the Legation Quarter could not have survived in the coming weeks.

Sir Claude also appointed a General Committee of Public Comfort, a Committee on Sanitation, and a Food Supply Committee, with others to be named shortly to oversee every detail of the besieged community's hazardous existence. The Food Committee went into action immediately and found a large variety of foodstuffs in various shops along Legation Street which had been abandoned overnight by their owners. Overlooked the previous day in the hectic moments before the ultimatum expired, several tons of yellow rice, which the foreigners would have to learn to like, were found in one store; white and yellow Indian corn, pulse (edible seeds), bags of coffee, sugar, and beans, and boxes of canned goods were requisitioned from other establishments. The prize cache, however, was 8,000 bushels of new wheat which had just arrived from the province of Hunan in cylindrical baskets. In the same shop was found eleven stone mills, also requisitioned, which would grind out much of the besieged colony's diet in the coming days.

In the sweltering heat, the confusion, the plunging fire from the Chinese lines, the various civilian committees organized themselves and set to work. Largely they were composed of missionaries, male and female, who were accustomed to working hard and making do with whatever materials were at hand. While the diplomats, the international society people, and globe-trotters among those present clapped their hands for chop-chop service from whatever Chinese servants had remained loyal, the missionaries labored in unison to sustain the rear areas of the defense of the Legation Quarter. It was already the custom to sneer at the homely dedicated people who, rightly or wrongly, had been laboring for and with the Asians for many years—it was the practice of sophisticates to view them as Bible-banging hypocrites, but without the organizing ability of the missionaries, their culinary, medical, and engineering services, the foreign colony at Peking would probably have succumbed.

Certainly it could not have made much of a fight without Dr. Gamewell's energetic presence. He seemed to be everywhere at once, pedaling furiously from one sector of the defense to another on his bicycle. Most of the legation guards were sailors or marines, and the few soldiers present had been trained in the old hollow-square, forward-with-the-bayonet school; their officers regarded military fortification as something unmanly and certainly undignified. But sandbags and bombproof shelters were more valuable than sword-waving panache against Krupp artillery and the Mauser rifles with which many of the Chinese were armed.

Stronger earthworks would be needed along the northern perimeter against the Chinese artillery; the hospital would have to be made bombproof; a blockhouse had to be built at the main gate on the east; Chinese attempts at mining under the defenses would have to be guarded against and thwarted. Dr. Gamewell's mind and spirit, so recently engaged by his ministry to the Chinese soul, were now preoccupied by mundane calculations that a Mauser bullet would pierce one-quarter inch of a brick wall, a Krupp shell fifty-four inches.

Everything had to be done at once—sandbags sewn and filled, trenches dug, earthworks thrown up, barricades erected on the glazed-tile parapet of the Tatar Wall. All that, and more, was Gamewell's responsibility. An admirer wrote:

> Often, four hours out of the twenty-four were his allowance for sleep. By means of a much-used bicycle he seemed to be everywhere at once, superintending the building of barricades, seeking reinforcements of Chinese laborers, and always watching for weak points in the defenses which were immediately to be strengthened. One day when Mrs. Gamewell was inquiring for her husband, someone replied: "If you stand right where you are for five minutes, he will be likely to go past." And the prediction proved true. Often after the furious attacks which came in the midnight hours, he would go to the threshold of the ballroom where the group of women were trying in vain to sleep, and would give them an account of what had happened, telling them it was never as bad as it seemed from the sounds. His reassuring words comforted them so that they could relax for a few hours' sleep before the morning sun summoned to the tasks of a new day.

They all must have wished for a General, or at least a Colonel, Gamewell to pull together the purely military aspects of the defense.

The guard force, largely composed of landing parties from the international fleet at Tientsin, was well drilled in presenting arms for distinguished visitors to a legation compound or at best making a "show of force" to confound ill-equipped natives. It had never been expected by their commanders that they would be called upon to conduct a last-ditch defense. Otherwise they would certainly have been equipped with something more lethal than four obsolescent rapid-fire guns. These included the American detachment's Colt heavy machine gun with 25,000 rounds of ammunition and an Italian one-pounder with only a few hundred shells. The Austrians had a serviceable Maxim machine gun, the British a five-barreled 1887 model Nordenfelt machine gun in which every fourth round jammed and had to be jacked out.

In the eight-nation force, including the military and naval attachés and other personnel with military experience from the legations, the British contributed 3 officers and 79 men, the Russians 2 officers and 79 men, the Americans 3 and 53, the Germans 1 and 53, the Austrians 7 and 30, the Japanese 1 and 24. The French contingent included 2 officers and 45 men, the Italian 1 and 28, but of those, 2 officers and 41 men had been detached to defend the Peitang Cathedral.

The professionals were supported by two groups of armed volunteers, including several with extensive military experience. Nigel Oliphant, a member of the Imperial Chinese Bank staff, had served in India with the Scots Greys. And there were several serving officers in transit. Lieutenant Vroublevsky had been sent to Peking by his regiment, the Ninth Eastern Siberian Rifles, to learn the Chinese language. Captain Labrousse was attached to the French Infanterie de Marine but happened to be passing through Peking on his way from Tonkin to Paris via Siberia.

These and other able-bodied and venturesome volunteers were organized into a group of seventy-five men with previous military experience which included thirty-two Japanese. It was a polyglot but disciplined and efficient force which helped man the front defense lines. The second outfit of franc-tireurs was more visibly ferocious but less professional, composed of about fifty men who were willing to fight with whatever was at hand. As Morrison of the *Times* described this colorful band, "They did garrison duties in the British Legation and were known as the 'Carving Knife Brigade,' from their habit of lashing cutlery of this type to weapons varying from an elephant rifle to the *fusil de chasse* [hunting rifle] with a picture of the Grand Prix. . . . The most experienced of them was he who had once witnessed the trooping of the colour in St. James's Park. They were formidable alike to friend and foe."

Aside from the scarcity of firepower, the defenders were handicapped by the lack of a skilled senior officer, with any sort of experience of siege warfare, to take overall command. No one really filled the bill except Colonel Shiba, the Japanese military attaché, whose ability and leadership were unquestionable. But he was an Asian, and that wouldn't do. The senior in rank on the scene, by unfortunate coincidence, was Captain von Thomann, the commander of the Austrian cruiser *Zenta*, who happened to be in Peking on a sight-seeing expedition. Nothing good had been heard from the Austrian Navy for at least a century, but Thomann announced late in the afternoon of June 21, after listening to wrangling between the various nationalities, that he was assuming command. At that point, twenty-four hours after the siege began, the Legation Quarter was in serious danger of being overrun. Two of the outlying legations, the Dutch and Belgian, had been abandoned in order to shorten the defense line. There had been frequent attacks on the main positions—that is, those around the British compound and Prince Su's palace—but none was pressed with sufficient vigor to overcome the defenders. The latter, however, as yet had little to protect them from the enemy fire but the overturned carts which formed the barricades. It was generally believed that they were opposed by up to 100,000 imperial troops and Boxers. The actual number was probably a quarter of that.

Direly threatened as they were, there were quarrels between the commanders of the various detachments and the proliferating committees appointed by Sir Claude and disputes over digging tools, bricks, timbers, and Chinese labor. "I forbid you to use a drop of that water!" the chairman of the Water Supply Committee shouted at the chairman of the Amateur Fire Brigade. Somebody had obviously had to take hold, but Captain von Thomann, with his explosive temper, was not the man for a coalition command. His self-appointed chieftaincy lasted less than twenty-four hours.

Roving the defense lines as one of the armed volunteers, Bertram Simpson found evidence of military efficiency only in the Japanese sector between Prince Su's palace ground and the French legation. The walls fronting their position were properly and alertly manned. Colonel Shiba was a bandy-legged little dynamo. "This man, working quietly, is reducing things to order, and in the few hours which have gone by since the dreadful occurrences of yesterday, he has succeeded in attending to the thousand small details which demanded his attention. He is organizing his dependents into a self-contained little camp; he is making the horde of converts come to his aid and strengthen his lines. . . . Already I honour this little man; soon I feel I shall be his slave." Elsewhere, Simpson noted, "half the officers are at loggerheads." Not only had Colonel Shiba taken a firm grip on his sector, but he was already gathering intelligence about the enemy's capability and intentions. He had sent a Japanese sailor to lurk around a Chinese camp a quarter of a mile away. The sailor brought back word that a group of snipers were about to slip away from the Chinese unit. Colonel Shiba immediately led out a reconnaissance in force, with Simpson going along as an observer of Japanese methods. The patrol probed along tortuous lanes leading in the direction of the abandoned Austrian legation and Customs Inspectorate on the northeast edge of the Legation Quarter. They killed a Boxer on a rooftop before returning to their own lines. Everyone was elated, Simpson observed, except Colonel Shiba, who had learned from his patrol that the outer walls of Prince Su's palace were longer than he had suspected.

Returning to the British legation, Simpson found his compatriots muddling through in their traditional fashion. Sir Robert Hart was sitting on an old mattress and looking dazed while Baron de Pokotilov of the Russo-Chinese Bank was striding up and down and muttering into his beard. "Already the British Legation has surrendered itself, not to the enemy, but to committees. There are general committees, food committees, fortifications committees, and what other committees I do not know, except that the American missionaries, who appear at least to have more energy than anyone else, are practically ruling them. This is all very well in its way, but it is curious to see that dozens of able-bodied men, armed with rifles [apparently he referred to the "Carving Knife Brigade"], are hiding away in corners so that they shall not be drafted away to the outer defences. Everywhere a contemptible spirit is being displayed. . . ."

Not everywhere, actually. If many of the 245 civilian males who had taken shelter at the British legation were proving a bit pusillanimous, the women and even many of the children were bearing up well. Most of the American women, drawing on any residual pioneer spirit they possessed, were busying themselves at sewing sandbags, making bandages, caring for the children. There were 149 women and 79 children of all American and European nationalities in the compound. Later it was one of the legends of the Peking siege that many women took turns at the loopholes and fought on the barricades, but aside from the rifle-toting American-born Mme. Chamot of the Hôtel de Pekin, this was all romanticizing. The women, except for a number of lily-fingered and languishing types, were fully occupied with tasks behind the defense lines. One major responsibility was the care and feeding of the 2,000 Chinese Catholics and 700 Protestants at Prince Su's palace.

Looking after the children kept many of the women busy from dawn to midnight from that first full day of the siege onward. Polly Condit Smith wrote:

> When we turn the room into a nursery for the children, for we cannot keep them always in their own room, nor can we allow them to be much in the compound, as half the time it is thick with exploding [sic] bullets, then it is a sight to behold. . . . Their one game seems to be "Boxers," and they copy in miniature what we grownups are playing in earnest. The younger ones are forced into being the attacking Chinese, and I am afraid when the big ones repulse them, they occasionally get very real bumps on their heads. They have small sandbags and barricades, and their Chinese war-whoop of Sha! Sha! (Kill! Kill!) is a creditable imitation of the real thing. . . . I help them to play, for it's a good thing that they don't realize what all this may mean, and we hope that relief will come before they lose their spirit and before they know.

All that day there was sporadic fighting, with the machine-gun squad of the American marine detachment killing six Boxers as they tried to loot and set fire to the Dutch legation, which was located next to the American compound. Both the Dutch and Belgian legations, however, had to be written off as indefensible later in the day.

The most daring feat was performed by a fifteen-year-old American boy. He was Fargo Squiers, who the day before had helped his father bring in supplies just before the Chinese ultimatum expired. Later he would serve with distinction as an aide to Captain Strouts, commanding the detachment of Royal Marine Light Infantry. At the moment Fargo was determined to make himself the No. 1 scrounger. Early in the afternoon he learned the Food Committee had considered the matter of the canned goods stocked by the two foreign stores, Imbeck's and Kierulff's, but decided it would be too dangerous to send a foraging detail that far up Legation Street.

Without telling any of his elders, the boy armed himself with a rifle and commandeered a cart and two unwilling Chinese assistants. He headed down Legation Street despite a peppering from Chinese riflemen. Polly Condit Smith recorded in her diary:

> On their way to Imbeck's, one of the Chinese was killed by a bullet in the head, and though the other survived to help him load the cart, after arriving in the courtyard of Imbeck's, he had difficult work, as coolie No. 2 tried to run away. Twice the boy had to point the muzzle of the rifle at him, indicating what he would do if he made any further attempts. On the return trip every yard of the way they were peppered by bullets, and the second coolie was wounded. . . . The cart came thundering into the British compound with the upper part of the cart riddled with bullet-holes.

Young Squiers was proceeding to his family's quarters with the provender when he was stopped by an officious member of the Food Committee, who called his group into emergency session to consider whether it shouldn't be confiscated for the communal stores. It was decided that Fargo could keep his loot from Imbeck's because he had "dared what no man in the compound had dared to do."

Everyone congratulated him as a "manly little chap" and a "plucky lad," but no one questioned whether several dozen tins of caviar, corned beef, and peaches were a fair exchange for the death of one "coolie" and the wounding of another.

At nightfall on June 21 many of the more knowledgeable Westerners, like Bertram Simpson, who had seen the haphazard arrangements of their defenders, with only the Japanese prepared to put up a good fight, believed they were doomed if an allied relief column didn't reach them within a week—if not sooner.

Even the bouncy correspondent of the *Times* was downhearted, "sapped by the spectacle of extraordinary incompetence around him," as his friend Simpson put it. "Of what good has all that rescuing of native Christians been—all that energy in dragging them more dead than alive into our lines in the face of Ministerial opposition, when we cannot even protect them ourselves?" Dr. Morrison asked.

The next morning, June 22, the defense of the legations almost collapsed without a shot being fired. Around nine o'clock there was a lull in the firing from the Chinese side. Then, suddenly, all the detachments except the British abandoned their positions and streaked for the British compound. Three-quarters of the defense lines were left open to the enemy.

What happened was later pieced together by Morrison of the *Times*. Someone (an "irresponsible American," according to Morrison) told the commanding officer, Captain von Thomann, that the Americans were quitting their positions for some unknown reason. Thomann himself panicked. He ordered the Japanese, French, Italian, Austrian, and German detachments immediately to fall back upon the British compound. Seeing that a general withdrawal was taking place, they were quickly joined by the Russians and the Americans. The 2,700 Chinese at Prince Su's palace were abandoned without a second thought. Everyone rushed for the British compound. The Chinese were so surprised that they did not take advantage of the withdrawal and order a general assault; they merely seized the opportunity to burn down the Italian legation.

It devolved upon the various ministers to sort out what had happened. Within half an hour, in emergency session, they ordered the various units back to their positions. Captain von Thomann was sacked on the spot. His post was assumed by Sir Claude Macdonald as the representative of the most powerful nation and as a veteran of several African campaigns with the Highland Light Infantry.

Fuming with disgust at the spectacle, Bertram Simpson had watched while the American marines came tumbling into the British compound "openly swearing at their officers. . . . With that smartness for which their race is distinguished, they see it is quite on the cards that they are forgotten up there [on the Tatar

Wall] if a rush occurs whilst the others are sitting safe in the main base. And the Americans are not going to be forgotten—we soon found that out." He also watched sardonically as the other ministers "crowded round his British Excellency in an adoring and trembling ring."

In two days four legations had been lost or abandoned. The foreigners would have to pull themselves together or their perimeter would be so shrunken the Chinese gunners could easily range on the choicest targets. Worse yet, according to Simpson, there was a deep distrust among the various allies, and "no one trusts the neighbouring detachment sufficiently to believe that it will stand firm under all circumstances and not abandon its ground." If one unit pulled out, the thin and fragile dike would be broken. Each detachment covered the others. The Russians and Americans had to hold the Tatar Wall to the south because it protected the British compound, the indispensable center and command post of the defense, from that direction and partly from the west; the French, German, and Austrian contingents covered the east flank; the Japanese the north and part of the east, with the Italians joining them. If one detachment quit—as the panic at 9 A.M. on June 22 proved—the whole system would crumble. Of all those multinational sectors, the most secure was the Japanese, who manned 1,000 feet of the wall around Prince Su's palace while the Italians covered only 100 feet and a hillock. With all their celebrated military aptitudes, the Germans of the See Battalion were "very indifferently" barricaded against attacks against their position in the southwest corner of the quadrant, where they joined hands with the French on their left and the Americans on their right.

At least Sir Claude infused the defense with some much-needed energy and sense of direction. He was only the nominal commander in chief and had to transmit orders for each nation's detachment through the proper fellow minister; thus he was more the chairman of yet another committee than the chief executive. He was also adept at delegating responsibility, mainly by unloading it on the sturdy shoulders of Dr. Frank Gamewell.

The most urgent task of the moment was fabricating thousands of sandbags to protect the defenders and bombproof the buildings. Overseeing this cottage industry, too, was the ubiquitous Gamewell. Parties of lady scroungers deployed to bring in the material needed for the bags. They raided Prince Su's palace and brought back bolts of costly Ningpo silks and tapestries. Lady Macdonald contributed the British legation's portieres, bedsheets, and table linen. The abandoned shops in Legation Street were searched for any sort of fabric, including men's suiting from the tailors' shops, and the deserted Chinese houses in the western section of the quarter were also looted. Some of the sailors and marines contributed their blankets.

The chapel served not only as the dining room for those sheltered in the British compound but as the sandbag factory. Between meals, almost around the clock, the women labored to provide the material for fortifying the outer defenses and protecting the various buildings. According to one account:

> There was never a day when someone was not making sandbags. A number of sewing machines appeared suddenly as if a magic wand had called them into being, and spools of thread multiplied in the same enchanted fashion.
>
> So expert did the bag-makers become that they could produce an average of one bag in four minutes, several hundred in two hours, and two thousand in a day. Between forty and fifty thousand were made in all. If the demand for bags was urgent, the women would leave their sewing and resort to the ditches where they held the bags and men shoveled in earth. One day Mrs. Conger was seen standing in a deep, dusty hole, holding bags open while a long-robed priest of the Greek Church filled them; a little Chinese boy tied the strings, and the English chaplain bore away the finished products. Sometimes Chinese and foreign children trotted rickashas full of bags to the gate or wall where eager men received them. A large part of the history of the siege is the story of these bags of many colors, made and filled by many hands, and saving from cannon-shot and bullet many hundreds of people.

A controversy arose over the proper size of the sandbags. One soldier stomped into the chapel to complain they were making the bags too small to afford much protection. The ladies then started turning out larger bags. That brought a complaint from a number of other marines that the bags broke when they were made too large. As usual it was up to Dr. Gamewell to resolve the problem.

He made some rapid calculations, then told the sewing circle, "No matter who tells you to do different, follow these measurements," and then pedaled away on his bicycle.

Late in the afternoon of June 22 it became apparent that the Chinese had decided on a change in tactics, that they would try to burn the foreigners out since shot and shell had thus far proved ineffective. Fire was one danger the defenders had not yet taken into account. They were taken completely by surprise when a number of Chinese infiltrators bearing torches suddenly approached the British compound close enough to heave in their torches. A few minutes later, about 5 P.M., other enemy soldiers set fire to a number of abandoned Chinese houses adjoining the southeast corner of the compound in the evident hope the fires would spread eastward. At the same time Chinese riflemen appeared on the roofs of the Mongol Market, overlooking the southwest corner of the quadrant, and directed heavy volleys at the compound and its surroundings.

Fire fighting was a utilitarian exercise which had never concerned the diplomatic colony. Its only equipment was two small, antiquated, hand-hauled fire engines—one of which immediately broke down—and a number of leather buckets, most of which leaked or were minus their handles. About all the fire fighters had going for them was the fact that there were eight wells of fresh cool water located within the walls of the compound.

As the flames approached the compound walls, there was confusion bordering on panic. "Where were the wells? where were water buckets? where was a water pump? where was a ladder, axes, and other utensils?" as the correspondent of the Shanghai *Mercury* described the frantic scene. "These were the questions of the excited throng trying to find out who was in charge of the firefighting." It was several hours into the evening before "the wood of the building of the servants' quarters adjoining the wall was torn down, water was poured on, and the flames destroyed the building outside our defence without doing harm to ourselves. The large water supply of the British legation proved its fitness for general headquarters."

That night someone, probably, should have meditated on the arson possibilities of the Hanlin Yuan, the great library with its halls crammed with the evidence of Chinese scholarship dating back for centuries. It was the repository of Chinese learning, in which so much justifiable Chinese pride was invested. The treasures accumulated through the centuries included the 23,000 volumes of the *Yung Lo Ta Tien*, an encyclopedia compiled under the direction of the second of the Ming emperors, which was finally completed in 1407 by a swarm of 2,000 scholars. It had never been printed; this was the only existing copy of an enormous work embracing the essence of all the literary, historical, philosophical, and classical product of the previous centuries and also including astronomy, geography, medicine, the occult sciences, Buddhism, and Taoism. There was no index of its materials, but the Hanlin Library undoubtedly rivaled that of ancient Alexandria as a repository of human knowledge and speculation.

The library was situated between the British compound and the wall of the Imperial City, with the Imperial Carriage Park to the west and the palace of Prince Su to the east. It was only a few yards north of the wall of the British compound. On the map, certainly, it constituted a threat. Yet everyone "knew" that the Chinese veneration of learning would not allow them to use the Hanlin Library—which was not only a library but the premier academy of the empire, the Chinese Oxford/Heidelberg/Sorbonne—as an instrument of military operations.

Yet they did, and with the dowager empress, it was later learned, watching with pleasure from a rockery high in the Forbidden City. With the currently favored General Tung Fuhsiang at her side, she murmured her approval as the flames destroyed something more precious than all her other treasures only because they also threatened to burn out the foreign devils.

At 11:30 A.M. on June 23 the fire from the Chinese lines suddenly ceased. The lull was quickly followed by a column of smoke and flame towering up from the Hanlin's halls and cloisters. The Chinese were running through the Hanlin complex with torches and kerosene, dashing from one courtyard to the next as the ancient buildings went up like tinder. The wind was blowing from the north, and the Chinese hoped the flames would quickly engulf the British compound.

That first attempt was beaten off when a Royal Marine detachment broke through the outer wall of the Hanlin Library and into the nearer cloisters, where they drove off the Chinese before the fire could spread. The alarm bell in the Jubilee Tower clanged to summon fire fighters of all ages, sexes, and nationalities to form a human chain from the wells in the British compound to the flames licking at the Hanlin buildings. It was a heroic effort. Mme. Pichon, the wife of the French minister, worked next to a coolie. Mrs. Conger's guests worked as a team in the bucket brigade. Lady Macdonald passed all sorts of utensils, everything from soup tureens to chamber pots, through her windows. In the compound itself the children were set to work beating out embers falling in from the north.

At first the foreigners, along with a large number of Chinese converts, seemed to be succeeding in their fight to save the library. Bertram Simpson described how "century-old beams and rafters were crackling. . . . The priceless literature was also catching fire, so the dragon-adorned pools and wells in the peaceful Hanlin courtyards were soon choked with the tens of thousands of books that were heaved in by many willing hands. . . . Beautiful silk-covered volumes, illumined by hand and written by masters of the Chinese brush, were pitched here and there with utter disregard."

Some of the more scholarly or opportunistic fire fighters, as Simpson observed (most of his published observations were anathema to his fellow Westerners in coming years), could not resist the chance to acquire a few treasures of their own:

> Sometimes a sinologue, of whom there were plenty in the legations, unable to restrain himself at the sight of those literary riches, would select an armful of volumes and attempt to fight his way back through the flames to where he might deposit his burden in safety; but soon the way was barred by marines with stern orders to stop such literary looting. Some of the books were worth their weight in gold. A few managed to get through with their spoils, and it is possible that missing copies of China's literature may be some day resurrected in strange lands.

Shortly after noon the flames licked dangerously close to the British compound; but then the wind suddenly shifted to the northwest, and the situation was improved. The fire was being brought under control. Hundreds of hand-carved wooden blocks on which the memories of antiquity were inscribed were passed in reverse down the lines of the bucket brigade, later to be used by the royal marines for lining loopholes and by the children in the British compound for building their own miniature barricades.

Later in the afternoon, however, the Chinese arson squads infiltrated the Hanlin again, and this time they managed to finish the job they had started shortly before noon. The missionary-correspondent Gilbert Reid told how:

> the Chinese started another fire in one of the largest buildings of the Hanlin. As the flames, thick and black, rose upwards the danger seemed great, but as the wind shifted it was decided to let the fire do the work of destruction with no restraint from us. Smaller buildings near the Legation wall were torn down for better security, and the whole Hanlin gradually became our northernmost point of defence with strong barricades. The library of the Hanlin was destroyed, except a few books which we ourselves saved.

The foreigners were almost as outraged by the self-destruction of China's greatest library as by the cannonading, in which two nine-pounder Krupp guns now took their dangerous part, arching their shells over the ruined tower of the Chien Men at a range of about a thousand yards and causing heavy damage to the Russian and American legations. Of the defenders, three had been killed and five were wounded during the past two days. The foreigners took their revenge with a cold calculation. Young Polly Condit Smith recounted the results in a few astringent sentences: "During the two fires in the Mongol Market and the Hanlin University Library a great many Chinese were shot by us, and when possible we straightway threw their bodies into the flames. . . . Some Boxers were captured during the almost hand-to-hand fighting that has taken place, and confined in this compound. They were all shot at dawn this morning."

While the Hanlin Library was falling into charred rubble, the Chinese launched attacks against the barricades covering Prince Su's palace and almost overwhelmed the Japanese and Italians. The alarm bell clanged repeatedly. The Chinese were coming from all sides. On the south they threatened the American and German positions on the Tatar Wall, the defenders of which had to detach part of their slender force to put out the fires set in the marine quarters and narrowly prevented from sweeping through the whole U.S. compound. The Americans, with the Germans and Russians on their flanks, had to hold their positions; otherwise the Chinese would haul artillery to the broad top of the Tatar Wall and bombard the whole Legation Quarter at will. From all accounts American morale was sagging, and their commander, Captain Myers, spent two sleepless days and nights with his marines behind their flimsy barricades on the wall. There was no rest from the daily sorties and artillery fire by the Chinese regulars and the nightly dirty tricks tried by their Boxer auxiliaries. The Boxers specialized in night attacks with clusters of flaming arrows, rockets, and showers of hot bricks apparently launched by catapults. They dashed up to the wall with flaring kerosene-soaked rags fixed to long bamboo poles. Another much-feared weapon was the jingal, a ten-foot musket fired by two men, which was a sort of primitive bazooka.

The marines were supported by one of the younger members of the U.S. legation staff, who not only acted as interpreter but recruited a Chinese labor force to help the marines at their nightly task of strengthening the barricades. He had other, less pleasant duties, as one of his compatriots recalled. "Many Chinamen who advance toward our lines too rashly are killed every night, and after hours of this work the number of corpses that accumulate is astounding. For the sake of the health of the community, Mr. Cheshire has to spend much of his time superintending his gangs in throwing dead bodies over the wall. Today he facetiously remarked that he thought he should be dubbed Major General of the Corpses, as he comes in touch with so many." There was a flowing of black humor of that sort. Another American asserted that the Chinese artillery had been so ineffective thus far because all the foreign-trained artillerymen were over in Tientsin reducing the Foreign Settlement to flinders.

It was a bad day, and it was followed by a night streaked by rocket and artillery fire. Most of the men were occupied by various duties, but many of the women sheltered at the British compound had little to do but soothe the children and try to sleep. A fatalistic attitude grew among some; others were convinced that the sailors and marines on the ramparts and their civilian auxiliaries couldn't hold out for another night.

Polly Condit Smith recalled that Mrs. Conger came into the room shared by the female members of the American diplomatic group and noted with surprise and dismay that Miss Smith was lying on her mattress and wearing a nightdress. The U.S. minister's wife demanded whether Miss Smith intended to await the massacre so flimsily clad:

It flashed through my mind that it made very little difference whether I was massacred in a pink silk dressing-gown, that I had hanging over the back of a chair, or whether I was in a golf skirt and shirtwaist that I was in the habit of wearing during the day hours of this charming picnic. So I told her that for some nights I had dressed myself and sat on the edge of the mattress wishing I was lying down again, only to be told, when daylight came, that the attack was over, when it was invariably too late for anything like sleep. . . . When one has so much to do in the day hours, I had come to the conclusion that, as it was absolutely of no benefit to anyone my being dressed during these attacks, I was going to stay in bed unless something terrible happened, when I should don my dressing-gown and, with a pink bow of ribbon at my throat, await my massacre.

Few others could contemplate having their throats slashed with such insouciance. The more religious among the besieged, oddly perhaps, seemed to be determined to hang onto their earthly lives as long as possible. A young female missionary later described her feelings during those long terrible nights when a massacre seemed likely, and they were nothing like as nonchalant as Miss Smith's. Miss J. G. Evans wrote in her diary:

Oh, such a night as we had! About midnight it seemed as though the powers of darkness were against us—it seemed as though the end were near. Abbie and I crept close together down on the floor, hoping to meet death together. How we all prayed! It was all we could do. The gentlemen who had guns and pistols could at least defend themselves. It was a fearful experience. We dared not have a light to attract the enemy; but in the darkness on the floor we waited for [what] at one time seemed would be the end. How the bullets whistled past the open windows!

Later that night, when the attack temporarily abated, Miss Evans was escorted to the barricades along the northern side of the compound to peer through a loophole at the moonlit battle-field. "I never realized so clearly how war looked—desolation—seven dead bodies, Boxers and soldiers, and several dead horses—nothing seemed alive but a dog—everything so still—no one to be seen—homes deserted—it was fearful. Those bodies lay unburied in the month of June . . . will not pestilence come next?"

The Chinese tendency to conduct their more aggressive operations at night puzzled the defenders of the legations. By day the Chinese rarely showed themselves in the sights of the defenders' sharpshooters, but invariably at night they fired every device in their arsenal and harassed the foreigners with infantry attacks at every section of the barricades. Never before, according to the allied military attaches, had the Chinese specialized in such nocturnal activities.

The reason for the Chinese switch in tactics became apparent when the copy of a report compiled by General Charles George Gordon was found in the files of the British legation. "Chinese" Gordon, who had died in yet another colonial siege years before, had served the Manchus as a military adviser during and after the suppression of the Taiping Rebellion. The Chinese government, expecting a war with Russia at the time, asked Gordon to advise them on how to wage war against a foreign army. Evidently General Gordon's advice was now being followed in the operations against the Legation Quarter.

"Amongst other things," Nigel Oliphant, who read the Gordon report, noted in his diary, "he strongly recommended that the Chinese never show themselves in an open attack but to gradually wear out their enemy by constant firing at night, so that the men should get no rest. It would be very interesting to know if it is in pursuance of this advice that the Chinese favour us with their erratic and annoying fusillades."

On June 24 it became apparent to the defenders of the Legation Quarter that unless they took some aggressive action, their lines would be compressed to the point they would be indefensible. They faced at least 20,000 Chinese with about 500 men, including civilian volunteers; the odds were no better than forty to one, and they were beginning to suffer an increasing number of casualties as the Chinese coiled tighter around their perimeter.

The northern sector, that covered by the Japanese and a smaller contingent of Italians, appeared to be especially vulnerable since they were facing the well-trained Peking Field Force. Colonel Shiba held his long line with groups of four or five Japanese riflemen posted behind shields formed by timbers, bamboo poles, and sandbags. Hundreds of Chinese kept moving closer and closer to his undermanned positions, and he was in danger of being overwhelmed. So he had craftily built a second and stronger defense line during the night of June 23–24. Before dawn the Japanese pulled back from their advanced positions and took up the shorter and better fortified line to the rear. Shortly after dawn Colonel Shiba watched Chinese scouts probing forward, then going back to report, presumably, that the Japanese had crumbled. The Chinese then attacked in force, only to find themselves caught in a death trap. The Japanese poured on enfilading fire and killed dozens of the attackers.

Later that day both the Germans and the Americans made sorties to improve their positions on the southern and southeastern sections of the front. Most of the Germans were posted behind hastily thrown-up earthworks, much less protective than the defenses of other nationalities. The Teutons, it was observed, had been behaving in a sullen fashion ever since Baron von Ketteler had been killed. A race of injustice collectors, they brooded over the fancied unconcern of the other nationalities over that event; actually the others were simply too busy worrying over their own skins, and national prejudices had nothing to do with the case. Pale eyes smoldering, the Germans decided to fight their own battle—as though their slice of the perimeter had suddenly been transformed into the East Prussian plain, with murderous Slavs just over the horizon—and refused to ask for their share of the "coolie labor" which the other nationalities used to build up their defenses. (A notable exception to this was the German chargé d'affaires, Herr von Below, who took Baron von Ketteler's place and acted as liaison between Sir Claude and the German See Battalion. Herr von Below, who styled himself on visiting cards as "*Chevalier de Below, Gentilhomme de la chambre de S. M. le Roi de Prusse*, was an amiable internationalist who spoke four languages and was considered by Sir Claude as the ablest of his associates in directing the defense.) On June 24, shortly after the Japanese success, the Germans spotted some of the crack Manchu Bannermen moving up through ruined houses on their front. They decided to demonstrate for their allies as well as the enemy the dire meaning of the ancient phrase *Furor Teutonicus*, fixed bayonets, swarmed out of their foxholes, and, according to one observer, "charged with a tremendous rush, killed everyone of the marauders, and flung the dead bodies far out so that the enemy might see the reward for daring."

Later that day the U.S. marines on the Tatar Wall also took aggressive action. They charged up the wall almost to the Chien Men (gate) to clear their sector of the enemy. Immediately afterward Dr. Gamewell and a crew of Chinese refugees climbed the wall and hastily built barricades from which the marines could sweep their sector. This apparently alleviated what one diarist referred to as "internal trouble in the American contingent." Later in the day, in fact, the Americans provided a squad of six marksmen, at the request of the British, to eliminate a bothersome group of Chinese riflemen who were peppering the compound from snipers' nests in a block of houses across the dry canal separating the compound from Prince Su's palace.

That night the situation seemed slightly improved, but that only meant the besieged could count on fighting another day. Everyone knew that a concerted effort by the Chinese, who seemingly were as disorganized as the defenders, would simply inundate the defenses. There was, in fact, a growing sense of mystery over why the Chinese did not accomplish what was clearly in their power.

Watchers on the walls that night kept straining their eyes for the star shells and rockets which would signal the advance of a relief column. That was their only real hope. But the allied forces to the east were having their own problems. There would be many more nights of watching for signal rockets.

The foreigners are like fish in a stewpan.

—DOWAGER EMPRESS *to* PRINCE TUAN

7. The Fish in the Stewpan

Another citadel of the Western presence in China, but one much closer to the source of naval and military power and comforted by the possibility of quicker relief, had been under siege for ten days before the Peking colony began its ordeal by fire. Tientsin's Foreign Settlement was imperiled by 25,000 Chinese, not only Boxers but imperial troops, and within a month their number would grow to 50,000. Contemplating their plight from her chambers in the Forbidden City, the dowager empress observed to her now-leading adviser, Prince Tuan, with satisfaction, "The foreigners are like fish in a stewpan." The problem, of course, was to winkle them out of the stewpan. And Tientsin, with allied forces almost within cannon-shot, was determined to hold out.

The defenses of the Foreign Settlement were thinly held, with the defenders outnumbered by more than twenty-five to one. They had no artillery with which to reply to the plentiful Chinese guns. More than 60,000 shells, it was later estimated, fell on the enclave during the siege. Their best hope of outlasting the Chinese was the fact that foreign military instructors had not finished their work with the imperial forces, that the Chinese attacks would be sporadic, ill-coordinated, and not pressed home at the weakest points in the defense system.

The Herbert Hoovers and other Americans took shelter in the compound of Edward Drew, the commissioner of customs, because it was near the center of the settlement and surrounded by godowns. Later it didn't seem such a happy choice because the Chinese gunners concentrated on leveling the godowns. All but two of the native servants had deserted the American households, and a number of American memsahibs had to rediscover their various domestic talents. On the first day of the siege a member of Hoover's staff, Wilfred Newberry, spotted the settlement's dairy herd grazing in a pasture about a mile away; he mounted a pony, rounded up the herd, and drove it into the Drew compound, though he was under fire most of the way.

The heaviest initial attacks came along the sector where the settlement's wall abutted the native city of Tientsin, where the Boxers and imperial troops were covered by the houses in their approach to the settlement's defense line. Had they attacked other sectors at the same time, they could have overwhelmed the foreigners, who, in some places along the barricades, had only one rifleman every hundred yards.

Another problem was the Chinese refugees. There were 500 or 600 minor officials and foreign-educated people who were certain to be slaughtered if the Boxers got hold of them. Most of them had been enthusiastic supporters of the "young emperor's" reform program, including Chang Yen-mao, who was director general of the Chinese Engineering and Mining Company, which employed Hoover, and Director of Railways Tong Shao-yi. Hoover not only supervised the construction of barricades and took charge of logistics but made himself responsible for the care of the Chinese refugees. He settled them in the mining company's compound across from Drew's. Every morning he and a number of Chinese volunteers, usually under fire, transported water, rice, and other foodstuffs from the warehouses to the Chinese compound. The Foreign Settlement's water supply was a constant problem. Water couldn't be taken from the canal, on which a large number of corpses floated. The only solution was to boil drinking water in the boilers at the municipal water plant, which was located outside the barricades. At night Hoover and his assistants slipped through the barricades with an escort of British infantry. While the Tommies stood on guard, they purified a day's supply of water, then slipped back through the lines before dawn with a train of municipal street-sprinkling carts containing the water. In Tientsin, as well as Peking, Americans with engineering degrees were more valuable than any number of West Point, Sandhurst, St. Cyr, and Potsdam graduates.

Caring for the wounded soon became a critical problem. The Foreign Settlement Club was turned into a hospital, with the one army doctor, one settlement physician, and one trained nurse as the only professional part of the staff. Soon not only the beds but the floors of the hospital were covered with the wounded soldiers and civilian volunteers from the barricades.

Lou Henry Hoover, a slim attractive brunette who twenty-eight years later made one of the more gracious First Ladies, displayed an energy and practicality to match her husband's. Mounting a bicycle, she pedaled between her various posts of duty, learned to ride close to the walls for protection against stray bullets, and coolly ignored it when sniper fire punctured her bicycle tires. Mrs. Hoover not only put in long hours at the hospital as a volunteer nurse but supervised a number of Chinese Christian women who milked the settlement's dairy herd.

Mrs. Hoover, as her husband later admiringly recalled, refused to lose her composure when the Chinese artillery launched its nightly bombardments. After the first week or so of the siege, the Hoovers moved to a bungalow near the Drew compound along with several members of his staff. During one drumfire barrage, as Hoover recalled, "a shell banged through a back window and then, exploding, blew out the front door and surroundings. Mrs. Hoover, after a long day at the hospital, was sitting in a side room playing solitaire. She never stopped the game." A few nights later a shell exploded in the Chinese compound and killed Tong Shao-yi's wife and baby. The other children of the Chinese railroad official were brought to the Hoover house and cared for by Mrs. Hoover. (One of Tong Shao-yi's daughters later became Mrs. Wellington Koo, the wife of a prominent Chinese diplomat. Years later Hoover met her at a dinner at the Chinese legation in Washington when she took his arm, saying, "I have met you before. I am Tong Shao-yi's daughter whom you carried across the street during the siege of Tientsin.")

Not all the besieged Westerners behaved with exemplary grace under the pressures of the siege. An infectious hysteria broke out when a number of civilians were struck or narrowly missed by snipers' bullets. A rumor cropped up, and quickly spread, that the shots had been fired by Chinese within the Foreign Settlement.

Before Hoover and the Russian commander, Colonel Wogack, could intervene, a number of the Christian refugees fell victim to summary justice; again Hoover's bête noire was the Briton whom he referred to as "the naval bully."

The first Hoover learned about a series of drumhead trials being conducted by Captain Bailey was from a Chinese messenger who appeared at the Hoover bungalow just as they were having dinner. His friends Chang Yen-mao and Tong Shao-yi and a number of other Chinese had been arrested and were to be placed on trial before an entirely unofficial court being held in one of the godowns. Hoover recalled:

> I rushed to the place, to find a so-called trial going on under torch-lights with Bailey a pompous judge and various hysterical wharf-rats testifying to things that could never have taken place. I attempted to intervene and explain who these Chinese were but Bailey ordered me to get out. I was told that some Chinese had already been executed on the nearby river bank. I made for the Russian headquarters a few blocks away on my bicycle and Colonel Wogack, quickly appreciating the situation, returned with me, accompanied by a Russian platoon. He stopped the trial immediately and the Chinese were turned over to me for return to their compound.

Day after day the foreigners in Tientsin defended themselves against artillery and infantry assaults that frequently threatened to overwhelm them. Their only advantages, as Hoover said, were "inside lines and intelligence." They could rush reinforcements to a threatened sector and stop one attack at a time. The superior skill of their artillerists made the most efficient use possible of their two small-bore field guns. Yet they knew the end could come at any moment—the moment someone on the Chinese side took command and ordered a coordinated attack on all sides of the Foreign Settlement. "Most of us made it a business not to think or discuss the possibilities," Hoover recalled. "We did have one dreadful person who periodically wanted to know if I intended to shoot my wife first if they closed in on us."

On the night of June 25, the fifteenth day of the siege, came a long-delayed glimmer of hope. A Chinese messenger got through the siege lines with word that reinforcements for the dwindling garrison would fight their way into the settlement the next day. The defenders were warned to be careful not to fire on them by mistake. The next day lookouts were posted on the roof of the tallest of the warehouses. During the morning the Chinese bombardment was suddenly suspended. Everyone strained his ears. Even before the allied column came into sight, a stirring refrain could be heard, that rowdy anthem of the Spanish-American War, "There'll be a Hot Time in the Old Town Tonight."

Within an hour a detachment of U.S. Marines and Welsh Fusiliers marched in with some machine guns and field artillery. They added only a few hundred rifles to the Foreign Settlement's defense, but they were a down payment on a more massive effort to relieve the siege. Then the siege ring closed again, tightened, and launched heavier and more dangerous assaults. It would be more than two weeks before substantial evidence of allied concern would manifest itself. Meanwhile, the foreigners, along with the 600 Chinese Christians, could only ask each other why it took so long to rescue them. It was the whole civilized world against crumbling China, yet they were still held hostage and daily threatened by massacre.

One of the American women in Tientsin, Mrs. James Jones, who had made what she called a "flying visit" to the city on a ship which docked just before the siege began, later recorded for a Shanghai newspaper her impression of those critical days, especially July 8, 9 and 10 with their "sharp times of shelling." The Chinese gunners, she wrote, performed so ably that "general admiration would have been expressed if only they had been shelling somebody else." Yet the low explosive power of the Chinese shells caused them to do relatively little damage, accurately though they were fired. On July 11 Mrs. Jones wrote:

> A few more holes in some houses, rooms wrecked and glass broken, and one house burnt in the American Board compound . . . and yet when the shelling was on it seemed as if the air was full of death and destruction, and so indeed it was.

> Many wonderful escapes are related. One old preacher of the American Board, who with his family had occupied a room for some weeks, was persuaded to change his quarters. Half an hour after, a shell came bursting into that very room and some hundred fragments, each enough to kill, were picked up there! A

mother with her children decided to leave the nursery for a while; they had just gone below when the room was wrecked. These hideous things come with such a combined infernal whistle, roar and howl that comparatively few people stand out in the open to watch them. . . . I heard of one house which had eighteen shells through it yesterday alone, so imagination can perhaps be left to picture the nervous strain of those who, however little they and their dwellings may suffer, cannot but remember that the next shell may strike them.

When would the allies arrive to silence those guns?

The allied command was almost as divided and uncoordinated as the Chinese mixture of regular and partisan forces. Almost every step of their progress inland from the forts guarding the mouth of the Pei Ho was a stumble that threatened to send the whole effort sprawling in the mud of the North China flatlands. This was the apogee of imperialism, almost all Western Europe, plus Russia, Japan, and the United States, ranged against a tottering Chinese Empire. For the first time in centuries, since Christendom itself was threatened by the Moslem incursions into Central Europe, the West was united in a common cause, Christianity against the heathen from the East, yet in practice they proved balky and self-centered allies. A pessimist of the Spenglerian school might have seized upon the quarrelsome councils outside Tientsin—and those *inside* Tientsin and Peking—as a symptom of the West's malaise. On the other hand, the allies were faced with a difficult and unfamiliar terrain, with language barriers, logistical problems, national jealousies and suspicions, and most of all, perhaps, a persistent habit of underrating the Chinese military capacity which marched in lockstep with the lordly Western disdain for all who might be categorized as heathen, barbarian, or racially inferior.

In Washington, as in London, the leading military and political figures were inclined to brush aside China as a sideshow. Nothing serious could really happen there in that quaint outmoded kingdom of pigtailed coolies. Britain's Foreign Secretary, Lord Salisbury, felt that a Chinese crisis piled on top of the Boer War, in which the sieges of Ladysmith, Kimberley, and Mafeking had just been lifted, was putting too much on his plate. Washington was equally inclined to turn a blind eye. The capital was preoccupied with the coming national election, and the Republican National Committee, determined to reelect President McKinley, kept grinding out press releases assuring the nation that the United States would not join the other powers in taking any drastic actions in China. It was content that Japan and Russia, as the two most interested powers, should be sending massive naval and military forces to the North China coast. But it would not be long before the United States, in a more limited way, joined that movement, especially after an admirals' conference off Tientsin on July 5 nervously declared that it would take an international force of 60,000 troops to batter its way to Peking.

For the time being the United States was content to reinforce from Manila, where the commanders spared whatever they could from the forces struggling to subdue the Philippine insurrection. Somewhat belatedly, it was decided to send the Ninth Infantry and a battalion of the First Marines to the international conglomerate of Tientsin.

Among those China-bound from Manila was a young marine lieutenant named Smedley D. Butler, an adventurous nineteen-year-old who was beginning a spectacular career. He would become Commandant of the Marine Corps and, eventually, unexpectedly, an outspoken opponent of American imperialism. Born in West Chester, Pennsylvania, he was the son of a Congressman and brought up as a Quaker. He did not allow his faith to inhibit him from obtaining a Marine commission when he was only sixteen years old (but claiming to be eighteen), and he had served in the Cuban campaign before being sent to the Philippines.

One June day young Lieutenant Butler was summoned to battalion headquarters near Manila to be told the battalion was being sent to Tientsin. His commanding officer, Major Littleton "Tony" Waller, told him, "The foreign concessions in Tientsin, twenty-five miles inland, are in desperate straits. Seventeen hundred allied soldiers, aided by several hundred civilians, are manning the defenses. They are surrounded by 50,000 Chinese." And that was about all the marines knew about their mission. They were hastily packed aboard a transport and on June 19 dropped anchor in the Yellow Sea off the Taku Bar. They ferried their stores to the side-wheeler USS *Monocacy* and waited aboard their sweltering ship to be given an assignment.

By July 7 the American command, uneasily divided between Marine Colonel Robert L. Meade and Colonel Emerson Liscum of the Ninth Infantry, had one Infantry regiment and two Marine battalions available for the allied assault designed to lift the siege of the Foreign Settlement and then drive the Chinese forces out of the Native City. They joined in the operations which broke the siege of the foreign concessions. But so far the American colonels had not been invited to participate in the allied war council which, eventually and after much disputation, agreed on a plan to take the Foreign Settlement, then immediately overwhelm the Chinese forces in the walled Native City. It wouldn't be enough merely to rescue the foreign colony because Chinese artillery would still command that enclave, and anyway a secure base had to be established for the rescue of the unfortunate Admiral Seymour's column, now reported in desperate straits fifteen miles north of Tientsin.

Lieutenant Butler with his platoon of Major Waller's battalion received vague orders to join in the advance on the Foreign Settlement. They were ferried ashore, and from there on more or less ad-libbed it. At the Tangku railroad station they confiscated a train and chugged slowly over shaky rails toward the front, wherever that might be. Along the way they came across a straggling column of 400 Russian infantry; the Russians were carrying their immensely fat colonel, whose feet had given out, on a litter. The marines invited the Russians aboard.

The whole operation was typical of the muddled tactics which governed, or failed to govern, the allied intervention. Somewhere on the outskirts of Tientsin the marines piled off their train, accompanied by the Russians, who had even less of an idea of what they were doing there than the Americans. Together, with much waving of arms, the two forces deployed in skirmish order and advanced until they came under fire from a zigzagging Chinese trench system. The marines' heavy-weapons detachment consisted only of one Colt machine gun and one three-inch field gun. For four days they fought their way forward through a North China dust storm, during which the Russians simply disappeared. Finally they more or less blundered their way past the barricades surrounding the Foreign Settlement. Dust-coated and staggering with weariness, they marched down Victoria Road, the main street of the settlement.

Their civilian compatriots, including the Hoovers, gratefully welcomed their appearance. That day, with the siege lifted, the wounded and the women and children who had been besieged in the Foreign Settlement were evacuated. Mrs. Hoover and a half dozen other women refused to join the evacuation because the more seriously wounded could not be moved and the military couldn't spare the doctors and nurses needed for their care.

There was no rest for the troops who had taken the Foreign Settlement. The allied command had decided to attack the Native City immediately. That day of partial victory the American commanders were informed by the allied war council that their forces would take part in the operation early the next morning, July 13. Again there was only the fuzziest outline of a plan. Seven thousand allied troops would be required to grapple with 50,000 Chinese waiting behind thick mud walls twenty feet high. The Russians and Germans were to attack the eastern side of the Native City while the British, American, Japanese, French and other detachments stormed the southern approaches. Brigadier A. R. F. Dorward of the British Army was placed in command of the Americans, the Ninth Infantry and the First Marines, as well as his own troops. The whole sector was under the nominal command of a Japanese, Major General Yasumasa Fukushima, who was the ranking officer on the scene but who apparently was too polite to issue any orders to any but his own forces.

The immediate objective of the attack on the southern side, launched at 3:15 A.M. on July 13, was the gate in the wall opposite the Western Arsenal. There were no maps available except rough sketches of the wall and other points of military interest, no one to guide the advance. Major Waller, commanding the Marine spearpoint, in desperation asked Herbert Hoover if he would act as their guide, thus unwittingly risking the life of the thirty-first President of the United States. Once they reached their jump-off position the Marines and the Ninth Infantry would deploy on the flank of the French, Japanese, and British units; the trick was to reach that position in the murk of the predawn hours. Hoover had taken horseback rides around the walls of the Native City before the siege began and thus was the only available, or at least the only willing, guide.

It was a scary assignment for a civilian, but Mr. Hoover bore it manfully. He later wrote:

> We came under sharp fire from the Chinese located on the old walls. We were out in the open plains with little cover except Chinese graves. I was completely scared, especially when some of the Marines next to me were hit. I was unarmed and I could scarcely make my feet move forward. I asked the officer I was accompanying if I could have a rifle. He produced one from a wounded Marine, and at once I experienced a curious psychological change for I was no longer scared, although I never fired a shot. I can recommend that men carry weapons when they go into battle—it is a great comfort.

Mr. Hoover was dismissed when the first light of dawn glimmered and the other attacking forces became visible.

A column of 600 French was forming to advance on the right, with the Japanese force in the center, and the two American regiments deploying on the left flank alongside the Royal Welsh Fusiliers, the British Naval Brigade, and about forty Austrian marines. A mist hung over the plain. When that curtain lifted with the dawn, their objectives showed up in a harsh and daunting clarity. The Western Arsenal was held by a small allied force equipped with a Maxim machine gun. Just to the north was the Taku Gate of the Native City. There were two mud walls surrounded by fifty-foot moats which would have to be surmounted under heavy fire. The moats had recently been flooded by the Chinese with water diverted from the canal, and it was a question whether the infantry would be able to flounder its way through the mudbath.

About 5 A.M. the French and the Japanese troops began the general assault. They advanced to the outer wall. The Japanese cut footholds and soon were swarming along its top. About a thousand yards ahead was the second obstacle, the City Wall, where the Chinese had concentrated most of their firepower. The French and Japanese were taking heavy casualties, so the Anglo-American-Austrian force on the left was ordered to advance and silence the Chinese gunners. They pushed forward in skirmish order while the Hong Kong Artillery, a battery manned by Sikh gunners, maneuvered into position, dug in their tailpieces, and began firing their heavy twenty-pounders. It was 7 A.M. before the left wing closed the gap between it and the Japanese in the center.

While the Germans and Russians were having an easy time attacking the Native City from the east, those in the southern sector were experiencing all the frustrations, mishaps, and misunderstandings of coalition warfare which would be magnified to an astronomic degree fourteen years later in the World War. Even officers who spoke the same language could not make themselves clearly understood.

Since the American regiments were taking a punishing fire in their exposed position, Brigadier Dorward sent a staff officer to Colonel Liscum with an order—or rather a polite suggestion—that "you move your command to the left of the Japanese."

A short time later the British commander rode up and observed that the Americans still had not finished crossing the moat protecting the outer wall. There was a discussion between Brigadier Dorward and Colonel Liscum over just where the Ninth Infantry was to fit itself in, which Dorward vaguely terminated with the comment, "It makes no difference which, to the right or left, as long as they get under cover." A typical muddle followed. Somehow the U.S. Infantry advanced to the right of the Japanese, where they had no business being. At this point heavy counterbattery fire from the Chinese knocked out four Japanese guns and the U.S. Marines' artillery ran out of ammunition and was forced to retire.

Meanwhile, the Marine rifle companies of the First Battalion, under Major Waller, along with the Welsh Fusiliers, were stalled until 6:30 A.M. for lack of orders. Then they got the go-ahead. Colonel Meade accompanied the advance elements of his regiment despite the fact he was suffering from inflammatory rheumatism and went into combat with his hands and feet wrapped in flannel bandages.

The marines and fusiliers crossed the outer wall and ventured under brisk fire into the paddies, burial mounds, dikes and ditches separating it from the City Wall. They advanced to within about 300 yards of the inner wall when they spotted a Chinese sortie from the South Gate. The Chinese were trying to get around the left flank of the advancing allies and cut them off. "It was a mudbath," as Lieutenant Smedley Butler later remembered the engagement. It was also a bloodbath. The marines were dropping all around under heavy fire from the inner wall. But the more immediate danger was the Chinese sortie. Butler asked permission to take the thirty-five men in his platoon through the paddies to confront the Chinese. As he advanced, another detachment from the Second Battalion worked around the Chinese to the right, brought them under a crossfire and drove them back to the Native City. During the firefight Lieutenant Butler was wounded in the thigh but refused to retire for treatment until he helped to carry a mortally wounded private off the field. Butler was given a battlefield promotion to captain.

Meanwhile the Ninth Infantry was blundering along, trying to follow the vaguely worded suggestions of Brigadier Dorward and taking heavy casualties in the process. Having appeared on the right instead of the left of the Japanese column, they were forced to proceed along a causeway on which they were exposed to withering fire from the Chinese. Then the regiment floundered through an area covered with ditches and ponds in which its slow advance again caused heavy casualties. The regiment was learning the hard way that it did matter very much whether it moved to the right or the left of the Japanese column, and now it came under heavy enfilading fire from the Chinese holding a series of huts about a thousand yards to the right.

To confront this new danger, Colonel Liscum ordered his battalions to change front and march on the right oblique. They held their fire while dodging toward the huts, taking cover behind burial mounds and struggling through ponds and ditches with three to eight feet of water in them. It was 8:30 A.M. before a sizable part of the regiment was in position to attack the Chinese-held huts in force. But they were confronted by a wide and deep pond and men were falling all around from the plunging fire of Chinese one-pounders. Their ammunition was down to about ten rounds per man, and the men were worn out and dispirited. The two battalions would have to be reinforced and resupplied before they could continue the advance.

About 9 A.M. Color Sergeant Edward Gorman was wounded in the knee and dropped the national flag. Soldiers were then very flag-conscious; a fallen banner was a terrible disgrace to the regiment, the army, and the nation. Colonel Liscum himself hobbled over to pick up the flag, was wounded in the abdomen, and gasped as he was being dragged to shelter, "Keep up the fire, men." A few minutes later Colonel Liscum, who had survived some of the bitterest fighting of the American Civil War, died in a Chinese rice paddy.

Major Jesse Lee as the senior field officer took over command. There was little he could do. His two battalions were pinned down, the Chinese were moving more troops into the huts ahead of him, and his ammunition was almost exhausted. A determined Chinese counterattack could have routed his battalions. There was nothing to do but send for help. Lieutenant Louis B. Lawton was dispatched with a message for Brigadier Dorward. Under heavy fire he made it to the British HQ, but on the way back he was wounded twice in the shoulder. Somehow he managed to crawl and stumble back to Major Lee to make his report. Later Lawton was awarded a Congressional Medal of Honor.

Heroic efforts were made to bolster the Ninth Infantry's shaky line. Brigadier Dorward sent a 100-man unit of the Naval Brigade as reinforcements, but they were pinned down before they could reach the Ninth Infantry's positions. The First Marines' artillery company was also dispatched to bolster the regiment's firepower but was decimated before it could dig in and provide fire support. In addition, Captain Ollivant of the British-officered First Chinese Regiment volunteered to take one man and a mule loaded with ammunition up to the Ninth Infantry's battered line. Along the way his companion was killed, then the mule. Ollivant gathered up as many belts of ammo as he could carry and lumbered along until he too was mortally wounded.

The Ninth Infantry was still stalled late in the day with its ammunition almost exhausted and the Chinese extending their advanced positions so close that the Americans could hear them talking. At one point the two salients were only seventy-five feet apart. By then the Ninth Infantry and its supporting elements were at least well dug in, but they could neither move forward nor retreat. Most of the infantrymen were in water up to their waists, some of them up to their armpits. Almost a quarter of the two battalions' strength lay dead or wounded.

By late in the afternoon the Third Battalion of the Ninth

Infantry, which had been assigned to various unnecessary guard details in the rear areas, arrived under the command of Lieutenant Colonel Charles A. Coolidge, who reported to Brigadier Dorward and asked to be sent forward to join the beleaguered regiment. The gloomy and reticent Dorward shook his head. It was useless trying to reinforce the Ninth Infantry by daylight; the Chinese had mustered too much firepower in that sector to make the effort worthwhile. Heavier artillery was wheeled up and emplaced behind the allied line, but successive barrages failed to dislodge the Chinese.

When night fell, it appeared that the only sensible move was to extricate those allied forces in the most exposed positions. The first day's attack on the Native City had been a failure. The Western military men accepted the situation with Occidental resignation, but the Japanese were not inclined to such a passive philosophy. When night came, they leapfrogged their forces closer to the South Gate. Meanwhile, the other allies were pulling back.

Darkness fell at 8 P.M. In two hours a full moon would rise. During that two-hour interval the Ninth Infantry and its supporting elements would have to be rescued. U.S. marines and part of the British Naval Brigade were sent out to cover their withdrawal and help carry back the dead and wounded. It was a dreary procession back to the main line. The Ninth Infantry had suffered decimation twice over, with Colonel Liscum and seventeen of his troopers killed, five officers and seventy-two enlisted men wounded, and one missing in action. All were victims of a classic foul-up, sacrificed to hasty planning and faulty liaison.

The Japanese had suffered even more grievously than their allies, but they were determined to batter their way into the Native City that night. They edged their skirmish line as close as possible to the South Gate of the inner wall, then sent sappers in to do the job. The Japanese engineers managed to place a tremendous charge at the gate but were spotted by the Chinese and came under heavy fire. A bullet cut the wire leading to the explosives. Three attempts to set off the bomb electrically failed. Then a brave little man whose chest should have been decorated with a sunburst of his emperor's medals, Second Lieutenant K. Inawe, dashed forward through the plunging fire from Chinese troops on the wall, and lit the fuse with a match.

Up went the gate in a fountain of masonry. In went the

Japanese infantry. Their banzai charge ended up, rather comically, in a pitch-dark courtyard typical of the ornate architecture the Chinese fashioned for their city gates. Fortunately the Chinese had been so frightened by the charge which destroyed the South Gate that all the defenders had fled; otherwise the Japanese troopers would have found themselves in a trap. They bashed in the gate to the courtyard and went howling into the narrow streets of the Native City.

The other allies were brooding over their watchfires when word came that the Japanese had stormed into the Native City. The news, no doubt, came as a shock to the more prideful and ambitious of their colleagues. The little "Nips" had done what the best colonial troops of three nations had failed to do, and the casualty figures indicated who had fought the hardest. The Native City had been taken at a cost of 750 men killed, wounded, and missing. By far the greatest sacrifice was made by the Japanese, who reported 320 men killed or wounded. For that price they proved something that Western military experts would note with increasing concern; they proclaimed the Japanese presence in eastern Asia, not merely as camp followers of the Westerners but as a growingly independent and aggressive power.

The sack of the Chinese section of Tientsin proceeded with dispatch. At that pursuit all the allies were equally efficient and diligent. Immediately after the Native City was taken, as the observant Mrs. Jones of Shanghai recorded, "the city and outskirts were given up to loot and many civilians as well as the military and bluejackets of all nations were indulging to their hearts' content all day. . . . After that the British were prohibited from looting but the troops of other nations seem far from giving over." Actually the British only systematized the pillage. Their troops were required to bring in whatever they seized to be divided equally as prize money.

The veteran British correspondent Henry Savage Landor viewed the legitimatized larceny with a philosophical eye. He was annoyed only by the spectacle of civilians outdoing the military in that pursuit. The foreign residents, he observed, "especially those who had not distinguished themselves in the fighting line, lost no time in making for the Mint, the Salt Commissioner's palace, the Viceroy's Yamen, or the nearest silk or jewelry store, where they knew that wealth was accumulated, and where they helped themselves to anything that took their fancy. Lump silver and bar gold were preferred."

Much of the Native City was in flames, he pointed out, and much looting had been done by the Boxers and Chinese soldiers before the allies took their turn. "It certainly seemed a pity to let so much beautiful and valuable property be wasted. Was it not, then, the lesser evil to allow these men, who had fought hard, to reap what benefit they could from the misfortune of others, especially since 'the others' were doomed to misfortune in any case?" Furthermore, Correspondent Landor maintained, the Chinese had it coming to them; "it was the only way by which the natives could be punished for their outrages on our men, women, and children; and, degrading as it may seem to those who had no chance of taking part in it, there is no doubt that the only portion of this war which will cause the Chinese some future reflection will be the burning and looting of Tientsin."

The different national styles in looting were studied with the detachment of an expert on colonial warfare and, Landor confessed, "afforded me more pleasure than anything else I could have carried away." That detachment might have vanished if he had been studying the sack, say, of Bristol or Wolverhampton, but anyway he noticed that the English were mainly interested in bringing home souvenirs for their families; they "loot, loot, loot, not for themselves, but for the friends and relations at home." The Japanese were dainty, "picked up and laid down the smallest and most minute articles with such neatness and grace that it was a real pleasure to see them, whereas the Yankees, or the French or the British or Russian, not to mention the German, could touch nothing that was not solid bronze without breakage or twisting or soil or injury of some sort." The Japanese looted, Landor wrote, "in a silent, quiet and graceful way."

The Americans he observed in that soldierly avocation were rather clumsy and lacked both finesse and appreciation. Landor thought it possible the American trooper "lacked some of the feeling and artistic taste to be found in some of the other nationalities, and as a rule he displayed much determined business capacity. . . . He will pick up a costly vase which has been preserved for centuries in the house of a high official, and to save himself the trouble of putting it gently down in the place from which it came will drop it on the floor . . . the noise of smashing crockery giving more wild delight to his unmusical ears than the beautiful design. . . . The visit of the American soldiers had about the same result on the interior of a Chinaman's house as a severe earthquake." Americans cast aside priceless porcelains, tapestries, and bronzes in a single-minded search for gold bars and the four-and-a-half-pound lumps of silver called sycee.

The toll taken by allied looters, military, naval, and civilian, was simply uncountable, but it ran into the millions.

Now also came the moment of reprisal against the Boxers, in which the Chinese enthusiastically joined. The native populace had generally believed the Boxers' boast of invincibility and supported them, but now Mrs. Jones wrote:

> troops and people turned on the Boxers and slew some hundreds, with their leaders, as responsible for the trouble come upon them and threatening them. Many Boxer proclamations and placards on yellow paper are yet prominent. These stuck on so many houses seem ludicrous now when not victory but utter defeat has overtaken them. . . . It is amusing to see how the natives in the city almost all go about with little flags, most of which bear a legend and the national emblem of the Japanese; some few have pieces of paper on which is written "France" or "England," but the many have professedly become "Submissive subjects of Japan."

The allied expeditionary force would linger in and around Tientsin to await reinforcement and refitting before proceeding, without undue haste, to the relief of Peking. They would also have to rescue Admiral Seymour's column. Those operations, however, would wait upon disputes in the allied war council, endless botheration over who was in command, and the leisurely attitude of colonial officers who would not be chivvied along until they were certain that their evening dress, tennis rackets, mustache wax, and other necessities were properly packed. There was a prescribed style for conducting oneself on campaign which could not be neglected in favor of other exigencies.

At the Herbert Hoovers' bungalow a rowdy group of Americans gathered. They were war correspondents just arrived from the States for whom Mrs. Hoover provided sleeping space on the floor in return for a pledge that they would help forage for food.

Among them was perhaps the oddest character who ever slipped into the rather primly conventional life of Mr. Hoover. He was a white-bearded old fellow named Joaquin Miller, self-styled "Sweet Singer of the Sierras," now working as war correspondent for the Hearst newspapers. Miller had shocked the more pedantic critics by rhyming teeth with Goethe, but he had won considerable fame as a lyric poet hymning the glories of California. During a lustily picturesque career he had been deported from Hawaii for appearing there with a pregnant young woman not his wife, and he had startled London society, which considered him an authentic representative of the Wild West, by picking up fish by the tails and swallowing them whole. After making a small fortune reading his poetry to vaudeville audiences, he had retired to a home on a ridge overlooking San Francisco Bay, where he distilled 110-proof whiskey. Now he had come out of retirement to cover an Asian war and was determined not to be outdone by his younger rivals.

Miller was told that Peking was under siege and there were thousands of hostile Chinese between the Foreign Settlement in Tientsin and the capital, but the Hoovers were unable to dissuade him from hiring a rickshaw to carry him to Peking. "We told him that the foreigners there were still under siege and that there were a few armies in between. But such arguments seemed to carry little weight with Joaquin. Mrs. Hoover finally bribed his rickshaw boy to desert him and he remained contentedly with us."

*For a week I have written nothing, absolutely
nothing, and have not even taken a note, nor cared
what happened to me or anyone else. How could
I when I have been so crushed by unending
sentry-go, by such an unending roar of rifles and
crash of shells. . . . My ego has been crushed out
of me.*

—BERTRAM SIMPSON'S *diary, July 3, 1900*

8. *A Mysterious Cease-Fire*

In Peking there was a momentary illusion of peace on June 25.
Five days of fighting had proved little beyond the fact that the
besieged were determined to hold out until a relief column arrived
and that the besiegers were willing to make enormous, near-sui-
cidal sacrifices to capture what one of their intended victims
called their "fortress slum." The only question seemed to be
whether the stubborn resistance of the besieged would outlast the
rage of the Manchus.

Most of that day was like the ones which preceded it. Relentless
heat from the cloudless sky. Eddying swirls of dust clogging the
nostrils and irritating the eyes. The dry heat of late spring being
replaced by the humidity of the North China summer months.
And the rotten-sweet smell of the high season in Peking, to which
was now added a thousand putrefactions of war.

Even in peace, as Polly Condit Smith noted, this was a bad time
of year, but now:

the temperature is like a Turkish bath without the clean smell.
Apropos of smell, a whole story-book could be written about the
Peking smell. The dry heat was nothing compared with this damp
temperature, which seems to soak out of Mother Earth the most
incredibly disgusting odors. There are so many dead dogs, horses
and Chinese lying in heaps all around the defended lines, but too
far for us to bury or burn them. The contamination of the air is

something almost overpowering. All men who smoke have a cigar in their mouths from morning until night as a protection against this unseen horror, and even the women, principally Italians and Russians, find relief in the constant smoking of cigarettes.

Around four o'clock that afternoon the sun began sinking, gilding the pink walls of the Imperial City and softening the stark barrier of the Tatar Wall looming over the Legation Quarter. It had been a hard day all along the outer works, many attacks, some casualties. Then the Chinese musketry slackened. In a few minutes there was only an occasional shot from the Chinese lines. The sudden cessation in the kettledrum of enemy fire was startling to the defenders. They began worrying about a change in enemy tactics, alert for some new production from the enemy's dirty-trick department.

Chinese soldiers were observed withdrawing from their advanced positions.

There was a blaring from massed groups of the long Chinese trumpets, a sound as stirring as bagpipes to the Western ear, "sobbing on a high note tremulously," as Simpson described it, "and then, boom, boom, suddenly dropping to a thrilling basso profundissimo."

The trumpeters were sounding the retreat. Troopers from the Moslem cavalry of Kansu Province in turbans and colorful tunics sauntered back from their front line evidently confident the enemy would not fire upon them.

A sentry posted on the roof of Sir Claude's stables shouted down a report that there seemed to be a lot of activity on the North Bridge.

In the British compound, scores of people rushed out to stare northward from various vantage points. Some brought field glasses with them, and reported that a Chinese soldier was waving a white flag from the bridge. A moment later another soldier appeared with a large sign, written with Chinese characters, held aloft. Sinologues among those present (including Sir Robert Hart, whom Simpson sarcastically referred to as "the great administrator") quickly translated the message from the other side:

IN ACCORDANCE WITH THE IMPERIAL COMMANDS TO PROTECT THE MINISTERS, FIRING WILL CEASE IMMEDIATELY. A DESPATCH WILL BE DELIVERED AT THE IMPERIAL CANAL BRIDGE.

On a large blackboard a reply was composed, stating that the message was understood and the dispatch would be received.

It was the first good news the foreign colony had received in many days. What else could the message mean than that the dowager empress and her advisers had experienced a change of heart, or mind, and decided to call off the hostilities? The siege, they assured each other, was over. The Chinese had decided that they could take the legations only at an incalculable cost. "Not one of us," one of them reflected, "had relished the idea of being massacred after the manner of the Indian Mutiny."

Yet none of the thankful Westerners was eager for the honor of crossing the lines under a flag of truce and receiving the enemy's message. A Chinese, as usual, was nominated for the distasteful chore, though he had more to fear from his own people, who saw him as a running dog of Christianity, than any foreigner. Seriocomedy ensued. The Chinese was outfitted with an "official" long coat and hat, given a small white flag and a noticeboard to carry, and then pushed out of the barricades. When he approached the North Bridge, however, the enemy soldiers began shouting at him, jocularly, but causing him to take fright, drop the noticeboard and bolt back to the Legation Quarter's barricades. No one else volunteered to venture out on the bridge and receive whatever "despatch" was awaiting delivery, important though it might be to the fate of almost a thousand Westerners and almost three times that number of Chinese Christians.

The people from the British compound mingled with their defenders on the barricades, milled around, debated, and speculated. They waited eagerly for definitive word from the Forbidden City that the dowager empress had relented, that they were reprieved. An hour passed. What were the Chinese up to? Had there been a palace revolution? Was an allied relief column so close to the city the Chinese had been scared into calling off their siege? Simpson described the scene:

> The setting sun now struck the Imperial City, under whose orders we had been so lustily bombarded, with a wonderful light. Just outside the Palace gates were crowds of Manchu and Chinese soldiery—infantry, cavalry, and gunners grouped altogether in one mass of colour. Never in my life have I seen such a wonderful panorama—such a brilliant blaze in such rude and

barbaric surroundings. There were jackets and tunics of every colour; trouserings of blood-red embroidered with black dragons; great two-handed swords in some hands; men armed with bows and arrows mixing with Tung Fu-hsiang's Kansu horsemen, who had the most modern carbines slung across their backs. There were blue banners, yellow banners embroidered with black, white and red flags, both triangular and square, all presented in a jumble to our wondering eyes. The Kansu soldiery of Tung Fu-hsiang's command were easy to pick out from amongst the milder looking Peking Banner troops. Tanned almost to the colour of chocolate by years of campaigning in the sun, of sturdy and muscular physique, these men who desired to be our butchers showed by their aspect what little pity we should meet if they were allowed to break in on us. Men from all the Peking Banners seemed to be there with their plain and bordered jackets showing their divisions; but of Boxers there was not a sign.

The moment of bloodcurdling pageantry passed with the fall of night. In the gloaming the leading members of the foreign colony debated over what to do. Somehow the truce had to be extended, the fighting replaced by parleying. Finally one of the diplomats who spoke Chinese ventured across the battle zone to speak informally with a Chinese representative. According to Simpson, the diplomat was informed that Generalissimo Jung Lu had ordered the cease-fire, that the Imperial Council was then in session, and that a peaceful gesture could be expected momentarily when the council had come to a decision.

Hours passed, but no further word came from the Chinese side. The defenders seized the opportunity to reinforce their sandbagged barricades, dig deeper revetments, and fashion more loopholes. Fresh stocks of ammunition and food were brought to the firing line. Then, at midnight, the truce ended as informally as it began. There were a few shots from the Chinese lines, then an outbreak of firing all along the perimeter. For whatever reason, the palace had changed its mind about the beauties of peace and reason.

It was not until long afterward that a fragmentary account of what had motivated the eight-hour truce could be pieced together. True enough, Jung Lu had ordered the armistice, and court intrigue and infighting had permitted the gesture. A circumstantial account of what had happened during the hectic hours of the afternoon of June 25 was provided by Ching Shan in his published diary. Much of what he related, considering his retirement from active service in the Forbidden City as a household functionary, was probably hearsay. It was partly verified, however, by what the Chinese representative had told the allied diplomat before the truce expired.

By Ching Shan's account the morning quiet of the Palace of Peaceful Longevity was shattered on June 25 while the dowager empress was still abed. Prince Tuan with a group of his toadies and some of the Boxer leaders were raising a clamor in the empress' antechamber. They shouted that the emperor was a traitor who sympathized with the besieged foreigners. The empress was not accustomed to being awakened in that rude fashion. She suddenly appeared at the top of a flight of steps, glowered at the unseemly demonstration, and denounced the demonstrators for committing *lèse majesté* by threatening the person of the emperor. That was the dowager empress' prerogative. Furthermore, she cut off the rebellious princes' allowances for one year and ordered them to stay out of sight until they had learned better manners.

The dowager empress was so outraged by Prince Tuan's conduct, his bold and noisy foray into her inner sanctum that she called Generalissimo Jung Lu and other advisers into conference on how to teach the war-hawk faction a sharp lesson. The result of their deliberations was the order for the cease-fire. The discussion continued until late in the evening when dispatches from Tientsin falsely claiming a great victory over the allied forces were received. Tzu Hsi then decided that the siege must be resumed. She was determined, she told her advisers, to "eat the flesh and sleep on the skins" of the foreigners. A figure of speech, of course.

Whatever the reason for its suspension, the siege was pressed with the utmost vigor during the remaining days of June. Night and day for a week the defenses of the Legation Quarter were pounded by a variety of weapons. One night alone 200,000 rounds were fired into the enclave by Chinese riflemen. The defenders were becoming exhausted by lack of sleep, improper nourishment, and constant strain. By the end of June there had been more than a hundred of the defenders killed or wounded, and many more suffering from dysentery. There was every indication now that the siege would go on to the bitter end: a massacre of all the survivors.

Night and day the men behind the barricades were summoned back to their positions, after snatching a few hours or minutes of sleep, by the ringing of the alarm bell. Bertram Simpson, a civilian volunteer fighting with the Japanese contingent, confided to his diary that he had been too weary to make any entries for the past week and that he had given up caring what happened to him or anyone else. "How could I when I have been so crushed by unending sentry-go, by such an unending roar of rifles and crash of shells, that I merely mechanically wake at the appointed hour, mechanically perform my duty and as mechanically fall asleep again. My *ego* has been crushed out of me." He had become "an insignificant atom in a curious thing called a siege."

The claustrophobic aspects of being bottled up like insects, of living constantly at close quarters with people one neither liked nor approved of before the siege, of the heat and boredom, almost outweighed the dangers of the siege. Danger did not make men and women comrades under duress, nor did it persuade them to forget their differences. People caught in a shipwreck, jammed together in a prison cell, or suddenly thrown together by some other disaster do not instantly tap the wellspring of brotherhood. A certain fondness for their fellow victims may develop only long after the event. A siege is one of the supreme tests of the human spirit; the danger without is no greater than that from within. Under stress, human folly and frailty, as well as the nobler aspects of the species, were heightened and made more apparent.

Sir Claude Macdonald had the devil's own job trying to unify the defenses. More the chairman of a committee of his fellow envoys than a commander in chief, he had to beg rather than order reinforcements for a threatened sector. In a situation calling for instant action, he had to write out a request for one detachment to send help to another, send it to the fellow minister whose unit was involved, wait while the minister consulted with the commander of his detachment, and hope that by the time the request was honored the Chinese were not pouring through a gap in the defense lines. He had to deal constantly with the touchy temperaments, national prides, and exquisite sensibilities of peoples as disparate as Latins and Teutons, Anglo-Saxons and Slavs.

Each contingent, it seemed, had developed its own peculiarities under stress, which may or may not have been fairly representative of its national character. The English were inclined to overdo their famous nonchalance and affect a languorous attitude toward imminent disaster, yet were capable of exhibiting explosive energy such as that of Captain Halliday of the Royal Marines when he led a sortie into the Chinese positions, killed thirty-four of the enemy, and was awarded the Victoria Cross. The French were temperamental and capable of a desperate gallantry only when sharply provoked. The Germans were sullen loners, convinced their allies hated them. The Japanese were the most dependable of all the forces present, fought stoically, steadily, and skillfully under all circumstances. The Americans were incredibly temperamental, tended to dog it except in an emergency. The Italians could only be regarded as a liability in any serious situation. So it appeared in the first week of the siege.

Sir Claude had no reserve force, unless one could so dignify the "Carving Knife Brigade," also known as "Thornhill's Roughs," who strutted around the compound with their fowling pieces and tried to look ferocious. If an emergency developed, Sir Claude could only plead with Russia to help Japan or America to aid Britain. The difficulty of his task was indicated in his journal for June 27:

> The Russian minister asks, twice, that the British should remove a sandbag barricade which is blocking his withdrawal route to the British legation. . . . Sir Claude replied that he is being heavily attacked from the north and can spare no men for this duty. "Indeed I may have to call upon you and Mr. Conger for help to repulse this attack—so please have some men ready." . . . Mr. Conger's comment is: "We are having the heaviest attack we have ever had here and every man is engaged." . . . At 2:30 P.M. Sir Claude writes again: "It is absolutely essential that the Fu [Prince Su's palace] should be held at all hazards. I hope therefore you will order over as many men as possible." . . . The Russian minister complies: "I am sending you my last ten men, but I must have them back as soon as you no longer need them."

When one considers that most of those scrawled urgencies required translation from or to Russian, German, Japanese, or whatever, it is apparent that the chain of command was anything but effective. As he surveyed his hastily contrived, often poorly sited defenses, Sir Claude must have felt like the captain of a leaky tramp steamer confronted by the onset of a South China Sea typhoon.

The Franco-Austrian position in the southeast corner of the quadrant was the most exposed, but it was not as crucial as two other sectors. If the Japanese could not hold Prince Su's palace and its fourteen-acre park along the northern perimeter, the Chinese would break through and cut off the British compound. Equally essential was the commanding height of the Tatar Wall, on which the Americans and a smaller contingent of Germans on their left were taking terrific punishment. The Americans and Germans each held barricades built across the forty-foot width of the wall, with the Chinese positions only a few yards away. They fought at such close quarters that the men posted there could be relieved only at night. Much of the difficulty with the Americans stemmed from the fact that they resented fighting in such an awkward, cramped position. Because of their discomfiture, having been trained to make gallant assaults over enemy-held beaches rather than cringe behind sandbags, the marines claimed the top of the wall couldn't be held and demanded the privilege of withdrawing. On June 25, in fact, U.S. Minister Conger informed Sir Claude that the Tatar Wall barricades would have to be abandoned. Sir Claude put his foot down. The Americans, with some assistance from the royal marines and the Russians, would have to stand fast or plunging fire from Chinese artillery would level the Legation Quarter.

So the marines reluctantly stuck it out but not without some very shaky moments. Captain Myers as commander of the detachment wrote Mr. Conger, "It is slow sure death to remain here. . . . The men all feel that they are in a trap and simply await the hour of execution."

The Americans were not the only ones who suffered from what the English called a blue funk. In the Franco-Austrian sector on July 1 a crisis arose when the Chinese brought up two field guns and began shelling the ruins of the French Legation in which the French and Austrians were holding out against incessant infantry attacks. A piece of shrapnel tore the face off a French trooper. The French commander ordered his bugler to sound the retreat, and the remnants of his force scrambled back to the Hôtel de Pekin, which had been sandbagged to form a strongpoint. They were firing from the windows as the Chinese advanced. Sir Claude, however, insisted that they had to recapture their former position. A half hour later the French and Austrians counterattacked and reoccupied the ruins of the French legation.

Sir Claude had his troubles behind the lines, too. There was the problem of caring for the hundreds of civilians in and around the British compound, rationing the food supply, guarding against epidemics, keeping the peace among so many different nationalities and diverse personalities, maintaining morale and preventing a panic from exploding.

Racial animosities, as well as international understanding, came into sharper focus under the stress of constant danger and discomfort. Always perceptive and usually fair, Polly Condit Smith would recall ten years later that "the British and Americans are almost one people here; although the expressions 'Damn Yankees' and 'Damn lime-juicers' are interchanged, they are used in a spirit of affection." As for the Russians, "they love us and we love them in as strong a fashion as they hate their English neighbors on the other side. . . . The Germans are somewhat by themselves and fraternize with no one . . . full of sullen rage at the unavenged death of their minister . . . notorious for their utter disregard of ordinary military precautions and unnecessary daredevil recklessness. . . . The Japanese are tremendously pro-English and anti-Russian."

Miss Smith's quick sketch of the various ministerial personalities indicated that Britain's stiff-necked Sir Claude was a paragon compared with some of his colleagues. The Italian minister, the Marchese di Selvago Raggo, an indolent and elegant fellow who dressed for dinner every night, "sits chatting with his wife, a very beautiful woman, in a *chaise longue* most of the time. M. Pichon, the French minister, nervously and ceaselessly walks about, telling everyone who speaks to him: '*La situation est excessivement grave; nous allons tout mourir ce soir.*' M. de Giers, the Russian minister, walks eternally between his legation and the British compound, and looks every inch a Minister. Mr. Conger, the American Minister, walks about. Poor Señor Cologan, the Spanish Minister, is very ill. M. Knobel, the Dutch Minister, offered his services as a sentry, but stated at the same time that he did not know how to shoot and was very shortsighted. Sir Claude Macdonald, the British Minister, is now the Commander-in-Chief and he tries sincerely to do his duty as such. His path is a thorny one, however; most of the Legations are so jealous of his compound being the centre and best stronghold *par excellence* that they are outrageously inconsiderate of all orders issued."

The diplomats and their families had an easy time of it compared with those who served as their defenders, particularly those who were wounded by a Chinese bullet, shell, arrow, or spear. By the end of June, as Miss Smith wrote, "the hospital is already full, men lying on straw bags in halls—crowded in every conceivable corner."

What was styled the International Hospital was actually a grim, anything but antiseptic "chamber of horrors," as Bertram Simpson called it, located in what had been the chancery of the British legation, where "on despatch-tables, lately littered with diplomatic documents, operations are now almost hourly performed and muttered groans wrung from maimed men . . . the stench is terrible . . . worse still are the flies, attracted by the newly-spilt blood. . . . Half the nationalities of Europe lie groaning together, each calling in his native tongue for water, or for help to loosen a bandage which in the shimmering heat has become unbearable. . . ."

In that cramped space during the course of the next six weeks 125 seriously wounded men, 1 woman struck by a stray bullet, and 40 cases of illness would be treated by the skeleton staff consisting of a German surgeon named Dr. Velde; the British legation's resident physician, Dr. Poole; the sickbay attendant from HMS *Orlando*; and a volunteer nursing corps.

The equipment with which the two doctors had to patch up the particularly nasty wounds inflicted by Chinese weaponry was pathetically inadequate. There were only four iron bedsteads and seven camp cots for patients who never numbered fewer than fifty or sixty after the first ten days of fighting; the less gravely wounded lay on straw-filled mattresses on the floor. There were only a few thermometers. Sawdust and powdered peat had to be used in making dressings to soak up the blood and pus from suppurating wounds.

The heat ranged upward from 100° F., the hospital was airless because the windows had to be sandbagged, and the wounded were tormented by swarms of flies and mosquitoes.

Even Bertram Simpson, who disdained and mistrusted many sides of the American character, had to concede that without the "Yankee missionaries" there would have been great difficulty caring for the wounded, as well as taking responsibility for the 2,000 Catholic converts in Prince Su's palace.

Most of the nursing was provided by the lady missionaries, though the more romantic accounts of the Boxer Rebellion, both fictional and documentary, doted on picturing the wives of diplomats and other highborn ladies as emulating Florence Nightingale; the spirit of the nineteenth century lingered, and the Lady Bountiful tradition was still strong, but it was the plain-faced missionaries who tended the wounded. They had some experience in that line and stronger stomachs for grisly sights and prolonged suffering. Certainly it took a sturdy female to serve in that lazaretto; she had to work in the narrow passages between the crowded beds and stoop constantly because of the mosquito nets overhead.

One American missionary recalled her endless days and nights:

> The supply of everything was short. . . . The patients were all wounded men, the supply of absorbent dressings was very small; of rubber protectives there were almost none. When the mattresses and pillows became bloodsoaked, there was nothing to do but wash them off as well as possible and use them again. The supply of proper sheets and pillowcases being inadequate, they were made up hastily out of any material that could be spared from the sandbags. Coarse, thin Chinese cotton covered one patient while his neighbor looked down on an expanse of slippery shining damask. As one patient remarked, "In this hospital it is every man his own tablecloth." Two dinner napkins made a cover for a feather pillow. A beautiful embroidered linen pillowcase did duty on a pillow made of the straw bottle-covers [the straw came from champagne bottles which, ironically, were in better supply than medicines].

Hospital gowns were often made of silk, damask, or brilliantly patterned Chinese cottons, so there was an incongruously gay costuming for even the most grievously wounded.

The missionary-nurse's account went on:

> The want of medical supplies was not so easily managed. An abundance of medical stores were destroyed at the different mission hospitals. But the besieged had only the small stock kept in the legations for the use of foreigners and a few things that had been for sale at the foreign store.
>
> At first the most approved surgical dressings were to be had, then bags of peat and finally, bags of sawdust served as dressings. At first bandages were used with a lavish hand, but before the close of the siege they had to be washed and do duty more than once. The small stock of the drugs most useful became pitifully small. The last bottle of chloroform was opened. No one can be impressed with the perishable nature of the hypodermic needle until he is obliged to use it many times every day with the knowledge that the last needle that can be procured from anywhere is in his hand.

The nurses were handicapped not only by the shortage of the most rudimentary supplies and pain-killers, but by the polyglot nature of their patients. "One needed to know most of the languages of Europe, besides Chinese, Japanese and one of India's dialects, to be equal to every emergency. . . . Often the sign language was the only one that could be understood."

Nurses' aides were recruited among the Chinese, but they proved a variable quality, often "conspicuous by their absence." The least reliable were the men detailed to operate the punka, which provided a minimum of ventilation in the officers' ward. "One night, after having herself pulled the punka for an hour rather than have the patients suffer, the nurse had to go to the American minister at midnight, call him up and ask him to go to the corridor where the Committee on Chinese Labor slept, wake up the committee and ask them to send another man to pull the punka for the rest of the night."

The first nights in the International Hospital were full of shadowy terrors, but the missionary-nurses soon learned to adapt themselves to the atmosphere:

Night was a dreary time, notwithstanding the pot of strong coffee kindly sent every evening by Mrs. Squiers to cheer the long hours for the nurses. No lights were allowed, for fear of attracting the attention of the enemy. The attendants worked by the light of small lanterns which were so covered with dark cloth that only a ray of light shone forth. When not in use even these were placed on the floor with their faces to the wall. Notwithstanding the smothering protection of sandbags and darkness, a bullet occasionally came whistling through the front door down the length of the hall over the beds of the patients lying on the hall floor.

The wounded men rarely complained but even more rarely exhibited any optimism over the outcome of the siege. "Other people might talk and plan for the coming of the troops; not so the hospital. The wounded lamented being deprived of their guns, spoke more often of the fear of falling unarmed into the hands of the Chinese, who seemed like demons to them. . . ."

Dysentery soon ravaged most of the people sheltered by the British compound. The only palliative was to drink gallons of water in which rice had been boiled, which helped quiet the spasmodic bowels. An epidemic of any sort would, of course, have caused the defense to collapse quicker than the full weight of the imperial army.

Polly Condit Smith recalled that whenever the kitchen was relatively unoccupied, she and her maid and Mrs. Squiers boiled up gallons of thick bland rice water, poured it into quart bottles, and placed them in a zinc-lined box filled with water to cool. "It is placed in a corner of our two-roomed quarters, and the constant stream of men coming and going to that box would lead an uninitiated observer to believe that at least a Hoffman House bar was hidden there and doing a steady business."

During the first days of July, when the dry season broke and torrential rains came down, the general health of the besieged suffered a decline, especially after the temperature went up to 110°. The children particularly were stricken by the heat and lack of proper food; there was only one cow in the compound, and it could not provide enough milk for all. Six European children, and uncounted Chinese, died just after the rains came. A baby, christened Siege, was born.

On July 1, just before the rains came, a critical situation arose when the Germans, holding the barricade facing east on the Tatar Wall (as the Americans held the one facing west), were driven off by a surprise attack of overwhelming force. This left the U.S. marines pinned down from two sides, with Chinese moving up their mobile barricades to within twenty-five feet of the American position. Captain Myers immediately informed Minister Conger and his colleagues that the position was now absolutely untenable; the marines simply didn't have the numbers to fight and face both ways.

To the besieged civilians that sounded like the death knell of the legations. "This sentence, 'to give up the Wall,' could be translated into siege language, 'the beginning of the end,'" Polly Condit Smith wrote in her diary that day, "and this news is most terrifying to us. I think that there are few who in their heart of hearts have given up hope of the troops coming soon. Nevertheless, the facts remain that if we cannot hold the place it would not take very long for us to be annihilated, and if the troops come a day after we are finished, a miss is as good as a mile, and we don't care then when they come." Miss Smith couldn't help wondering what monstrous forms of incompetence and maladministration were holding up the relief column. "Are the allied Powers fighting each other, or are they fighting their way up here?"

One thing was certain, the Council of Ministers, which also served as the General Staff of the defense, agreed: The Tatar Wall had to be held at all costs. Without it, the defense could not survive for more than a few days made horrible by a rain of shells. One observer wrote, "a council of war was hastily convened very much after the style of the Boer commandos, with everybody talking at once." The decision was that the Americans would be strongly and secretly reinforced for a sudden dawn assault on the Chinese position.

Fifteen Russian sailors and twenty-six British, including royal marines and English volunteers like Nigel Oliphant, formerly of the Scots Greys, were assembled along with Captain Myers and fourteen U.S. marines to conduct the foray.

Just before they went over the top, Captain Myers addressed the assault force in an emotional style which Oliphant, as a Proper Briton, considered a bit, well, unseemly:

Captain Myers made a speech, which was interesting because it was so utterly unlike what a British officer would have said under similar circumstances. He began by saying that we were about to embark on a desperate enterprise, that he himself had advised against it, but that orders had been given, and we must do it or lose every man in the attempt. . . . He ended up by saying that if there was any man whose heart was not in the business he had better say so and clear out. One man said he had a sore arm and went down—not one of ours, I am glad to say.

With fewer than sixty men at his heels, Captain Myers led his mixed force over his own barricades and into the Chinese position. It was just before dawn on July 3. Rain was pouring down. The men slipped and stumbled forward over the glazed surface of the Tatar Wall.

Captain Myers fell with a spear wound in the leg, and two of his marines were killed before the desperate little storm troop reached the Chinese. They kept going, knowing that it was, as one of the missionaries later put it, "a struggle which more than any other was the pivot of our destiny."

Once into the Chinese position, they went to work with the bayonet. The Chinese had been taken completely by surprise. They were routed, but only after twenty or thirty of their number had been killed; there was no time for a careful body count. Many Chinese rifles and bandoliers of ammunition were captured. Pistol shots disposed of any of the enemy who had not succeeded in fleeing. When dawn came up, the wall had been cleared and the situation was saved, temporarily.

The next day was the Fourth of July, and the victory on the wall had given the Americans in the British compound something to celebrate. They took the action on the wall as an American success, though their marines had been outnumbered by both the British and the Russians. They could hold up their heads again after all the snide remarks made about how *cautiously* the celebrated United States Marine Corps had been performing. Conger and all other members of the legation staff appeared with miniature Stars and Stripes in their buttonholes. The U.S. minister also insisted on showing everyone a framed copy of the Declaration of Independence which had hung in his office; it had recently been pierced by a Chinese bullet just through the lines condemning George III. Some of the British considered his display in the worst of Yankee taste.

Not all the Americans celebrated, however. Baroness von Ketteler, the former Maud Ledyard, was still distraught over her husband's death. Her sheltered girlhood as the daughter of a railroad president had not prepared her for this. Mrs. Frank Gamewell tried to comfort her, but she said, "I am so alone. . . . No title, no position, no money can help us here . . . these things mock us."

Mrs. Conger observed the Fourth by going alone to the plot in the courtyard where six American marines were now buried and placing a silk American flag over their graves.

Peking must be stormed and levelled to the ground.

—KAISER WILHELM *to* CHANCELLOR VON BÜLOW

9. *The Shock Wave from Peking*

When the news of the siege of the Peking legations reached the outside world, an obscure Russian exile named Vladimir Ilyich Ulanov, later known as Lenin, was living in Switzerland and spending his days plotting at café tables with fellow Bolshevik fugitives. He saw the event as a signal demonstration of his own teachings and promptly called upon "enslaved humanity in China to break its chains."

Comrade Lenin correctly evaluated the significance of the uprising but overestimated its potential.

Anyway his attitude toward events in North China was atypical in the Western world, where the Boxers' outbreak, followed by the support of the Manchu dynasty, was viewed as testimony to support the belief that there were still large areas of the earth's surface in which the clarion call of "Onward, Christian Soldiers!" must reverberate.

The first definite word that the Peking legations had been placed under siege and the lives of the foreign colony were imperiled reached the outside world on June 29, nine days after the siege began. A Chinese courier had slipped through the countryside and brought a ten-word dispatch from Sir Robert Hart, as alarming as it was brief, to the allied command at Tientsin.

"Foreign community besieged in the Legations," it read. "Situation desperate. MAKE HASTE!"

At the moment there was little the naval commanders could do but forward the message to their capitals. For the international fleet on that date there was only the prospect of hard fighting merely to reclaim the Foreign Settlement in Tientsin. At a conference between the British admirals and Admiral Yevgeni Alexeiev, the governor-general of Port Arthur, who had come down the coast for consultations and a tour of inspection, it was decided that for the time being nothing could be done about the relief of Peking. As the British representatives at that conference cabled the Admiralty, the Russian agreed that "with all the reinforcements expected, Russian and Japanese, it will only bring the total to about 20,000 men, which would enable us to hold the base," but it would be "impossible to advance beyond Tientsin."

In the homelands of the various nationalities represented at Peking preparations were ordered for expeditionary forces, warships were being dispatched, stern notes were being written. The news of the siege was bad enough, but it was made incomprehensible by the attitude of the Chinese diplomats in the various capitals who blandly kept offering assurances that diplomatic personnel in Peking would not be harmed despite the alarming tenor of Sir Robert Hart's dispatch.

The British government, for one, was not satisfied by such assurances. On July 5, it gave the Chinese envoy a warning message for Peking stating that the Chinese authorities would be "held personally guilty if the members of the European Legations and other foreigners in Peking suffer injury."

In the Western capitals there was a growing sense of alarm because, at the very least, their Peking legations were cut off from the rest of the world. There may have been some doubt whether they were under actual attack, but undoubtedly they were in great danger. This feeling was only partly dispelled by an appeal, supposedly signed by the captive emperor, to Queen Victoria, the Czar of Russia, and the Emperor of Japan asking for their help in bringing about a settlement of Chinese problems with other nations.

Then on July 16 the London *Daily Mail* published a horrifying dispatch under a Shanghai dateline. The headline told the story: THE PEKING MASSACRE!

According to the *Daily Mail*'s anonymous special correspondent, the Chinese had massed their artillery on the night of July 6–7 and systematically destroyed the defenses of the Legation Quarter in Peking. In all-night fighting, the defenders had hurled back wave after wave of Chinese assault troops. Then their ammunition supply ran out. There was a desperate last stand around the British legation. The legation guards were wiped out to the last man, and then everyone else was "put to the sword in the most atrocious manner."

The Shanghai correspondent added other blood-dripping details, supposedly from accounts given him by "authoritative" Chinese sources.

His story was accepted to the last comma as an accurate account of the legations' last hours. Without further checking, without demanding substantiation from any independent sources, other newspapers picked up and reprinted the story around the world and even added a few embellishments of their own, such as reports that many men in the legations shot the women and children, then themselves, rather than submit to rape and torture. The usually magisterial *Times* of London declared in an editorial: "It would be foolish and unmanly to affect to doubt the awful truth."

The news that traveled like a shock wave around the world was, in fact, a tissue of false rumors. The *Daily Mail* account wove together reports circulating in Shanghai, some of them perhaps maliciously concocted by Chinese dissidents, and offered them as verified truth rather than unverified rumor. Other Shanghai correspondents had forwarded such tales to their newspapers but had refused to vouch for their truthfulness. Rival editors then picked up the *Daily Mail* story after having refused to publish similarly gory accounts from their own correspondents.

It was an outstanding case of journalistic irresponsibility, a symptom of the sensationalism with which the new mass-circulation newspapers in both England and the United States competed for readership. Not long before the Hearst and Pulitzer newspapers in New York had more or less created the *casus belli* of the Spanish-American War with their atrocity tales from Cuba. The dashing foreign correspondent who flitted around the globe in sun helmet and riding boots, starting wars and lecturing prime ministers, was the most glamorous figure imaginable.

Just how the "Peking massacre" hoax was concocted, and by whom, was investigated months later by the *Times* of London. Its investigator, fittingly enough, was Dr. E. G. Morrison, who was supposed to have been among those massacred in Peking. Morrison confidentially wrote the manager of the *Times*:

I see that *The Times* whitewashed the *Daily Mail* [Morrison apparently was referring to the fact that on August 20 the *Times* had conducted a preliminary investigation and concluded that the *Daily Mail* had published its special correspondent's account in good faith] and bore witness to the good faith with which they had published that disgraceful telegram from Shanghai which caused misery to so many families. The man who sent the telegram was I understand F. W. Sutterlee. This man was manager of the firm of Keen, Sutterlee and Co. of Philadelphia who in 1896, after the failure of the firm, sold thrice over by means of forged warehouse certificates the same stock of wool and then skipped with the proceeds to Tientsin under the name of W. F. Sylvester.

In Tientsin Sutterlee had entered into a partnership with one Louis Spitzel, a naturalized Englishman, "who had been in trouble with the police in England for being in possession of goods knowing them to have been stolen. These two men carried on business in Tientsin under the name of Taylor & Co. and with them was a man named Baker . . . who had been the warehouse clerk whose forgery of certificates enabled Sutterlee to effect his swindle in January 1896."

After the outbreak of the Spanish-American War, Sutterlee and Spitzel, joined by a new partner named Louis Etzel:

went down to Hongkong and Manila and engaged in a lucrative trade selling arms to the Philippine insurgents [who, of course, were then engaged in resisting the American occupation forces in the archipelago]. On one occasion the firm loaded a vessel with firearms in Canton and shipped them to the Philippines. They made a sworn declaration that the arms were for Singapore and they entered into bail of $15,000 with Mr. Drew, the Commissioner of Customs at Canton, that they would produce within six weeks a certificate from the American Consul in Singapore that the goods had been landed in Singapore or their bail would be forfeit.

The Consul in Singapore—Pratt—was in their pay, engaged in the smuggling of arms to rebels at war with his own Government. This treachery was just at this juncture discovered and he was removed from his post. Sylvester was never able to produce the certificate that the goods had been landed at Singapore and he was called upon to forfeit his bail. He had the impudence to contest the case *Drew vs. Sylvester.* He admitted that he had signed the undertaking with Mr. Drew but contended that the contract was void *ab initio.* He lost his case and since has been living as Sutterlee in Shanghai at the Astor House and acting as the trusted Correspondent of the *Daily Mail.*

Dr. Morrison concluded that "the *Daily Mail* did not exercise a very wise choice in the appointment of their Correspondent."

Certainly that was an understatement. To the editors in London, Sutterlee was merely a name on the payroll; they knew little or nothing of his background, yet they published his dispatch without questioning its credibility, just as the New York *Journal* bannerlined accounts of wholesale slaughters in Cuba which had been imagined in Havana bars. The story not only brought grief to the families of the people involved but influenced the actions of the various governments.

Certainly Mr. Sutterlee's tale had anything but a salutary effect on some of the more hotheaded rulers and statesmen.

One of those most affected by the "massacre" news, following as it did the report of the killing of his ambassador, was the German Kaiser. Wilhelm II was the inventor of the "Yellow Peril" and for several years, on occasion, had been clamoring that barbaric hordes one day would swarm out of the Asian deserts and imperil Christendom. Some of his fears may have been genuine, but they also served the purpose of his venturesome foreign policy. He wanted to "nail down Russia in Asia," as he informed his foreign ministry in 1895, "so that she may occupy herself less with Europe and the Near East." The idea was that Russia would be so preoccupied with imaginary threats from the Far East that the czar would give Wilhelm a free hand in the Balkans, the Middle East, and elsewhere.

To make his message as graphic as possible, Kaiser Wilhelm commissioned the court painter, Hermann Knackfuss, to execute a heroic canvas illustrating the point for his simpleminded Russian cousin. It was not art, but it was effective propaganda. Knackfuss' painting showed ravaging Asian hordes being held at bay by the Christian powers. Leading the Christian world were a highly idealized Germany and Russia, the German figure a winged Siegfried, the Russian clutching the true Gospel, with Britannia lurking demurely to the rear. Underneath this garish daub, Wilhelm scrawled, "Nations of Europe! Guard your most sacred possessions." Then he sent the painting to St. Petersburg, where Czar Nicholas expressed his childish delight. "So it worked all right," Wilhelm congratulated himself. "That is very satisfactory."

As the self-appointed "First Gentleman of Christendom," Wilhelm took off like a skyrocket when he heard the false report of the Peking massacre. Without consulting his military or diplomatic advisers, he volunteered to send an expeditionary force of 30,000 men to Tientsin. The relief of Peking would be a Wilhelmine project, an opportunity for the glory thus far denied him. A German field marshal would command the interallied operation. Uhlans would drive the hideous Boxers into the Gobi Desert and skewer them with their lances.

Wilhelm's imagination ran riot with the possibilities of a new Crusade until his Foreign Office and the more sober-minded generals managed to calm him down. But he did insist that German marines be dispatched immediately to the Far East, declaiming that such an operation was "no business of the Foreign Office" but must be directed "from the saddle as it were."

His tendency to view everything in primary colors was still dominant July 27 when his yacht *Hohenzollern* brought him to Bremerhaven to preside over the departure of the troopships. He had already declared to Chancellor Prince von Bülow that "Peking must be stormed and levelled to the ground."

His speech to the departing marines was a monument of kingly indiscretion. He began calmly enough by exhorting the troops to "open the door for culture"—that was the smarmy sort of phrase most Westerners used in expiation of their actions in China—but then he was overcome by the intoxication of the moment. Drunk on fancies of his historic mission he bellowed at his embarking troops:

"You must know, my men, that you are about to meet a crafty, well-armed foe! Meet him and beat him! Give no quarter! Take no prisoners! Kill him when he falls into your hands!

"Even as, a thousand years ago, the Huns under their King Attila made such a name for themselves as still resounds in terror through legend and fable, so may the name of Germany resound through Chinese history a thousand years from now so that never again will a Chinese dare to so much as look askance at a German."

The Hun allusion not only was historically inept—the Huns, after all, were Mongols bent on conquering Western Europe—but in the coming World War gave Germany's enemies the label for all Germans. The Kaiser's advisers, in fact, heard his oration with concealed horror. They did their best to tame it down and handed the international press a heavily expurgated copy of the Kaiser's remarks. One reporter, however, got a true copy of the harangue, and it was sent winging around the world. When the Kaiser read a censored version of his speech in a German newspaper, he still could not understand what all the fuss was about and complained to Prince von Bülow, "You have struck out the best parts of it."

Then he happily occupied himself with persuading the other nations involved that the commander in chief of the Joint Relieving Force, as it was grandly styled, should be Field Marshal Count Alfred von Waldersee.

The reaction to the *Daily Mail*'s dispatch from Shanghai was somewhat milder in other capitals, but it did hasten the sending of troopships and lent urgency to the measures being taken in the various Western capitals. The Russian government seized the opportunity to inform the Chinese minister to St. Petersburg that it was moving its Far Eastern army into Manchuria on the pretext of "protecting our interests" in that sphere of influence.

The *Times* of London reported from Rome that the news had produced a "painful stupor" in Italy.

The fate of the foreign diplomats in Peking got the top play in newspapers throughout the world through the last two weeks of July. For at least a week the *Daily Mail* account was accepted journalistically, if not officially, as the gospel truth. Then doubts began to seep in, especially after the State Department in Washington reported receiving a coded cablegram from Minister Conger, though there was considerable doubt about its authenticity. "For one month," Conger's dispatch read, "we have been besieged in British Legation. Quick relief only can prevent massacre." That message indicated the legations still endured more than two weeks after the *Daily Mail* said they had been overwhelmed.

London was virtually in mourning. A memorial service for the supposed massacre victims was scheduled for St. Paul's Cathedral on July 23. Thousands planned to attend, with one newspaper reporting that "in the selection of the psalms special care has been taken to avoid those which seem to breathe a spirit of revenge." The service was canceled, however, because of the growing uncertainty over the truthfulness of the *Daily Mail*'s scare story.

Washington, perhaps oddly, was the least volatile of all the capitals and maintained the ponderous calm of the McKinley administration.

President McKinley was renominated for a second term. His first term having been adventurous enough, what with the Spanish-American War and the occupation of the Philippines, McKinley now preferred the plumage of the dove to that of the hawk. The generals and admirals would be kept on a tight leash and follow the State Department's lead. Preparations for the modest American role in the relief of Peking went forward at deliberate speed, though American public opinion was almost as aroused by the plight of the missionaries as Britain's or Germany's and, as Henry Adams commented, "The drama of the Legations interested the public much as though it were a novel by Alexandre Dumas." Church groups, of course, were pouring out a torrent of propaganda for the rescue of the missionaries by whatever means necessary. More for show than anything else, the administration announced the appointment of a senior general, Adna R. Chaffee, renowned for exploits on the frontier and in the Civil War, a satisfactorily hard-bitten old cavalryman with a face like the map of a battlefield, to take command of the land operations in North China.

More than any of the other nations involved, however, it was the paramount aim of American policy to avoid alienating China. In one of the alternating currents of America's historic attitude toward China, governed by a rheostat which could have been marked "love," "hate," and "occasional indifference," America then was in a sympathetic mood toward Chinese problems. China was regarded with great pity. Every church had its barrel in the vestry for the deposit of secondhand clothes for the underclad Chinese. A nightly refrain at American dinner tables was the injunction to children to clean their plates and "think of the starving Chinese." China was omnipresent in the American consciousness. It was an unstated national priority to help the Chinese restore themselves to their ancient dignity.

And President McKinley himself reflected those attitudes, according to his latest biographer, Margaret Leech:

> His tolerant mind was quick to comprehend the distress and confusion of an isolated people, whose homogeneity and seclusion had been disturbed by the inroads of the powers. Though keenly worried about Conger and the other members of the American legation, he refused to acknowledge doubts of their survival even in the dark days of July, when it was . . . almost universally believed that the entire foreign colony had perished. The reports of a general massacre came from an apparently reliable source, but they were insistently denied by the Chinese minister at Washington, and the President continued to hope. His optimism was a matter of policy, as well as personal inclination. To abandon hope for the legations was to divest the intervention of the motive of rescue and relief. When Secretary [of State] Hay submitted the draft of a telegram to Kaiser Wilhelm, conveying the President's condolences on the murder of the German minister, McKinley took care to delete a reference to "the only too real apprehension that the other foreign representatives may have shared his fate."

In furtherance of its low-keyed approach, the McKinley administration maintained the most cordial relations with the Chinese minister to Washington, Wu Ting-fang. It was this friendly relationship which resulted in Washington's being able to put the quietus to the *Daily Mail* massacre story and, incidentally, caused the cancellation of the premature memorial service in London.

Early in July Secretary of State John Hay asked Minister Wu to forward a cipher message to Minister Conger asking for assurance of his survival. Ten days passed before Conger's reply was received, since it had to be passed through the siege lines between the Forbidden City and the Legation Quarter. On July 20 Conger replied that the legations were under siege but after a month of fighting were still holding out. When the British in particular questioned the authenticity of the Conger message, Secretary Hay cleverly asked Minister Wu that a second query be cabled. Conger was asked to give the name of his sister. "Alta," came the correct reply. That one word relieved the despondency in hundreds of homes throughout the Western world.

I have always found that there is a corrective for everything in this world. Action is the best one of all, people say. It is not always so. . . .

—B. L. Putnam Weale, *Indiscreet Letters from Peking*

10. *The Fabrication of "Old Betsy"*

The defenders of the foreign colony in Peking were still holding out in those mid-July days when the outside world was hearing that they had been hacked to death by Chinese swords.

As the siege went on, day by day, the symptoms of "stockade mentality," a sort of mass persecution complex, proliferated. Behavior became erratic even among those formerly noted for a sturdy sense of the fitness of things. Several times a certain German officer imagined he saw a searchlight playing its beam on the night horizon, signaling the approach of a relief column; it was a German naval searchlight, he loudly asserted. Nonsense, Sir Claude Macdonald firmly replied at each imagined sighting, it was a British searchlight. Once, to hammer the point home, he posted a bulletin on the board at the Jubilee Tower which served as a community newspaper, declaring: "This morning at about two o'clock I saw the searchlight of Her Majesty's ship *Terrible*. I recognized it as the searchlight of that ship because it has a very characteristic searchlight." No one dared ask him how anyone could say for certain whether a searchlight, whose beam was seen in the distance against a distracting pattern of rocket and artillery fire, was British or German, army or navy; or for that matter, what the searchlight of a British warship would be doing almost ninety miles inland. Searchlight sighting became a nightly pastime, undiminished by the fact that each sighting proved to be false.

The bizarre and hallucinatory spread like fever dreams in a pesthouse, and in diaries and memoirs of the siege there were frequent references to madness, delusion, and dementia.

In at least one case the epithets were justified and not merely the small change of a community under constant stress. There was a Norwegian missionary named Nostegarde who suffered a complete crackup early in July and made such a nuisance of himself that he narrowly escaped being shot by his companions in misfortune.

Early on the morning of July 3, when the strike force was assembled to clear the Tatar Wall, Nostegarde suddenly showed up wearing a long black robe and a top hat and crying out that he wanted justice done his reputation. "Someone, he said, had been speaking ill of him and taking away his good name. The more the men tried to pacify him the more excited he got," Nigel Oliphant recalled. "He shouted, he howled, he appealed to King Oscar and the whole of the Norwegian royal family to right his wrongs. Nothing would quiet him; at last he was gagged and taken away struggling and stifling." The marines and volunteers exhibited considerable forbearance at that; the noise he made endangered the secrecy of their sortie against the Chinese position.

Nostegarde was kept tied up in the stables, where his howls only added to the tension of life in the British compound. A few days later he broke loose and slipped through the defense lines. Ironically, he was better treated on the Chinese side than among his own kind, probably because the Chinese regarded madness with a superstitious awe. He was taken to General Jung Lu's headquarters as a more or less honored guest. His personal papers were examined by Jung Lu's officers, including a letter of apology he had written to the Russian minister after he had "indecently exposed himself" before Mme. de Giers.

Nostegarde repaid the Chinese hospitality in full measure. As he later admitted, he answered the questions of the Chinese officers regarding the remaining strength of the legation guards, which positions had been damaged by shellfire, which were the strongest held, the state of the ammunition supply, the effectiveness of the Chinese gunnery. Deranged as he apparently was, he provided the enemy with sensible advice and valuable information. He even volunteered the suggestion that Chinese riflemen should lower their sights, that their shots were flying harmlessly overhead.

After four informative days, Nostegarde was sent back to his own people, to whom he boasted about what he had done. Some of the more hotheaded civilians, claiming that Chinese marksmanship had clearly improved after Nostegarde had offered his critique, urged that the missionary be shot as a traitor. Because the man's fellow missionaries, who were doing all the donkey work around the beleaguered compound, wouldn't have liked that and might have gone on a sympathy strike, Nostegarde was put back in the stable under a more secure guard and kept there for the duration.

Others besides the unfortunate Norwegian thought they might go around the bend or up the wall, when someone broke out a stock of gramophones which had been snatched from Kierulff's store. The record industry being in its infancy, there were only a few selections to be played—"Marching Through Georgia," "There'll be a Hot Time in the Old Town Tonight," "Home Sweet Home," and other selections with themes more ironic than comforting. To this cacophony, loosed without regard for the wounded men trying to sleep within earshot, were added the offerings of a group of American missionaries who gathered at the chapel door nightly to sing "Nearer My God to Thee," a thought which did not uplift all their auditors, and the carolings of a Russian lady with an impressive thorax and a powerful voice box, who claimed to have been an opera singer. From that medley of ragtime, hymns, and classical arias, some sought refuge in the library of the first secretary of the British legation, who had collected a number of works on the Sepoy Rebellion. Those who sought a clue to the fate of the Peking legations in the history of a somewhat similar incident in Indian history, it was said, cheered themselves up by reading about the relief of Lucknow but avoided accounts of the dismal end of Cawnpore.

Food had now become a primary concern, since there was no way of knowing whether the supply would suffice for the duration of the siege or whether bullets and shells might give out before the rations. The mutton had given out and was replaced by horse and mule meat. Each night the Food Supply Committee was convened to survey the remaining stocks and decide on the next day's menu, which was then posted on Sir Claude's bulletin board along with his nightly report on searchlight sightings. A typical menu:

BREAKFAST
Porridge of Ground Wheat
Steak
Wheat bread and butter

DINNER
Stew with brown flour dumplings
Crackers and jam
SUPPER
Brown rice pancakes and syrup
Bread

As one of the American missionary ladies in charge of the victualing wrote, "We had to vary the bill of fare with boiled beans, rice puddings, and anything we could make without eggs, butter or lard." Her committee also was charged with overseeing the water supply:

> The second day we had been in the Legations, one of the servants came in and said: "What shall we do for water? They have locked the well." My heart sank, for I feared the reason of a locked well was scarcity of water. On asking one of the members of the general committee what was to be done, he explained that there was plenty of water to be had in the many other wells on the premises, and that the large well had been locked up only to save its supply as a near well, and to send people to farther ones first. Hard cold water was used for laundry purposes as our heating facilities were limited. The chapel food committee succeeded in keeping a supply of cold boiled water in bottles for those who feared to drink from wells.

That the besieged did not lack for protein was due to several hundred horses, ponies, and mules rounded up shortly before the siege began. The small amount of mutton available was kept for distribution in the hospital, where the wounded were given mutton broth and mutton stews; the rest of the beleaguered community adapted itself, with surprising ease and swiftness, to the idea of horse and mule meat. The French and Belgians, of course, already regarded that as a staple. Polly Condit Smith wrote early in July:

There are a lot of horses, ponies, and mules in the compound which we have kept alive by feeding with straw, and every day two animals have been slaughtered and distributed among the messes. Then the coolies have a kitchen, where they can come whenever their work makes it possible, and they get rice and horse-meat. It is queer to see how many people acknowledge that they like it, having eaten it now for two weeks. Of course, a great deal depends on the animal, but they agree that mule and pony are better than horse. Some people who have among their stores plenty of canned or tinned beef even prefer the horse-meat. At our mess, however, we have a prejudice against it, and as long as we continue to have the tinned beef we will not send for our share of the animal.

Much of the meat on the menu was provided by the racing ponies which fortunately were on hand for the race meeting which ended just before the siege began and which their once-proud owners surrendered to the butcher with hardly a quiver of sentiment. Children's pet ponies were also sacrificed, though not without stormy protests. Miss Smith observed:

The May races having come off before the siege, most of the diplomats had not disposed of their horses and polo ponies, and the all-important question now is not if "Cochon" will win more cups in future, but if his steaks will be tender. Things are so queer now. The one cow which still gives a small amount of milk, needless to say, has not been killed for her beef, but is carefully tended for her baby-saving fluid. The president of the largest and most influential bank in Peking, besieged here with us, has received a wound which incapacitates him for active work. He can only hobble around on a crutch. He has volunteered to tend "Miss Cow" and assist her to find the few blades of grass which are still to be had.

By the time the legations had been under siege for two weeks it was evident that help from the outside would not be coming for some time, though the community was enlivened almost daily by

大清國當今慈禧端佑康頤昭豫莊誠壽恭欽獻崇熙聖母皇太后

Tzu Hsi, the Dowager Empress of China.

(The Bettmann Archive)

Drawing of a Boxer in full regalia.

(The Granger Collection)

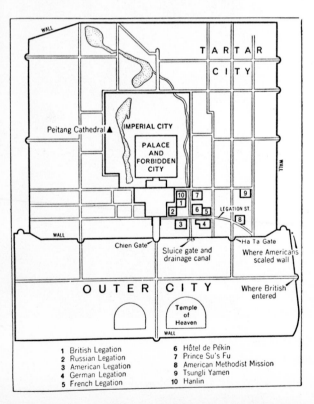

Map showing locations of the Imperial City and Legation Compounds.

(Historical Pictures Service, Chicago)

Artist's rendition of marines defending the U.S. Legation.

(Wide World Photos)

The fighting at Tientsin, from a drawing by H. M. Paget.

(Historical Pictures Service, Chicago)

The Tientsin relief column attacked by Boxers at Langfang, from a contemporary drawing.
(The Granger Collection)

Artist's representation of Japanese cavalry charging Boxers outside Tientsin.
(The Granger Collection)

Drawing of the allied forces marching on Peking.
(Historical Pictures Service, Chicago)

The Ninth United States Infantry entering Peking. Drawing by
Frederic Remington.

(The Granger Collection)

Boxers on trial before the Chinese High Court.

(Historical Pictures Service, Chicago)

Execution of Boxer chiefs.

(Culver Pictures, Inc.)

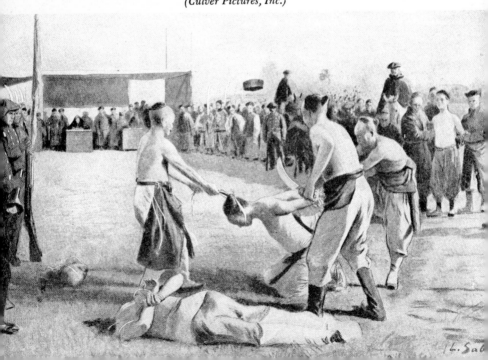

A Boxer undergoing torture.

(Historical Pictures Service, Chicago)

Russian soldiers watch as a chief of the Boxers is led by on the executioner's cart.

(Historical Pictures Service, Chicago)

Execution of Boxers at Kowloon near Hong Kong.
(Historical Pictures Services, Chicago)

rumors which kept hope alive and morale afloat. The defenders began giving more thought to conserving ammunition, strengthening their defenses, and using the technical ingenuity with which Westerners were supposed to be endowed as a birthright. The siege was tightening like a noose around the legations. Mass infantry attacks having been costly failures, the Chinese had adopted new tactics; under cover of darkness they moved their barricades closer and closer to the foreigners' positions until various outposts either had to be abandoned or held at an unbearable cost. Each night the Chinese breastworks, earthworks, and redoubts seemed to have inched a little closer—the tactics of the boa constrictor. The enemy had also begun mining underneath the Legation Quarter, until the overly imaginative could visualize a squadron of Moslem cavalrymen popping up from the floor of the mess and joining them for supper.

Counterfortification and countermining were the only possible response, and in that effort the heroic labors of Dr. Frank Gamewell, the missionary turned military engineer, made him the least expendable man among the besieged. He saw that the stable gate in the northwest corner of the quadrant was vital to the defense and built a wall eight feet thick behind it. The Chinese burned the heavy wooden gate but found themselves confronted by the wall when they tried to storm into the British compound from that direction.

In the southwest corner of the perimeter overlooked by the rooftops of the Mongol Market, one of Gamewell's admirers wrote, "solid barricades five feet in thickness were constructed. In exactly five hours after these defenses were finished, the Chinese had loopholed every house opposite, thus showing how necessary it was to have this remote corner protected."

Gamewell, now officially designated the director of fortifications, the overseer of scores of women sewing sandbags and a much greater number of Chinese pressed into a shovel brigade, "gave endless time and thought to the eastern side of the compound, which was the strategic section. The Su Wang Fu [Prince Su's palace] was separated [from the British compound] only by the narrow canal road. If the Fu should have to be abandoned, as had already seemed likely, the enemy could mount their guns on the mounds of the flower garden, only fifty yards away from the residence of Sir Claude Macdonald. To prepare for such an emergency, thick, high walls were built of earth and braced by heavy timbers. Counter-mines were dug in order to stop mines projected by the enemy. This elaborate barricading was a herculean task, and literally could not have been accomplished without the patient, uncomplaining labor of the Chinese Christians, whose presence was at first deemed by some to be a menace and a nuisance."

Laying down counterbattery fire had also become a serious problem, because the defenders were so outgunned it was no contest. They had exactly one artillery piece, backed up by the three balky and unreliable machine guns. The gun was the Italian one-pounder, which barked like a terrier at the heavy Krupp cannon available to the Chinese.

Bertram Simpson, who was becoming a military expert under fire, considered the Italian one-pounder "absolutely useless. Its snapping shells are so small that you can thrust them into your pocket without noticing them. This gun is merely a plaything. And yet being the best we have, it is wheeled unendingly around and fired at the enemy from a dozen different points. It may give confidence but that is all it can give." Worse yet, there were only about 120 rounds of ammunition left. Simpson watched it chipping away at a brick-walled Chinese breastworks: "Each time, as ammunition is becoming precious, the gun was more carefully sighted and fired, and each time, with a little crash, the baby shell shot through the barricades, bored a ragged hole six or eight inches in diameter. Then, suddenly, as the gun was shifted a bit to continue the work of ripping up the barricade, attention would be distracted, and before you could explain it the ragged holes would be no more. Unseen hands had repaired the damage by pushing up dozens of bricks and sandbags. . . ." Yet the one-pounder was the only artillery piece they had, it was useful in bolstering the defenders' morale, and its accuracy when employed against specific targets was remarkable. Three days after the siege began, according to Nigel Oliphant, it knocked out two three-inch Krupp guns which had been punishing the American position on the Tatar Wall. In one week of the siege the toy cannon was shifted from the British stables to the Tatar Wall to the British legation library to Prince Su's palace to the earthworks covering the Hanlin Library, back to the palace and stables again, and finally to the main gate. Mobility was not the least of its charms.

With their reputation for tinkering and fabricating, the Yankee talent for improvisation, the Americans finally decided to do something about equalizing the artillery situation. They found the barrel of an old cannon, which fortunately had been rifled, lying in a corner of the blacksmith's shop. It was believed to be a relic of the 1860 Anglo-French expedition. A few days after the old gun was found on July 7, with international cooperation, they had a mongrel sort of fieldpiece in action against the enemy.

An American sailor, Gunner's Mate Tom Mitchell, took charge of the project with a Welshman named Thomas as his assistant. They chipped off the rust and mounted the barrel on an Italian carriage. Then they found a number of nine-pounder shells which had been dropped down a well the second day of the siege, when it was feared the defense lines would be overrun. The shells had been imported for a Russian nine-pounder which the Russians had absentmindedly left behind in Tientsin. Though they had been soaked in well water for days, the shells were found to be still usable, once the damp charges had been replaced by dry gunpowder, and better yet, they fit the barrel of the reconstituted gun.

The French and British, pointing out that the cannon had an Italian mounting, fired Russian ammunition, was left over from an Anglo-French operation, and was rehabilitated by an American sailor, christened it "The International Gun." Fair enough, perhaps, but the Americans insisted on calling it "Old Betsy" as their ancestors on the frontier had often called their long hunting rifles.

Military experts on the scene were inclined to scoff at Old Betsy and predicted it would be more dangerous to its gun crew than the enemy. But Old Betsy confounded its critics. The first time it was fired, its shell went straight through three separate walls. The enemy, fearing some devilish new secret weapon, scattered like quail.

The gun, however, had its drawbacks. Its sights had rusted away, and it could not be aimed for long-range accuracy. Fifty yards was about the limit of its effectiveness. Furthermore, the recoil was terrific, and black smoke poured out its muzzle after every shot, making its operators a target for the enemy gunners. Nevertheless, Old Betsy devastated the Chinese barricades with one shell, then was loaded with grapeshot—old nails, scrap iron, nuts and bolts—for a followup, antipersonnel shot which cut down the enemy exposed by the first shell.

Gunner's Mate Mitchell, of course, appointed himself as chief proprietor of the cannibalized cannon and demonstrated his prowess as a gunner with a certain swagger which other nationals found a bit obnoxious. On July 12 Chinese troops infiltrating through the Hanlin Library complex came so close to the defense lines that they leaned a banner against the wall of the British compound. Mitchell briefly considered blowing up the enemy standard with a round from Old Betsy, then opted for more direct action. He dashed over to the wall and grabbed the Chinese flag. A Chinese soldier clutched the other end of the staff. All firing ceased on both sides as the two men engaged in a tug-of-war over possession of the red and black banner. Mitchell threw fistfuls of dirt in the Chinese soldier's face, wrenched away the flag, and ran back to his own lines with the trophy.

Until mid-July there were few such moments of comedy relief. Day and night the defenders took their turns at the loopholes, often finding the duty more tiresome than dangerous or exciting. Bertram Simpson confided to his diary:

> It is such dull work in front of the eternal loopholes, with nothing but darkness and thick shadows around you, and the rest of the post of four or five men vigorously snoring. . . . And when your two hours are up, and contentedly you kick your relief on the ground beside you, he only moans faintly but does not stir. Then you kick him again with all that zest which comes from a sense of your own lost slumbers. . . .

The strain was telling on those with nerves already stretched beyond the endurance point. Baroness von Ketteler, for one, was behaving oddly, unbalanced as she was by her personal tragedy. She was rarely allowed out of the sight of one or more of her fellow Americans. One afternoon Polly Condit Smith was sitting with her near the tennis court, on which she and the late baron had sometimes played, and trying to cheer her up. A sniper had taken a bead on them and began firing from a concealed position somewhere above them and beyond the compound wall. The first shot sent Miss Smith scrambling for cover. She looked around and saw Baroness von Ketteler sitting in the same place and seemingly inviting death. The bullets began flying all around, but she refused to budge. Finally Miss Smith's screams attracted the attention of one of the men in the compound, and he carried the melancholic baroness to safety.

A black-letter day in the calendar for the superstitious, Friday, July 13, was what Sir Claude later termed "the most harrowing day for the defence during the whole siege." The firing grew so relentless that M. Pichon, never the last to take alarm, burned the French legation's archives—always diplomacy's signal of despair —in a corner of the compound. A breeze came up and started scattering charred fragments of forgotten notes and *démarches,* whereupon the equally excitable Mme. Pichon rushed out to her husband's assistance, collected the windblown pages, and returned them to the archival bonfire. The British couldn't help wondering what nasty things M. Pichon might have said about them in the documents he was so bent on destroying.

That day the Japanese, who had built a defense in depth, abandoned the seventh of their nine lines under unremitting pressure. The Germans were forced out of their corner of the quadrant and regained their position only after a counterattack with fixed bayonets. The Jubilee Tower's alarm bell rang with special urgency around four in the afternoon. On the Tatar Wall the Americans had all they could do to hang on. The royal marines were also having trouble holding their barricades near the British compound. Had the Chinese, everyone wondered, finally started applying the tactics of concerted attack on all sides which inevitably would carry them to victory?

Two hours later, around dusk, the firing slackened. But a few minutes after six o'clock an emergency occurred in the southeast sector held by the French and a few Austrians. It had been suspected for several days that the Chinese were mining under that section of the defenses. Later Bertram Simpson told a rather wild and incredible story related by one of the young French volunteers. The latter, on duty at night behind the barricades, watched the Chinese disappearing into a tunnel in no-man's-land to work on a mine only twenty feet away. The Frenchman waited for them to come out, bayoneted each sapper as he appeared, until he had disposed of thirteen of them. He was so weary of the bayonet work that when three more Chinese came out of the tunnel he took them prisoner, marched them behind the French barricade, where he and his comrades beheaded them. With the guillotine figuring so large in French history, beheading did not cause any queasiness among the Frenchmen. The severed heads were then heaved into the Chinese lines.

If that account was true, it is remarkable that the French were so surprised on July 13, when a Chinese mining operation was completed with explosive results.

The Chinese sappers had tunneled under the French positions and planted two huge charges of gunpowder under the French legation and a fortified house nearby. In the gloom of early evening the mines were exploded. Two French sailors were killed, and only the foot of one of them was later found. Professor Destalon of the Imperial University faculty, a volunteer fighting with his country's naval detachment, and the Austrian chargé d'affaires, Von Rosthorn, were injured when they were buried under the debris. They added to the day's casualty list of five men killed and ten wounded.

After the explosion the French and Austrians moved back into the ruins of the houses, determined to hang onto their corner of the defenses. The British, having heard tunneling noises under their section of the perimeter, started a countermining operation. It was a bad night. The defenders were exhausted and depressed. Bertram Simpson was raging inwardly, and on the pages of his diary, over the fact that many in the British compound were shirking their duty despite the critical turn of events. Nothing, apparently, could jar some of those conscious of rank and position, of wealth and influence, out of the notion that fighting for survival was an endeavor reserved for the lower orders. Simpson estimated that there were about 200 men of all nationalities, young and able-bodied enough to take part in the defense, who dogged it or merely made a show of joining in. The dangers and sufferings of the past three weeks had not ennobled many characters. "The universal attitude is: spare me and take all of my less worthy neighbours. In gaining skin-deep civilization we have lost the animal-fighting capacity." A few days before, he noted, several able-bodied men had fought over the privilege of supervising a newly established laundry in the British legation. He was also depressed by the spectacle of French Minister Pichon and his staff, "all armed with *fusils de chasse,* and looking *très sportsman,* on a tour of inspection when everything is quiet. Each one is told by his tearful wife to look out for the Boxers, to be on the alert—as if Chinese banditti were lurking just outside the Legation base to swallow up these brave creatures!—and in a compact body they sally forth. They are married men; marriage excuses everything when the guns begin to play."

If there was anything to cheer up the defenders, it was the valiant little Japanese, who held such a long and vital sector with their decimated original detachment of twenty-five men, plus a scattering of volunteers who preferred their company to that of other units, plus the dispirited Italians. The Japanese military attaché, Colonel Shiba, was by all odds the most respected of the various commanders on the scene—"a splendid small person," as Polly Condit Smith called him. Originally the officers of the detachments from Western nations had ignored him in their councils. All that was changed. "He has done so splendidly in his active and continuous fighting in the Fu, and has proved himself such a general that his opinion and help are asked by all the commanders. His men are all so patient and uniting in their long, long hours behind the barricades, and so game. . . ." The contrast between the dedicated Japanese and the listless Italians was appalling. "One can only hope," young Miss Smith tartly added, "that for Italy's sake her soldiers in Peking are the worst she has."

To the missionaries and the few others concerned about the 2,700 Chinese Christians gathered in and around Prince Su's palace, the condition of the refugees, for whom the Westerners had the highest moral responsibility, having induced them to alienate themselves from the rest of their countrymen, was as depressing as the military situation that night. Certainly the Chinese, though many of the men were undertaking the heaviest labor in constructing defensive works while others risked their lives trying to run messages to Tientsin, were not receiving their share of the rations. They were barely able to exist on handfuls of low-grade rice; second-class citizens, second-class Christians in their own land, they were mostly viewed with a lordly indifference by their appointed protectors across the canal. Already the Chinese children were eating the leaves off the trees in the palace grounds, and they wandered around naked in the heat-dazed afternoons with the swollen bellies produced by near starvation.

To at least one Westerner who fought along the wall protecting Chinese refugees, who shared his food with the Chinese children, whatever glory there had been in defending the legations had long departed, and there was nothing left but "brutal realities." He wondered whether they deserved to survive and guessed they didn't.

The next day, when things were looking their blackest, when the men at the barricades could hardly face another day of fighting, there was another of those curious moments of reprieve offered by the enemy.

It was signaled by the nerve-shattering chorus of Chinese trumpets which denoted a request for a cease-fire. When the guns stopped firing, an elderly Chinese who several days before had volunteered to carry a dispatch to Tientsin was shoved into the no-man's-land and tottered back to the lines around the legations. The courier was one of a number, always Chinese, who had been dispatched to Tientsin and who had invariably been captured; the Chinese cat watched all the mouseholes. A Roman Catholic convert, the old man too had been captured and given a ritual beating. That was four days before. The courier had been taken to General Jung Lu's headquarters, where his message was studied and he was treated kindly for three days, then given a letter for Sir Claude and told to bring back a reply.

A conciliatory approach had been adopted by the enemy. This was July 14, the day the allied forces stormed into the Foreign Settlement at Tientsin. The letter, signed by "Prince Ching and Colleagues" (Prince Ching being the moderate who had been replaced as head of the Tsungli Yamen by the violently immoderate Prince Tuan), was prefaced by this remark: "For the last ten days the soldiers and militia have been fighting, and there has been no communication between us, to our great anxiety." The Chinese Foreign Office, however, had learned from the captured courier that the foreign envoys were well; that "caused us very great satisfaction." Because of the violent hatred expressed by the Boxers, it was no longer practicable to consider escorting the ministers to Tientsin; therefore, the ministers should proceed to the shelter of the Tsungli Yamen, "but at the time of leaving the legations there must on no account whatever be taken any single armed foreign soldier, in order to prevent doubt and fear on the part of the troops and people, leading to untoward incidents." A reply was requested by noon the following day. "This," the note added, "is the only way of preserving relations that we have been able to devise in the face of innumerable difficulties. If no reply is received by the time fixed, even our affection will not enable us to help you."

What sort of ploy was this? Had the Chinese begun to realize that backing the Boxers had been a lunatic gesture? Sir Claude's reply was firmly self-righteous. The Chinese had broken the old rule that even in time of war the persons of diplomatic representatives were not to be endangered. If harm did come to the envoys in Peking, there would be "grave problems of personal reprisals against all those in official positions in the city."

The Chinese courier carried that message back through the lines under a flag of truce, and then the fighting was resumed.

Once again there was trouble and dissension in the American defense of the Tatar Wall. Despite their vaunted discipline the Marine detachment was in a state bordering on mutiny. Much of the trouble stemmed from the questionable leadership of Captain Newt Hall, who had replaced the wounded Captain Myers in command. It was not helped by the tendency of Minister Conger and First Secretary Squiers, as former Army officers, to interfere in Marine affairs. On July 10 Morrison of the *Times* had written in his diary:

Today on the Wall there were 13 men under Captain Hall. He is never put on the Wall, his men having no confidence in his judgment. He has no control over his men who get blind drunk and insult their NCO with impunity. One man was brought down from his post where he tried to kill a Russian NCO. . . . What punishment will he get? I asked. The Captain says when he gets him back to his ship he will give him a mighty rough time. But for striking the NCO? That he said is more serious. He would probably have his chew of tobacco stopped.

Morrison perhaps tookAmerican slackness in discipline a little too seriously—the loose rein had always been a principle of American command—but undoubtedly the morale of the U.S. Marine detachment left something to be desired.

Not that all the marines present had taken to boozing and

insubordination. There was the undersized Private Dan Daly, the reticent Irishman from Manhattan, for instance. On the night of July 14 the American command had decided that their barricade must be advanced to cover a larger portion of the Tatar Wall. The decision had been pressed on Captain Hall by Conger and Squiers, who prided themselves on their military expertise, though Conger's Civil War record had been undistinguished and Squiers had spent fourteen years as a second lieutenant. The two diplomats insisted that a new and wider expanse of the wall could be held, and Captain Hall finally yielded to their arguments.

That night Hall and Daly conducted a two-man reconnaissance, the idea being that Daly alone would hold an advanced position during the night, after which the rest of the detachment would move up. The two men crawled along the wall for about a hundred yards until they came to a low stone wall, more of a parapet than a bastion, which might serve Daly as a defensive position. "Daly," Captain Hall whispered, "I can't order you to stay here. But if the Chinks can be held back tonight, we can dig in so they'll never break through."

"See you in the morning, Captain," was Daly's reply.

Obviously there was nothing wrong with Private Daly's morale. Alone with his Lee rifle and a bandolier of ammunition, he fired whenever an enemy silhouette appeared against the backdrop of burning houses which had been set afire by a group of Boxers operating in the vicinity. Time after time the Boxers attacked Daly that night, with groups of two or three men trying to rush him, meanwhile loosing spears, steel-tipped arrows, and bullets. By dawn there were heaps of the dead Boxers in front of the low stone wall which had sheltered him through the night.

Private Daly, in the laconic manner which was to make him a Marine Corps legend, had bought enough time for his comrades to extend and bolster their position. When he crawled back to rejoin them just before dawn, he asked his fellow marines, "Anyone know what *Quon-fay* means? Those Chinamen been yelling that at me all night."

"It means devil," he was told by a veteran of China Station duty. "Very bad devil."

Daly cleaned his rifle before leaving the barricades for a few hours' sleep, then returned to duty before noon, modestly unaware that his deeds that night would win him the Congressional Medal of Honor. Several years later he was awarded another one in Haiti, and before his lengthy career ended, the Commandant of the Marine Corps would pronounce him the greatest marine of all time.

That same morning, July 15, when everyone was still puzzling over the latest approaches from the Chinese side and awaiting the next move, there were two fatalities to depress the defenders, all the more because the victims were brave and spirited young men. Every morning Captain Strouts of the Royal Marines and Dr. Morrison of the *Times* joined an early-breakfast session which included First Secretary Squiers, his wife, and Dr. Frank Gamewell. They formed a like-minded group, an elite, who viewed the actions of the senior members of the diplomatic colony with a sardonic amusement.

That morning the breakfast circle was depressed by news of the death on the barricades of Henry Warren, a bright young consular student. About eight o'clock Morrison and Strouts went out to the British lines a few hundred yards away to supervise the relief of the night pickets. They were returning over a stretch of open ground when they were caught in a Chinese fusillade. Both fell with serious wounds, and Colonel Shiba was grazed by a bullet when he went to their assistance.

The Squierses and Polly Condit Smith were still lingering over coffee when Strouts and Morrison were brought in on litters. The captain died three hours later. Morrison had suffered a thigh wound and would be out of action indefinitely. The death of Strouts and the wounding of Morrison were hard blows, particularly for Miss Smith and their other American friends. "Morrison," she wrote, "was the most attractive at our impromptu mess—as dirty, happy and healthy a hero as one could find anywhere." That evening Strouts and Warren were buried as a warm drizzling rain fell on the mourners.

The service was interrupted by still another truce which, if it had come earlier, would have spared the lives of the two young men being lowered into the North China mud.

Perhaps it was that after weeks of rifle-fire and cannon-booming, the colourless monotone of complete silence was nerve-destroying. Yes, it must have been that, a perpetual, aggravating, insolent silence is worse than noise. . . .

—B. L. PUTNAM WEALE, *Indiscreet Letters from Peking*

11. *Not Peace, Not War*

What interrupted the Strouts-Warren funeral service was yet another cat-footed approach of Chinese statesmanship. The elderly Roman Catholic convert who had been pressed into messenger service by both sides had returned to his own lines with two messages.

One was the U.S. State Department's coded query to Mr. Conger ("Communicate tidings bearer," it read) which was the first message to reach the besieged legations. After being deciphered, it turned out to be an inquiry into the health of the diplomatic colony. Conger's reply, of course, assured the Western capitals that the Peking community had survived but was still in desperate danger. Aside from easing the anxieties of people throughout the world with relatives and friends among the besieged, the State Department's approach, via the Chinese minister to Washington, evidently persuaded some members of the Manchu hierarchy that they had better begin thinking about what would happen after the Boxers had their fling.

Certainly those Manchu aristocrats and bureaucrats with a normal sense of proportion realized that, with the Peking legations holding out, the situation around Tientsin turning against the Chinese, and a large expeditionary force being organized for a march inland, it was time to think about consequences. Another factor was the polite resistance of the viceroys and provincial governors against joining in the antiforeign crusade. As early as

July 7 a memorial submitted to the Manchu court from the
provinces pointed out that the Boxers had proved a broken reed
when the test came, that they had been gloriously efficient at
hacking the heads off missionaries but hung back when it came to
attacking foreigners capable of defending themselves. "When the
Boxers first came," the Memorial of July 7 read, "they claimed
that they had supernatural powers, that they were invulnerable to
guns and swords, and that they were capable of burning the
foreign houses and exterminating the foreigners as easily as
turning over a hand. Now they are different; first they evade by
artifice, then they retreat and make no advance. Only the army of
Tung Fu-hsiang [that is, the Moslem forces from Kansu] has
attacked with all effort night and day."

Some of this growing doubt was reflected in the second of the
two messages forwarded by the Tsungli Yamen. It also was signed
by "Prince Ching and Colleagues." The offer to shelter the foreign
diplomats in the Tsungli Yamen, while the other members of the
foreign community presumably took their chances and shifted for
themselves, was not mentioned. Instead, the envoys were assured
that the Chinese government would "continue to exert all its
efforts to keep order and give protection."

Thus began an uneasy interlude of armed truce—not peace, not
war, but something nervous and tentative in between. There was
no firing that night, but much argument and debate over just what
the latest gesture really signified. Most agreed that they couldn't
count on the truce's lasting any length of time; in any case, the
privations, if not the extreme danger, still went on. Bertram
Simpson remarked on how jittery the sudden silence made
everyone. "Perhaps it was that after weeks of rifle-fire and
cannon-booming, the colourless monotone of complete silence
was nerve-destroying. Yes, it must have been that, a perpetual,
aggravating, insolent silence is worse than noise."

If the twenty-five days of fighting had seemed like a fever
dream, with the inability of hordes of Chinese, at least 25,000 of
them, many well armed, to overwhelm a mere 500 Caucasians and
Japanese not the least striking aspect of unreality, the truce also
partook of hallucination.

The truce was declared on July 16, and on the following day
there was a cautious fraternization between the two camps. First
the Chinese in the multicolored uniforms which signified their

various formations came out on their ramparts and sprawled in the sun. The foreigners studied them warily for a while, wondering whether it might be a trick to lure them out of cover. Then some of the bolder spirits wandered over to the Chinese positions and found the enemy troopers in an amiable, hospitable mood. With appalling indiscretion, possibly out of simple vanity, they conducted tours of their own fortifications. The Westerners were surprised by the diligence in Chinese military engineering, the intricacy of the enemy's fortifications. One of the sightseers later recorded:

> Nothing surprised us so much as to see the great access of strength to the Chinese positions since the early days of the siege. Not only were we now securely hedged in by frontal trenches and barricades, but flanking such Chinese positions were great numbers of parallel defenses, designed solely with the object of battering our sortie-parties to pieces should we attempt to take the offensive again.

Once an atmosphere of goodwill, of whatever duration, was established, everyone got down to business. Everyone, that is, but the Moslem troopers from Kansu Province, who were inclined to glower and hang back from any friendly relations with the Westerners. The people of the Legation Quarter were able to buy fresh eggs from the Chinese, and some of the Japanese even managed to buy rifles from the Chinese infantrymen.

Otherwise the scene was something that might have been executed by Goya in one of his darker moods. "Skulls and bones littered the ground," Bertram Simpson noted, "and represented all that remained of the dead enemy after the pariah dogs had finished with them. Broken rifles and thousands of empty brass-cartridges added to the battered look of this fiercely contested area." Conversations with the Chinese soldiers provided Simpson with several surprises and "made us begin to understand the complexity of the situation around us. The Shansi levies and Tung Fu-hsiang's men—that is, the soldiery from the provinces—had but little idea of why they were attacking us; they had been sent, they said, to prevent us from breaking into the Palace and killing their Emperor."

The temporary thaw produced some whimsical effects, as when

a Chinese trumpeter, formerly a member of Sir Robert Hart's Customs Service brass band, sought admittance to the legations' lines. The trumpeter had been struck on the head by his commanding officer's sword for some unexplained lapse, and one of his ears had almost been severed. He was blindfolded and brought to the hospital, where Dr. Poole sewed up his ear.

Occasionally there were misunderstandings. An English marine tried to steal a watermelon from a Chinese soldier and in the process knocked him down. The Chinese began running for their weapons when an unofficial armistice commission managed to pacify them with apologies. The English marine would be punished, and the Chinese would be paid a dollar in compensation. Peace was restored.

One of the bolder and more inquisitive spirits was a young French volunteer, M. Paul Pelliot, who was on leave from his diplomatic post in Tonkin. With the spirit of inquiry which later made him renowned as an Oriental scholar, Pelliot announced that he was going to "make some social calls," clambered over the Chinese barricades, and disappeared. Bets were taken on whether his head would soon be displayed in a cage over one of the ceremonial gates. Two hours later he sent back a note saying he was being entertained at General Jung Lu's headquarters. Pelliot himself, head intact, reappeared that evening with a tale to tell:

The young Frenchman had been really well treated, fed with Chinese cakes and fruit, and given excellent tea to drink. Then he had been led direct to Jung Lu's headquarters, and closely questioned by the generalissimo himself as to our condition, our provisions, and the number of men we had lost. He had replied, he said, that we were having a charming time, and that we only needed some ice and fruit to make us perfectly happy, even in the great summer heat. Thereupon Jung Lu had filled his pockets with peaches and ordered his servants to tie up water-melons in a piece of cloth for him to carry back. Jung Lu finally bade him goodbye, with the significant words that his own personal troops on whom he could rely would attempt to protect the legations, but added that it was very difficult to do so as everyone was fearful of their own heads and dare not show too much concern for the foreigner.

Pelliot's companions not only welcomed his reappearance and his gift of fresh fruit, but the assurances he had been given by the enemy commander in chief. Here was definitive testimony to what many suspected: that some very highly placed personages in the ruling circle were opposed to the dowager empress' policies and were only waiting for a chance to end the conflict.

Most agreed that their situation had improved immeasurably, that the truce proposed by the Chinese was a sign of weakness on the enemy side.

Yet they were also conscious of the Alice-in-Wonderland aspect of the situation, epitomized by the arrival of carts loaded with melons, fruit, ice, and vegetables from the Forbidden City. They had been sent by the dowager empress and were followed by a whole cartload of cabbages. The gifts posed a moral problem for some. The puritanical types said the fruit and vegetables ought to be sent back to the imperial palace; otherwise it would appear that they were condoning her actions. Others suspected that poison had been injected into the fruit. Few, however, did not manage to swallow their objections and suspicions, along with the melons and peaches.

Two days after the truce began a messenger who had been sent to Tientsin by the Japanese on June 30 returned with information for Baron Nishi, the Japanese minister. It was posted on the bulletin board at the Bell Tower as a morale booster:

"A mixed division consisting of 2400 Japanese, 400 Russians, 1200 British, 1500 Americans, 1500 French and 300 Germans leaves Tientsin on or about July 20 for the relief of Peking. The Foreign Settlement has not been taken by the enemy."

The information proved highly misleading, but it was greeted joyously. Certainly Peking would be relieved in a week or ten days. If only the truce could be stretched out. . . .

Occasionally there were alarms, indications that the rickety arrangement not to fight, but not to lay down arms, might break down. Several times there were unexplained bursts of rifle fire at night from the Chinese side, but the attacks were not resumed.

Meanwhile, the diplomatic corps and the Tsungli Yamen returned to the congenial occupation of exchanging notes. It was a baffling correspondence, with much waffling and equivocation from the Chinese, who referred obliquely to the "general ferment, absolutely beyond our control." To the more knowledgeable among the foreigners, it was apparent that many highly placed Chinese wanted to regain favor with the outside world, knowing the Boxers had led the court into a monstrous blunder, but could not seem to be making peaceful gestures until they were certain that more sensible elements were prevailing over the Boxers' partisans around the dowager empress. There was a long dialogue between Sir Claude and "Prince Ching and Colleagues," as the collective at the Tsungli Yamen continued to sign themselves, on a proposed evacuation of the diplomatic personnel and their families. Sir Claude prolonged the bootless intercourse only because he wanted the Chinese to keep negotiating instead of fighting. Occasionally Sir Claude protested violations of the truce, but "Prince Ching and Colleagues" soothingly replied that such outbreaks of nocturnal shooting was "more or less on the same footing as the sounding of the evening drum and the morning bell—an everyday matter—and really hardly worth a smile."

Meanwhile, the semibesieged foreigners were occupied by more immediate matters than the *pourparlers* traveling between Sir Claude's study and the Chinese Foreign Office. The food supply was running dangerously low, and the positions protecting the legations had to be reinforced for the day, which many believed inevitable, when the Chinese resumed the fighting. Bertram Simpson wrote in his diary on July 20:

Fortification of the inner lines is going on harder than ever. The entire British Legation now has walls of immense strength, with miniature blockhouses at regular intervals and a system of trenches. If our advanced posts have to fall back they may be able to hold this legation for a few days in spite of the artillery fire. French digging, in the form of very narrow and very deep cuts to stop the enemy's possible mining, is being planned and carried out everywhere, and soon the general asylum will be even more secure than it has been since the beginning.

Undoubtedly we are just marking time—stamping audibly with our diplomatic feet to reassure ourselves, and to show that we are still alive. For in spite of all this apparent friendliness, which was heralded with such an outburst of shaking hands and smiling faces, there have already been a number of little acts of treachery along the lines showing that the old spirit lurks underneath just as strong.

Except for the withdrawal of immediate danger, the situation of the foreigners was not greatly improved. They were still imprisoned, unable to move beyond the siege lines, always fearful that they might be caught out in the open if hostilities were suddenly resumed. The squalor of their compressed living quarters was certainly unrelieved. A missionary lady wrote:

> I can think of nothing but the immigrants landing at Castle Garden as I look about from time to time. Men, women and children lying in all kinds of places on the floor, nearly all dressed, gave us indeed a title to be called "refugees." Many had no pillows, or sheets, or even a blanket. It was a time when he who had shared with he who had not. If one had two [shirt] waists or handkerchiefs, one went to his neighbor who had none, so in spite of lacking many things which we had thought positively necessary, we yet made ourselves comfortable.
>
> The distribution of the different families and individuals who occupied the chapel at night is something not to be forgotten. On the left hand of the front entrance a Presbyterian Doctor of Divinity had his bed on the floor. Then came the "Methodist bed." At right angles to this a Presbyterian pastor and his wife slept on the floor, the bed being rolled up in the daytime.
>
> Next an American Board [of Missionaries] mother and two children had a bed made by two chapel seats put together. Within the altar rail on one side was another American Board mother with two children. . . . The pulpit was pushed back and served as our china closet. . . . Another family of mother and three children camped at night somewhere near the middle of the chapel floor, and near them, two more chapel seats served as a bed for a Methodist brother. There was a deep bay window on the right hand side of the chapel. Two families of three members each lived on either side of the baptismal font, which was in the window, and the font itself was decorated with books, bottles, and toilet articles of various kinds. There were two or three whose resting (?) place at night could not be accounted for, as their beds were invisible during the day.

Lives were so inextricably woven together that there were seriocomic episodes. It was perfectly possible for a man to kiss another man's wife good-night without lecherous intent. A young mother also stumbled into an embarrassing moment. "In the farther end of the room near the door a baby slept on a little couch in the corner, while his mother slept on the floor. One night the mother got up to attend to the baby, but becoming confused in the darkness she found herself patting the head of a gray-haired man and singing a lullaby to him."

Another room had been added to the hospital to care for the wounded. Some of the legation guard detachments had suffered heavily by this time, the Japanese forty-five killed or wounded, the Germans thirty, the French forty-two. A plague of flies had descended to bedevil the wounded and fever-stricken in the hospital. A missionary nurse recalled:

> When we complained, the surgeon quietly remarked: "They always follow an army." That put a new aspect on affairs. In a military hospital one might not complain of anything that belonged to an army.
>
> The daily adjusting between the civil and military went on with remarkably little friction. The steward, who was an independent factor on his gunboat, learned to work with women of varied degrees of training and of many nationalities. They in turn came to know what he considered his work and what was an indignity. Doctors worked under the authority of nurses. All hearts were controlled by one desire, to give every possible help and comfort to brave men who were giving their lives to defend men, women and children unknown to them.

The Food Supply Committee was increasingly nervous over the dwindling food stocks and making daily calculations. The last of the ponies was being slaughtered, and one owner, whose pony had been a family pet, wrote in his diary, "Went to say goodbye to poor old Memory. He was wretchedly thin. Very sad."

Even sadder was the plight of the 2,700 Chinese Christians, who were becoming feverish-eyed skeletons. There is no record of an official decision having categorized them as expendable but obviously the mathematics of siege were not in their favor. In the eyes of many of their countrymen, they were second-class devils. To their fellow white Christians, they were racial inferiors to be relegated to the subhuman category. A Chinese life simply did not weigh as much as a Caucasian one on the emergency scale of values, no matter what the Gospels said about the equality of all souls before the Judgment Seat.

Few of the diarists and only two of the memoir writers even mentioned the ordeal of the Chinese converts. It was something one did not care to discuss later. The Chinese and their sufferings were carefully ignored by all but some of the fighting men posted near the walls of Prince Su's garden. And by Bertram Simpson, whose subsequent candor on that and other subjects his fellows found so obnoxious. He wrote on July 24:

> Down near the Water Gate, which runs under the Tartar Wall, the miserable natives imprisoned by our warfare are in a terrible state of starvation. Their bones are cracking through their skin; their eyes have an insane look; yet nothing is being done for them. They are afraid to attempt escape even in this quiet, as the Water Gate is watched on the outside night and day by Chinese sharpshooters. It is the last gap leading to the outer world which is still open. Tortured by the sight of these starving wretches, who moan and mutter night and day, the posts nearby shoot down dogs and crows and drag them there. They say everything is devoured raw with cannibal-like cries. . . .

The equally frank and clear-eyed Polly Condit Smith, likening the scenes in and around Prince Su's palace to Doré's engravings for Dante's *Inferno*, provided an equally graphic account.* By the last week of July, she wrote, not only the leaves had been stripped off the trees in Prince Su's compound but the bark had also been removed and eaten. She continued:

> Diseased or not, these wretched people have been forced to remain here all together, as there is no other place for them. Carrion crows and dogs are killed and dragged to the Fu by sentries whenever possible, and these ravenous creatures pull the flesh from their bones and eat it without a pretence of cooking. Every morning when the two horses are shot at the slaughter-house, for distribution to the [British legation] messes, half of the inedible parts are eaten with relish by these starving people.

---

* Though Miss Smith's account parallels Mr. Simpson's, it is quoted here because later Simpson was heavily criticized for overemphasizing the negative aspects of human behavior under the duress of the Peking siege.

The heat is intense, the ground in the Fu is brown and hard, the children are naked, and the adults wear little, but one and all are enveloped with the agony of relentless, hideous starvation. The white rice which we have used in the compound has been finished, and we now use the yellow or uncleaned rice, which is very sandy and gritty, and which even the coolies in ordinary times would never think of using. It is made into curries or eaten plain, but one has to swallow it in spoonfuls without closing one's teeth on it, or it would be too much like chewing sand.

Unmilled rice may have been hard to get down, but there was enough to feed the white refugees and keep them relatively healthy. Yet there was never even a consideration of whether it should have been shared with the Chinese. Even more depressing is the fact that the Chinese expected no better treatment from their preceptors; perhaps therein lies a clue to the ultimate failure of the Christian effort in China.

On July 28 another messenger slipped through the siege lines with further word from Tientsin. Two weeks earlier a fifteen-year-old Chinese boy who had attended Sunday school at an American mission had been lowered from the Tatar Wall with little hope that he would make it to the coast. The boy, disguised as a beggar and carrying the mendicant's rice bowl, succeeded in reaching allied headquarters near Tientsin, then returned fourteen days later with a message from British Consul Ronald Carles sewed in the collar of his coat. It was one of those hallucinatory side effects of the siege that rarely has such a long and desperately awaited message been greeted with such heartfelt cursing. The message read:

Your letter of 4 July. There are now 24,000 troops landed and 19,000 troops here. General [Alfred] Gaselee is expected at Taku. When he comes I hope to see more activity. The Russians are at Peitsang. Tientsin city is under foreign government and the Boxers' power here is exploded. Do try and keep me informed of yourselves. There are plenty of troops on the way if you can keep yourselves in good for a time, all ought to come out well. The Consulate is mended to be ready for you when you come. Almost all the ladies have left Tientsin. Kindest remembrances to all in the Legation.

A backward schoolboy, it must have seemed to Sir Claude, who excised several phrases before posting the message on the bulletin board, could have composed a more informative and cogent dispatch. What did Carles mean by "24,000 troops landed and 19,000 troops here"? The siege of Peking had begun more than five weeks ago, and still the international force at Tientsin was waiting for the arrival of a general before "more activity" could be expected. The chatty banality of the message for which a fifteen-year-old Chinese boy had risked his life made it all the more grating.

The reaction to Mr. Carles' cheery note was a unanimous denunciation. "Never has a man been so abused," wrote Bertram Simpson, "as was that luckless English Consul who penned such a fatuous message. . . . We would have more weeks of it [the siege]. Perhaps even a whole month. The people wept and stormed, and soon lost all enthusiasm for the poor messenger-boy who had been so brave."

Morrison of the *Times* was amused by the "petulance with which the British were forced to admit that this somewhat incoherent production was really written by a Consul still in the British service. From this document it was impossible to know whether the troops were on their way to Peking from Tientsin, or to Tientsin from Europe, who were the troops, and how many, or whether the number landed was 24,000 in all or 43,000, while the observation that the troops were coming if our provisions held out seemed to imply that if our provisions failed the troops would return to Tientsin."

Shortly after receiving the dispatch from Tientsin, the defenders noted signs of activity behind the Chinese lines. Much blaring of the long-throated Chinese trumpets. Much marching and counter-marching of large enemy units with banners flying. A resumption of the tapping noises underground which indicated Chinese sappers were mining under the legation defenses.

The soldiers read the omens as a sure sign that the Chinese would shortly resume the fighting, while the diplomats—except for the eternally pessimistic M. Pichon—pointed out that they were still "in communication" with their counterparts at the Tsungli

Yamen. A large amount of quibbling rice-paper documents was piling up on Sir Claude's desk.

The soldiers rightly prepared for the worst while hoping for the best. They put in their time burrowing underground in an attempt to tap one of the Chinese tunnels, though the odds of bursting in on a team of Chinese sappers were heavily adverse. Digging through the subsurface clay was a miserable job those sweltering late-July days, but occasionally there were rewards. At one place ten feet below the surface they broke through to an abandoned underground storeroom with hundreds of ancient stone cannon-balls. Some of the experts from the Imperial University faculty believed they were relics of Kublai Khan, who had built the Tatar City part of Peking in the thirteenth century. In other places they came across the splendidly tiled drains, four feet high and three feet wide, which had once caused Marco Polo to marvel at the cleanliness of the city.

Aboveground the watchful foreigners observed the Chinese building new barricades and digging trench systems, though they had agreed to stop such construction while the truce was in effect. Immediately after the truce began, the British had started organizing cricket matches, and sailors had rafted up and down the canal in wistful remembrance of their naval calling; but now everyone was turning to strengthening the legations' fortifications. There was no pattern to the enemy troop movements, much of the parading seemed aimless, but there was a growing feeling that a "storm was about to break on us."

Meanwhile, the battered community occupied itself with the consideration and embellishment of rumors that, as Bertram Simpson listed them, "all Manchuria is in flames; that the Yangtze Valley has been trembling on the brink of rebellion; that Tientsin city has at last been captured by European troops and a provisional government firmly established; and that many of the high Chinese officials have committed suicide in many parts of China. . . ." The rumors, he believed, were a symptom of a sort of siege sickness, of psychological traumas inflicted by the tension of the past two months. He noted that "many people behaved almost as if their minds had become unhinged" and that in the hospital "the wounded became more sick."

They might quarrel over which rumors to believe, but most agreed that the dragon was beginning to breathe fire again.

And indeed it was. A high-tempered and hyperactive general newly arrived from the provinces was infusing the Manchu court with a fresh determination to destroy the foreigners, to quell the increasingly influential voice of the moderates, to rectify the mistake of having called a truce and reprieving (to recall the dowager empress' baleful metaphor) the "fish in the stewpan."

The diary of Ching Shan, who still lived in the Forbidden City though he had retired as comptroller of the imperial household several years before, indicated that morale had slipped badly at the court when the attacks on the Legation Quarter failed to attain their objective. He had been the tutor and was still the confidant of Duke Lan, who told him "an extraordinary story of how the Heir Apparent called the Emperor a 'Devil's pupil' this morning, and when rebuked for it, actually boxed His Majesty's ears." The dowager empress, who reserved to herself the right to punish the emperor, flew into a rage when she heard about the incident and "gave orders to the eunuch Tsui to administer twenty sharp strokes of the whip on the Heir Apparent's person. Prince Tuan is much enraged at this, but he is horribly afraid of Her Majesty and when she speaks to him 'he is on tenter-hooks, as if thorns pricked him, and the sweat runs down his face.'"

There were quarrels not only within the imperial family but among the dowager empress' closest advisers over how to proceed. A growing and newly emboldened faction of moderates was urging that the truce be extended. Meanwhile, Prince Tuan and Duke Lan, as leaders of the pro-Boxer clique, were recommending that mines be dug from the Hanlin on the north side of the Legation Quarter and a huge charge of explosives be set off under the British compound.

Then came the inspiriting presence of General Li Ping-heng, who harangued the dowager empress on the necessity of wiping out the legations and killing the "traitors"—or moderates—in her advisory circle. A man of violent disposition, a traditionalist who hated all aspects of modernization, General Li had been governor of Shantung when the two German missionaries were killed; it did not improve his opinion of foreigners when German pressure resulted in his removal from that post. Recently, as imperial inspector of the Yangtze Naval Forces, he had alarmed the peace-loving southern viceroys by proposing the bombardment of all foreign vessels approaching Shanghai.

"The Old Buddha," Ching Shan confided to his diary, "places much confidence in Li Ping-heng." She had always been greatly impressed by men with positive opinions. So many of her generals were pallid characters inclined to raise pedantic difficulties and complain about the superiority of European arms.

Li Ping-heng had arrived on July 26 after the truce had been in effect for ten days. The dowager empress was so enchanted by his flamboyant personality, so taken by his conviction that the foreigners could be wiped out, that she issued an imperial edict granting him the privileges of riding a horse within the Forbidden City and being carried in a sedan chair inside the Winter Palace, both prerogatives rarely granted in the inner sanctum of imperial power where the functionaries spent most of their time falling on their knees in abasement before some Manchu princeling. She also gave him command of a group of four armies which was to interpose itself between Peking and any relief force advancing from Tientsin.

Once again the Boxer cause was in the ascendant in the Forbidden City. It was a bad time for Hsü Ching-cheng, the president of the Imperial University and former minister to St. Petersburg, and Yung Chang, a minister in the Tsungli Yamen, to present a memorial to the throne urging that all partisans of the Boxers, no matter how high their rank, should be silenced. According to a notice circulated by the latter's family several months later:

> In this document they declared that the situation was becoming desperate, that even the Princes of the Blood and the Ministers of the Grand Council had come to applaud these Boxers, and to assist in deceiving Their Majesties. There was only one way left to avoid dire peril and hold back the foreign armies, and to do this it was necessary to begin by beheading their leaders among the Princes and Ministers. Having sent this Memorial, our father said to our mother, "Things have come to such a pass that, whether I speak out or keep my silence, my death is certain. Rather than be murdered by these treacherous Ministers, I prefer to die at the hands of the public executioner."

That fate was meted out to Hsü Ching-cheng and Yuan Chang, along with the president of the Board of War and two other moderates, only two days after the fire-eating Li Ping-heng arrived. The charge against Yuan Chang, "a crime of gross disrespect," was that he had suggested that a coffin be provided for Baron von Ketteler's corpse. The dowager empress was so enraged by the moderates that, according to the diary of Ching Shan, she screamed that "their limbs should be torn asunder by chariots driven in opposite directions."

Gentler counsel prevailed, and decapitation was prescribed. The next morning, Ching Shan wrote, the moderates went to the chopping block, brave and defiant to the end:

> Just before the sword of the executioner fell, Yuan remarked that "he hoped that the Sun might soon return to its place in the Heaven, and that the usurping comet might be destroyed." By this he meant that Prince Tuan's malign influence had led the Empress Dowager to act against her better instincts. Duke Lan, who had been superintending the execution, angrily bade him be silent, but Yuan fearlessly went on, "I die innocent. In years to come my name will be remembered with gratitude and respect, long after you evil-plotting Princes have met your well-deserved doom." Turning to Hsu, he said, "We shall meet anon at the Yellow Springs [that is, in the spirit world]." Duke Lan stepped forward as if to strike him, and the headsman quickly despatched him.

General Li Ping-heng continued to deliver fire-eating sermons against the foreign devils and their sympathizers, accounted for the renewed activity noted by the defenders of the legations, and promised that their ordeal would shortly be renewed.

12. *The International Relief Force*

Certainly one of the most laggard and cumbersome operations
to lift a siege in modern military history was the International
Relief Force which was assembled at Tientsin and finally went
slogging toward Peking.

There were a number of factors tending to slow down the effort.
Army and navy commanders, particularly those of different
nations, found cooperation difficult and distasteful. Many of the
troopships had to travel most of the way around the world.
Deciding on a supreme commander took long vexatious hours of
deliberation. There were international rivalries, particularly those
between the Russians and Japanese, to be taken into account.

In addition, there were more serious and practical matters
inhibiting a swift completion of the operations. For one thing,
there was the dismal situation of the first expeditionary force
launched in the direction of, but not anywhere near, Peking. Sir
Edward Seymour's relief force itself had to be relieved; it was
holed up at the Shiku Arsenal fifteen miles north of Tientsin. A
rescue column had to be sent out to bring Admiral Seymour and
his force, including 300 sick and wounded borne on litters, back to
Tientsin.

Besides all that, there was the threat to other foreign enclaves in
China. If everything were thrown immediately into the Peking
operation, what would happen if the Boxers erupted elsewhere?
Though the peace-minded viceroys kept things largely under

control throughout the rest of China, there were occasional uprisings to contend with.

At Newchwang, for instance, 150 Boxers attacked the foreign settlement, opposed only by a squad of Russian cavalry, some volunteers, and two Russian gunboats, soon reinforced by twenty Russian marines.

The Boxers, led by a beribboned bravo whose "facial expressions reflected those of a hardened sinner," according to a Shanghai newspaper account, were contained in the native city. According to the newspaper dispatch:

> In the meantime, the Russian gunboat *Gremiastchy* had moved to a position opposite the native city and another gunboat took up a position near the fort. The *Gremiastchy* opened fire with shrapnel, directing her shots well beyond the heart of the city, and the enemy was seen streaming out of the city in an opposite direction. The slaughter of the Boxers became general. . . . The Boxer element is completely wiped out and there is at present no fear of attack from local rowdies or soldiery, and the whole place is policed by Russian forces. The only fear of attack to be anticipated is from the north where the Imperial troops and hordes of brigands have joined hands. It means a deal of hard fighting to subdue the entire district. Where a few days ago Boxer flags were seen there are now innumerable miniature Russian flags and foreign signboards over Chinese shops, taken down before, are being restored. . . . The railway between this and Port Arthur remains still interrupted.

Meanwhile, the buildup at Tientsin had proceeded at a deliberate pace, with no visible signs that the project was being hurried along by visions of several thousand compatriots undergoing the perils of a siege at Peking. Brass hats are not overendowed with imagination; it is one of their most valuable qualities to be unaffected by emotional considerations. They held endless councils of war, pored over their maps, counted their mountains of supplies, studied a blizzard of intelligence reports, and remained impassive, if not completely immobile.

Originally the advance on Peking had been scheduled for August 1. Instead of moving out, the commanders of the various contingents met on that date for another council of war, having decided they didn't have enough troops on hand. The Russian commander, General Linivitch, was insistent on that point. As usual, the Japanese were more aggressive and businesslike. Lieutenant General Yamaguchi announced that he would march on August 4 whether or not his allies joined him. The attitude of General Chaffee, the U.S. commander who had arrived in Tientsin only two days earlier, was not made known.

By then a colorful array of regiments, the cream of the colonial armies, had been transported to Tientsin. The Americans had on hand the First Marines and Ninth Infantry, plus two battalions of the Fourteenth Infantry newly arrived from the Philippines, the Sixth Cavalry from the mainland, Battery F of the Fifth Artillery, also on consignment from Manila, not all of which would join in the excursion to the Chinese capital.

In all there were about 25,000 troops available, about 20,000 of whom would be detailed to the International Relief Force. Originally it was believed that from 40,000 to 60,000, plus line-of-communications forces, would be needed for the operation, but waiting for that many to arrive would mean Peking might not be relieved for another year at the present rate of increment. Mostly they had to depend on forces closer at hand than the 30,000 troops Kaiser Wilhelm so eagerly offered—the U.S. forces fighting the *insurrectos* in the Philippines, the French colonial troops eternally occupied with putting down uprisings in Indochina, Russia's Far Eastern garrisons, and the relatively nearby troop and supply bases of the Japanese home islands.

The logistics of that effort often took a rather exotic turn, particularly among the British, whose officers shuddered at the thought of campaigning without an adequate supply of fly whisks, solar helmets, canned goods from Fortnum's, shooting sticks, and the latest cricket results from Lord's pavilion. One historian of the campaign cites a number of the items laboriously collected by the British, not all of them as nonsensical as they sound, because there was a probability of campaigning in the bitter cold of a North China winter as well as its searing summer months.

A War Office intelligence report of a year later showed that Her Majesty's supply officers collected oxen and tongas to be used as field ambulances, lamb's-wool drawers, puttoo gloves and posh-teens, all drawn from Indian Army stocks. Goat's-hair socks for cold-weather campaigning were imported from Norway. Firewood being hard to obtain in North China, 2,000 tons were forwarded from Australia. Nor was aviation neglected, though the first military airplane had not yet taken wing. A horse-drawn balloon section was sent from Southampton on July 28; it would arrive weeks after the campaign was over to be asked, "What the hell are you doing here?" The French commander, General H. Frey, also felt uneasy without his own aerial service and cabled Paris for an observation balloon and a *section d'aerostatiers.* None of these requests were regarded as frivolous by their colleagues. A successful general accumulated as many supplies, and as many types of equipment, as he could wheedle from his general staff.

The British were usually accorded the senior partnership in such ventures, so no one was greatly put out when General Alfred Gaselee was placed in charge of the expedition. He was a mild and easygoing man, with the offhand manner patented by Sandhurst, but at least he had enough energy to insist on an "early forward movement." Colonel A. S. Daggett, commanding the Fourteenth U.S. Infantry, sided with him during the endless palavering in Tientsin, despite the reluctance of his superior, General Chaffee, to move without receiving more artillery.

Only General Gaselee's insistence that the first priority was succoring the besieged in Peking, not gathering more exotic specimens of armament, succeeded in getting the combined force under way. The Japanese of course were eager for action, and they had the largest troop strength among the allies. The others knew they couldn't let the British and Japanese march forth without them. Furthermore, intelligence reports agreed that the Boxers had lost their steam and that morale among the Chinese regular forces, as well as the home defense units, was disintegrating.

The makeup of the expeditionary force was approximately as follows: Japanese, almost 10,000; Russians, almost 5,000; British, 3,000; Americans, 2,000; French, 800; Germans (with what they exuberantly styled the East Asiatic Corps still on the high seas), Austrians, and Italians, a combined total of several hundred. The Sixth U.S. Cavalry had arrived off Taku, but the voyage had made their mounts temporarily unfit for service, so only one troop (the equivalent of an infantry company) joined the column.

It was the last flaunting of old-style imperialism, which had been so severely tested and found wanting by the Boer War and the Philippine insurrection. It was also the last flourish of the old premechanized style of compaigning; just over the horizon were the tanks, aircraft, chemical warfare, zeppelin bombardments, monster cannon, mess-levied armies of World War I. There was still something elite, prideful, and picturesque about professional soldiering.

On the high road to Peking, colonial warfare made its last appearance in full panoply, with so many of the fabled regiments dating back to the Napoleonic Wars, to India's conquest and the Sudan, to North Africa and the American frontier soon to be destroyed in the European trenches, on Gallipoli, and in the Mesopotamian desert.

They represented a Victorian world which could still afford certain illusions, largely based on theories of racial superiority. Just before the International Relief Force set out under a rainbow of guidons, the New York *Times* ran a headline announcing with evident surprise that CHINESE CAN SHOOT STRAIGHT.

As an elderly retired Marine general Smedley D. Butler would remember the spectacle presented by the multiflagged army that marched out of Tientsin on the morning of August 4, 1900— "French Zouaves in red and blue, blond Germans in pointed helmets, Italian Bersaglieri with tossing plumes, Bengal cavalry on Arabian stallions, turbanned Sikhs, Japanese, Russians, English." Young Captain Butler and his Marine company trudged along the dusty road in company with the Royal Welsh Fusiliers, whose standards were decorated with ribbons honoring their charge up Bunker Hill. Now the Americans would become so friendly with the Welshmen that they presented the Fusiliers with a silver cup before leaving China.

The route they followed was that taken by the Anglo-French expedition to Peking in 1860, along the Pei Ho River, which served as their artery of supply. A fleet of junks and sampans containing food and ammunition was towed or poled up the Pei Ho in a supply train six miles long.

"Infernal" was Butler's one-word description of conditions on the march. The daytime temperature was about 104°F with not a breath of air stirring, not a cloud in the sky. North China is uncomfortably close to the deserts of Mongolia.

The troops marched through villages with "dead Chinese piled in the courtyards," testimony of parochial bloodlettings never to be recorded or explained, symptoms of a self-destructive fury among the Chinese masses.

"Most of the time," as Butler remembered the ninety-mile march, "we pushed through fields of grain ten feet high. It was like walking through a blast furnace. For days we struggled through those jungles of grain. We even bivouacked in them at night, eaten alive by mosquitoes."

The amiable General Gaselee pushed the advance at a punishing pace, fighting whenever the Chinese offered resistance, then resuming the march immediately, leaving whatever mopping up was necessary to the rear echelon. His tactics were sensibly simple, as was ordained by a multilingual force with differing national interests and commanders of diverging ambitions. Whenever the expedition suspected it would run into opposition, the inadequate cavalry (one Japanese regiment whose chargers were not up to vigorous campaigning, a few Cossacks, and the peerless Bengal Lancers) fanned out on a reconnaissance. Then the leading elements of the column redeployed in skirmish order, the horse artillery came up and bombarded the enemy positions, and the infantry swept forward. The Chinese generally abandoned their positions without much of a fight. Such tactics were serviceable enough, given the lack of cavalry for thorough reconnaissance, flanking movements, and pursuit, but they would never be studied at West Point or St. Cyr.

The first battle en route occurred the second day on the march, August 5, at the railroad town of Peitsang a few miles north of the Shiku Arsenal. Most of the fighting was done by the Japanese and Russians, both clad in the white tunics of their summer issue, and both charging over the blazing plain in close, bayonet-hedged formations which inflicted unnecessary casualties on them. The Japanese and Russians seemed to be in a sort of contest, trying to outdo each other in a rivalry which would be more severely tested in the Russo-Japanese War over Far Eastern spoils several years later. They were supported by two of the British Navy's twelve-pounders, and it was an easy victory. With the sort of low-grade resistance offered by the Chinese, many of those accompanying the column wondered why it had taken the allied command so long to organize the enterprise.

The next day, ten miles up the road to Peking, the Chinese

again offered battle at Yangtsun, which was where the railroad crossed the Pei Ho and was protected by an elaborate system of trenches and earthworks. It was also garrisoned by a sizable force.

This time the British and the Americans were ordered to lead the assault, with the Russians and French supporting their attack and the Japanese held in reserve. When they went in, shortly after midday, the heat was so oppressive many collapsed from sunstroke or exhaustion. The water supply was inadequate; the designated troops, burdened with the heavy rifles, packs, and accouterments judged necessary for taking the field in 1900, stumbled forward against an intricate maze of Chinese fortifications and more often than not foundered from heat stroke rather than Chinese bullets. Somehow they managed to take one Chinese defense line after another. Because of language difficulties between the assault force and its supporting elements, the attack was poorly coordinated. It was an action undertaken at the company and platoon level rather than the regimental, or as the disapproving French General Frey put it, they fought "rather as bands of partisans than as regular troops taking part in a planned operation."

One tragic instance of the difficulties of a combined operation was the accidental shelling of a company of the Fourteenth Infantry. Four American soldiers were killed by the shrapnel from their allies' guns, and eleven were wounded, some of them fatally. The misdirected fire came from an artillery position manned by the Royal Artillery and a Russian battery. At a later inquiry the British claimed that the Russians asked for the range. They were given the distance in yards instead of meters, and since the Russians used the metric system, their salvo fell short and landed on the advancing Americans.

Despite such mishaps, the international column had stormed into the center of Yangtsun by nightfall.

There was a pause for consultation among the generals. When they had set out from Tientsin, they had agreed that the expedition would pause after taking Yangtsun to rest the troops and bring up reinforcements (including the balance of the Sixth U.S. Cavalry). They had expected much stronger resistance and a longer casualty list. The weakness displayed by the enemy both at Peitsang and Yangtsun, indicating a collapse of Chinese morale, encouraged the generals to consider pressing the advance. Each commander now saw the chance for a quick grab at glory and promotion. Others remembered how certain participants had enriched themselves in 1860, when the Anglo-French expedition sacked Peking. The junk-and-sampan supply train was far to the rear, however. So the leaders of the force agreed that the next day, August 7, should be spent resting the troops, the horses and mules and allowing their supply train to catch up.

Another generals' conference was held outside the tent of Russian General Linivitch the morning of August 7, at which General Frey had to confess that his French contingent would not be able to maintain the pace of the advance. It was a grievous blow to General Frey and, as he believed, to the prestige of the French nation. He had come to China hoping the tricolor at least would stay in the vanguard beside the Union Jack and the Stars and Stripes; like most French generals he was obsessed by words like "grandeur" and "glory," as his massive memoir of the campaign indicated. Not only had he been given inadequate resources to promote the grandness of France, but his contingent was universally despised by the other nations present. A British naval officer and future hero of a much wider conflict, Roger Keyes, told his biographer that it consisted of "the scum of the French army and was quite disgraceful." The French unit consisted of two battalions of Infanterie de la Marine, plus three mountain and field batteries, mostly undersized Tonkinese with French officers. Their uniforms were as ragged as the clothing of Chinese peasants. Their supplies were hauled along, not by mule pack but wheelbarrows and even rickshaws.

General Frey, who noted in his memoirs with a trace of envy that Japanese officers were able to "sacrifice hecatombs of men in order to gain for Japan the leading role in the action," had to inform his fellow generals on the morning of August 7 that his contingent simply could not stand the pace. His chief assistant, Colonel de Pelacot, had just sent a message stating that "the men are exhausted and, according to the doctors, incapable of doing a full day's march tomorrow." His troops would have to stay behind, garrisoning Yangtsun, waiting for fresh troops from Tientsin and hoping that "a sense of military confraternity forming an almost international Order of Chivalry"—as he grandly described colleagues more intent on grabbing for glory and loot than recapturing the knightly atmosphere of the War of the Roses—would allow them to share the honors of taking Peking with him. General Frey did manage to scrape up a ragtag force and chase his rivals up the road to the capital, but the French were losers in an unofficial contest of military prestige, just as the Japanese were clearly the winners.

The next objective was the walled commercial city of Tungchow, only fourteen miles from Peking and slightly farther up the Pei Ho than the distance from Tientsin to Yangtsun. More hard marching over a dusty road and through fields of millet ten feet high. The now rather cocky Japanese formed the vanguard, followed by the Russians, the Americans and smaller detachments, with the British constituting the rearguard. The British contingent looked like a durbar, with colonial regiments bearing the guidons of the Royal Welsh Fusiliers, the First Sikhs, the Twenty-fourth Punjab Infantry, the Seventh Rajputs, the Weihai-wei (Chinese) regiment, the Hongkong Artillery, the Twelfth Royal Field Artillery, and a detachment of Royal Engineers. The fabled Bengal Lancers were usually off serving as a cavalry screen for the advance guard.

There was some difficulty with the Russians, who wanted to leapfrog over the Japanese and lead the way toward Peking. More than once the expedition threatened to degenerate into a footrace between the Russians and the Japanese for the honor of planting the first flag on the city's walls.

The Americans refrained from joining in the scramble, if only because they were too exhausted to care who got to Peking first. Most of them had campaigned in the Philippine jungles, yet on the North China plain they succumbed to the heat and other hardships, especially the lack of water. March discipline suffered accordingly, though there were no deserters, only temporary dropouts. The officer commanding the Seventh Rajputs reported that they had to leapfrog an American outfit "marching slowly along at about two miles an hour, with heads bent and eyes closed. . . . I do not think they even noticed us as we passed them." Smedley Butler agreed that "nearly fifty percent of our men fell behind during the day," but "in the cool of evening they would catch up with us and start on again next morning."

On August 12, several hours before dawn, looking back over

their shoulders to make sure the Russians weren't trying to steal a march on them, the Japanese vanguard pulled up before the south walls of Tungchow.

They blew up the South Gate, then marched into the city—once one of the richest in North China—and found that the Chinese garrison had fled. Before the enemy forces quit the city, however, the Boxers had run amok, looted, killed those they suspected of having been lukewarm or antipathetic to the Boxer cause. The Japanese and their allies, in training for the greater loot ahead, ransacked the stores and houses for whatever the Boxers had not chosen to carry off.

Young Smedley Butler, holding his marines back from the fun and games, later noted that Tungchow "must have been a rich town before it was struck by war. Now corpses, with skulls smashed in, lay sprawled across the streets. Brocades and fragments of porcelain spilled out of the broken fronts of shops. The gilded archways were shattered. Carved teakwood furniture was being split up by the Allied soldiers for firewood. . . ."

The relief expedition paused that day to rest and refit while the generals conferred on whether to make an immediate lunge at Peking. A captured dispatch indicated that Chinese resistance was swiftly collapsing. General Li Ping-heng, who had revitalized the Manchu court only a few weeks before and since had taken charge of the forces defending the capital, wrote his superiors in the Forbidden City that the jig was up. No longer breathing fire but exuding despair, he wrote:

I have retreated from Matou to Changchiawan [between Yangtsun and Tungchow, where his forces had fled without a fight]. For the past few days I have seen several tens of thousands of troops jamming all roads. They fled as soon as they heard of the arrival of the enemy. As they passed through the villages and towns they set fire and plundered. . . . From youth to old age I have experienced many wars, but I never saw things like these. . . . The situation is getting out of control. There is no time to regroup and deploy. . . .

The next day General Li Ping-heng ended his life by taking poison.

At the generals' conference the evening of August 12 it was

decided to send the cavalry out on reconnaissance the next day to determine how much resistance could be expected between Tungchow and the walls of Peking. During the thirteenth, also, the allied forces would move up to jump-off positions from which the attack on Peking could be launched. They would draw up parallel to each other, like sprinters, and then make a dash for the prize. Little mention was made of the besieged legations or the possibility they might be within hours of being overwhelmed and the defenders massacred. Purely military considerations and behind them the determination that no single contingent would be allowed to make a sneak play for the honor of first entering the city were uppermost on the agenda.

General Gaselee, it should be noted, tried his best to prevent the final stage of the operation from turning into a grab bag instead of what it was designed to be, a rescue mission. His innate decency still casts a mellow glow on the half page of history he occupies. Shortly after Tungchow was captured, a former missionary serving on his staff as an intelligence officer proposed that the marketplace be set afire so its flames could be seen by the people in the Legation Quarter a dozen or so miles away.

"Well, you know," General Gaselee replied in his mild ruminative voice, "we do not wish to antagonize the 350 million people of China."

It was hardly his fault that the International Relief Force soon became involved in two kinds of relief work, first relieving the legations, then relieving Peking of its treasures.

All thoughts of relief have been pushed into the middle distance—and beyond—by the urgent business we have now on hand.

—B. L. PUTNAM WEALE, *Indiscreet Letters from Peking*

13. *The Ordeal Comes to an End*

Janus-faced seemed to be one way of describing the oddity of the imperial government's behavior toward the legations it was trying to obliterate.

One face was diplomatic and conciliatory; the other wore the murderous scowl of the fanatic.

The truce ended, as unofficially as it began, and by August 4 the firing from both sides was heavy. That eventuality did not take the legations by surprise. Despite protestations from the Tsungli Yamen, they expected that the fighting would be renewed and had taken advantage of the truce by bolstering their defenses and shoring up the weak points. In the southwest corner of the quadrant, an assault group led by an ex-officer of the German army named Heinrich Otto Von Strauch had captured and fortified some of the houses in the Mongol Market, thereby strengthening a weak hinge in the defenses.

A Chinese infantry division was reported to have arrived from Shansi; this did not seem reassuring to the defenders who were constantly being informed by the Chinese Foreign Office that their safety was the imperial government's primary concern. With one hand, that apparatus seemed to be offering the olive branch while the other still brandished the sword, and it was vexing to be simultaneously shot at and receive the shooter's congratulations on having not been hit. Even as the fighting was resumed, a stream of messages was still forwarded from the Tsungli Yamen. In its mysterious way the Chinese Foreign Office sent along coded dispatches which could only raise the morale of the defenders, including one from General Gaselee on August 10 ("Strong forces of allies advancing. Twice defeated enemy. Keep up your spirits"). The Chinese diplomats also passed along word that the respected Li Hung-chang had arrived in Shanghai and would soon negotiate by telegraph with the foreign envoys in Peking. What telegraph? The lines had been cut weeks before. With a vexation undoubtedly shared by her companions, Polly Condit Smith acidly remarked on that last advisory from the Tsungli Yamen: "Not a word was mentioned about our leaving for Tientsin, nor an apology for the continued sniping at night, and the occasional attacks which make us realize the lie that we are being 'tenderly cared for and watched over by the Empress.' "

The two faces of the official Chinese also puzzled Bertram Simpson, though as a volunteer rifleman he usually saw only the menacing one. The Tsungli Yamen, he wrote in his diary August 4, enclosed with each cipher telegram it forwarded "a formal despatch in Chinese, generally begging the Ministers to commit themselves to the care of the Government. They now even propose that everyone should be escorted to Tientsin—at once. And yet we have learnt from copies of the *Peking Gazette* that two members of the Yamen were executed exactly seven days ago for recommending a mild policy and making an immediate end of the Boxer regime. . . . Our fate must ultimately be decided by a number of factors, concerning which we know nothing."

The strangeness of their equivocal situation, still menaced by an enemy who alternated shouts of "Kill, Kill, Kill!" with murmured assurances that the dowager empress hoped they were all in the best of health, made everyone feel that the earth had tilted slightly on its axis. Everything was out of focus, blurred by uncertainty, and certain moral distinctions tended likewise to become hazy. Increasing hunger also weakened the basic supports of human conduct. One evening Polly Condit Smith was strolling in the compound with Dutch Minister Willem Knobel. They heard a hen clucking in some nearby shrubbery. They knew it belonged to a Russian family, but that didn't inhibit a Dutch diplomat and a wellborn American girl from instantly becoming chicken thieves. Knobel pounced on the chicken, thrust it under his coat, and with Miss Smith fled into the dusk for a secret and illicit cookout.

Their own privations, though relatively minor, allowed them all to ignore the increasingly tragic situation of the Chinese converts. No count was kept of those who died among the Chinese, but Cecile Payen, one of Mrs. Conger's Stateside guests, one night found herself listening approvingly to a missionary's explanation that the Chinese "really liked to eat" the mangy cats and starved dogs which supplemented their diet of bark and leaves.

Not the least incongruous aspect was the nightly concert being presented on the steps of the Jubilee Tower. A missionary choir, earnest Christian voices raised above the occasional shots from the defense lines, provided a rousing rendition of "Tramp, Tramp, Tramp, the Boys Are Marching," which the audience could only hope was true of the relief force from Tientsin. The powerful voice of Mme. Pokotilov, the wife of the head of the Russo-Chinese Bank, who claimed that she had once been a diva with the St. Petersburg Opera, pierced the night with her offering of the "Jewel Song" from *Faust*. One night the Chinese in apparent protest loosed a volley in her direction. It was snidely suggested by some of Mme. Pokotilov's critics that the Chinese would rather charge the American machine gun barehanded than listen to another rendition of the "Jewel Song."

The Japanese, meanwhile, were waging war in their usual pragmatic fashion. They went their own way, seldom joined the pontification at councils of war, and rarely consulted with their allies. A study of their methods might have been instructive for those Westerners who suspected that the Western Hemisphere would one day face industrialized Japan as an enemy. The Japanese were guided only by practicality. They would just as soon buy an enemy as kill him. Early in the siege Colonel Shiba and his men had acquired a large stock of Shanghai dollars by burrowing into the cellars of abandoned Chinese houses. During the truce, in the course of bargaining sessions, they latched onto a Chinese soldier who agreed to sell them military information. On learning his information was false, they told their spy that they would pardon him if he would agree to procure ammunition for them. Thereafter their man made nightly runs, through a tunnel between the lines, to a cellar in the Japanese sector. One Westerner who witnessed the nightly transactions recalled the Chinese "crawled in like a dog; got up painfully, as if he were very stiff, and silently began unloading. Then I understood why he was so stiff; he was loaded from top to bottom with cartridges. It took a quarter of an hour for everything to be taken out and stacked on the floor. He had carried in close to six hundred rounds of Mauser ammunition, and for every hundred he received the same weight in silver. This man was a military cook, who crept round and robbed his comrades as they lay asleep, not a hundred yards from here."

The stolid Japanese suffered from none of the psychological trauma, or combat fatigue, which afflicted some of the European defenders. One Russian soldier went out his mind and made a solitary assault on the Chinese barricades. The Chinese respected insanity but not when it came charging at them with a bayoneted rifle. They cut down the Russian, then hauled his body over the barricade with long poles, supposedly because Chinese commanders offered a sizable reward for European heads. A more troublesome case was that of a British marine. Early in the siege he had driven his bayonet into the chest of an attacking Chinese, then fired every shot in the magazine of his rifle into the dying man. Soon thereafter he began behaving oddly and had to be confined, strapped to a bed in the hospital. Every night he kept shrieking, "How it splashes! How it splashes!"

On August 8 there were increasingly alarming signs of a buildup behind the Chinese lines. The fresh division of Shansi infantry was taking its place in the enemy positions, Bertram Simpson noting in his diary that "the enemy has planted new banners on all sides, bearing the names of new Chinese generals unknown to us." The new flags were planted only twenty to thirty feet from the legations' barricades and seemed to mock the continued assurances from the Tsungli Yamen. It seemed ominous too that the Chinese had moved so close to the defense positions that they could heave rocks at the outposts and seemed to be preparing for an assault that would swarm over the barricades in overwhelming numbers.

The Chinese reinforcements, it developed, were bringing a surprise for the defenders: new repeating rifles. On August 9 the Shansi division, having taken a mass oath to finish off the legations "leaving neither fowl nor dog," attacked in the southwest sector against the recently bolstered defenses covering the Mongol Market. They stormed through the rubble-strewn marketplace behind scythelike sweeps of rapid fire. But they encountered a surprisingly stubborn resistance. The defenders were well sheltered and popped up to fire only when the attackers came into the open.

A little later in the day the men from Shansi got their own unpleasant surprise when a huge and intricate barricade collapsed in front of them. Their commander and twenty-six others, suddenly exposed, were cut down before they could scramble to safety. To the Tsungli Yamen this seemed unsporting conduct. It sent over a note bitterly complaining: "This was far from being a friendly procedure." On such occasions the vagaries of the Chinese mind, in both its military and diplomatic convolutions, so mystified their opponents that even old China hands could only mutter something about the Mysterious East.

On August 10 arrived a definitive bulletin from General Fukushima, the chief of staff of the Japanese vanguard of the International Relief Expedition. "Probable date of arrival at Peking August 13 or 14," the dispatch read. Everybody believed that businesslike message, but it was lent further credence by the arrival of a note from the Tsungli Yamen stating that the Chinese troops which had been attacking the legations were being severely punished, with many decapitated—an obvious ploy from the Forbidden City, which had long been in the habit of underestimating the intelligence of all foreigners. The frustrated court, with the possibility of its dynastic doom not to be dismissed, evidently believed it could persuade the Westerners that for almost two months the imperial army, as well as the Boxers, had been trying to exterminate the foreign colony in Peking without the consent of the imperial government.

Meanwhile, all the evidence during the next two days indicated that the enemy command, or at least its more aggressive part, was determined to have one more fling at overrunning the Legation Quarter.

"All thoughts of relief," Bertram Simpson wrote August 12, "have been pushed into the middle distance—and beyond—by the urgent business we have now on hand." The firing had become hot and heavy on all sides. "Some of our barricades have been so eaten away by this fire that there is but little left, and we are forced to lie prone on the ground hour after hour. . . . So intense has the riflefire been around the Su wang-fu [Prince Su's palace, where the Japanese held that section of the perimeter] and the

French legation lines that high above the deafening roar of battle a distinct and ominous snake-like hissing can be heard. . . . It is the high-velocity nickel-nosed bullet tearing through the air at lightning speed. . . . The Chinese guns are also booming again, and shrapnel is tearing down trees and outhouses, bursting through walls, and wrecking our strongest defences. . . ." The defenders could also hear Chinese artillery targeted on the Peitang Cathedral, and the hundreds sheltered there, the separate ordeal of which will be related further on. Simpson could visualize the courageous Favier like an ancient warrior-priest "urging his spear-armed flock to stand firm." It was, in fact, a fairly accurate image.

The Chinese effort may have been entering its last-gasp phase but it was still capable of deadly effect. That evening, with the fire from the enemy barricades slackening, Captain Labrousse of the French Marines was taking a breather with his friends behind the French legation position. He had been a leading spirit in defending that position and displayed a reckless courage when the fighting was hottest. Now he counseled his companions to think more of their own safety and not expose themselves needlessly. "It would be a pity to be shot the last moment before we are relieved," he remarked. A few minutes later he was struck by a bullet in the head and died immediately.

That night, too, watchers on the Tatar Wall noticed a curious side effect of the relief operation. It was driving in from the west masses of Chinese troops fleeing before the advancing relief columns. Inadvertently the relief force was adding to the weight of enemy numbers pressing on the legation defenses. Before dusk fell, the watchers from the American position focused field glasses on the area beyond the western wall of the city. The western and southern gates to the capital were clogged by soldiery panicky in their determination to get behind the capital's defenses, hopeful that the matriarch on the Dragon Throne would protect them.

One observer saw hundreds of infantrymen, no longer in formation, but a fleeing mob, entering the capital, and behind them "long country-carts laden with wounded, driven by savage-looking drivers, powdered with our cursed dust. . . . Sometimes a body of cavalry, with gaudy banners in the van and the men flogging their steeds with short whips, have also ridden by escaping from the rout. . . ."

Most were convinced that the next day or two would be the worst of ordeals. The civilians among the besieged were edgier than the soldiers, and even the missionaries fell to squabbling. The Methodist faction announced that they would no longer operate the punka, which circulated the stale air in the dining mess, while the Congregationalists were at table. A couple of Mrs. Conger's guests from the States formally complained to the U.S. minister because a squad of marines, bone-weary from a long watch on the Tatar Wall, passed them without snapping the customary salute. Minister Conger took the complaint under advisement.

Mrs. Conger maintained her almost unearthly serenity, reinforced by her ardent belief in and practice of Christian Science. Polly Condit Smith, who described her as "conspicuous for her concise manner and an open follower of Mrs. Eddy," recalled that a bullet whizzed through the window of a room full of women and children, missing one baby's head by no more than an inch. Mrs. Conger "earnestly assured us that it was ourselves, and not the time, that were troublous and out of tune, and insisted that, while there was an appearance of war-like hostilities, it was really in our own brains. Going further, she assured us that there was no bullet entering the room; it was again our receptive minds which falsely led us to believe such to be the case."

On Monday, August 13, the Chinese made a supreme effort to overwhelm the defenders of the Legation Quarter.

And even while their army was launching its most furious and sustained attacks, the Chinese diplomats continued to exude a moonstruck, incomprehensible solicitude for the people their soldiers were intent on killing. In one of the few quiet sectors, under a truce flag, a messenger from the Tsungli Yamen arrived with one of the familiar red envelopes containing that day's pious sentiment. Among their confreres in the Chinese Foreign Office, the Western diplomats were informed, "it was hoped that, dating from today, neither Chinese nor foreigner would ever again hear the sound of a rifle." If the attacks then being pressed with the utmost energy succeeded, it was, of course, unlikely that many of the foreigners would ever hear anything again except Gabriel's trumpet.

Sir Claude Macdonald's report for that day took note of the contents of that message and wryly commented, "I read this sanguine aspiration to the accompaniment of a violent fusillade from the Chinese troops, which began shortly after a shell had burst in my dressing-room. Three times during the night it was necessary to call up the reserves in support of the firing line, the attacks being more frequent than on any previous night."

More than once it appeared that the International Relief Force might come charging down Legation Street only to find the legations overwhelmed and their occupants massacred. The Chinese hammered all around the perimeter during the day, trying to find a weak point, their trumpets blaring the charge, the enemy troops screaming *Sha! Sha! Sha!* The alarm bell in the Jubilee Tower clamored incessantly. Whatever spare weapons there were in the British legation were broken out and distributed to everyone, for self-defense or suicide—it was up to the individual. Chinese-speaking people in the British compound could hear the Chinese officers urging their men, "Don't be afraid, don't be afraid—we can get through!"

Toward the end of day the Chinese attacks reached their crescendo. Dr. Frank Gamewell dashed from one barricade to another to shore up the defenses. Gunner's Mate Mitchell stoked and fired Old Betsy until its barrel was close to cracking, then fell with a bullet which shattered his arm. In the northern sector covering Prince Su's palace the Japanese, with their Italian cohorts, were being driven back to the last of their nine lines. A desperate Colonel Shiba ordered his men to bang on pots and pans to persuade the enemy his force was stronger than it was.

The Shansi regiments, armed with the new Mannlicher carbines, renewed their assaults and endangered the western side of the British compound. By pouring into the Mongol Market, the enemy was threatening perhaps the weakest point on the perimeter. It was a desperately close call. Bertram Simpson, who was among the volunteers fighting beside the British marines in that sector, related that "God willed that just as the final rush was coming a Chinese barricade gave way; our men emptied their magazines with the rapidity of despair into the swarms of Chinese riflemen disclosed; dozens of them fell killed, and the rest were driven back in disorder. Ten seconds more would have made them masters of our position."

Just before the light faded on that murderous day, there was another menacing development. A modern gun was being emplaced high above them on the Imperial City wall: a two-inch, rapid-firing Krupp field gun, as it was later learned. The devastation it could wreak was immediately apparent to Sir Claude Macdonald, who didn't have time to wonder why the Chinese hadn't thought of it before. By eight o'clock the Krupp cannon was beginning to fire from behind its embrasure in the towering wall. By then, however, Sir Claude had ordered the Americans' Colt machine gun and the Austrians' Maxim into position to deal with it. The Colt was sited to fire at 350 yards' range, the Maxim at 200. The Krupp gun had got off seven rounds and "did more damage" in ten minutes, as Sir Claude later wrote, "than the smoothbores had effected in a five weeks' bombardment." Too late, however, to do the Chinese much good. Firing over fixed sights, the machine gunners knocked out the Krupp's gun crew and silenced the cannon.

The roar of musketry only increased for the next six hours and rose to its maximum pitch around 11 P.M. Bertram Simpson, who had been fighting in one sector, then another for the past forty-eight sleepless hours, wondered whether this was "the last night of this insane Boxerism, or merely the beginning of a still more terrible series of attacks with massed assaults pushed right home on us." Every available man, including some walking wounded, was now manning the loopholes in the barricades.

The roar of battle continued until shortly after 2 A.M., August 14, when "a distant boom to the far east broke my ears," as Simpson would recall. From a slightly different quarter came the answering boom of another heavy gun. With his customary precision, Sir Claude, sitting in his study in the British legation and working on his journal of the day's events, recorded that artillery firing miles to the east was audible at 2:15 A.M. and "no one doubted that they were those of our relief."

There was a sudden cessation of firing from both the Chinese and legation lines. Both sides were listening to the cannonade, the cadence of the heavy guns with a crackling undertone of Maxim machine-gun fire. It was unmistakably the overture to the relief of Peking. It seemed as though the God of Battles, finally impatient with the ineptitude of the Chinese, had taken over the orchestration of events.

We stood transfixed. It seemed to us as if the whole world had come to our rescue.

—MARY HOOKER, *Behind the Scenes in Peking*

14. *The Footrace to Peking*

That distant booming of artillery heard by the defenders of the Legation Quarter in Peking was a sign that the Russians were trying to steal a march on their fellow participants in the International Relief Force. Welcome as it was to the ears of those under siege, it should not have been heard for hours. At the generals' conference it had been decided that the various national contingents would start out together, as in a footrace, just before dawn on August 14. It wasn't until hours later that various generals learned that their Russian comrades had jumped the gun in their determination to beat the Japanese into the city. To the Russians and the Japanese, of course, the march to Peking was merely the prelude to a grappling for greater prizes—principally the rich and varied resources of Manchuria.

The agreed-upon plan of the various commanders was simple enough to prevent interallied misunderstanding. The Russians would advance along the ancient paved road that ran along the north bank of the Tungchow-Peking Canal. Japanese columns would flank them on both sides of the road. The U.S. contingent would press forward on a road running just south of the canal, and the British on a road paralleling the American route a mile and a half farther south. The other detachments would bring up the rear.

By nightfall on August 13 the various forces were in position to advance by daybreak. They went into bivouac for the night—all but the Russians. The latter were astir before midnight and moving out on the paved road north of the canal, and they had not taken the trouble of advising their allies of their early departure. Early that evening scouts had returned to the Russian headquarters with word that they had reached to within 200 yards of the outer wall guarding the Tatar City without being fired upon. A *coup de main,* it seemed to the Russian commander and his staff, was a sure thing.

With rumbles of Muscovite laughter the Russian officers urged their troops on. What a joke it would be on the Japanese when they saw Russian banners planted on the ramparts of Peking. The joke, however, turned on the Russians.

Crossing unfamiliar and poorly mapped terrain, over a jumble of cornfields, irrigation canals, and sunken roads, would have taxed better-led troops than the Russian levies. The vanguard was commanded by General Vassilevski, the chief of staff, and consisted of one infantry battalion and one section of artillery. It slogged through the rainy night hopeful of achieving a surprise victory not only over the enemy, but over its allies.

In the early morning hours the Russian troops approached their objective—or, actually, the Americans'. In their night march the Russians had committed a serious violation of the canons of military practice. According to the battle plan they had agreed upon, they were supposed to strike off on the right oblique and attack the Tung Chih Gate, the northernmost of the four gates in the east wall. Instead they cut diagonally across the allied front, on the *left* oblique, and attacked the Tung Pien Gate, which was the American objective. In less polite times commanders had fought duels over one column crossing the front of another; seizing another detachment's target only compounded the felony. The Russian action was refought on sand tables by military academy instructors for years afterward, but no sensible explanation could ever be found except the old "fog of war" excuse. The Russians did steal a march, it seems, but they attacked the American objective only by accident.

Their more or less stealthy operation was not a great success, though they tried to bring it off with all the courage and skill at their command. They brushed past resistance on the outskirts of Peking, then directly assaulted the Tung Pien Gate. Vassilevski himself led a small party of troops across the bridge over the moat and killed the Chinese guards on duty at the gate. Then they called up their two field guns, which blasted open the outer gate. Vassilevski and his troops found themselves under heavy fire in a courtyard, overlooked by a tower, between the inner and outer gates of the city wall. By sunrise they had seized a short section of the wall but had not broken into the city itself; instead of dashing in to relieve the siege of the Legation Quarter, they found themselves pinned down—and they had to wait for hours until General Linivitch's main body, moving with the sluggishness generally attributed to the czarist army, came up to reinforce them.

The other elements of the International Relief Force learned they had been foxed by the Russians when Vassilevski's artillery section opened up on the Tung Pien Gate. At both the American and British headquarters it was believed that the Chinese were attacking on another front. After listening to the sounds of firing, everyone went back to sleep. Around daybreak, however, a Japanese staff officer rode up to General Chaffee's tent wanting to know whether he had any information on the Russians' activities. The Russians, Chaffee replied, must either be on the north side of the canal, where they were supposed to be, or back in Tungchow struggling along to reach their jump-off position. No, the Japanese officer insisted, the Russians were not to be found.

Chaffee didn't much care about the Russians. A single-minded fellow, he would push forward on his designated route and be damned to the other forces on his flanks. At 5 A.M. he sent M Troop, Sixth Cavalry, out on the road to Peking to reconnoiter. About two miles east of the city walls Troop M was fired upon as it entered a village. Then enfilading fire came from the rear. Captain De Rosey C. Cabell and his troopers took shelter in a walled enclosure and sent word back to General Chaffee that he was meeting with strong resistance.

That dispatch greatly alarmed General Chaffee, who had commanded the Sixth Cavalry for many years during its Indian-fighting campaigns; it was his regimental home. He hurried over to the headquarters of the Fourteenth Infantry and demanded the services of a battalion, commanded by Captain Frank F. Eastman, to rescue "my boys."

General Chaffee and the infantry battalion hotfooted up the road only to find their way blocked by a French column, which was hastening to the front and *la gloire*. The French were not even supposed to *be* on that road; they had been assigned, as an afterthought, to bring up the Russians' rear. The hot-tempered Chaffee shouted in English, the French commander replied haughtily in his own language, and the sun was rising toward its midmorning meridian by the time the Frenchman was bullied into yielding the right of way to the American advance. Chaffee then found that Troop M wasn't in nearly so dangerous a predicament as he had been led to believe. The cavalrymen were lying on the roofs of houses in the village exchanging fire with a Chinese force no larger than their own.

Chaffee pressed on with his cavalry troop and his infantry battalion, having decided to reconnoiter as far as the northeast corner of the Native City of Peking. Then he halted, remembering the agreement was not to attack the outer wall of the capital until the Russians, Japanese, and British were in position on his flanks. At about 10 A.M. he got word that the Russians had made a premature attack on his objective hours before. His left flank was unprotected except for a troop of the Bengal Lancers, the main body of the British force not yet having advanced.

By then General Gaselee had ordered all the allied detachments to move forward, devil take the hindmost. The plan for a coordinated assault on the eastern defenses of Peking was abandoned. It was every outfit for itself.*

What had been designed as a military operation turned into an international footrace. Each contingent tried to bash its way through the walls and into the capital before its rivals. That the British won in a saunter must have seemed proof of something— British luck, the superiority of the playing fields of Eton, the efficacy of nonchalance—to their rival commanders.

Those who tried hardest, the Japanese and the Russians, seemed to meet with the greatest frustrations. The Russians were held up most of the day around the Tung Pien Gate until their reinforcements arrived and they were able to link up with the Americans on their left for a general advance into the city. The Japanese ran into heavy opposition at the Chi Hua Gate. They

---

* As General Gaselee put it, "Owing to the premature advance of the Russians, the intended concentration was abandoned, and the troops all hurried forward to assault the city of Peking."

brought up their nine batteries of artillery, fifty-four guns in all, and fired more than a thousand shells into the Chinese defenses. But the enemy refused to give ground. It wasn't until nightfall that Japanese engineers were able to approach the gate and blow it open with high explosives, and their infantry didn't march into Peking until the next day, August 15.

Meanwhile, the Americans were making the best of a situation ensnarled by Russian overeagerness. Instead of attacking their originally assigned objective, they launched their assaults on the wall of the Native City to the south of the Tung Pien Gate and north of the Sha Huo Gate, which was the British objective. They fetched up with the northeast corner of the Native City wall looming before them. Chinese riflemen were firing down on E Company, Fourteenth Infantry, which had been ordered to lead the American advance. One platoon dashed for shelter under the wall while the rest of the company provided covering fire. Within a few minutes the whole company, plus Company H, had made it to the wall.

Colonel Daggett of the Fourteenth Infantry joined the huddle under the wall just in time to confront the next question: How do you get over a thirty-foot wall without scaling ladders or grappling hooks? Answer: Look for an agile and gung-ho volunteer.

Colonel Daggett held a hurried conference with his adjutant. "I wonder if we could get up there?" he asked, looking up the blank face of the wall, which was as high as a three-story building.

Among those who overheard the question was the bugler of Company E. He was Calvin P. Titus, a modest and soft-spoken youth of twenty. Compared to the strapping troopers around him, he was scrawny and undersized, five feet seven, weighing about 120 pounds.

Somewhat shyly, he volunteered to make the climb. Colonel Daggett looked him over, stroked his beard, and waited for some brawnier specimen to volunteer. None did.

"If you think you can do it," Daggett said finally, "go ahead and try."

Titus removed his haversack, canteen, hat, belt, and pistol and made his bid for glory. Fortunately the ancient wall was made of large bricks, eighteen inches long and four inches thick, from which the mortar had eroded. The spaces between the bricks provided handholds. Hand over hand Titus clawed his way steadily to the top. Crenellation along the top of the wall prevented anyone standing below from seeing whether the embrasures were defended. If they were, Titus would be a dead bugler. But this was his lucky morning, and he hauled himself over the top without being spotted by the enemy. Obviously the Chinese defense was utterly disorganized. In certain places along the walls it provided a hot and heavy reception for the attackers, and in others it was nonexistent.

Titus took a quick look around. To his right were three huts made of matting which leaned against the outer parapet of the wall, and beyond them loomed the pagoda which towered over the gate. Several hundred yards away Titus could see some Chinese soldiers firing down on the bridge across the moat. He ran over to the huts and, though unarmed, banged on the doors of each to make sure there was no one lurking inside. Then he returned to the place where he had climbed up and shouted down to Colonel Daggett and the others, "The coast is clear. Come on up."

At 10:45 A.M. the others began scaling the wall. Captain Henry G. Learnard was the first to follow Titus and brought a ball of twine with him. After lowering the twine, Titus hauled up a rifle and an ammunition belt and began firing on the Chinese, which may have been unwise. The enemy replied with rifle and artillery fire as the tiny force of Americans on the wall increased with a painful slowness. About a score of men from Company E managed to scale the wall before one trooper lost his handhold and was seriously injured. Fearful that other allied troops might mistake his men for the Chinese, Colonel Daggett sent up the regimental colors. At 11:03 A.M. the Stars and Stripes were unfurled, whipped in the breeze, and were cheered by the rest of the Fourteenth Infantry and the Russians pinned down on the right. Part of Company H also began scaling the wall with a ladder improvised from bamboo poles and wire. By noon the Fourteenth Infantry had enough men on the wall to force the Chinese to retreat from the Tung Pien Gate, which the Russians then succeeded in clearing. For his actions in bringing this about, Bugler Titus was awarded the Congressional Medal of Honor and given an appointment to West Point.

By then the Ninth Infantry and the Marine battalions had swept up the approaches to the wall on the left of the Fourteenth Infantry. They laid down covering fire for the dashing Captain

Henry F. Reilly's Battery F, which came clattering up with its gunners riding the caissons and whipping up the gun teams, ready to dig in their trails and begin battering at targets of opportunity. Still farther to the left the British had finally bestirred themselves and were nonchalantly deploying near the Sha Huo Gate.

By then General Chaffee arrived on the scene with First Lieutenant Charles P. Summerall's section of the Sixth Artillery and found both his infantry and artillery impeded by Russian carts, disabled guns, corpses, and other debris from the night attack on the Tung Pien Gate. On command from the exasperated Chaffee the Americans literally began shouldering and shoveling their way through the untidy Russians' leavings.

For several hours Chaffee's troops were occupied by dogged street fighting in the southeast corner of the city. Reilly's battery moved forward with the infantry, firing up streets and alleys whenever there was Chinese resistance, battering down houses, and laying down a barrage for the infantry squads darting from one doorway to the next. It was hard dirty work. Chaffee and his officers drove their troops forward in hope of winning the race to the Legation Quarter. By midafternoon Reilly's gunners were pounding at the Ha Ta Gate in the Tatar City wall, and within minutes the ancient pagoda crowning the gate burst into flames. It was about 4 P.M. when the advancing Americans spotted a U.S. marine waving a flag from the top of the Tatar Wall.

Half an hour later they learned that, for all their grim exertions, for all of Bugler Titus' heroism, for all the street-by-street fighting, the honor of relieving the legations had gone to another force.

The British had simply strolled in and walked off with the prize. Starting off around noon, hours later than the other contingents, they had marched up to the Sha Huo Gate with their sepoy regiments and the Twelfth Regiment Royal Field Artillery. One of the latter's guns blew a hole in the gate. A sepoy of the Twenty-fourth Punjabs climbed over the wall and opened the gate from the inside. The Indian troops with their British and native officers then filed in. Their approach lay closest to the Legation Quarter of any of the allied columns.

With hardly a shot fired at them, the British force approached the Ha Ta Gate, which was still held by a few Chinese. They moved farther along the Tatar Wall until they came to the positions held by the U.S. Marines. On the wall they could see three flags, British, American, and Russian, hanging limply from their staffs. There was no sound of firing from within the Legation Quarter. For a moment General Gaselee and his officers believed that they had arrived too late, that all the defenders had been killed. "We feared the worst had happened," one of Gaselee's staff later wrote, "and the flags were only a ruse to lead us on."

While they fearfully paused, a sailor with blue and white semaphore flags suddenly appeared on the wall above them. He signaled them to enter by the sluice gate of the Imperial Drainage Canal. It was now about 2:30 P.M., and in other quarters of the city the Americans, the Russians and the Japanese were hotly engaged while the British were puzzling over how to get over or through the Tatar Wall without soiling their uniforms. The sepoys of the Seventh Rajputs surged forward to the rusted iron bars which formed a grillwork barring a tunnel seven feet high. The drainage canal from the Imperial City, fortunately, had almost dried up. In a few moments the sepoys broke down the grill while a squad of U.S. Marines cleared obstacles on the other side. Marines and sepoys rushed into each other's arms and danced in the mud of the canal bottom.

Just which of the British troops were the first to burst into the British compound was later disputed. By the testimony of Mrs. W. P. Ker, who was watching the green gate opposite the counselor's house, it was a representative of one of the Empire's lesser breeds:

> The first man through the green door was a Sikh. He rushed up to the lawn and then toured the compound; an unforgettable sight, naked to the waist, sweating like a pig, hair tumbling from his shoulders. He kept waving his rifle and shouting "Oorah!" There was no doubt about his joy at our relief. The next man was Tom Scott (Bengal Lancers) hard on the Sikh's heels. . . . Major Vaughan, the cousin of the Headmaster of Rugby, *really* was the first man to reach the gate, but sat himself down in a ditch to light his pipe, and so got left.

Sir Roger Keyes, then a lieutenant and naval aide to General Gaselee, remembered it slightly differently: "Major Scott of the 1st Sikhs, four or five of his men, Captain Pell, the General's ADC, and I were the first to arrive at the Water Gate. . . . Some American Marines were pulling down the bars which closed the entrance, and being very slim, I managed to slip through ahead of the others. I then ran up the bank of the drain and through a gate into the American Legation. Running through it and through the Russian Legation, I arrived on the lawn on the British Legation." Lieutenant Keyes, though he had taken a more circuitous route, claimed to be the first man into the beleaguered compound. He had brought a white naval ensign, which Major Scott then hoisted on the staff over the British legation.

The siege of the legations was broken. Fifty-five days in an earthly hell had ended for some 3,700 people.

For twelve hours that day the people penned up in the Legation Quarter had been awaiting their deliverance. There had been heavy firing until dawn, and the alarm bell had rung to repel an all-out attack. First Secretary Squiers of the American legation regarded the situation so critical that he posted himself behind the Marine barricades on the Tatar Wall during the predawn hours and sent hourly reports to Sir Claude in the British legation. It almost looked as though they might be overwhelmed with relief only a few hours away. A last-minute surge of pessimism manifested itself largely through the unfortunate presence of William N. Pethick, a longtime American resident in China, who had accompanied Squiers to the Marine post. Pethick convinced Squiers that the sound of guns they heard could not be coming from the relief force but from the Chinese lines. "No sign of the approach of our troops beyond the firing of machineguns," Squiers informed Sir Claude under persuasion from the gloomy Pethick. "The other guns were *certainly* Chinese. Pethick tells me Li Hung-chang [whose secretary Pethick had been for many years] in '95 bought some 50 Maxims, a number of which were issued to the troops."

Later that morning, however, it was apparent that Pethick's pessimism was unwarranted. Captain Hall of the U.S. Marines watched shells exploding around the Tung Pien Gate (Reilly's battery going into action) and reported that the allies were fighting their way through the eastern section of the city. The missionary ladies broke out their last supplies of coffee and cocoa in celebration, and at noon the dinner menu featured the last of the pony meat. Then the whole quarter sank into its midday torpor; some people even took a siesta. Polly Condit Smith debated with her maid over whether or not to take a bath. Dr. Frank Gamewell, conscientious to the last, set out on his bicycle for a last tour of the defenses to make sure the northern barricade was sufficiently sandbagged. Mrs. Conger was staying at the bedside of Gunner's Mate Mitchell, who had been wounded in the eleventh hour as he worked Old Betsy to its last round. In the grounds around Prince Su's palace many of the Chinese converts were so close to death from starvation that they couldn't raise a cheer when they learned the siege was within hours of ending.

Shortly after 2 P.M. the advancing British colors were sighted among the turbaned heads of the sepoys, and everyone in the British compound began shouting, "They're coming, they're coming!" and dancing with joy. Bertram Simpson had clambered over the debris between the fortified Hôtel de Pekin, in which M. and Mme. Chamot were already opening the champagne for a victory celebration, and the battered walls of the French legation, when his nose told him that relief was only a few yards away:

> I put my leg up to swarm over a wall, and suddenly a thick smell greeted my nostrils, a smell I knew, because I had smelt it before. . . . It was the smell of India! Into this quadrangle beyond hundreds of native troops were filing and piling arms. They were Rajputs all talking together. . . . I noted without amazement that tall Sikhs were picking their way in little groups, looking dog-tired. . . . Pioneers, smaller men, in different turbans, were already smashing down our barricades and clearing a road. . . . Around all our people were crowding a confused mass of marines, sailors, volunteers, Ministers—everyone. Many of the women were crying and patting the sweating soldiery. . . . People you had not seen for weeks, who might have, indeed, been dead a hundred times without your being any the wiser, appeared now for the first time from the rooms in which they had hidden and acted hysterically. They were pleased to rush about and fetch water and begin to tell their experiences. . . .

There was still fighting up along the Tatar Wall toward the Chien Gate, where Chinese riflemen were holding out behind barricades, but nobody paid any attention to stray bullets.

General Gaselee, splendidly mounted, suddenly appeared in a mass of red-turbaned Sikhs, and that made the relief official, at least for the British. It all seemed like a page torn from a volume of Kipling's stories. "He jumped off his horse on seeing us, and showing on every inch of him the wear and tear of an eighty-mile midsummer relief march, he took our hands, and with tears in his eyes said, 'Thank God, men, here are two women alive,' and he most reverently kissed Mrs. Squiers on the forehead." Polly Condit Smith wrote.

She and other Americans had to wait for more than an hour before their own troops arrived. The sense of anticlimax was almost ludicrous. General Chaffee and the vanguard from the Fourteenth Infantry pushed in from the east and appeared before the sluice gate through which the British had entered the Legation Quarter. Instead of grateful voices raised in thanksgiving, the American commander heard the sardonic voice of an American marine greeting him from the top of the Tatar Wall.

"You're just in time," the marine called down to the general. "We need you in our business."

"Where can we get in?" General Chaffee shouted back.

"Through the canal," was the reply. "The British did it two hours ago."

For the Americans in the Legation Quarter at least, the sight of the American flag and its bearers was warmly welcomed. The British forces had passed on to grapple with whatever Chinese forces were still resisting, and "now came long lines of khaki-uniformed Americans, and General Chaffee, and well-set up Marines under Colonel Waller," Polly Condit Smith wrote in her diary that night. "They came on and on, stumbling through the hot August sunlight, line after line, without end, and we were nonplussed when they told us they were but a small detachment." Before nightfall French and Russian troops paraded in. "We stood transfixed. It seemed to us as if the whole world had come to our rescue. . . ."

General Chaffee and his staff repaired immediately to the American section of the British compound to report to Minister Conger. The old war-horse, according to Mrs. Conger, was deeply affected. "General Chaffee warmly greeted us with tears in his eyes. 'We heard the fierce fighting last night,' he said, 'and knew that you were still alive. We pushed forward, but when the firing ceased for a time, we were sure that we were too late, that all was over, that you were massacred. The awful thought of defeat, of failure, came over me. But it was not defeat!' "

For most of the International Relief Force and those whom it had relieved it was a night of celebration, though in the northeast corner of the city the Japanese were still trying to batter their way through some of the remaining Chinese defenses. The tables at the Hôtel de Pekin were crowded with officers from the various commands and many of them succumbed to the effects of M. Chamot's iced champagne, for which they paid in gold coins which they had not received from their paymasters. "Most of the officers at the tables," one participant recalled, "soon became highly elated. That is the way when your stomach has been fed on hard rations and you have had fourteen days of the sun. I left them in the remains of the little barricaded and fortified hotel disputing away in rather a foolish fashion because they were more or less inebriated."

The more sophisticated folk, like the well-connected and much-traveled Polly Condit Smith, celebrated the lifting of the siege less alcoholically the night of August 14. In her corner of the British legation, wearing a freshly laundered frock thanks to the services of her maid, she received Colonel Churchill of the British Army. Because of her social position, she was able to get word that night to her family that she had survived, Colonel Churchill being the British military attache in Tokyo and having access to the field telegraph. The first official telegram dispatched from Japanese headquarters, to which he was attached, transmitted the news via the Japanese War Office to Lieutenant James M. Key, the American naval attaché in Tokyo and Miss Smith's brother-in-law, that she was alive and well. She wrote:

> How wonderful to think that as the troops were marching up to Peking the engineers were steadily placing the telegraph wires, so that six hours after we were relieved a message went flying down the coast with the tidings! To know that my dear sister in Japan and my family at home may have been relieved from the uncertainty of my condition already causes my heart-strings to loosen up a bit. . . .

Obviously the globe-trotting Miss Smith had learned from living in embassies around the world how to pull the right wires. Her second caller that evening was General Chaffee, with whom she had lunched in Havana the year before. She charmed him into agreeing that she could leave with the first convoy of boats carrying the wounded down the Pei Ho to Tientsin, "where the consul will be instructed to look out for us until we take passage for Japan." Among those who would accompany her was the wounded Nigel Oliphant, who regretted not having been able to finish the golf course he had laid out but was consoled, as a golf-mad Scot, that he had "introduced at least one branch of civilization in Peking."

After a brief respite that night the fighting was resumed the next morning. Large patches of the capital, particularly the Imperial City, still had not been occupied by the allied troops, and the Russians and Japanese were still trying to subdue enemy forces in their allotted sectors. In addition, the Peitang Cathedral with almost 3,500 people crammed together in conditions which made the ordeal of the Legation Quarter a summer on the Riviera by comparison, also had to be liberated. It wasn't until the third day, August 16, that the generals and ministers in charge of operations got around to sending a column to the relief of the Peitang, only two miles away.

The morning of August 15 the city bustled with troop movements. The French contingent had finally marched in, and the Americans, apparently on the sole initiative of General Chaffee, were preparing to assault the Imperial City. On learning of that venture, the French, though they had marched in not long before dawn, insisted on taking part. Their infantry was exhausted by the march; but their mountain guns, packed in by a mule train, could be employed, and General Frey was determined not to be cheated of his share of *la gloire.*

A large group of spectators gathered on top of the Tatar Wall to watch the action. Most of them, Bertram Simpson observed, "had been spectators rather than actors in the siege. I remember being seized with strange feelings as they looked down towards the Palace in pleasurable anticipation. They imagined, these self-satisfied people who had done so little to defend themselves, that a day of reckoning had at last come. . . ."

The American assault began shortly after dawn under the personal supervision of General Chaffee. Four of the six guns in Captain Reilly's Battery F were placed on the Tatar Wall to fire ahead of his advancing infantry, which was composed of the Fourteenth Infantry and the Marine battalions. The whole operation was a sort of bullheaded charge, pointless from the strictly military viewpoint (with the Chinese troops abandoning their positions and fading away) and deplorable from the diplomatic standpoint. Furthermore, American policy was to deal gently with China. Chaffee, like his French colleague, had to have his moment of unshared glory. At the same time he had neglected to order up scaling and other necessary equipment for his troops and to give precise orders how the operation was to be conducted. His harshly peremptory manner was transmitted to his staff. Colonel Daggett, whose regiment undertook the assault, later recalled that a member of Chaffee's staff clanked up to him with a ten-word directive from the commanding general: "There is the gate. My duty ceases, yours begins."

Chaffee posted himself with four of Reilly's guns on the Tatar Wall next to the Chien Gate and the bombardment began at 8 A.M. Skirmish lines from the Fourteenth Infantry went forward, accompanied by Lieutenant Summerall's section of the Sixth Artillery. They met little resistance in the streets separating them from the outer gates of the Forbidden City, which were made of heavy beams faced with sheet iron. Lieutenant Summerall calmly walked up to the outer gates, chalked an X where the bar securing them was located, and strolled back to his section. He brought one of his guns up to within ten feet of the barrier and opened fire. The first shot went through the gate, the second broke the beam which locked it from the inside, and Fourteenth Infantry troopers poured into a large courtyard and came under heavy fire.

Meanwhile, the French, uninvited, had joined in the operation. Apparently they did not understand this was an all-American caper. Under General Frey's direction, however, a battery of mountain howitzers was hauled on a ramp to the top of the Tatar Wall. It was a gala occasion, with the ladies of the French legation attending. The French minister, M. Pichon, pointed out suitable targets in the Forbidden City. The four little howitzers barked on orders from General Frey and the ladies squealed with joy as the shells burst among the gleaming tiled roofs of the Forbidden City.

Everyone thought it was a splendid demonstration of Gallic ardor, of the élan on which the French prided themselves, and not least among their considerations was the fact that the German contingent was dourly tramping along miles away on the road from Tientsin while French guns were pounding the inner citadel of the once-mighty Manchus.

Not, perhaps, understanding how important the demonstration was to the collective French ego, General Chaffee soon put a stop to it. An American staff officer came over to General Frey with a suggestion that the French shells might fall short and endanger the American infantry. Nonsense, replied General Frey, his bombardment was "calculated to enhance his [Chaffee's] prospects of success." Frey ordered the barrage to continue. M. Pichon pointed out more targets. The ladies from Paris and Dijon clapped their hands with pleasure.

Less than thirty minutes later another American officer handed General Frey a direct, tactless, and brusque order to cease firing at once. The French guns stopped firing. American manners, M. Pichon and General Frey agreed, left a great deal to be desired. They escorted the ladies back to the British compound for a round of morning chocolate.

Meanwhile, the Americans were fighting their way through the Chinese nest of boxes, a series of forecourts, one leading into the other, which guarded the palaces of the Forbidden City. In the first courtyard they were met with heavy sniper fire until they got a few men on the surrounding walls to pick off the snipers. Then Lieutenant Summerall brought up his section and blasted the gate leading to the next courtyard. Here resistance had thinned out, and the lead platoon of Company M, Fourteenth Infantry, soon secured it. Three hundred yards away there was yet another gate, and the assault troops were beginning to wonder whether the Forbidden City wasn't some kind of Oriental joke. Again resistance thickened as Company E leapfrogged Company M and advanced across the open space to the next gate. The rest of the Fourteenth Infantry, followed by the Ninth Infantry and the Marine battalions, was coursing into the forecourts of the Forbidden City. Summerall's guns were brought up to shatter the third gate, actually the final portal to the palaces, courtyards, and temples beyond. The American regiments were within minutes of seizing the gilded but sclerotic heart of the Manchu empire.

Just before the final assault a command arrived from General Chaffee to halt in their tracks. Then came orders for them to withdraw. Fifteen men had been killed and many more wounded —now they were ordered to call off the operation. Why had they advanced in the first place? They cursed the brass hats with justifiable vehemence, but retreated in good order and closed each splintered gate behind them.

They soon learned that the withdrawal wasn't General Chaffee's idea. He had been instructed by higher authority not to enter the Forbidden City.

Bertram Simpson, who had followed the assault, watched the Americans pulling back and calling out "with curious oaths" and loudly demanding "why in hell this fun was being stopped." He looked over the battlefield on which the palace guards, armed with weaponry only Kublai Khan might have found usable, had tried to comply with their oath to protect the Dragon Throne. "Old-fashioned Chinese jingals, gaudy banners, and even Manchu long-bows were scattered on the ground in enormous confusion. The palace guards, belonging to the old Manchu levies, had evidently been surprised here . . . and had fled panic-stricken, abandoning their antiquated weapons and accoutrements as they ran."

At that the Americans retreated in better humor than Simpson discovered in the ranks of a company of French colonial infantry, travel-stained men from metropolitan France, who were demanding of their officers when they would be allowed to break into the Forbidden City. "They wanted to loot; to break through all locked doors and work their wills on everything. Otherwise, why had they been brought? These men knew the history of 1860." Already officers of the various contingents were finding it difficult to keep their men under control; the tradition of pillaging a conquered city was still strong among the European nations.

Probably it was that secretly treasured tradition which caused higher authority to recall the American troops from their admittedly unauthorized lunge at the Forbidden City. When their allies learned of the Yankee enterprise, they summoned a conference of the commanders and the various ministers at which M. Pichon and General Frey, still smarting over the insulting order they had received from General Chaffee to stop firing their popguns, obtained their revenge on Yankee insolence. Along with the

Russians they advocated a conciliatory attitude toward the Manchu court. Invading the sacred territory of the Forbidden City would only make it more difficult to deal with the dowager empress, they pointed out. It was known that Tzu Hsi and her intimates had fled the night before, but her property must be sequestered, held in trust. All sorts of pious sentiments wafted over the conference table.

With considerable relish the Europeans snapped the leash on the Yankees despite their protests that they had suffered heavy casualties to no purpose. It may have been ungenerous, but the Americans believed that the chief motive of their allies was to see that they got an equal opportunity at the treasures of the Manchu palaces. In no time at all the "sacredness" of the Forbidden City was repealed by general consent. Peking was to be so thoroughly and ruthlessly ransacked that the operation could have served as a model for Marshal Göring when he assembled his collection of stolen property during World War II.

The Americans were outraged, of course, and, as they brought their dead and wounded back to the Legation Quarter, did not attempt to conceal their feelings. Among them was Captain Reilly, the much-esteemed commander of Battery F, who had been killed by a stray bullet as he directed the barrage from the Tatar Wall. He was buried in the compound of the U.S. legation with full military honors that afternoon. Minister Conger, a frugal man, moved forward to retrieve the American flag before the coffin was lowered into the ground.

"Don't touch that flag," General Chaffee rasped. "If it's the last American flag in China it will be buried with Reilly."

It wasn't until late afternoon of August 15, or slightly more than twenty-four hours after the Legation Quarter was entered by the International Relief Force, that the directors of that enterprise took up the matter of the Peitang Cathedral. It lay only two miles to the northwest of the Legation Quarter. Still it wasn't until the third day of the occupation that a column was sent to find out what happened to those other victims of the Boxer uprising.

No word had been received from the cathedral during the fifty-five days, though firing and shelling had been heard from that direction. Its occupants might be considered officially and socially inferior to the *Corps Diplomatique,* yet on simple grounds of humanity they might have been spared a thought. Even the French commander and the members of the French legation had ignored the fate of Bishop Favier and his flock while they dallied on the Tatar Wall with their toy artillery and later on argued with their colleagues over a fair running start at the treasures of the Forbidden City. Late in the afternoon of August 15, however, the council of ministers and generals ordered that a column be sent to the Peitang Cathedral early the next morning.

Shortly after dawn on August 16 a column of French, British, and Russian troops set out through shattered streets for the cathedral. En route they passed an ominous sight: the head of Father Addosio, an Italian priest, stuck on the point of a lance and displayed outside the recent headquarters of General Tung Fu-hsiang. The previous day Father Addosio, who did not share the general unconcern over the fate of those besieged at the Peitang Cathedral, had wandered out of the Legation Quarter, highly distracted; during the siege his hair and beard had turned white and his mind had become unbalanced. "We had considered the Italian priest so quiet and docile that he was not restrained at all," Polly Condit Smith wrote in her diary, "and yesterday he quietly wandered out into the Chinese lines, and undoubtedly he was killed before they knew his mind was gone. . . ." Possibly unaware that large sections of the city still had not been pacified, Father Addosio had mounted a donkey and rode off to the North Cathedral to find out what had happened to his coreligionists. If the siege of Peking had need of a martyr, he would serve. Who could say that, in the eye of heaven, he was madder than the men and women who plundered Peking?

The dilatory relief of the Peitang Cathedral turned out to be an anticlimactic gesture. Twelve hundred men marched to its rescue without risking so much as a sniper's bullet. And when they arrived in battle formation, they found a detachment of more than 200 Japanese troops "whose presence," as General Frey rather grimly remarked, "nobody could explain." The Japanese contingent had arrived from a different direction, having just broken through the outer wall of the city. Thus a Christian citadel was liberated by infidels. Nevertheless, the bearded, jovial, and high-spirited Favier greeted his compatriots by sounding the anthem "La Casquette du Père Bugeaud" on a bugle and embraced them with a truly Christian generosity. Nor did he ask what kept them so long.

The ornately carved, white-marble façade with its inscription ("Catholic church built by order of the Emperor, tenth year of the Emperor Kuang-sü, of the great dynasty of the Tsings") was shattered by the 2,400 shells which had exploded over Favier's compound. It was a splendid example of church architecture. As described by a British correspondent who accompanied the rescue column, "the main entrance opened on three flights of steps guarded by two Chinese sea lions. . . . Four statues of artistic merit adorned the lower portion of the façade. A handsome circular window, encased in a marble frame, and two side windows, gave light to the church from the south. Probably the most interesting detail was the marble high relief in the upper centre of the façade. It represented the Good Shepherd and His flock. The interior of the Cathedral was in the purely Gothic style of the fourteenth century. . . . The roof was supported on thirty-six pillars, standing on handsome marble bases, and sur-mounted by prettily-ornamented capitals. The Cathedral was lighted by twenty-four windows of coloured glass, those of the transept representing such subjects as the Virgin, Christ in His glory, and portraits of the Saints and the twelve Apostles. The glass was all imported from Paris. There were in the Cathedral ten altars all beautifully carved by Chinese workmen and delicately lacquered and gilt. . . . Alas, all this is now wreck and ruin!" The bishop could only bemoan "our work of nearly half a century destroyed."

Certainly Favier had proved himself the good shepherd so many missionaries earnestly considered themselves. Under his inspiration and that of the aged sister superior, who died the day before the siege ended but not until her work was finished, the defense of the North Cathedral was a much more remarkable feat of arms—and of the human spirit—than that of the Legation Quarter.

His only armed defenders were 2 young officers and 41 French and Italian sailors. And in his care he had approximately 3,900 souls, most of whom were Chinese converts. Among them were 850 Chinese schoolgirls, 22 Sisters of Charity, and an uncounted number of small children, 166 of whom died during the siege. Not only did the cathedral lack an adequate force of defenders, but there had been no opportunity to increase the food stocks, no nearby stores and godowns to ransack for supplies. But what they had, they shared equally, Chinese and Caucasian, and while the relief of the legations was a matter for congratulation, the survival of Favier and his people was truly a triumph of the Christian spirit, one that still glows across the intervening decades.

Henry Savage Landor, the first British correspondent to reach the scene, interviewed Bishop Favier immediately after the allied column arrived at the cathedral, and found him still exclaiming over their deliverance. "It is a miracle from Heaven that we are alive today," the bishop said. "Without a miracle it would have been impossible to resist for fifty-five days the bombardment, the ferocious attacks of the Chinese, the starvation, and the moral trials of such a siege."

The journalist, who considered Favier the "greatest of all the heroes" among the Westerners caught in Peking, quoted him as marveling over the fact that not one of the Chinese flock had tried to save himself at the expense of his European protectors:

> The Boxers constantly sent in arrows with letters to our Christians promising to spare the lives of all converts if they delivered up the Bishop and other Europeans. Among 3,000 of our Catholics, not one man wavered for an instant, nor showed any sign of treachery. . . . They one and all behaved like heroes, ready at any moment to sacrifice their own lives for the sake of the others. Our attempts to communicate with the Legations and the outside world failed, and alas! with disastrous results.
>
> Our first messenger, who volunteered to take a message to the legations, was seized by the Boxers on leaving our compound. He was skinned alive. The skin and head hung outside our main gate. During the fifty-five days we neither sent nor received a single message, nor did we have a single day of truce, the hatred of the Boxers being shown in a fiercer way towards us than the Legations, probably because the cowardly crowd knew that we were weaker. . . .

Even a Protestant could admire Favier in a day when the ecumenical spirit was far in the offing and presently unthinkable. One of the chroniclers of the Peitang Cathedral siege was the

Reverend Gilbert Reid, who gathered the stories of the survivors within hours of its relief and published his account in the Shanghai *Mercury*. Bishop Favier, he wrote, "while untrained to martial deeds, maintained cheerfulness and hope, and by calmness of spirit and trust in God, kept in check any panic amongst the converts and all despondency among the marines. However desperate the situation, the Bishop never lost heart. . . ."

The cathedral complex included a foundling hospital and other facilities, and normally there were several hundred priests, nuns, nurses, teachers, and other persons living on the grounds. When the Boxers struck, there were food supplies for about 500 people instead of the 3,000 men, women and children who sought refuge there. There was no horse, pony, or mule meat available. The daily ration for each adult, at first, was a pound of rice, millet, or beans a day, but subsequently this was reduced to two or three ounces. By August 10 the food was exhausted; leaves and grass found in the cathedral grounds were eaten, and a soup of dahlia and lily roots was concocted for those suffering from wounds or disease. Nor did those besieged in the cathedral have the opportunity to trade for food as the legations did during the unofficial truce. "The men worked well so long as their strength remained," Reid wrote, "but afterward could not do much more than crawl around and keep up mere existence."

Favier's spiritual valor was matched by the courage of the French and Italian sailors. Though they had a shorter perimeter to defend than the Legation Quarter, they could muster only forty-one rifles against attacks launched by as many as 2,000 Boxers and imperial troops. The enemy artillery fire was much heavier, with as many as fourteen guns brought to bear on the cathedral and its auxiliary buildings. "There were twenty-eight days of successive shelling, being four days longer than the whole period in which there was shelling on any of the Legations," Reid reported. "During these days as many as 2,400 shells were fired, and on one day, June 24th, 380 shells burst into the grounds." When Mrs. Conger and her daughter visited the scene a few days later, the former noted "thousands of bullet-holes in the fine windows . . . the large organ is shot through and through."

The first attacks, as recounted by Bishop Favier, were terrifying affrays hardly made more bearable by evidence of religious fanaticism:

They advanced in a solid mass and carried standards of red and white cloth. Their yells were deafening, while the roar of gongs, drums and horns sounded like thunder. . . . When the Boxers, led by the Buddhist priests, were within a few yards of our gate, diabolical incantations were made by their leaders, a number of men being quickly placed in a hypnotic trance. Joss-sticks and images were burned and other exercises, accompanied by weird chanting, took place. When the mob had been worked into a state of uncontrollable excitement, a terrific rush was made by the Boxers for our front gate.

They waved their swords and stamped on the ground with their feet, yelling and gesticulating like madmen. They wore red turbans, sashes and garters over blue clothes. Their leaders wore yellow instead of red. The Buddhist priests were urging them on, and now they were only twenty yards from our gate. Three or four volleys from the Lebel rifles of our sailors left more than fifty dead on the ground. A great many others were wounded.

The bishop did not attempt to conceal a certain unepiscopal relish in recalling the scene: "There was a stampede but they sneaked back during the night and set fire to many houses around us. The flames threatened us on every side, and we had much difficulty in saving our buildings. Luckily we had plenty of water, and by the grace of God we managed to save our buildings. . . ."

Until July 30 the leader of that small force of French and Italian defenders was Lieutenant Paul Henry, a twenty-three-year-old Breton, whose inspirational and martial qualities, by all accounts, were almost as valuable as the unshakable determination of Bishop Favier. Most of the thirty-man French naval detachment came from the maritime province of Brittany, part of the sturdy and often contentious Celtic minority in the French nation. Lieutenant Henry himself was a throwback to more chivalrous times. "I am sure God will not let me die," he told one of the Marist fathers, "as long as I can be of use in defending you."

Knowing the disparity of the odds against holding the cathedral, Lieutenant Henry conducted himself with the fire and dash of a D'Artagnan. On June 20, the beginning of the siege, the Chinese began "firing with one gun straight into the main entrance of the Cathedral grounds," Reid recounted. Lieutenant

Henry led a sortie to take the cannon, which they hauled back into their own lines and turned on the attackers.

With his limited supply of ammunition, Lieutenant Henry had to make every shot count. During one massed attack by the Boxers early in the siege, his sailors fired fifty-eight rounds in two volleys. Their marksmanship was spectacularly effective. After the attack was over, they counted the bodies of twenty-seven Boxers and twenty of their partisans. Reid reported:

> The forty [sic] defenders who fought at the Cathedral were stationed at six different places, where stronger fortifications were made. The French were supplied with 2,000 rounds of ammunition, but the Italians had less. As soon as one of the number was killed a Chinaman would take his place. Night and day this small number had to keep watch and be ready to resist every device of the enemy. The shelling left its effect on nearly every building as well as the Cathedral itself. Four mines were dug and exploded, all being at the north end, where the Foundling Hospital was situated. As many as eighty persons were killed from one explosion. . . . The loss among the natives was almost entirely from the mines. The Foundling Hospital is now a total wreck, and a fitting illustration of the total design of the enemy.

A lot of the heart went out of the defense on July 30, when Lieutenant Henry was shot in the throat and died a short time later. But his example served to keep the surviving members of the Franco-Italian detachment at their posts. Only toward the last few days did the defenders and those they were protecting abandon hope of surviving.

On August 12 the Chinese sappers exploded the largest of their mines under the Foundling Hospital and the nuns' quarters. Five Italian sailors, as well as scores of Chinese children, were killed in the explosion. One of the heroines of that dreadful occasion was a tiny Neapolitan nun, Sister Vincenza, the hospital pharmacist, who was in charge of sixty-six of the Chinese infants, whom she would take out for an airing, six at a time, under an open umbrella. All sixty-six of her charges were killed by the mine and, she said, "I never felt young again."

Lieutenant Olivieri, the twenty-year-old Italian officer who took over command of the defense force after Lieutenant Henry's death, was lying in bed with a severe inflammation of the throat when the mine exploded. He was buried under tons of rubble, beams, and iron bars. Sister Vincenza rallied a force of sailors and helped them haul off the debris. Miraculously he was still alive. "He was sitting on his bed with his chin pressed against his knees because of a heavy beam which weighed down on him," Sister Vincenza recalled. "What had saved his life had been the mosquito curtain. The net was wound round his head and kept the dust from his face. But how had he been able to breathe down there during the hour and a half or two hours? His first words were: 'And the nuns? Are there any victims among the nuns? And my sailors?' "

The next day another mine destroyed about eighty yards of the compound wall which the defenders used as their first line of resistance, but by then the enemy was so demoralized that he lacked the spirit to attempt a breakthrough.

Hardly a person who sought refuge with Bishop Favier escaped being wounded, ravaged by disease or malnutrition, or deprived of a wife, husband, or child; most were barely half alive when the relief arrived, but their morale was higher than those in the Legation Quarter who suffered so much less. Their undaunted spirit was epitomized by the good shepherd Favier sounding his bugle to welcome the relief column. And the durability of Christianity, at least on the humblest level, was demonstrated by those French, Italian, and Chinese who held the Peitang Cathedral against the most violent assaults. The enemy may have stayed his hand when it came to destroying the Legation Quarter, because on the contemporary scale of values the life of one minor diplomat outweighed that of any number—say, a thousand—Chinese Christians. But he went all-out to level the Peitang Cathedral. "To the credit of Catholic France and Catholic Italy this calamity was prevented," the Protestant missionary Reid observed. "The defense was one of sublime heroism."

In the Legation Quarter the rejoicing over their deliverance was generally short-lived. Some of the more religious persons, no doubt, would give thanks for their timely rescue to the end of their lives. Many others, who had performed heroically, who had sacrificed themselves for others, felt a moral or psychic letdown.

Their roles in a historic drama, which many of them consciously enacted, were ended, and they were left on a darkened stage. Never again would they be the focus of the world's interest and concern. They felt suddenly deprived of a stimulus which had given their otherwise-humdrum lives an intense meaning for fifty-five or more days. They could only pride themselves, now, on having been luckier than the sixty-six persons killed in the Legation Quarter, the two adults and six children who succumbed to disease or illness, the uncounted Chinese who had died in Prince Su's palace.

The sudden absence of danger was something like withdrawal from a narcotic. An English missionary (the Reverend Roland Allen, who published his chronicle of the siege the following year) remarked that the "whole aspect" changed within twenty-four hours of the relief and that the "moral atmosphere was as changed as the outward aspect."

Many missed the daily routine of standing watch at the barricades, tending the wounded, or serving on one of the many committees. "Then each one had his own place, his own work. . . . Now the whole compound was in turmoil . . . everyone had to forage for himself. . . . For the moment it seemed as if confusion was worse confounded and supplies were more difficult and scanty than ever."

Even more worrisome to the Reverend Mr. Allen was the evidence of "a good deal of jealousy" between the allies and the predictions of the more worldly-wise that "they could not remain long together without strife."

The troubles in Peking were only beginning.

III. THE RECKONING

I made up my mind not to go out of the Palace at all. I am an old woman, and did not care whether I died or not. . . .

—DOWAGER EMPRESS *to* PRINCESS DER LING

15. *The Flight of the Empress*

In the early morning darkness of August 15, about twelve hours after the Legation Quarter had been liberated and while the enemy was still clearing out pockets of resistance in scattered parts of the capital, the dowager empress, part of the imperial family and the court, with a minimum of retainers, took flight from the Forbidden City. They had led the most sheltered of lives, protected by successive walls, by endless barriers of custom, and by a huge corps of servants and guards; now they were being flung into the real world, like rare orchids transplanted from a hothouse to a kitchen garden.

The decision to abandon the Forbidden City had been taken on August 10, though the dowager empress three years later told the Princess Der Ling, her first lady-in-waiting and confidante, that she had protested against the move.

Less partial sources indicated, however, that the old beldame of the Manchus was not so reluctant to get away from the predictable vengeance of the allied forces and that she could not bear the thought of watching the conquerors trampling over the fragile beauty of her beloved palaces, gardens, and pagodas. Early in August she had received a sternly worded memorial from Li Hung-chang in Shanghai, where that elder statesman had given an interview to the London *Times* correspondent in which he made it clear that he would not journey to Peking until "convinced by clear proofs that the Empress Dowager had seen the folly of her ways and was prepared to adopt a conciliatory policy toward the foreign powers."

Rarely had any of her advisers addressed Tzu Hsi so bluntly, but as Li Hung-chang wrote in his memorial he was too old for polite lies. "I am nearly eighty years old, and my death cannot be far distant; I have received favors at the hands of four Emperors. If now I hesitate to say the things that are in my mind, how shall I face the spirits of the sacred ancestors of this Dynasty when we meet in the halls of Hades?"

There was nothing left to do, he wrote, but throw themselves on the mercy of the victors:

> It is to be remembered that between our Empire and the outer barbarians hostilities have frequently occurred since the remotest antiquity, and our national history teaches that the best way to meet them is to determine upon our policy only after carefully ascertaining their strength as compared to our own. . . . Needless for me to say how greatly I would rejoice were it possible for China to enter upon a glorious and triumphant war; it would be the joy of my closing days to see the barbarian nations subjugated at last in submissive allegiance, respectfully making obeisance to the Dragon Throne. Unfortunately, however, I cannot but recognize the melancholy fact that China is unequal to any such enterprise, and that our forces are in no way competent to undertake it.
>
> Looking at the question as one affecting chiefly the integrity of our Empire, who would be so foolish as to cast missiles at a rat in the vicinity of a priceless piece of porcelain? It requires no augur's skill in divination to foresee that eggs are more easily to be cracked than stones.

The court must recognize that it had gambled everything on the Boxers and their false promises, had lost and must now arrange a peace on the best possible terms:

> When betrayed by the Boxers and abandoned by all, where will your Majesties find a single Prince, Councillor, or Statesman able to assist you effectively? The fortunes of your house are being staked upon a single throw; my blood runs cold at the thought of events to come. Under any enlightened Sovereign

these Boxers, with their ridiculous claims of supernatural powers, would most assuredly been condemned to death long since. Is it not on record that the Han Dynasty met its end because of its belief in magicians, and in their power to confer invisibility? Was not the Sung Dynasty destroyed because the Emperor believed ridiculous stories about supernatural warriors clad in miraculous coats of mail?

Li Hung-chang urged the dowager empress to "appoint a high official who shall purge the land of this villainous rabble."

For himself, Li Hung-chang added, he would delay his journey to Peking until some measure of order had been restored; otherwise "the end of my journey would most probably be that I provide your rebellious and turbulent subjects with one more carcass to hack into mincemeat."

On August 10, with the allies still far from the city walls, the dowager empress had issued a decree ordering General Jung Lu, Hsü Tung, Kang I, and Chung I to stay in Peking and form a sort of caretaker government while she exiled herself to some distant province. Somehow the next day, with a swiftness unequaled by the telegraph, the southern viceroys heard of the decree and sent a memorial protesting her plans for evacuation. They were saying, in effect, that their ruler ought to stay and take the bitter medicine of defeat, assume responsibility for having committed the central government to ruinously supporting the Boxers. Their memorial did not reach Peking until after August 15, but doubtless it would have failed to persuade Tzu Hsi that an abstraction like the government was more important than the dignity of her person.

Undoubtedly the effect would have been powerfully persuasive if she had stayed: the tiny imperious figure of the empress in her Hundred Butterfly Robe, seated on the Dragon Throne, defiantly confronting the powder-stained invaders of her capital. It would have been a moment of psychological victory. Who could resist its dramatic appeal? The world, which could still entertain romantic fancies about royalty rising to a heroic occasion (the last emperor of Byzantium dying in battle against the Ottoman Turks, Marie Antoinette in the tumbril), would have applauded her courage and forgotten, for the moment, her costly miscalculations. But this was Peking, not Constantinople, and the Manchus were not given to romantic gestures.

Yet the possibility of confronting the allies from the imposing platform of the Dragon Throne seems to have occurred to her, only to be dismissed as quixotic. Several years later she told the Princess Der Ling: "I made up my mind not to go out of the Palace at all. I am an old woman, and did not care whether I died or not, but Prince Tuan and Duke Lan suggested that we should go at once."

It is difficult to believe that Prince Tuan and Duke Lan, as proponents of such disastrous policies, could have then influenced her decision. Undoubtedly Tzu Hsi herself decided it would be best to seek exile, not because she lacked the courage to confront the invaders of her capital, but because she would be in a better bargaining position far from Peking and would not be subjected to the distasteful necessity of dealing directly with foreigners.

For the titular head of the Manchus it was a moment of supreme humiliation when she and her followers, like escaping footpads, slipped out of the northwest gate of the Forbidden City only a few hours before allied forces entered it from the south. Tzu Hsi was disguised in the blue cotton garments of a peasant. She had hastily snipped off her six-inch fingernails. Her hair was done up Chinese fashion with a plain black band substituted for her bejeweled Manchu headdress. "Who would ever believe that it could have come to this?" she wailed as she surveyed herself in the mirror.

There was just time for one bit of unfinished business: settling accounts with Chen Fai, Emperor Kuang Hsü's secondary wife, better known as the Pearl Concubine. During the crisis of 1898 the Pearl Concubine had suggested to the dowager empress' face that her consort was the lawful sovereign, that he bore the Mandate of Heaven, and that the dowager empress could not usurp his powers. Tzu Hsi had neither forgotten nor forgiven the Pearl Concubine's insolence.

At 3:30 A.M. all the concubines were summoned to her presence to hear her announcement that none of them would accompany the court in its flight from Peking. According to the diary of Ching Shan, both the emperor and the Pearl Concubine implored her that the latter be made an exception. The Pearl Concubine further enraged her by suggesting that if she couldn't go along, the emperor should stay with her in Peking.

"Throw this wretched minion down the well!" Tzu Hsi shouted to the eunuchs.

The Pearl Concubine, by Ching Shan's account, was wrapped in a carpet by two eunuchs and thrown down the well outside the Ning Shou Palace.

Many others died in the hours following the flight from the Forbidden City. Grand Secretary Hsu Tung hanged himself, despite his orders to act as one of Tzu Hsi's caretakers, and eighteen of his womenfolk followed his example. Everyone feared the vengeance of the allied forces more than death itself. "From all sides," wrote Ching Shan in his diary, "I hear the same piteous story; the proudest of the Manchus have come to the same miserable end. The betrothed of Prince Chun, whom he was to have married next month, has committed suicide, with all her family." By that evening Ching Shan and all his womenfolk were also dead; suicide was the only honorable course.

That the flight from the Forbidden City was undertaken in a panicky haste was attested by an Englishwoman, Mrs. W. P. Ker, who was permitted to visit Tzu Hsi's inner sanctum at the Ning Shou Palace a few days later:

> Tzu Hsi's room was just as she left it. On the rich coverlet of the bed lay an embroidered coat of black satin; beneath a pair of Manchu shoes. Nearby were two large boxes of silk handkerchiefs, overturned; one box of pale yellow handkerchiefs and one of pale blue. A handful had been hurriedly snatched from each. In the adjoining rooms, along the walls, were huge camphorwood boxes, filled to the top with coats and trousers of every colour, embroidered with gold and with pearls; all were new, all were neatly piled. In other boxes were rich sable coats, and silk coats lined with white fox fur; untailored sable skins and fur of every kind, stored and ready for the winter.

In the Kung Ning throne hall Mrs. Ker explored a "suite of many rooms, each one more magnificent than the other, divided not by doors but by wood carvings, rose, sandal and peach woods in different patterns. . . . Carved screens, tables, chairs and stools lined the walls, and on the tables lovely porcelain, jade, lacquer and jewel-trees. On a long table, the length of one room, were dozens of foreign clocks, some handsome, others hideous, all ticking cheerfully, regardless of the ominous silence around." And nearby was the Sheng We Men, the Gate of Military Prowess, through which Tzu Hsi and her retinue had fled on their Via Dolorosa to the interior.

A further humiliation of that predawn flight, as the dowager empress later recalled, was the disloyalty of her servitors, whom she had been allowing for decades to cheat on the household accounts. Even the chief eunuch, Li Lien-yeng, who had helped her memorize the Boxer incantations, "feigned illness and followed a little later," evidently reluctant to abandon the comforts of the Forbidden City. Though opium smoking was a forbidden pastime within the Imperial City, Tzu Hsi had indulged Li Lien-yeng and allowed him his nightly pipe. She later complained to the Princess Der Ling:

> How badly I was treated by my own servants.
>
> No one seemed anxious to go with me, and a great many ran away before the Court had any idea of leaving the Capital at all, and those who stayed would not work, but stood around and waited to see what was going to happen.
>
> I made up my mind to ask and see how many would be willing to go, so I said to everyone: "If you servants are willing to go with me, you can do so, and those who are not willing, can leave me." I was very much surprised to find that there were very few standing around listening. Only seventeen eunuchs, two old women servants and one servant girl. . . .
>
> Those people said they would go with me, no matter what happened. I had 3,000 eunuchs, but they were nearly all gone before I had the chance of counting them. Some of the wicked ones were even rude to me, and threw my valuable vases on the stone floor, and smashed them. They knew that I could not punish them at that important moment, for we were leaving.
>
> I cried very much and prayed for our Great Ancestors' Souls to protect us. Everyone knelt with me and prayed. The Young Empress was the only one of my family who went with me. A certain relative of mine, whom I was very fond of, and gave her everything she asked, refused to go with me. I knew that the reason she would not go was because she thought the foreign

soldiers would catch up with the runaway Court and kill everyone.

Tzu Hsi never forgave that kinswoman, who owed her status entirely to her, for thinking more of herself than the person of her empress. Seven days after the royal fugitives fled from the capital, she sent a eunuch back to Peking to find out what was happening. Her relative, as she told Princess Der Ling, "asked this eunuch whether there were any foreign soldiers chasing us and whether I was killed. Soon after the Japanese soldiers took her palace and drove her out. She thought she was going to die anyway, and as I was not yet assassinated she might catch up with the court and go with us. I could not understand how she traveled so fast. One evening we were staying at a little country house, when she came in with her husband, a nice man. She was telling me how much she had missed me, and how very anxious she had been to know whether I was safe. . . . From that time she was finished for me. . . ."

Distressed by the self-centered attitude of her retinue, accompanied mainly by those who had more to fear from staying than from facing the rigors of the journey to a destination as yet not determined, the dowager empress of China began the hegira, which would take them along the high roads to the west for more than two months in which they wandered like a band of mendicants. She set out as a passenger in Duke Lan's cart while the emperor rode with General Ying Nien and the empress and the heir apparent in a commoner's cart. The emperor, much as he had affronted her by advocating westernization, despite the fact that he had been her prisoner for two years, was required to join the flight. To leave him behind, doubtless, would have resulted in the Western powers placing him on her throne. The other members of the court-in-transit included Na Yen-tu, Pu Lun, Ting Chang, Chih Chun, Chao Shu-chiao, and Pu Hsing. Two days later Prince Tuan, fearful of falling into allied hands, forgetful of a vow to fight to the bitter end, caught up with the court. Three days later they were joined by Kang I in defiance of his orders to stay behind and join in the caretaker government; only the dowager empress' intervention spared him from being sent back to his post in the capital. Perhaps she realized, in a rare moment of pity, how thin the royal Manchu blood was running.

The governing urge of the imperial caravan was to get away from any pursuing enemy troops. Their first day on the road, after a wistful pause at the Summer Palace, they covered more than twenty miles and slept that night in a ruined temple at Kuanshih. A rural magistrate who watched their carts race through his village later described their appearance as that of "defeated jackals."

On August 17 the dowager empress and her bedraggled retinue reached the city of Huailai. They appeared so suddenly the local magistrate (equivalent to a mayor or burgomaster) didn't have time to put on his official robes or receive them in fitting ceremony. A large crowd gathered and pressed close to the dowager empress, but she would not allow them to be dispersed. In extremity she was learning something about the art of public relations. "Let them crowd around us as much as they like," she said. "It amuses me to see their honest country faces."

She and her followers needed time for rest and rehabilitation. "So hurried was the flight," Grand Secretary Wang Wen-shao recalled in an account published years later in a Shanghai vernacular paper, "that no spare clothes had been taken; the Empress was very shabbily dressed, so as to be almost unrecognizable, and the Chinese mode of hairdressing producing a very remarkable alteration in her appearance." Ironically, it seemed to him, Tzu Hsi had disguised herself as one of the Chinese whom her dynasty had conquered centuries before:

> They slept, like travelers of the lowest class, on the raised brick platform of the inn, where not even rice was obtainable, so that they were compelled to eat the common porridge made of millet. . . . The number of personal attendants and eunuchs was very small, and not a single concubine was there to wait upon the Old Buddha. . . .
>
> The dangers of our journey are indescribable. Every shop on the road has been plundered by bands of routed troops, who pretend to be part of the Imperial escort. These bandits are ahead of us at every stage of the journey, and they have stripped the countryside bare, so that when the Imperial party reaches any place, and the escort endeavor to commandeer supplies, the distress of the inhabitants and the confusion which ensues are

really terrible to witness. The districts through which we have passed are literally devastated.

Certain by now that they weren't being pursued by allied troops, the dowager empress and her party stopped over in Huailai for three days, rested and were supplied with more nourishing food and more suitable clothing. Magistrate Wu, who later wrote a book published in England under the title *The Flight of an Empress*, looked after them so well that he became an imperial favorite. He also furnished a yellow sedan chair in which the dowager empress could travel in a more becoming style. A member of the Grand Council, bearing the imperial seal, and a number of bureaucrats caught up with the party. Now decrees could be issued and edicts solemnly promulgated, although how much obedience they would engender was questionable. First things first: all the surrounding districts were ordered to send all the money they could raise to the traveling court. Wandering bands of defeated soldiery must be kept off the roads and away from the villages and towns; just where they were supposed to go or what they were supposed to do was not stated. The caretaker government back in Peking was ordered to negotiate with the British minister, and Viceroy Li Hung-chang, who had succeeded in staying away from the seat of government during the Boxer uprising, was commanded to begin talking peace with the other foreign powers.

The court felt it was back in business again, all was not lost, somebody had to rule China, and the foreigners had no real alternative to the Manchu dynasty. There would be months of bargaining, diplomatic approaches, mutual recriminations, but eventually the dowager empress would be restored to the Dragon Throne. In the meantime, it was the better part of discretion to deal at a distance with the allies—a great distance—because they were more likely to be amenable if they didn't have the dynastic rulers in their physical power.

It was decided that the court would seek shelter deep in the interior, at Sian, the capital of the province of Shensi, 700 miles to the southwest of Peking. Shensi was fiercely loyal to the Manchus. The provincial governor was ordered to prepare a temporary palace in Sian for the self-exiled rulers.

So the journey continued, not without complaints from the old lady traveling in the imperial sedan chair.

"I had a very hard time, traveling in a sedan chair from early morning, before the sun rose, until dark and in the evening had to stop at some country place," she told the Princess Der Ling. "I am sure you would pity me, old as I am, that I should have had to suffer in that way."

She continued to have trouble with her retainers, whose loyalty to her person did not stand up well under the court's reduced circumstances. Tzu Hsi must often have had reason to reflect on how respect for power waned when that power was deprived of its trappings. An empress in road-stained traveling costume was not nearly so awesome in her majesty as one in an embroidered robe and cape made of 3,500 perfectly matched pearls. She related:

> One day something happened. It rained so much and some of the chair carriers ran away. Some of the mules died suddenly. It was very hot, and the rain was pouring down on our heads. Five small eunuchs ran away also, because we were obliged to punish them the night before on account of their bad behavior to the Magistrate, who did all he could to make me comfortable, but of course food was scarce. I heard these eunuchs quarreling with the Magistrate, who bowed to the ground, begging them to keep quiet, and promised them everything. I was of course very angry. . . .

She did not elaborate on the fate of the "five small eunuchs," but it could not have been a pleasant one.

The weary travelers, so unaccustomed to the daily rigors faced in much greater degree by 350,000,000 of their subjects, finally arrived in Sian on October 26. Their ordeal as wanderers lasted slightly longer than the siege of the Peking legations—a measure, perhaps, of poetic justice.

Once the dowager empress and her retinue established themselves in Sian, surrounded by some of the trappings and comforted by most of the obeisances they regarded as their hereditary privilege, they felt a resurgence of their former self-confidence. The court occupied both the provincial governor's and the viceregal palaces. "Both Yamens," according to one account, "had been prepared for Their Majesties' use; the walls had been painted Imperial red, and the outer Court surrounded with a palisade, beyond which were the quarters of the Imperial Guards [that is, the Banner Corps], and the makeshift lodgings of the Metropolitan Boards and the officials of the nine Ministries on Palace duty." As much as possible the arrangements of the court in Peking were re-created in Sian, where the two yamens were now designated the "Traveling Palace."

The ceremonies attending every function of the court, which had to be abandoned in transit, were restored:

> Behind the main hall was a room to which access was given by a door with six panels, two of which were left open, showing the Throne in the centre of the room, upholstered in yellow silk. It was here that Court ceremonies took place. On the left of this room was the apartment where audiences were held daily, and behind this again were the Empress Dowager's bedroom and private sitting-room. The Emperor and his Consort occupied a small apartment communicating with the Old Buddha's bedroom, and to the west of these again were three small rooms, occupied by the Heir Apparent. The chief eunuch occupied the room next to that of the Old Buddha on the east side.

The imperial budget was so strained that only 200 taels (about $125) was allotted daily for their majesties' table—only about a tenth, as the dowager empress remarked, as was spent for that purpose in Peking—but the menu soon included such delicacies as swallows' nests and *bêche-de-mer* imported from the South Pacific.

Once again the dowager empress and her court were hermetically sealed against the realities of the world their dynasty had ruled for centuries. The world had slipped back onto its axis. To the dowager empress, with her confidence returning, unconditional surrender to the allies was unthinkable. From his study of the court memoirs and documents, Professor Tan concluded: "Argument for continuation of war was not infrequently heard in Sian. It was asserted, for instance, that the fall of Tientsin and Peking was due to the betrayal of traitors, that the Allies could never penetrate deep into the interior, and that if Tung Fu-hsiang's army was augmented to 50,000, the Allied forces could be defeated."

Unrealistic, if not hallucinatory schemes and proposals obsessed the court-in-exile. The men in Peking who had been ordered to negotiate peace terms were denounced in Sian for "currying favor with the barbarians." The stab-in-the-back delusion common to defeated causes soon made its appearance among the dowager empress and her advisers, who were reinforced by other fugitives from Peking, many of them spring-heeled opportunists who saw their opportunity of sharing in the imperial favor by catering to Tzu Hsi's understandable preference for believing that she had been betrayed, not defeated. A bureaucrat named Hsia Chen-wu gained temporary popularity by advocating "continued resistance" if the allies were not generous in their terms. When his aggressive proposals became ludicrous even in that vacuous atmosphere, the dowager empress rebuked him for his ignorance but praised him for having a "loyal heart."

During that period of exile in Sian, the dowager empress must have been greatly concerned by the question of how many truly "loyal hearts" there were in the higher echelons of her government, whether they had supported to the utmost the policies which resulted in the foreign occupation of Peking and Tientsin, how much of that support had been *pro forma* to the extent necessary to escape her wrath. Perhaps if she had been more willing to hear opinions contrary to hers . . . but that sort of thinking was a form of self-betrayal. A Manchu ruled absolutely.

She was often observed pacing her chambers in the temporary palace, deep in the velvety Shensi nights, and sighing loud enough to be heard by her servants. Somehow, she must have realized, she had been deliberately let down, her orders circumvented, her will blunted. Why had not the rest of China mobilized to support her? Why had thousands of imperial troops, some of them equipped with the most modern weapons, failed to crush the fewer than 500 men defending the Peking legations? Why had the Boxer movement not only failed to muster the legions of spirit soldiers but collapsed so quickly? It would be some weeks before she looked to some of her closest advisers, Prince Tuan and Duke Lan foremost among them, for one part of the answer. They had, of course, given her bad advice in overstating the potential of the Boxer societies—and they would pay for it.

A philosopher might have told her that the Boxers were an anachronism unworthy of survival in the modern world; that the incongruous was always fated to shrivel under the stress of reality;

that spirit soldiers, sprites, and demons could not coexist with railroads, the telegraph, and Krupp cannon.

Tzu Hsi, however, was not one to dote on philosophy or be satisfied with abstract answers to concrete questions. She would ponder over her resounding defeat to the end of her life, but probably never comprehended the deviousness and the subtlety of the means used to undermine her policy. She had simply been defied by her satraps. Men like Li Hung-chang who saw modernization as China's only hope preferred that the Boxer cause be crushed as just one more wayward episode in the history of a temporarily declining nation; they were as patriotic, even as antiforeign as any of the dowager empress' more fanatical advisers, but they regarded the uprising as doomed, suicidal. Their role was to pick up the pieces and guide their country to a more progressive future.

The resistance to the Manchu court took many forms. Commanders in the southern provinces responded to the call to arms by sending only driblets of troops to Peking; many of them never actually reached the capital but seemed to lose their way en route or found excuses for malingering. Meanwhile, the southern viceroys were maintaining diplomatic contact with all the foreign capitals and trying to present the events around Tientsin and Peking as purely localized disturbances. Yet the political leaders outside Shantung and Chihli provinces were protective in their attitude toward the dynasty; they took the position that the empress dowager and the Manchu court had been forced to side with the Boxers and could not be held accountable. Only six days after the attack on the Legation Quarter began, some of the viceroys plotted a *coup d'état,* but one which would spare their rulers. It was proposed that General Yuan Shih-kai lead his army north to purge the court of "undesirable elements," meaning the pro-Boxer faction led by Prince Tuan, and "protect" the dowager empress and the emperor. In the process, of course, the Boxers would be put down. "Your army," the general was told, "may not be strong enough to resist the foreign aggression but it is more than sufficient to suppress the internal disturbances." Yuan was a cautious fellow, however, and replied: "The critical illness is undergoing a change; better not hurry with the medicine." By the time the dowager empress reached Sian she must have realized that the South had badly let her down.

The full implications of the tragic death of General Nieh, probably her ablest field commander, must also have impressed themselves upon Tzu Hsi by then. Nieh commanded the most efficient of her armies, German-trained, clad in European-style uniforms, equipped with weapons from Western arsenals. He had first tried to suppress the Boxers encroaching on the Tientsin-Peking railroad. His reward was an edict from Peking warning him that if he did not ally himself with the Boxers and if he failed to halt the first of the allied relief columns moving toward Peking, he would be court-martialed.

General Nieh, believing it was hopeless to integrate the Boxers with his trained forces, sought death on the battlefield. Deliberately exposing himself to artillery fire, he was killed by a shell a few days later. Shortly thereafter the allies took Tientsin, were reinforced, and marched on Peking with little resistance. The Boxers had failed utterly to live up to their promises. Once violently pro-Boxer Viceroy Yu Lu admitted that the Boxers were concerned only with pillaging and "never had any intention of fighting the foreign troops." Time after time he had asked the Boxer leaders to join in opposing the foreigners; but they always refused, and by early August they had vanished into the hinterland. Yu Lu pronounced himself guilty of error and committed suicide when the allied forces marched into Yangtsun. His confession could only remind Tzu Hsi of the warnings of some of her more trustworthy advisers that the Boxers movement was rooted in the underworld and the chief motive of its leaders was to gain sudden wealth and power for themselves.

If any one man saved the foreigners in North China, however, it was Generalissimo Jung Lu, with the help of the Chinese military establishment and its abhorrence of losing yet another confrontation with the Western powers at a time when China needed all its strength to ward off Japanese and Russian ambitions in Manchuria. Jung Lu, as the dowager empress' oldest friend and reputedly her favorite former lover (an Oriental version of the Potemkin Catherine the Great relationship), was the only man who could have got away with a barefaced betrayal of her policy of destroying the foreigners.

Just before his death in 1904 he wrote a memorial congratulating himself on having averted the "crowning misfortune which would have resulted from the killing of the Foreign Ministers."

True enough: the diplomats in Peking and all the others owed their lives, not to the blundering relief expedition they welcomed as their saviors, but to the man whom they reviled as a barbarian and a monster.

Some of the foreigners, particularly those with a modicum of insight into the Chinese psyche, realized that something besides God, the Union Jack, and Manifest Destiny had intervened on their behalf; that without a friend in court they would have been obliterated at the enemy's leisure. None of them knew until several years later that their protector was the enemy commander in chief. Arthur H. Smith wrote that "there were occasions, as on the day when the gathering at the British Legation took place, when it would have been easy by a strong, swift movement on the part of the numerous Chinese troops to have annihilated the whole body of foreigners, and without serious risk to the attackers, but the opportunity was not seized." The perceptive Bertram Simpson realized that "were the Chinese commanders united in their purpose and their men faithful to them, a few determined rushes would pierce our loose formation."

Sir Robert Hart, the inveterate Sinophile, was even closer to the mark when he noted in a book published the year following the Boxer Rebellion:

That somebody intervened for our semi-protection seems, however, probable. Attacks were not made by such numbers as the Government had at its disposal—they were never pushed home, but always ceased just when we feared they would succeed—and, had the force round us really attacked with thoroughness and determination, we could not have held out a week, perhaps not even a day. So the explanation gained credence that there was some kind of protection—that somebody, probably a wise man who knew what the destruction of the Legations would cost the Empire and Dynasty, intervened between the issue of the order for our destruction and the execution of it, and so kept the soldiery playing with us as cats do with mice, the continued and seemingly heavy firing telling the Palace how fiercely we were attacked and how stubbornly we defended ourselves, while its curiously half-hearted character not only gave us the chance to live through it, but also gave any relief forces time to come and extricate us, and thus avert the national calamity which the Palace in its pride and conceit ignored, but which someone in authority in his wisdom foresaw and in his discretion sought how to push aside.

"Someone" could only have been Generalissimo Jung Lu. Perhaps his military opponents realized that, though they did not mention the possibility in any of their memoirs, when allied officers found scores of new Krupp cannon in the Peking arsenals. They could have pounded the Legation Quarter to rubble in a few hours. Yet they had never been employed, except for the one which fired exactly seven shells the last night of the siege, merely a token of what could have been accomplished with massed batteries of the guns. Instead, Jung Lu contented himself with firing an estimated total of 3,000 cannonballs and shells into the Legation Quarter during the siege, many of them from guns which belonged in a military museum. According to one Chinese source, Jung Lu stopped the belligerent Moslem General Tung Fu-hsiang from using high-explosive shells on several occasions.

Tung Fu-hsiang was so outraged at being muzzled that he overestimated his own influence with Tzu Hsi and tried to have Jung Lu cashiered for treachery. One day, after Jung Lu had refused his appeal for the use of heavy artillery, he approached the dowager empress as she was painting a bamboo design on a silk panel in the Hall of Imperial Supremacy. "I have come to ask your Majesty's permission to impeach Jung Lu as a traitor and a friend of the barbarians. He has guns which my army needs, but he has sworn never to lend these guns even though Your Majesty should command it."

"Be silent!" replied the dowager empress, who did not like being addressed in the barrack-square tone. "You were nothing but a brigand to begin with, and if I allowed you to enter my army it was only to give you an opportunity of atoning for your former misdeeds. Even now you are behaving like a brigand, forgetting the majesty of the imperial presence. Of a truth, your tail is becoming too heavy to wag. Leave the palace forthwith, and do not let me find you here again unless summoned to audience."

The dowager empress trusted Jung Lu completely, even if she did not comprehend his motives. Besides, as she frequently complained, the firing of artillery gave her a headache. Without that trust and affection, dating back to their early youth, the generalissimo would not have dared to circumvent the imperial policy.

The antiforeign faction in the court was strong enough and had sufficiently influenced the dowager empress so that he was forced to make noisy demonstrations against the Legation Quarter, and some of the attacks almost got out of hand (as the foreigners' casualty list showed); but his real attitude toward the venture was expressed in a letter written on July 9 to two political leaders in South China:

> If we can save the foreign ministers, it will be good for the future. But after the death of the German Minister, the British Minister had Prince Su driven out of his palace and ordered thousands of Christian converts to live there. [Actually Prince Su had voluntarily evacuated his palace, along with his concubines, some days before the siege of the Legation Quarter began.] The various legations were united and daily fired their rifles and guns, killing innumerable officials and people. . . . It was therefore impossible for the Headquarters Army [that is, the Peking Field Force] and Tung Fu-hsiang's troops not to defend their positions and make counterattacks. Meanwhile the Boxers stirred up more disturbances. I have tried to give protection and to bring about a reconciliation. I have put up notices allowing the Christian converts to redeem themselves. On June 25 I had a notice written in big characters saying that in accordance with the Imperial decree we will protect the legations, that shooting is forbidden, and that we should communicate with each other. . . . We can only do what is humanly possible and await the Mandate of Heaven. . . .

The restraint which Jung Lu exercised in command of the Peking Field Force, compared with the ferocity of General Tung Fu-hsiang and his Kansu divisions, over which Jung Lu evidently did not have complete control, was mentioned in one of his dispatches by Sir Claude Macdonald:

> There were noteworthy differences, however, between the troops on different sides of us, those to the north and west—all Kansu men under Tung Fu-hsiang—remaining sullen and suspicious. [Sir Claude was writing about the period of the mid-July

truce.] From other directions, and especially on the east, where Jung Lu's troops were posted, it was possible to obtain supplies (small, but welcome) of eggs and vegetables, the sellers being smuggled through the Chinese soldiers' lines in spite of the prohibition of their officers, and it was from this side that the messengers came with all later letters. They declared, in fact, that they could not get through the troops on our western side without being shot.

Toward the end of the siege Jung Lu tried to have Tung Fu-hsiang's troops withdrawn from their positions and sent away from the capital. They would be replaced by his own forces. One of the pro-Boxer partisans at the court caught on to the scheme and protested, successfully, that the Moslem troops should be kept in the battle line. In a memorial to the throne, Duke Lan declared that word of Jung Lu's proposed action was having a bad effect on civilian morale. He informed the dowager empress on August 10:

> The people in Peking feel alarmed and apprehensive. Yester-day so many inhabitants and shopkeepers went to urge Tung to stay that the streets were jammed. This shows how he had gained the heart of the people, who regard him as the Great Wall. The Wu Wei Headquarters [Peking Field Force] troops are newly recruited and have no experience of war; they cannot be much relied upon. It is requested that an Imperial decree be issued, ordering all Kansu troops to remain and to collaborate in the work of defense and extermination. . . .

Obviously Jung Lu was a man of considerable moral and physical courage. Even though he risked his career, and possibly his life in the effort, he opposed the pro-Boxer faction in the court headed by Prince Tuan and Duke Lan, used his great and long-standing influence on the dowager empress, and warned her against involving the dynasty with the Boxer cause.

One day in the spring of 1904, while sojourning at the Sea Palace, the dowager empress recalled for her young lady-in-wait-ing how Jung Lu, who had just died, tried to persuade her against her disastrous course. Jung Lu had been ill and on leave when he heard of the demonstrations of Boxer "invulnerability" which had been conducted for the court by some of Prince Tuan's friends.

Jung Lu, regarding such rituals as an obscenity and an insult to the throne, returned hurriedly from sick leave.

"Jung Lu," the dowager empress told Princess Der Ling, "looked grieved . . . said that these Boxers were nothing but revolutionaries and agitators. They were trying to get the people to help them to kill the foreigners, but he was very much afraid the result would be against the government. I told him that he was probably right, and asked him what should be done. . . ." The dowager empress, of course, did not explain that she was most likely to be impressed by the last person who talked to her. Willful as she was, she bent like a willow to changing currents of opinion. Eventually she acted on whatever prejudice ruled her. Then and later, as subsequent conversations showed, her dominant passion was a hatred of Christians and what she conceived to be their practices.

Jung Lu, she said, confronted Prince Tuan on the Boxer question, and the two men quarreled, upon which the prince warned her that "all of Peking had become Boxers, and if we tried to turn them, they would do all they could to kill everyone in Peking, including the Court; that they had the day selected to kill all the foreign representatives; that Tung Fu-hsiang, a very conservative general, had promised to bring his troops out to help the Boxers to fire on the Legations."

No doubt with relish, Tzu Hsi then presided over a struggle for her favor between her old favorite, Jung Lu, and her new, Prince Tuan. She kept sending for each man and telling him what the other had just said. Jung Lu suggested that:

> I should issue an Edict, saying that these Boxers were a secret society and no one should believe their teaching, and to instruct the generals of the nine gates to drive all the Boxers out of the city at once. When Prince Tuan heard this he was very angry and told Jung Lu that if such an Edict was issued, the Boxers would come to the Court and kill everybody. When Prince Tuan told me this, I thought I had better leave everything to him.
>
> After he left the palace, Jung Lu said that Prince Tuan was absolutely crazy and that he was sure these Boxers would be the cause of a great deal of trouble. Jung Lu also said that Prince Tuan must be insane to be helping the Boxers to destroy the Legations; that these Boxers were a very common lot, without

education, and they imagined the few foreigners in China were the only ones on earth and if they were killed it would be the end of them. Then they forgot how strong these foreign countries are, and that if the foreigners in China were all killed, thousands would come to avenge their death.

Jung Lu assured me that one foreign soldier could kill one hundred Boxers without the slightest trouble, and begged me to give him instructions to order General Nieh to bring his troops to protect the Legations. Of course I gave him this instruction at once, and also told him that he must see Prince Tuan and Duke Lan at once to tell them that this was a very serious matter and that they had better not interfere with Jung Lu's plans. Matters became worse day by day and Jung Lu was the only one against the Boxers, but what could one man accomplish against so many?

Thus, deftly, the dowager empress portrayed herself as the helpless bystander to a power struggle. She absolved herself of responsibility—a mere woman beset by quarreling magnates. Yet her own words picture her as refereeing the jousting matches between her commander in chief and the men who had become powerful under her patronage; she made the ultimate decision. Out of affection for the historic truth or for the general himself, she also made it clear that Jung Lu had opposed the Boxer movement to the full extent of his capability.

After the fall of Peking, Jung Lu was ordered to remain in the capital as one of the representatives of the imperial authority. He disobeyed that decree, retreating with some of his beaten troops to Paoting. The reason for his disobedience, on the testimony of Chinese documents, was the hostility of the foreign envoys. Sir Claude Macdonald, as indicated above, realized that someone in high military authority must have been throttling down the Chinese attacks, but the diplomatic corps as a whole and the outside world from its reading of newspaper accounts largely fabricated in Shanghai insisted on viewing Jung Lu as one of the prime villains of the Boxer Rebellion. No doubt he would have been seized by the allies and possibly executed.

Under those circumstances Jung Lu wisely departed from the capital. The elder statesman Li Hung-chang, who had taken charge of negotiations with the foreign powers, furthermore agreed that it would be best for Jung Lu to rejoin the court-in-exile and exercise a moderating influence. He arrived in Sian on November 11, 1900, by which time the Grand Council had been purged of its pro-Boxer members.

Jung Lu assumed leadership of the Grand Council and prevailed over those of the dowager empress' advisers who had been advocating a continued resistance in North China. From then on, the still-supreme authority in China took a more realistic attitude toward its situation and realized that survival could be guaranteed only by making peace as quickly as decently possible.

Not the least of Jung Lu's duties was to console the aging empress when she wept over the failure of her plans to restore China to its ancient and austere ways. Freshets of tears would fall when she learned what the crusaders from the West were doing to the lustrous beauty and preserved antiquity of Peking.

Some allowance should be made for the fact that during the excitement of a campaign you do things that you yourself would be the first to criticize in the tranquil security of home.

—Smedley D. Butler, *Old Gimlet Eye*

16. *The Sack of Peking*

The world outside China exulted over the salvation of the legations in Peking. It seemed a demonstration of the righteous force of Christianity. Once more the heathen had been sent scattering. The relief of Peking was presented as the apotheosis of one of the less fratricidal crusades to the Holy Land, conveniently ignoring the fact that the Crusaders sacked Constantinople when it was known as the second Rome.

"History has repeated itself," it seemed to the *Times* of London, under whose stately phrases there seemed to be sacred music playing. "Once more a small segment of the civilized world has exhibited those high moral qualities the lack of which renders mere numbers powerless."

While sermons and editorials by the thousands sounded the self-congratulatory note, while all Christianity celebrated the victory over the dark insensate forces of paganism and superstition, the situation in Peking developed in a manner far less pleasing to those who believed the relief of the besieged foreigners had been a demonstration of the *Gott mit uns* spirit which would expand into colossal irony during the coming World War.

Anarchy prevailed over Peking and most of North China and Manchuria. The rule of law had been abandoned. The authority of the Chinese central government had vanished into the interior with the dowager empress, and the allies, having made no preparations for a temporary military government, being as ill prepared for success as for their several setbacks, failed to fill the vacuum.

Peking was divided into pie slices occupied by the various national contingents. Only a quarter of the capital's population remained, thousands having been murdered by the Boxers and other thousands having fled into the countryside. Attempts to protect the lives and property of the Chinese were, to say the least, fainthearted.

Looting quickly became the sole preoccupation of the allied garrisons and civilians alike (including members of the legations), who, after a brief hour of thanksgiving, quickly fell upon the shops, palaces, homes, and government buildings of the conquered city. It was not Western civilization's finest hour. Within twenty-four hours of their deliverance, as the Reverend Roland Allen wrote, regarding the people of the legations, "men in small parties were beginning to go out in search of loot."

Several days after allied troops entered the city ten fires were still burning within the Imperial City without attracting any official interest. Looting parties had invaded the famous Lama Temple with its invaluable library of Buddhist literature without a sign of disapproval from the occupying powers. They savaged the library as thoroughly as the Boxers had wrecked the Hanlin, but without the excuse of ignorance. A British correspondent observed:

> Attempts were made to keep soldiers and civilians in order, and threats of "shooting looters on sight" were issued, but never carried out except in the case of Chinese. . . . Long lines of mules were to be seen all day long, carrying away loads of silver, grain and silk from various government and private stores to the quarters of the allies. Missionaries, male and female, were frequently observed collecting curios in uninhabited houses. . . .

The correspondent also came across the story of a "disgraceful case of blackmailing" involving "a man who called himself an Englishman" who "made several thousand dollars by selling small British flags and a certificate guaranteeing the life of the purchaser. When he could not obtain cash, he was satisfied with title-deeds of Chinamen's property. He was eventually arrested, court-martialled, and condemned to be shot; but, much to everyone's surprise, the British authorities released him. He made a hasty journey to the coast with his ill-acquired wealth."

Although the Americans had been prohibited from taking the Forbidden City, those sacred imperial precincts were looted as thoroughly as the Mongol Market. The Americans began to suspect that their assault had been called off just before it could penetrate the final gateway because their allies did not want the treasures of the imperial palaces placed under the protection of the U.S. forces. A Washington directive had forbidden, in advance, any of its citizens from participating in any sack of the capital or the countryside.

This did not prevent many Americans from exercising their inalienable rights of individual enterprise. One citizen of Peking who begged an American soldier to write a notice that would keep looters away from his premises was rewarded with a sign proclaiming: "USA Boys—plenty of whiskey and tobacco in here." Many Chinese, however, still had faith in the goodwill so often, so piously proclaimed by Americans, and as Mrs. Conger related, a large number came to the U.S. minister for help in preserving their possessions. "A little paper from him often protects their goods and provisions and enables the owner to sell them." Actually Mr. Conger's bits of paper only served as homing devices for looters.

Most Chinese, though innocent of participation in the Boxer outrages or any other actions against the foreign community, expected nothing less than the barbaric treatment they received. Polly Condit Smith wrote that the wealthier Chinese had abandoned the capital and taken with them their favorite wives and concubines, upon which the lesser creatures of their households, the always superfluous children and women, "promptly committed suicide, usually by hanging themselves, or drowning themselves in the wells of their courtyards. The men who are throughout Peking now looting constantly run into these silent testimonials, showing how these people all preferred self-inflicted death to what they knew they could expect when the civilized and Christian soldiers of the West should be turned loose."

The whole city stank of death, of unburied corpses and rotting garbage, and through it coursed the victors in an orgy of acquisition. Peking had become a gigantic thieves' market.

Bertram Simpson described how hundreds of rolls of silk,

looted from some town on the route of the International Relief Force, were thrown on the market. "Someone who had some gold in his pocket got an enormous mass for a hundred francs. The next day he was offered ten times the amount he had paid. In the dark he had purchased priceless fabrics from the Hangchow looms which fetch anything in Europe. Great quantities of things were offered for sale as quickly as they could be dragged from haversacks and knapsacks." He was told that "everything had been looted by the troops from the sea right up to Peking, that the men had got badly out of hand in the Tientsin native city. . . . Every village on the line of march from Tientsin had been treated in the same way. Perhaps it was because there had been so little fighting that there had been so much looting."

Only the briefest consideration was given to halting the sack of Peking. Since some of the highest-ranking officers and diplomats were involved in the same endeavor, it would have taken more brazen hypocrisy than even a Victorian colonial general could muster to issue such a fiat. An American witness testified to a "very animated generals' conference" held a few days after the relief of the legations:

> the great question being whether there should be a unanimous effort to stop all looting and sacking, or whether it should be continued. The Japanese, French, and Russians were absolutely *pro;* English and Americans, *con,* the latter having the strictest orders from President McKinley against any looting.
>
> The English, although giving their vote for no looting, added they should continue to place "in safe-keeping all valuable things" found in the district given them to police. This, of course, gives them practically the right to loot, although whatever is brought in has to be placed in one place, where they have an auction later, and the officially prescribed amount *pro rata* is given to the officers and men, so that they are really doing just what the other nations are doing, only in a somewhat more legalized way.

The Victorian moral fiber, though it became legendary to other generations, though it was passed down as a legacy of inestimable worth, apparently lacked something in tensile strength. Few found themselves capable of resisting the temptation to share, indirectly if they did not go out on smash-and-grab expeditions themselves, in the gutting of the imperial city.

The wellborn and otherwise-scrupulous Polly Condit Smith, as she frankly related, found her own inhibitions melting away almost hourly. Her first experience with the temptations of buying what was, strictly speaking, stolen property came when a Sikh trooper of the British contingent approached her near the British legation with the proposition: "Mem-sahib give me two dollars, I give mem-sahib nice things." Miss Smith handed the man two dollars and received in return a gold-mounted cloisonné clock and two fat hens.

Perhaps, she may have reflected, her scruples had eroded when she and the Dutch minister some days earlier had stolen a chicken belonging to the Russians. A few hours after she made her purchase from the Sikh she breakfasted with her genial bearded Russian admirer, Baron von Rahden:

> He told me he had procured for me a good sable coat—and when a Russian speaks of sables they are good, for that nationality are expert judges of furs. I wanted to accept the coat in the spirit it was offered, as a testimonial of a charming friendship, formed under extraordinary circumstances, but owing to the intrinsic value of the garment I had to decline it. I don't think he understood very well my refusing it, and I had within an hour the pleasure of seeing him present it to another woman, who accepted it without a qualm, and without giving him, I thought, very many thanks.

She confessed that her soul was "torn with conflicting emotions all day." Late that afternoon another admirer, a Belgian, brought her a tortoiseshell bracelet handsomely set with pearls. "I surprised myself by promptly accepting it. My nerves could not have stood it, and I took it rather than have a repetition of the sequel to the sable-coat episode."

No nationality, it must be said, was immune to the fever of petit and grand larceny that was coursing through the city. Russian general, French diplomat, British lady, American officer, Japanese marine—all joined in the sack. Shortly after his arrival as supreme commander of the occupation forces, Field Marshal Count Von Waldersee observed: "Every nationality accords the palm to some other in respect to the art of plundering, but it remains the fact that each and all of them went in hot and strong for loot."

The Purple City of the Manchus lay as helpless as the coolie hovels in the Native City. Within hours after the Americans were prohibited from seizing the Forbidden City, it was being invaded by gangs of looters while the remaining eunuchs and other servants stood around and watched. Some Americans tentatively joined in the forays, though their government did not recognize the "spoils of war" doctrine. One of them was Captain Smedley D. Butler, whose company was bivouacked in the Palace of the Eighth Prince.

Later, as he candidly recalled in his memoirs, it seemed to him: "Some allowance should be made for the fact that during the excitement of a campaign you do things that you yourself would be the first to criticize in the tranquil security of home." His own efforts as a pillager were ludicrously unproductive. Butler and some of his comrades broke into an empty palace, where they found a number of candlesticks, boxes, and trays they believed were made of gold. They buried their loot in a rear courtyard, then several days later dug it up for examination by an expert. The ornaments were brass. Several days later he and his company tramped through the Forbidden City and were disillusioned by the fact that its gold pillars were actually covered with a thin, flaking gold leaf. "As we swung out the north gate we were filled with contempt for those Chinese rulers who were satisfied to live in musty old palaces."

By all accounts the Japanese were the most successful, systematic and efficient at the business of looting, just as they had been the most professional and energetic in defending the Legation Quarter and in the march from Tientsin to Peking.

Bertram Simpson, by his own account one of the shrewder and more enterprising of the entrepreneurs, illustrated how masterful were the Japanese at acquiring plunder. The Japanese weren't looking for trinkets and *objets d'art* to decorate their homes, but for the fabled negotiable treasures of the Manchus. One trove was the Treasury of the Board of Revenue.

The Treasury was located in the Russian sector, so Simpson went to the Russian commander in chief, General Linivitch, with information that a fortune in precious metals was secreted in the cellars of that building. The deal was for Simpson to receive a quarter share of the proceeds if his information was correct. Young Simpson's fortune would have been made, since the Treasury was said to hold bullion worth 10,000,000 to 12,000,000 francs. With two companies of Russian infantry doing the donkey work, Simpson and General Linivitch supervised a search of the cellars beneath the Treasury building; walls were broken down and tunnels dug, and after hours of labor they discovered that the Japanese had beaten them to the treasure. The latter had acquired more than 1,000,000 pounds sterling in bullion. Linivitch was furious and "accused us all of making a fool of him, of knowing from the beginning that it was a wild-goose chase. We retired from the Chinese Treasury with indecent haste."

Yet the testy Russian general did not leave Peking empty-handed. One of the most prominent Russian statesmen, Count Sergei Witte, had General Linivitch in mind when he wrote in his memoirs, "It was rumoured that Russian army officers took part in the looting, and I must say, to our shame, that our agent in Peking [presumably the Russian minister] unofficially confirmed these rumours to me. One lieutenant general, who had received the Cross of St. George for the capture of Peking, returned to his post in the Amur region with ten trunks of valuables from the looted Peking palaces. Unfortunately, the general's example was followed by other army men." The only lieutenant general on the scene was Linivitch.

If the Japanese were the craftiest among the plunderers, the French operated with an effective combination of guile and gall. They had their eye on the palace of Prince Li, which was reportedly stacked with bars of silver bullion but which unfortunately was located in the American sector south of the Tatar Wall and north of the temples of Heaven and of Agriculture. A high-ranking French officer presented himself at Minister Conger's office with a bland request for a slight adjustment in the sector lines. Without inquiring into the reasons for the request, and with his accustomed naïveté, the U.S. envoy agreed. The French immediately swarmed into Prince Li's palace and recovered 60,000 pounds sterling in silver bullion from its cellars. When word of how they had conned the Americans out of that considerable trophy got around, the French announced they were transferring part of the booty to an indemnity fund for reconstruction of the Peitang Cathedral, a curious way of financing the renovation of church property. "The consequence," one American noted, "is that there are a lot of indignant American military men wandering about trying to understand why this change in the map should have been made without consulting them."

Meanwhile, the French and the Germans were squabbling over the antique bronze astronomical instruments at the Peking Observatory; this especially distressed Mrs. Conger. "Each nation represented here is standing on its honor," she recorded in her diary. "Each one is acting for itself, and no other nation can say, 'Hold;' 'Stop;' 'Going too far.' One of the most heartrending acts to me is the removing and carrying away of the exquisite bronze instruments at the Peking Observatory. These old, historic treasures were more than valuable and beautiful. They have stood on their sentinel watch between four and five hundred years. They belong to China and can never act as honorable and beautiful a part elsewhere." She brooded also over the disappearance of the bonds which had united the various nationalities during the siege. "What war means I can now comprehend. It is selfish, destructive, cruel."

After quarreling over the relics at the observatory, France and Germany made a thieves' bargain and divided the loot. But France brooded over the injustice of it all. One of the first demands victorious France made of defeated Germany after World War I was for its share of the Peking Observatory loot.

The Franco-German squabble was decorous compared to the scenes daily and nightly enacted in the helpless city. Rape, robbery, and mayhem went on around the clock. Chinese suspected of having been Boxers or having sympathized with the movement were tortured and killed. Even Chinese innocent of any involvement in the uprising were stripped of their possessions, saw their daughters raped, watched their shops looted and their homes burned. An uncontrollable, blood-lusting madness seemed to have seized the occupation forces from many lands.

Nor was any effort made to control what many of their commanding officers regarded as a just retribution. Almost as rare was the missionary who spoke out against vengeance.

Some of the scenes as described by Bertram Simpson read like a page torn from a history of the Hundred Years' War. One was that of a plunderbund of French sailors and Russian Cossacks storming a series of warehouses. They ripped open chests, boxes, and bales in search of silver bullion or gold coins—nothing else interested them. "Rich silks and costly furs, boxes of trinkets, embroideries, women's headdresses, and hundreds of other things were flung to the ground and trampled underfoot. . . . They wanted only treasure, these men, gold if possible, something which possessed an instant value for them." Long Chinese robes made of sable were cast aside, although they would have brought thousands of dollars outside China.

Simpson was the definitive chronicler of the sack of Peking. Candidly admitting his own depredations, he took a certain satisfaction in revealing those of more important personages:

> Even some of the Ministers have made little fortunes from so-called official seizures, and there is one curious case, which no one quite understands, of forty thousand taels in silver bullion being suddenly deposited in the French Legation, and as suddenly spirited away by someone else to another Legation, whilst no one dares openly to say who are the culprits, although their names are known. Silver, however, is a drug on the market. . . .

His account continued with a description of a "huge Russian convoy" he saw traveling through the city. "It was a curious mixture of green-painted Russian army-waggons and captured Chinese country-carts, and every vehicle was loaded to its maximum capacity with loot. The convoy had come in from the direction of the Summer Palace. . . ." One cart was overloaded, so the driver casually heaved off "three beautiful porcelain vases of enormous size . . . then some bulky pieces of jade carved in the form of curious animals." The day before, at the villainous Prince Tuan's palace, "I had seen the incredible sight of thousands of pieces of porcelain and baskets full of wonderful *objets de vertu* smashed into ten thousand atoms by the soldiery who first forced their way there."

Soon the leaders of the occupation forces placed a guard around the walls on the Forbidden City and stationed pickets at the gates, but at night it was simple enough to get over the walls and into the palaces. By the end of August Simpson watched:

> lumbering military trains going back to Tientsin, laden with countless chests of loot. . . . Every place of importance, indeed,

has been picked as clean as a bone. Now that the road is well open, dozens of amateurs, too, from the ends of the earth have been pouring in to buy up everything they can. The armies thus have become mere bands of traders eternally selling or exchanging, comparing or pricing, transporting or shipping. Every man of them wishes to know whether there is a fortune in a collection of old porcelain or merely a competence, and whether it is true that a long robe of Amur river sables, when the furs are perfect and undyed, fetch so many hundreds of pounds on the London market. . . . Yet it is noticed that the very best things always disappear before they can be publicly sold. A phrase has been invented to meet the case. *"Cherchez le general,"* people say.

Peking during the first months of the occupation became a paradise for bargain hunters. Simpson told of coming across a private market established by some English soldiers at which various stolen property was on sale. "There were enamels and miniatures which must have lain undisturbed for countless years watching the Manchu emperors come and go. There were beautiful stones and snuff-boxes, and many other things." One soldier-trader showed him a Louis XIV gold belt buckle set in diamonds and rubies, "one of the countless presents made during the early days of the Jesuits in Peking." Simpson bought it for a few gold coins excusing himself on the grounds that "such things have an international value, and were not merely the sordid pickings from deserted private dwellings. Who would not rob a fleeing Emperor of his possessions?"

The Chinese could understand the principle of sacking their capital. In Asia, as well as Europe, robbing a defeated enemy was an ancient folkway, a crime sanctified by custom. They barely resented the looting of private houses and shops, accepted it with a Confucian calm and fatalism. What they could not bear was the dishonor of their womenfolk. Simpson visited several Chinese families of the burgher class, old friends of his, and they gave scarcely a thought to their vanished possessions. But they wept inconsolably because they had "lost the intangible—their honour. Each one had women of their households violated. One, with many hideous details, told me how soldiers came in and violated all his womenkind, young and old. . . ."

By the end of August the outside world learned through

newspaper correspondents of the widespread and continuing mistreatment of Peking by the occupation forces. Messages began rocketing from the chancellories and war ministries in foreign capitals: Stop the pillage; restore order. Most of those on the scene, however, could not abandon the opportunity of a lifetime. As late as October a British officer wrote home that the quality folk as well as the common soldiery were still at it; the wife of the British Minister was included in the group: "Lady Macdonald was out with a small force . . . and devoted herself most earnestly to looting."

That tidbit of correspondence forms an amusing background to the dressing down Sir Robert Hart gave Bertram Simpson on the subject of his extraofficial activities. What was right for Lady Macdonald was reprehensible in a mere employee of the Chinese Customs Service:

> My own chief eyed me very severely the other day and said that everyone reported that I had developed into a species of latter-day robber-chief and had slain hundreds of people. He said all sorts of other things, too, and I let him exhaust his oratory before I replied. Then I inquired regarding the definition of the term treasure-trove, which has become the consecrated phrase for all our many hypocrites. The generals and many of his colleagues had much treasure-trove, I said; I had some too. Of course, I admitted that if there were investigations, and everyone had to render a strict account, I would do the same; but for the time being, I wanted to know that there was going to be only one law for everyone.

Simpson considered that a telling reply because:

> some of the biggest people in the Legations are so mean and so bent on covering up their tracks that *they are using their wives to do their dirty work.* . . . I believe my chief thought for a moment that I knew something about an affair in which he was involved, for he said only one word, *"Bien,"* and looked at me in a strange way. I knew I had frightened him, and that he must have thought that if I chose to speak later on there would be trouble. I had no such intention, of course. . . .

As the pack trains loaded with booty moved in convoys to Vladivostok and Tientsin for transshipment to homes and auction rooms all over the world, those few who deplored what was happening to Peking may have found a glimmer of hope in the arrival of a German field marshal who had been appointed supreme commander of the International Relief Force. German discipline and German rectitude were celebrated—although more in Germany than elsewhere—and the Teutonic distaste for disorder of any kind was equally legendary.

Count von Waldersee was reported to have diplomatic talents and was married to an American. His disposition was said to be more congenial than most jackbooted Prussians. Even so Kaiser Wilhelm experienced much difficulty in obtaining the appointment for Waldersee. President McKinley supported it because he had a reelection campaign coming up and the then-powerful bloc of German-American voters had to be considered. The British, Russians, and Japanese all reluctantly agreed, though Britain was growing anxious over Germany's construction of a High Seas Fleet to rival the Royal Navy. France held out the longest because every loyal French liver was upset by the idea of French troops serving under the nominal command of a veteran of the Franco-Prussian War.

Waldersee and the troopships bearing the East Asiatic Corps sailed shortly before the news that Peking had been captured was received, with the Kaiser throwing a tantrum over the deflation of his hopes that a German officer would lead the forces of Christendom on the crusade. "The Kaiser," Waldersee remarked, "got it fixed firmly in his head that the Allied advance on Peking, till now regarded as impracticable on account of the rainy season, would begin under my supreme command, and mine would be the glory of capturing Peking. Now that dream was over. . . ."

For a German militarist, Field Marshal von Waldersee displayed a rather elfin sense of humor, though it tended to evaporate, judging from some of his actions, in the astringent atmosphere of North China and what he regarded as his duty to punish the Chinese. In his memoirs he recalled that the Kaiser had detached two members of the Imperial Bodyguard and "told them that they would be held personally responsible for my life and that they must never let me out of their sight. To Sergeant Major

Nasser he allotted the duty of holding me back should I ever ride too much to the front in battle." Regarding the French so reluctantly serving under his command, he observed that "they are in universal disrepute—even the Russians do not want to have anything to do with them."

Waldersee and his command arrived in early October and soon demonstrated that *Schrecklichkeit*, or calculated frightfulness, was still a part of the German military doctrine. After tarrying in Tientsin, the troops were eager for their share of the loot. A Briton who watched Waldersee march into Peking at the head of the East Asiatic Corps couldn't help sneering at their overly picturesque appearance:

> He made a sort of entry which seemed to me farcical. I only noticed that he was very old, and that the hats that have been served out to the special German expeditionary corps are absurd. They are made of straw and are shaped after the manner of the Colonial hats used in South Africa. . . . This must be some Berlin tailor's idea of an appropriate head-dress for a summer and autumn campaign in the East. The hat is quite useless, and had it been a month earlier all the men would certainly have died of sun-stroke.

The Britisher also observed that there was a resurgence of the looting and raping with the appearance of the German corps, that "as soon as night closes down, all these men fall to looting and outraging in any way they can. They say that the Kaiser, in his farewell speech to his first contingent, told the men to act in this way. They are strictly obeying orders."

The field marshal was determined to prove what German troops could do in the field and therefore undertook a number of punitive expeditions, some of them in cooperation with the British forces, which only increased the agony of the woebegone population of North China. "The only thing that worries me," he said, "is our slackness with the Chinese."

Much as he had done himself to impoverish the Chinese, Bertram Simpson was disgusted by the attitude of the German newcomers. He attended a conference at the British legation with one of Waldersee's fire-eating young staff officers. It was the latter's opinion that "could Waldersee only act as he wished, they would have proper punitive expeditions which would shoot all the headmen of every village for hundreds of miles. . . . I hated him immediately. . . . Since we all are still armed, I told him he could have satisfaction, at once if he wished, and at any number of paces he chose to name." Cooler heads intervened to prevent a duel. And his compatriots soon were marching out with the Germans to wreak vengeance on Chinese villages. Politics had dictated that decision, as Simpson learned. "It was highly important to placate the Germans because of South Africa." British policy of the moment was to play up to Germany and defeat Russia's territorial ambitions in the Far East. For that policy decision nameless Chinese villagers would die of English bullets.

What the allies had done to North China in the guise of mounting a relief expedition to Peking, the unabashed pillage which victimized thousands of innocent Chinese, was shocking even to the man who commanded General Sherman's cavalry in the march through Georgia, which to Americans epitomized all that was ruthless about warfare. Major General James H. Wilson was one of those dashing cavalry brigadiers in their twenties who had distinguished themselves in the Union Army during the Civil War, at the end of which he was commanding all the Union cavalry in the West. His troops captured Confederate President Jefferson Davis.

General Wilson, like many other old war-horses, had come out of retirement to serve in the Spanish-American War, had commanded a corps in the invasion of Puerto Rico, and had served as military governor of Cuba. Citing his travels in China fifteen years before, Wilson begged for a chance to serve with the American expeditionary force over there and, though senior to General Chaffee, agreed to assist Chaffee as his second-in-command. On July 24 Wilson got his orders to sail for China. He arrived in Tientsin two weeks after the relief of Peking.

Even with memories of devastated Georgia in mind, he was shocked by the ravages of the countryside between Tientsin and Peking inflicted by the allied advance. He noted that "the sedgy banks of the Pei Ho were reeking with the stench from the floating bodies of dead Chinamen" and that it was evident "that the allied armies had spared no Chinaman with arms, or even the appearance of arms in his hands, but had been conducting war on the old plan of kill, ravish, burn, and destroy."

Wilson was so upset by what he had seen on the way to Peking and in and around the capital itself that several weeks later, on being introduced to the allied generalissimo, Field Marshal von Waldersee, he burst forth with a denunciation of the way the European troops had behaved and compared it, not altogether accurately, with the forbearance of the American forces. Somewhat priggishly, to the European mind, he proclaimed that "while our forebears appeared to have left the customs of the Middle Ages behind when they came to America, their racial kinsmen from European countries, greatly to my surprise, seemed to return naturally to the cruelties of primitive man."

Waldersee tactfully agreed with him and replied, "Ah, General, I regret to say the Europeans, no matter whence they come, have never abandoned the cruel and outrageous practices which you so justly condemn."

Wilson was placed in command of most of the American troops occupying a sector of the Native City, with special responsibility for guarding the main gate of the Forbidden City. From his headquarters in the Temple of Agriculture, he issued instructions based on General Order No. 100 governing the conduct of U.S. armies in the field, which he considered a "just, liberal and humane code." The orders were translated into Chinese and posted in the streets. The Chinese, he later wrote, "came to understand that not only life but property of every sort was safe in the American quarter."

Certainly he did his best to prevent American troops from participating in the ongoing sack of the city. The marine legation guards had participated in the looting, but whatever they stole was confiscated, sold at public auction, and the funds diverted to the quartermaster. He was confident—unduly confident, perhaps—that "no part of the regular army got off with either silks, carvings, lacquers, or porcelains in the way of loot, and that whatever they carried back to the States they purchased at the regular daily sales in the British quarter or at the special sales of our own quartermasters." Stolen property, it seemed, was sanctified if it filtered through enough hands.

About ten days after General Wilson arrived in Peking he was given command of a joint Anglo-American force charged with driving off a sizable force of Boxers, the only remaining band of the insurgents, gathered at Patachow, also known as the Eight Temples, twelve miles northwest of the capital. He had visited the Eight Temples as a tourist in 1885 and was determined to destroy nothing of cultural value, unaware that the British had other ideas. The centerpiece of the temple area was the lustrous White Pagoda, which had been standing in all its porcelain glory for more than a millennium.

On the afternoon of September 16 General Wilson moved out with his combined force of 2,000 troops. They included two battalions of the Sixth Infantry, one battalion of the Fourteenth Infantry, a section of artillery, plus the Welsh Fusiliers and two battalions from the Indian Army of Baluchs, Sikhs, and Pathans, followed by a Hindu pack train. The force spent part of that night in bivouac, then resumed the march early in the morning to attack shortly before dawn. The Eight Temples, occupied by the Boxers, were located on the crown of the foothills. Wilson detached the Fourteenth Infantry battalion and the Baluch battalion, guided by First Secretary Squiers from the American legation and two other Americans, to circle the temple area and attack from the rear. The remainder of the force was deployed as a blocking force to cut off the Boxers' escape. The main idea was to prevent any damage to the temple area.

Wilson's simple plan was executed with little difficulty. On being attacked from the rear, most of the Boxers fled into the hills. A few who offered resistance were killed. The whole operation, or at least that part of it foreseen by Wilson, was completed by 8 A.M. He reported:

> When I reached the Boxer shrine, I found the altar still smoking with incense and the few native women that were left behind, running hither and yon with heart-rending shrieks and frenzied excitement. . . . A number of prisoners were taken, the affair was soon ended and the main body of the attacking force went into bivouac for breakfast and rest while the Baluchs went to looting. . . . Nine Boxers in uniform were killed, while many more were wounded and carried off . . . the only wounded person I actually saw was a Chinese woman who had been hit in the elbow by a stray rifle shot.

British and American officers congratulated each other pro-fusely on the surgical swiftness and efficiency of the operation.

The mood of allied amiability was, however, soon broken.

Brigadier Richard Barrow, adjutant general on General Gase-lee's staff, had accompanied the strike force as the representative of British interests. And those interests, the brigadier made plain, made it necessary that the punitive aspects of the expedition be emphasized. The Boxers had occupied the Eight Temples, and the Chinese had to be impressed with the fact that allowing Boxers to remain in their midst was punishable by destruction of their property, no matter what its cultural value.

Poor old Wilson, who had watched Georgia bleed without a quiver, was something of a Sinophile and definitely an admirer of Chinese art and architecture. He was appalled when Brigadier Barrow, "in the name of Sir Claude Macdonald," asked permis-sion to "destroy the beautiful white porcelain pagoda which had stood on the brow of a hill overlooking the plains beyond for a thousand years, and was still as fresh in appearance as the day it was built."

An argument broke out. The British not only requested but demanded the right to blow up the White Pagoda. General Wilson replied that such an act would reek of "barbarism," and he would not permit it while he remained in command of the joint force. Simple enough, replied Brigadier Barrow. Let General Wilson remove himself from command of the British troops.

What justification did the British have for such an action? Wilson demanded. The brigadier's reply was "still more amazing, for he explained at once that if the Christians did not destroy this famous Chinese temple, the Chinese, who had destroyed many missionary churches, would conclude that their gods to whom the Pagoda was dedicated were more powerful than the God of the Christians." Thus the destruction of the White Pagoda would be a service to Christianity, as well as would impress the Chinese with the futility of worshiping the gods whose counsel the Boxers had sought.

Wilson could hardly order his American troops to guard the White Pagoda and fire on any British forces which endangered it. His decision was to dissolve the joint command and return to Peking early the next day, "after which the British Minister and the British commander would, of course, be free to take such action as they might think proper."

By the time Wilson and his troopers had moved only a few miles on the road back to Peking the British contingent, "which had already undermined the foundation of the pagoda, exploded a charge of gunpowder under its base and toppled the world-famed structure." Shards of porcelain were all that remained of the White Pagoda.

By a cruel and galling irony, it was General Wilson who was charged with destroying the pagoda, and it took some effort for the American to clear his name. He related in his memoirs that "the Chinese correspondent of the London *Times*, a Mr. Middleton, I believe"—he meant Dr. Morrison, who was not usually so careless with the facts—"cabled that journal that the White Pagoda had been destroyed by my command and authority."

General Wilson demanded and received a retraction, but "the event left a most unfavorable impression in my mind, both on account of the views brought forward by the British Minister and of the unfair account the British correspondent made haste to give of it. . . . The whole performance, although but seldom mentioned, was generally regarded by the allies as an act of superstitious vandalism, alike discreditable to the British officers concerned and to the British civilization which they represented."

During the next several weeks Wilson supervised smaller expeditions sent into the countryside to pursue Boxer bands and confessed he was puzzled by the fact that "everywhere outside of the line of the allied operations they found peace, order and industry prevailing." He also obtained a disillusioning insight into the workings of colonialism at the social affairs sponsored by the American command. Officers of the other allied detachments were invited to the Temple of Agriculture for a taste of American hospitality. The regimental bands played, and punch was served as the occupation of Peking took on something of a gala air. Such occasions were revealing to Wilson, as a sturdy nonracist democrat, in the segregation of British officers from Indian officers, both commanding Indian troops. (The same social gulf, he might have been surprised to learn, separated American officers serving with the Philippine Scouts and their Filipino officers—but that was in another country.) General Wilson was struck by "the fact that the lowest ranking white officers took social precedence of even the Indian field officers [that is, majors, lieutenant colonels and colonels; a British sublieutenant thus was graded socially above a Sikh major]." Prophetically enough, Wilson believed that "if this is the common rule in the native army, it must ultimately give our British cousins a good deal of trouble before they are through with it."

Before the year ended, General Wilson closed out a long and distinguished military career by returning to the States and, over his objections, being placed on the retired list. He then wrote a book on his experiences in North China which was of little consolation to those who believed the Chinese must be severely punished for the Boxer Rebellion.

As early as September 3, the newspapers in Vienna, reflecting the world-weary cynicism on which the Viennese prided themselves, were predicting that the suppression of the Boxers would not inaugurate an "era of good feeling" (as so many less pessimistic people believed) but would result in conflict between the great powers. As their troops came to blows over the loot in Peking, their chancellories and war ministries back home girded themselves for disputes on larger matters than a stolen candlestick.

Germany, for the moment, was happily occupied in making the Chinese tremble at the sight of a field-gray uniform. German punitive columns, often accompanied by British forces, marched in all directions to teach the Chinese the error of their recent ways. At Paoting a number of town officials were executed and other reprisals carried out. Once Bertram Simpson came across a German battalion driving villagers before them like cattle. Such actions, Waldersee maintained, were "exerting a moral influence of far-reaching importance."

His colleagues were not so impressed by the efficacy of German moralizing, and the British were getting weary of leveling pagodas and temples simply because they were there. A British officer who had accompanied one of the Waldersee operations wrote home: "We fired about 2,000 rounds, mostly at inoffensive people, I believe, and killed about fifteen of them." It seemed a poor return for the money spent on high explosives. General Chaffee, to his credit, refused to allow his forces to participate in the shoot-ups.

He told a "war" correspondent that "where one real Boxer has been killed since the capture of Peking, fifteen harmless coolies or laborers on the farms, including not a few women and children, have been slain."

Waldersee, however, persevered in his vengeful mission and sent enthusiastic reports to his colleagues in Potsdam on the excellent performance of his Krupp artillery, which was splendidly effective in knocking down peasants' huts and village archways, all very useful practice for his gunners and with no enemy to shoot back at them. Kaiser Wilhelm, of course, was delighted by his reports and wrote Waldersee in his own hand, "How glad I am to hear of the satisfactory working of our heavy howitzers! Our whole Field Artillery is cock-a-hoop over this."

The Russians were particularly pleased that their German confreres were childishly content with bashing up North China villages instead of interfering with the Russians' more serious and profitable undertakings.

At the start of the Boxer Rebellion the czar's ministers saw that, like previous instances of Chinese resistance, this one could be used as a pretext for acquiring more Chinese territory. They coveted the three provinces of Manchuria. There is considerable evidence that Russia was delighted by the opportunities offered by the Boxer Rebellion and may even have intrigued to bring it about.

When the news reached St. Petersburg that the foreign legations in Peking were under siege, General Alexei Kuropatkin, the Minister of War, was delighted. According to the memoirs of Count Witte, Kuropatkin exclaimed, "I am very glad. This will give us an excuse for seizing Manchuria. We will turn Manchuria into a second Bokhara." Russia had recently "pacified" and annexed the Central Asian emirate of Bokhara.

According to reports circulating in the czar's court, Count Mikhail Muraviev, the Foreign Minister until his mysterious death shortly after the outbreak of the Boxer Rebellion, either committed suicide or died of a heart attack after a stormy interview with Czar Nicholas. Princess Radziwill and many others leaned toward the suicide theory. From her Polish estate on August 15, 1900, she wrote a confidante that Count Muraviev killed himself over the failure of his intrigue with Prince Tuan, the leading pro-Boxer at the Manchu court, which would have resulted in Russian suzerainty over Manchuria. Princess Radziwill wrote Count di Robi-lant:

> With all the means in his power, Muraviev had urged upon the Czar a policy of aggression in China, against the advice of Witte. . . . Muraviev had come to an understanding with Prince Tuan and was convinced that he could count on Tuan's friendship to obtain the gradual evacuation of all foreigners from China. At the same time the Russians would push on their railway in Manchuria, which would give itself to them *for love.* . . .
> The trick was to have been played within two years. Tuan did not keep his promises. The [Boxer] movement broke out two years too soon. . . . Muraviev saw all his diplomacy turn against what he had foreseen, and himself betrayed by Prince Tuan. . . . Not knowing how to extricate himself, he committed suicide. All this is spoken of quite openly in St. Petersburg. . . .

Whatever secret maneuvers it had undertaken before the Boxer Rebellion, Russia moved swiftly to take advantage of the Far Eastern crisis to extend its hegemony over Manchuria, which was then based on its Port Arthur leasehold and the Chinese Eastern and South Manchurian railways. Germany and Britain were so alarmed by those moves that they entered into an agreement affirming that the Open Door doctrine recently proposed by the United States must be upheld. They agreed that this principle was to be maintained "so far as they could exercise influence."

Russia was not to be dissuaded by such a feeble proclamation or by a more vigorous Japanese effort to checkmate the Russian power play. The Russian minister to Tokyo rather scornfully reported to St. Petersburg: "The immediate objective of the Japanese Government is to bring about a combination against Russia, like the one as a result of which Japan, after the war with China, was prevented from establishing herself on the Liaotung Peninsula."

With more than its usual subtlety, Russia was playing a double game. On August 18, only three days after the International Relief Force established itself in Peking, a joint council of the foreign envoys and military commanders was held in the Russian legation. The Germans clamored for revenge, citing the assassina-tion of Baron von Ketteler, and along with some of the other allies proposed that the whole Imperial City be leveled to the ground and the walls of the city razed. Russia, however, intervened on behalf of the Chinese government and played the "honest broker" role. It prevented any wholesale destruction in the capital. In return for that service it wanted China to make sizable concessions in Manchuria.

Ten days later Russia proposed to the United States that the two powers withdraw all their troops from Peking to Tientsin. The Russian note was taken so seriously in Washington that President McKinley and his Cabinet held a special all-day session composing a reply, the language of which was so turgid that newspaper correspondents were unable to report, on quick analysis, just what it meant. In effect, Washington told the Russians they agreed it would be a good idea to clear out of Peking but not until the other powers acted likewise. McKinley's biographer has summarized his attitude:

> Political interest urged the removal of Chaffee's force before the national election, but the campaign issue of "McKinley's imperialism" did not tell the whole story. The involvement in military occupation was on every count objectionable to the President. He was informed of the atrocities which some European troops inflicted on the Chinese people, and of the difficulties in supplying a large force at Peking during the winter. Both Chaffee and Conger strongly advised withdrawal. . . . Above all, the jealous quarrels among the powers made the President anxious to extricate the American troops from an equilibrium of tensions which might momentarily break into violence, invasion, and world war.

There was some substance to President McKinley's fears about an explosive aftermath to the joyously proclaimed relief of the Peking legations. The various powers involved in that crusade were tangled in conflict like a basket of snakes. France was intent on thwarting Germany. Japan regarded Russia as its next opponent in a showdown over control of East Asia. Britain and Russia came close to an open conflict regarding certain railway lines which were financed by British bondholders but over which the Russians had assigned themselves operational control. Those and other disputes were sorted out by Field Marshal von

Waldersee with a fairly capable exercise of his diplomatic talents. Waldersee perforce had become a supreme referee instead of a supreme commander.

But there was nothing Waldersee or even the foreign ministries back in the Western capitals could do about the Russian expansion in Manchuria. Shortly after the siege in Peking began, there were Boxer-fomented disturbances in Fengtien Province of Manchuria, though the other two provinces of Kirin and Heilungkiang remained quiet. The Chinese themselves provided an excuse for the Russian intervention. Several days after the attacks on the Peking legations began, an imperial decree was issued to General Tseng Chi, the Tatar governor of Fengtien, ordering him to organize a Boxer movement in his province; perhaps the Manchu court believed that disturbances in Fengtien would serve as a diversion. There was a popular basis for antiforeign activity because the people of Fengtien greatly resented the railroad building undertaken by the Russians.

Within a week the partisan bands were endangering Western and Russian interests in southern Manchuria. A Boxer-inspired mob destroyed the Protestant missions in Mukden, where the French mission was attacked and burned several days later. Russian workers and guards were attacked along the South Manchuria Railway. The partisan activity continued for several weeks until the Tatar generals who governed the Manchurian provinces were warned by the Chinese minister to St. Petersburg that the Russians were concentrating large forces at Vladivostok and Port Arthur. The elder statesman Li Hung-chang at the same time cautioned the Tatar generals against allowing the Boxers to get out of hand or foreign property to be destroyed.

By then, however, the Russians were determined to seize their opportunity to send large numbers of troops into Manchuria, not only to protect its railroad system but to claim seniority over the right to develop the vast coal and iron deposits. Eleven troopships, escorted by seven warships, carried Russian forces down the Amur to Aigun, from which point they invaded the northern province of Heilungkiang. Another invasion force rapidly engorged the province of Kirin. A Russian division based on Port Arthur swarmed over Fengtien Province and on October 1 entered the city of Mukden.

All three Manchurian provinces were now under the control of the Russians, who had all the forces needed for such an enterprise readily available in their huge Far Eastern army based on Vladivostok. Tortuous negotiations between St. Petersburg and the Chinese caretaker government in Peking followed. The Chinese, of course, were forced to make sizable concessions. Under terms of an agreement signed by General Tseng Chi and Admiral Alexeiev, the Russian governor-general of the Liaotung Peninsula, the former had to promise he would keep Manchuria "pacified" and would summon Russian troops if further disturbances occurred; all military installations in Fengtien Province not occupied by the Russians had to be destroyed in the presence of Russian officials; Russian troops would be stationed in Fengtien to protect the railroads, and the Russians would turn over the civil administration only after they were satisfied the peace would be kept; and a Russian resident would be stationed in Mukden to serve as liaison between General Tseng Chi and Admiral Alexeiev.

It was a humiliating agreement for the proud Tatar generals to suffer, as the suicide of one of them indicated. Russia in effect was establishing a protectorate over Manchuria. The appointment of a Russian resident, functioning much like a British resident in India, signified that Manchuria was being reduced to a colonial status. When the fugitive Manchu court in Sian learned of the terms of the agreement, which was concluded without its knowledge, it issued a decree for the punishment of General Tseng Chi. That decree had to be rescinded when St. Petersburg announced that the ongoing negotiations over Manchuria would be endangered if Tseng Chi were punished.

A trail of gunpowder led from Manchuria to the outside world. The eastern provinces were so rich in mineral resources, with a railway network available to develop them, that both Japan and Russia were willing to go to war over the prize. During months of haggling over a final agreement, the allies which had marched together in one moonstruck hour of international amiability to relieve their besieged legations in Peking now began choosing up sides. France supported its old ally, Russia. Britain tentatively lined up with Japan. Germany also tended to favor the Japanese cause, if only because France favored the Russian. The Japanese sense of outrage grew as the Russians increased their demands on China for larger concessions in Manchuria as a punishment for the antiforeign outbreaks lasting only a few weeks in Fengtien Province. Actually other foreigners had suffered more than the Russians in those Boxer disturbances. At any rate, what the Russians demanded as compensation for a few skirmishes between their railway guards and the Boxer bands was wildly out of proportion to the damage suffered. The Russian Foreign Minister, Count Witte, was now insisting that all the gold mines in Fengtien and all the petroleum resources of the three Manchurian provinces be turned over to Russia; that Russia be granted forest rights in the Yalu Valley; that the Chinese Eastern Railway take over all coal mines within five miles on both sides of its right-of-way; that the South Manchuria Railway lines be extended, and Russian warehouses and oil depots be established at the mouth of the Yalu and at Chinwangtao.

The Japanese were so outraged by the Russian proposals that they inquired of the British government, "How far may Japan rely upon the support of Great Britain in case Japan finds it necessary to approach Russia?" Britain becomingly waffled. Neither it nor Germany was willing to go to war with France and Russia just so Japan, instead of Russia, could enjoy the fruits of exploiting Manchuria. In any event the Russians decided against pressing their demands for an agreement which the Manchu court, with a growing confidence engendered by the progress of peace negotiations between Sian and Peking, refused to sign. The Russians, however, did not withdraw their occupation forces from the Manchurian provinces.

An uneasy sort of twilight zone, with Russia assuming squatter's rights, enveloped the Manchurian provinces for several years until the Russo-Japanese War in which the czar's forces were soundly beaten on land and sea. Then Japan took its turn squatting on Manchuria, the Balkan cockpit of the Far East.

The worthiness of the international crusade which marched with crossed banners to Peking was tested in the acid bath of historical reality—which was that of the European rivalries approaching the flashpoint of Sarajevo—and was found wanting.

*To divide China among the nations would mean
wars and a standing army large and strong. The
bitterness of the Chinese would grow deeper and
more active, and they would sting their venom
into the foreigner with a poison not yet calculated.*

—SARAH CONGER, *Letters from Peking*

17. *Peace, Indemnity, Decapitations*

In conquered Peking, the Chinese were impressed with the fact
of their defeat by the various national flags which fluttered over
the palaces and pagodas of the Imperial City. The I-luan Tien, the
palace of the dowager empress, served as the headquarters of
Field Marshal von Waldersee and echoed with the rattle of Uhlan
spurs on marble floors.

As a further demonstration that the Manchu dynasty had been
humbled, the allied command ordered a victory march through
the Imperial City. The British minister considered that gesture
necessary, otherwise, as Sir Claude put it, "the Chinese with their
infinite capacity for misrepresentations" might spread the word
that "some supernatural power had intervened, so that the Allied
forces had been affected by fear of the consequences of invading
the sacred precincts" of the Forbidden City.

Making the arrangements for the ceremonial march were
almost as difficult as agreeing on peace terms to be submitted to
the Chinese government. Besides the language barriers among the
various commands, there were touchy questions of precedence,
with the Russians and the Japanese squabbling over which
contingent should lead the parade. Perhaps it was no deficiency in
musicianship that caused the Russian band to bungle the Japanese national anthem as the Japanese trooped their colors before
the reviewing stand. There were other gaffes. The spectators
barely managed to suppress guffaws at the comic waddle of the

German contingent goosestepping along the line of march. Another band was still playing the revolutionary "Marseillaise" for the troops of republican France just as the troops of monarchist Italy passed the reviewing stand. The French colonial infantry wore such ragged and filthy uniforms they hardly lived up to the image of collaborators in a much-heralded victory. Sikhs puffing away on bagpipes also seemed more than a trifle incongruous—almost as much as if their pink-cheeked British officers appeared tootling on snake charmers' flutes.

The most elaborate description of the ceremonies was provided by Henry Savage Landor, the British war correspondent who had hastened to North China from the Philippines, where he had bestowed his imprimatur on the American regiments engaged in pacifying those islands. In his massive two-volume account of the Boxer Rebellion, which he fashioned in time to be published the following year, Landor limned the diplomatic corps gathered nearby in the reviewing stand with a not altogether admiring eye:

> In front stood the lumbering, bony figure of Sir Claude Macdonald, in an ample grey suit of tennis clothes and a rakish Panama slouch hat. He walked jauntily and with gigantic strides, moving his arms about as if preparing for a boxing match. To his right the Russian minister seemed reposeful by contrast. He was clad in dark clothes and bore himself with dignity. Next to him came the representative of the French Republic in a garb which combined the requirements of the Bois de Boulogne on a Sunday with the conveniences of tropical attire on a weekday. Mr. Conger, the American minister, strode ponderously behind, dressed in white cottons and military gaiters. The march through the Imperial City being a military affair, it seemed as if the Ministers were sulky and attached no importance to the occasion. In fact, some appeared quite bored.

Even the diplomats were capable of betraying well-bred surprise, however, during a disgraceful incident which ensued in the Forbidden City. They and some of the senior military officers were taken on a tour of the emperor's quarters. When they reached the emperor's private apartments, Landor recorded, they found some magnificent jade, solid gold vases, and lacquered coffers containing gold embroidery, jade imperial seals, necklaces, decorations, and other gewgaws.

Without shame or hesitation:

> a number of officers made direct for those coffers, smashed them open, and filled their pockets with what they could get, regardless of the feelings of the spectators, who stood aghast. A worse thing happened. Out in the court, as one of the Chinese officials who was escorting the visitors stood impassive, with his white tasseled hat and a long necklace of amber and jade with pendants, the emblem of his rank, dangling on his chest, a military officer approached him and with a bow removed the valued necklace from the Chinaman's neck, placed it round his own, and with a "Ta-ta" and graceful wave of the hand, walked away with it. A complaint was later made of this to Sir Robert Hart but, unfortunately, the necklace could never be recovered.

Ministerial minds just then were concentrated on more serious matters than the peacockery of the military. They were engaged in the protracted negotiations which would ultimately lead to peace with the Dragon Throne and meanwhile acted as conduits for the views of their respective chancelleries, most of which were at odds with one another. They also had to decide how long to keep the occupying forces, which were turning from acquiring loot to other pursuits resulting in an alarming increase in venereal disease, in Peking.

Everybody proclaimed a desire for peace, but how to arrange it was another matter. Quibbles over protocol, conflicting aims, and the intricacies of intergovernment dealing took endless hours of conversation and "exchanges of views." It was almost four months before all that confabulation resulted in a meeting between the envoys and the Chinese negotiators, who had their own problems in persuading the fugitive government in Sian that peace would be made on allied terms and that it was certain to be costly and humiliating.

The Germans, still burning with outrage over the killing of Baron von Ketteler, insisted that the members of the imperial government who promoted the Boxer cause must be punished before there could be any talks between the allied and Chinese negotiators. With the dowager empress this demand was not altogether repugnant; those who wrongly advised, no matter how intimate with her they had been, were customarily punished by death, imprisonment, or exile. When the allies demanded that nine princes and ministers closely associated with the Boxer movement be executed, however, the dowager empress temporized. She responded by degrading the nine men named by the allies and dismissing them from their posts.

The allies were particularly determined that the Moslem General Tung Fu-hsiang, whose troops from Kansu had launched the fiercest attacks against the legations, be deprived of his command, if not his life. That demand the dowager empress simply could not comply with. Tung was very popular with the people of Kansu and Shansi provinces; his troops, numbering 15,000, were the most reliable in the realm and were presently stationed around Sian. The Moslem troops were needed not only as a bargaining counter but to put down any rebellions which might erupt in North China. For the time being the Allies had to be satisfied with the dowager empress' decision to strip the general of his honors but retain him in command. In addition, he and his troops were ordered to return to their home province.

There was endless haggling at ministerial conferences in Peking over just what would be demanded of the Chinese. The Germans and, to a lesser extent, the British favored the harshest possible peace terms. The Russians in their preoccupation with Manchuria and in further consideration of the fact that Russian Orthodox missionaries had not been stationed in China were pressing for gentler terms and were generally supported by the Japanese and the Americans (for diverse reasons of their own).

The Americans alone, at least those in the State Department, tended to distrust Li Hung-chang as the chief Chinese negotiator. Secretary of State Hay considered him an "unmitigated scoundrel," while the Far Eastern desk believed that the revered elder statesman was "deeply involved" with Russia. The latter viewpoint was supported by the evidence that Li Hung-chang had practically turned Manchuria over to the Russians, but it was also true there was little he could have done to prevent the Russian take-over.

Then, too, the Americans had begun yearning for a bit of Chinese soil they could call their own. The Navy was proposing the establishment of a coaling depot on the Chinese coast. President McKinley waited until he had been reelected to suggest that the U.S. be granted a concession in the southeastern province of Fukien. None of the other allies was inclined to support this bit of Yankee presumption, Fukien having recently been designated as part of a Japanese sphere of influence. Tokyo was approached but coldly refused to consider the U.S. proposal. The rebuff was received in Washington with the sullenness of a child caught reaching for the cookie jar.

The serious negotiating began on October 10, when Li Hung-chang arrived from Tientsin and was coldly received by the German and British representatives. He called at the American legation and was received with only a degree or two more warmth. The Chinese sense of humor was a trifle too callous for Mrs. Conger. "After his official call," she related in her diary, "he asked to see the ladies and remained about thirty minutes. He seemed to think eating horse-meat during the siege quite a joke and talked and laughed about it. We told him that it was not our food that we remembered with feeling, but the killing of our people, and the effort on the part of his countrymen to take our lives."

It was obvious to the Congers that Li Hung-chang, though he had always been conciliatory toward the Western powers, was still a patriot through and through. His main concern at the moment was persuading the allies not to demand too harsh punishment of the dowager empress' intimates; Prince Tuan, after all, was the father of the heir apparent, and there were dynastic considerations to be taken into account. The business of dynastic succession, of regarding certain personages above any law except that of the venerable Manchu institution the Clansmen's Court was naturally difficult for Americans to understand. It might have been made more comprehensible if Li Hung-chang had been able to present it in a homelier context, passing down the inheritance of Standard Oil to the Rockefellers, for instance.

"I wish you would use your influence with your colleagues," Li Hung-chang murmured to Mr. Conger, "and persuade them to think that these punishments [that is, degradation] are sufficient for my people."

"I must first persuade myself," Conger stiffly replied, "that they are sufficient before I can use my influence with my colleagues in that direction."

Privately, however, the Congers were among the more enlightened Westerners who realized that the days of overt and oppressive Western influence in China were numbered and that the peace negotiations ought to take that fact into account. "China belongs to the Chinese, and she never wanted the foreigner upon her soil," Mrs. Conger wrote a relative back home. "The foreigner has never lost sight of the fact that the Chinese officials wished to show them all the concealed disrespect that they dared. . . . Heretofore, the foreign Ministers, on their official visits to His Majesty, have been escorted through a side or back gate and received in a simple, inferior throne room, poorly furnished, and arranged for this special occasion." The Tsungli Yamen, where the daily details of diplomacy were transacted, was "a dirty, cheerless, barren building." The Chinese, she believed, had nothing but concealed contempt for all foreigners and were willing to make "untold sacrifices" to rid themselves of the interlopers. Nothing, certainly not a retributive attitude, could reverse the xenophobic tides washing over China. "To divide China among the nations would mean wars and a standing army large and strong. The bitterness of the Chinese would grow deeper and more active, and they would sting their venom into the foreigner with a poison not yet calculated."

Sarah Conger was neither a trained observer nor an intellectual, but she showed a deeper understanding of the foreigners' position in China than most of the professionals—the Germans in particular. They seemed to view vast and inherently powerful China as another Alsace-Lorraine to be ground underfoot. Their representatives in Peking kept demanding that the guilty members of the imperial government be turned over to the Western powers for punishment and hoped to prolong the negotiations so the Chinese, in despair, would agree to almost anything. When Li Hung-chang sailed from Shanghai for Tientsin, the Germans considered the possibility of intercepting his ship, kidnapping him, and holding him at Tsingtao, largely because, like the American State Department, they believed he was pro-Russian. Privately Li Hung-chang regarded the Russians and Germans as "equally pernicious and brutal."

The difficulty in arranging even the most preliminary discussions between the Chinese plenipotentiaries, Li Hung-chang and Prince Ching, was that each of the "victorious" nations had its own set of capitulations to be forced upon the Chinese. France was taking an independent position, though inclined to side with Russia if necessary, and its Foreign Minister, Théophile Delcassé, proclaimed that it had "no interest in provoking or desiring the break-up of China" but wanted the "maintenance of equilibrium in the Far East." France proposed a six-point program as the basis for peace negotiations; this included the prohibition of arms imports to China, indemnities for persons and organizations suffering loss or injury during the Boxer Rebellion, dismantling of the Taku forts, and the establishment of a permanent legation guard, actually an occupation force, in Peking. The further punishment of the culprits around the dowager empress was a necessary precondition. France's allies agreed this might be a reasonable starting point in dealing with the Chinese.

The first session between Chinese and allied representatives took place on Christmas Eve. Li Hung-chang was ill and could not attend, but Prince Ching, blandly competent, was equal to confronting the eleven foreign envoys around the conference table in the Spanish legation. Much of the haggling during the previous four months had centered on the allies' demand that the Chinese representatives present credentials precisely stating that they were empowered to negotiate for the Chinese government. Therefore, Prince Ching opened the proceedings by presenting each of the ministers with an envelope containing a document plastered with the imperial seals proclaiming that he had the authority to speak for his government.

Now, Prince Ching added, would each of the ministers produce his own document proving he had the power to negotiate for his own government?

None of the ministers, obsessed as they had been with Chinese credentials, could produce such a document. The meeting then was adjourned in an atmosphere of Occidental bemusement. Somehow, they felt, they had lost face.

On January 4, 1901, the Chinese plenipotentiaries transmitted to Sian, the dowager empress, and the Grand Council the definitive terms on which peace might be arranged. The Joint Note to China, as it was termed, contained twelve main points and nineteen annexes stating just how the Chinese government was to be humbled and the Chinese people made to pay for that government's missteps. The principal provisions were:

—A mission headed by a prince of the ruling house was to proceed to Berlin and express to Kaiser Wilhelm official regrets for the murder of Baron von Ketteler. At the scene of that crime the Chinese were to erect a monument inscribed in Latin, German, and Chinese confessing to and asking forgiveness for the murder.

—An "honorable reparation" was to be made Japan for the murder of Chancellor Sugiyama of the Japanese legation.

—"Expiatory monuments" were to be erected by the Chinese government in each of the foreign cemeteries where the graves had been desecrated.

—All "official examinations" were to be suspended for five years in towns where foreigners had been massacred or mistreated.

—The "severest punishment in proportion to their crimes" was to be meted out to persons designated by the foreign powers.

—Arms and "materials serving exclusively for the manufacture of arms and ammunition" would no longer be imported.

—Twelve places between Peking and Tientsin were to be garrisoned by the foreign powers to guarantee communications between the capital and the coast.

—The Taku forts were to be leveled.

—Indemnity of foreigners and foreign governments and missionary societies for losses suffered during the Boxer Rebellion was to be arranged.

—The Legation Quarter in Peking was to be fortified if necessary, legation guards were to be maintained, and Chinese would not "have the right of residing in that quarter."

—Membership in any antiforeign society was to be made punishable by death. Furthermore, any viceroys, governors, provincial or town officials who failed to suppress any antiforeign disturbances promptly would be dismissed from their posts and never reemployed by the Chinese government.

—The Chinese Foreign Office was to be refurbished and made suitable for receiving foreign diplomats. Furthermore, court ceremonial was to be "modified," and foreign envoys calling at the Imperial Palace were to be received with an appropriate dignity. In other words, they would no longer have to enter through the back door.

In Sian the empress dowager and her advisers were taken aback by the severity of the Joint Note and more than a little irked by suggestions from their plenipotentiaries in Peking that the virtual ultimatum be complied with. If peace was not soon arranged, the Peking representatives emphasized, "the existence of the nation would be in danger." Li Hung-chang and Prince Ching did not need to add that several measures the Manchu court had feared would be imposed were not even broached by the allies.

As certain members of the Grand Council and various provincial officers who gathered in the viceregal yamen in Sian pointed out, the allies did not demand, as had been greatly feared, the partition of China. Nor was control of the Salt Administration, further industrial or mining concessions, or direct control of the armed forces demanded by the allies. Of the greatest interest to the dowager empress, as they pointed out, was the fact that the foreign powers did not demand her dethronement and replacement by the Western-minded emperor.

Nevertheless, the Grand Council, isolated as it was in remote Shensi Province from conditions in other parts of China, was inclined to argue over certain points. The plenipotentiaries were instructed to dicker, to seek gentler terms, to move the negotiations from Peking to Shanghai as a diversionary move. A further proposal, indicating the surrealism which seemed to afflict the deliberations in Sian, was that a "temporary capital" be established in the upper Yangtze Valley in which the foreign envoys would reside. The councilors in Sian seemed to believe that most of their problems would be solved if only, somehow, foreign influence could be isolated in some remote part of the realm. Li Hung-chang replied that such an idea was "nonsensical" and cautioned that "those who are not responsible can make comments easily."

Several days after the Joint Note had been forwarded to Sian, Li Hung-chang dispatched a cautionary to the Manchu court and the Grand Council declaring that postponement of a decision on acceptance of the peace terms, in hopes of obtaining a more satisfactory settlement, was dangerous:

> The demands in the Joint Note are not open to discussion; any argument would only lead to the rupture of the negotiations. . . .
> A decree has been issued ordering acceptance; if we do not sign, they would consider the Court breaking its word and the

plenipotentiaries possessing no authority. In that eventuality not only would it be impossible to request them to withdraw their troops, but also impossible to stop their military advance.

Sian yielded to Li Hung-chang's arguments and on January 10 ordered him and Prince Ching to sign the protocol. That left two other matters to be adjudicated—the punishments and the size of the various indemnities—and those negotiations took more months of bargaining.

Meanwhile, the army of occupation stayed on the scene. There were quarrels among the various detachments; morale disintegrated in the boredom of garrison duty, and there was little to do but prepare for the endless "grand reviews," with which the generals tried to overawe one another. America's brave lads in khaki were no saintlier than the other nationalities, but Mrs. Conger beamed with maternal pride over them. She was certain that the Chinese had come to like and trust the American troops and wrote in a letter home on January 5, 1901, that "Colonel Wint has just returned from an expedition into the country. The natives fled as he and his men approached but, when they learned who they were, they remained in the villages, brought food to them, and formed long lines with buckets of water for the cavalry horses." Peking shopkeepers, she added, were flocking into the American sector of the capital. "The humane way in which our army has treated the Chinese has been a bright star in America's crown." A short time later the proprietors of 2,000 Chinese shops in that sector memorialized the U.S. provost marshal that "you have opened charity eating houses, you have employed policemen to prevent crime, gambling houses and opium dens have been closed and thieves driven from the district."

In distant Sian, too, there was a resurgence of self-esteem. Some of the old resplendency had been restored to the dowager empress and her entourage. The viceregal palace was furnished in a more pleasing style, and dinners once again were served on gold plate. Tzu Hsi's fingernails had regrown to mandarin length and flashed like tiny sabers. The dynasty, her first concern, seemed to be secure again. She was delighted by reports of quarrels among her enemies, and as two English historians working from native source materials later observed, "it was becoming clear to the Empress

Dowager that along the well-worn path of international jealousies she could return unpunished, and even welcomed, to Peking."

The foreign powers *needed* her on the throne. So did her people. There was no feasible substitute for the Motherly and Auspicious Tzu Hsi. So she was able to deal confidently with the allied demands for retribution and in a surprising measure to thwart them.

The allies nominated twelve men as "deserving death." Their note delivered to the plenipotentiaries and forwarded to Sian included the following names and citations:

—Prince Tuan, "principal author of the Boxer movement, into which he dragged the Chinese government by persuading them that this was the best way of ridding China of all foreigners."

—Prince Chuang, the Peking prefect of police, accused of being "commander-in-chief of the Boxers" and responsible for a poster offering a reward for anyone who captured foreigners or killed anyone protecting foreigners.

—Duke Lan, Peking's assistant prefect of police, "one of the official chiefs of the Boxers."

—Ying Nien, also an assistant prefect, same charges as Duke Lan.

—Kang I for promoting the Boxer cause at court and being "mainly instrumental in obtaining entire freedom of action" for the Boxers.

—Chao Shu-chiao, who "lavished encouragement on the Boxers" in his official position.

—Yu Hsien, governor of Shansi Province, for reorganizing the Society of Boxers and "bringing about the Shansi massacres."

—General Tung Fu-hsiang, for collaborating with Prince Tuan and planning "the destruction of foreigners in China."

—General Li Ping-heng, nominated for posthumous degradation because he "employed his influence to get the Boxers recognized as a loyal and patriotic sect" and "from 27 July besieged the legations with troops which he had brought from Kiangsu, and later fought the allied armies on their way to Peking."

—Hsü Tung, for being "one of the Mandarins most hostile to foreigners, whose extermination he advised," for having praised the Boxers, "whose accomplice he has never ceased to be," and supporting them with all the prestige of "a great personage of the Empire and guardian of the heir presumptive."

—Hsü Cheng-yu, son of Hsü Tung, for being "equally responsible with his father" and "principal cause of the execution of the Mandarins who had endeavoured to stop the attacks on the Legations."

—Chi Hsiu, "one of the Mandarins most hostile to foreigners," who "made bloody reprisals on the party which disapproved of the attack on the Legations."

On orders from the dowager empress, the plenipotentiaries negotiated with the ministers in Peking for reduction of some of the sentences. During February, 1901, the Council of Ministers functioned as a high court of justice to determine which of the twelve men in the "deserve death" category might be spared. As members of the imperial family, Prince Tuan and Duke Lan could not be treated like ordinary mortals; only the Clansmen's Court, presumably, could exact the extreme penalty. On behalf of some of the others the right to commit suicide was argued. A particularly vigorous effort was made to spare the life of Chao Shu-chiao, who apparently had had little real effect on the growth of the Boxer movement. Petitions were sent from all over China to the viceroys of the Yangtze region asking their intervention on behalf of Chao Shu-chiao. The Council of Ministers might well have been lenient in his case, but most of the envoys were still in a hanging-judge mood.

After a number of exchanges between Peking and Sian, it was agreed that Prince Tuan and Duke Lan—though probably the most vociferous in promoting the Boxer cause, though without their patronage the Boxers could not have made their case before the dowager empress, though they had been instrumental in causing the execution of anti-Boxer or moderate officials—would not be put to death. As monarchies, Japan, Germany, Russia, Italy, Spain, and Belgium were required to sympathize with dynastic considerations; killing people of royal blood had always set a dangerous precedent, and the world had never been quite the same since Louis XVI and Marie Antoinette were sent to the guillotine.

The allies therefore reduced considerably their demands for the punishment of what later would be called war criminals. Prince

Tuan and Duke Lan were exiled to Turkestan for life. (Prince Tuan's son, the fifteen-year-old heir apparent, was disinherited by the dowager empress, not because the allies demanded it but because she was irked by his loutish behavior.) Yu Hsien, Ying Nien, Hsü Cheng-yu, and Chao Shu-chiao were sentenced to decapitation. Prince Chuang was to be allowed to commit suicide. Kang I, Hsü Tung, and Li Ping-heng were posthumously degraded. Chi Hsiu and General Tung Fu-hsiang were dismissed from the imperial service. At the last moment Ying Nien and Chao Shu-chiao were reprieved, after a fashion, and along with Prince Chuang allowed to commit suicide. Only Yu Hsien and Hsü Cheng-yu, finally, were decapitated. By the end of February all the sentences had been carried out.

Although two of the enforced suicides turned out to be rather messy affairs, Prince Chuang ended his life with a stately dignity that was felt to be a credit to all, in a manner worthy of the Manchu tradition.

The business of informing Prince Chuang that he had been nominated as one of the sacrificial goats for the failure of the dowager empress' policies was conducted with the prescribed delicacy and indirection. Prince Chuang had retired to a village in the southern part of the province with his No. 1 concubine and his favorite son to await Tzu Hsi's verdict. Imperial Commissioner Ko Pao-hua appeared at the prince's house early one morning, at first denying that he brought word of the dowager empress' decision. They talked of other affairs; then Ko Pao-hua wandered off to the rear of the house and selected a room in an abandoned temple, from the beam of which he slung a strong silk cord. Ko Pao-hua then went back and read the imperial decree to Prince Chuang.

"So it is suicide," Prince Chuang remarked. "I always expected that they would not be content with anything less than my life." He turned to his son and said, "Remember that it is your duty to do everything in your power for your country; at all costs, these foreigners must not be allowed to possess themselves of the glorious Empire won for us by our ancestors."

Prince Chuang then followed the imperial commissioner to the temple in a rear courtyard, where he glanced up at the cord hanging from the beam and complimented Ko Pao-hua, "Your

Excellency has indeed made most admirable and complete arrangements." The direct descendant of Nurhachu, the conqueror of the Ming dynasty, then strangled himself.

The other two condemned men, Chao Shu-chiao and Ying Nien, were lamentably unable to summon up a similar dignity and serenity for making their exits. Ying Nien spent a whole day lamenting his fate and the injustice of it all, then swallowed mud and choked himself to death. The court chroniclers agreed that his method was graceless and unbecoming to a Manchu aristocrat. The death of Chao Shu-chiao turned into black comedy. He took poison immediately after the death sentence was read to him; but it seemed to have little effect, and he continued chatting, Roman-style, with friends who gathered in his chamber. The governor of Shensi, who was assigned to supervise the affair, became impatient and ordered that a strong dose of opium be administered. Chao Shu-chiao only became more animated in recalling happier times for his friends. He was then given a heavy dose of arsenic that subjected him to agonizing pain. A squad of eunuchs finally put an end to his suffering by stuffing twists of rice paper into his nose and mouth.

After the punishment or degradation of the principal pro-Boxer conspirators, the Council of Ministers on March 31 presented a much longer list of lesser personages, ranging from princes of Mongolia to petty local officials, who were to be dealt with. They had the bad luck to be presiding over districts in Chekiang, Szechuan, Hunan, Kiangsi, and Kweichow, where there had been short-lived disturbances. One hundred and nineteen were given sentences ranging from death to official reprimand. Most of them could have escaped punishment simply by fleeing to the interior, but all of them submitted to the edicts of Sian and thereby testified to a strong residual loyalty to the Dragon Throne.

During the rest of the spring and throughout the summer of 1901 the Council of Ministers and the Chinese plenipotentiaries debated the indemnity question. They had to decide how much China would have to pay, the length of time in which payment would be made, and the revenues from which the indemnity would be taken.

China was bankrupt, had been for years, but only the United States was willing to go easy in this regard, knowing that the indemnity would be sweated out of the already-overburdened Chinese masses.

W. W. Rockhill took over as American plenipotentiary during the fiscal negotiations while Minister Conger and his family went home on leave. On instructions from Washington Rockhill proposed that the total indemnity be no more than 40,000,000 pounds sterling ($200,000,000 at the current rate of exchange). That, the State Department's economic advisers believed, was the outside limit of China's ability to pay.

Some of the European nations were outraged at so low a figure. France and Germany, accustomed to levying heavy indemnities on each other when one side or the other lost a war, were particularly loud in their protests against the American proposal.

"Only America," complained Field Marshal von Waldersee in tones better suited to the Little Match Girl, "seems to desire that nobody shall get anything out of China."

At a council session on April 25 the various allied representatives finally got down to totting up their combined demands, including occupation costs. They came to just over 67,000,000 pounds sterling. On May 7 the figure was increased to 67,500,000 pounds sterling.* That came to 450,000,000 taels in Chinese gold. Some of the allies came around to the American view that such a sum would be insupportable, but Germany and Britain held out against any charitable inclinations. Sian was warned that if it wasted time haggling, the amount would only be increased by additional costs run up by the occupation forces. On May 26 an Imperial edict guaranteed payment of 67,500,000 pounds.

China was given thirty-nine years in which to pay the Boxer indemnity. Its maritime customs were to be placed under foreign control to facilitate collection of the damages, import duties were to be increased to 5 percent, a special tariff was to be placed on the inland merchandise traffic largely borne by junks and sampans, and new taxes were to be levied on such imports as flour, cheese, soap, spirits, and clothing. Every peasant in the land would pay for the excesses of a relatively few Boxers and their collaborators in the Forbidden City.

Elsewhere hailed as a righteous exaction, the Boxer indemnity seemed especially outrageous to the aging Mark Twain, who had

---

* About $335,000,000 at the 1900 rate of exchange.

recently joined the Anti-Imperialist League and who was now antireligious to the extent that he considered the Protestant clergy no more than apologists for the "dollar civilization." Introducing the young Winston Churchill on his first American lecture tour, Twain remarked that "England sinned when she got herself into a war in South Africa, just as we have sinned in getting into a similar war in the Philippines." A few weeks later he wrote a salute to the twentieth century for a New York newspaper beginning, "I bring you the stately matron named Christendom, returning bedraggled, besmirched, and dishonored from pirate raids in Kaio-Chou, Manchuria, South Africa and the Philippines, with her soul full of meanness, her pocket full of boodle, and her mouth full of pious hypocrisies. Give her soap and a towel, but hide the looking-glass." A short time later in a magazine article titled "To the Person Sitting in Darkness," he attacked the "Blessings-of-Civilization Trust," whose managers he identified as President McKinley, Joseph Chamberlain, the Kaiser, and the czar, and its emissaries, the Christian missionaries, whom he pictured as marching forth under the double standard of the cross and the black flag. He charged the missionaries with acting as collectors of the Boxer reparations and with demanding the life of a Chinese for each Christian killed during the uprising. Neither charge was true. He ended his tirade with an atrocious pun which he placed in the mouth of a "typical" missionary: "Taels I win, Heads you lose." Twain's hyperbole served no useful purpose. There was more truth and justice in Nathaniel Peffer's summation that the conclusion of the Boxer episode was "still another sore to fester until it ultimately released its pent-up poison in the years from 1925 to the Chinese intervention in Korea in 1950."

Despite its most famous writer's public distress, America ended its connection with the Boxer Rebellion on a note of much-needed grace. It devoted its share of the Boxer indemnity to a special account out of which thousands of Chinese students, for almost half a century, were educated in the United States. The coming of Chairman Mao, of course, ended that arrangement.

Look at those colored glasses in the windows and these beautiful paintings. They were all spoiled by the foreign troops in 1900. I don't intend to have it repaired as I don't want to forget the lesson I have learned and this is a good reminder.

—DOWAGER EMPRESS *to*
PRINCESS DER LING

18. *Tzu Hsi Returns to the Dragon Throne*

To those who struggled to get the Chinese giant back on his feet after the Boxer Rebellion, it seemed essential to restore the dowager empress and the Manchu court to their rightful places in the Forbidden City. Until the court returned from Sian, there would be no strong central government, and the country, in effect, would be ruled by provincial viceroys of varying quality. Tzu Hsi, however, had no intention of returning to Peking until the vermilion sealing wax had been affixed to various treaties and protocols, and she was able, meanwhile, to remain aloof from the haggling over terms. Perhaps, too, she was wise enough to realize the longer she stayed away from the capital, the quicker certain passions, not least of all the foreigners' thirst for revenge, would subside.

Nor was she eager to view what the allied soldiery had done to mar the ancient perfection of the Forbidden City, its palaces and gardens. She knew that the Americans had been diligent in protecting certain of her possessions, but as she later told Princess Der Ling, "All the valuable things at the Sea Palace had been taken away, and someone had broken the fingers of my white jade Buddha, to whom I used to worship every day. Several foreigners sat on my throne and had their photographs taken." She worried over the safety of the vast treasure secreted in the Winter Palace, which (according to Mrs. Conger) the Americans had also taken under their protection and was to be returned intact. On the other hand, she would be glad to leave Sian, where court intrigues were thickening and the discipline of the eunuchs had eroded despite an almost daily ritual of wholesale whippings. "When I was at Sian I was just like being sent into exile," she complained several years later to Princess Der Ling. "Although the Viceroy's Yamen was prepared for us, the building was very old, damp and unhealthy. The Emperor became ill. . . ."

Late in June, 1901, an imperial decree signed by the otherwise shadowy emperor announced that the dowager empress had decided to return to the Forbidden City:

"Our Sacred Mother's advanced age renders it necessary that we should take the greatest care of her health, so that she may attain to peaceful longevity; a long journey in the heat being evidently undesirable, we have fixed on the 19th day of the Seventh Moon [September 1] to commence our return journey and are now preparing to escort Her Majesty by way of Honan."

What was labeled a Penitential Decree was also issued, supposedly to apologize for and explain the events of the previous summer. It was something less than a *mea culpa* the allies might have hoped for. The decree admitted "disastrous mistakes" had been made, but assigned them to other than imperial personages; the flight to Sian was described as a "Western tour" of the provinces. In bold defiance of what had become common knowledge, the decree asserted: "There are ignorant persons who believe that the recent crisis was partly caused by our government's support of the Boxers; they must have overlooked our reiterated Decrees of the 5th and 6th Moons, that the Boxers should be exterminated and the Christians protected. Unfortunately these rebels and their evil associates placed us in a position from which it was impossible to escape. . . ."

The dowager empress and her court claimed to have been appalled by the attacks on the Peking legations and regarded with horror the possibility that any foreigners might be harmed. "To the Throne's strenuous efforts is really due the avoidance of such a dreadful catastrophe, and the gifts of wine, fruit and watermelons to the besieged Legations were an indication of Her Majesty's benevolent intentions." The supposedly penitential document also took note of the failure of the southern provinces to join in the late struggle. "Caring nothing for the innumerable difficulties which beset our Throne, they stand idly by, contenting themselves with delivering oracular opinions and catch-words, and they even go so far as to reproach their sovereign, the father of his people." As in the case of most such self-serving documents, it was signed by the powerless emperor, but the real author was the empress dowager.

Shortly before Tzu Hsi's triumphal procession appeared before the walls of Peking, the man largely responsible for making it possible, Li Hung-chang, died in the capital. Of lowly origin, his career bore testimony to the best qualities of the examination halls, in which all aspirants to office had to prove they were worthy of advancement on the basis of ability and aptitude, although the tests were formulated on the ancient wisdom. The system stultified any progressive tendency in education, but it did guarantee that capable men rose on their merits and was one of the main buttresses of the long supremacy of the Manchus. Foreigners, who perhaps did not understand that Li Hung-chang was as antiforeign as any Boxer hetman but was worldly and intelligent enough to know that mere belligerence would not drive away the uninvited guests from the outside world and met such incursions with intellectual suppleness and the delaying tactics of a Fabius Cunctator, greatly mourned his passing.

The U.S. minister and his wife joined other residents of the foreign colony in paying their respects to the great statesman. Viewing it all through eyes accustomed to the austerities of Mary Baker Eddy's church, Mrs. Conger was astounded at the complexity of Chinese mourning procedures when she called at the 175-room ducal palace in which Li Hung-chang died. "We passed through court after court filled with people and with quantities of gifts. . . . The sounds of wailing music, the coarse white sackcloth of the mourners and servants, the many banners, the food, the altar with its shrine and shrine accessories, all combined to make the scene weird, yet so intense that we partook of the spirit of the solemn occasion. . . . The ceremonies were prolonged into days and weeks." Then, at last, a lengthy cortege began the journey to South China, where Li Hung-chang was to be buried in his birthplace, with shrines and pavilions especially erected along the route:

Any language would beggar a description of this wonderful procession bearing the remains of Viceroy Li Hung-chang out of Peking. It extended for miles and was brilliant in its colorings.

. . . There were rich silk and satin embroidered canopies, umbrellas, chairs and emblems representing high Imperial, official and scholarly honors. The great number of uniformed bearers and escorts were in accordance with this Viceroy's high rank. . . . This whole picture was, to me, out of the realm of reality, and yet I knew that each part of this wonderful procession held its deep meaning and was real to these people. I mentally cried out, "Halt! Tell me!"

The remains of the great compromiser had hardly been borne out of the imperial capital when the still-lively lady who headed the House of the Manchus arrived on January 7, 1902. There had been several delays before the journey finally began on October 24, 1901, and was completed by a wonderful variety in modes of transportation—palanquin, sedan chair, railway train, and barge. First the departure was set back from September 1 by reports of roads ruined by the summer rains. Then there were urgent consultations with the court astrologers, whose readings governed the dowager empress in such matters.

Magistrate Wu Yung, who had become an imperial favorite by taking charge of the court's living arrangements, serves as our eyewitness to the ceremonial progress from Sian to Peking. It was like a city on the move. Although the dowager empress had fled with a handful of the faithful, she was returning with a following and in a style which advertised that the dynasty was flourishing again. She and the members of the ruling house were carried in sedan chairs which formed the nucleus of a procession including 2,000 carts. The baggage wagons transported not only the court's personal effects, but the tributes of silks, jade, furs, and bullion which had come in from the provinces during the stay in Sian. Ten thousand varicolored banners, with imperial yellow predominating, whipped above the cortege. Preceding and following the caravan were hundreds of mounted Manchu Bannermen. Mounted trumpeters galloped ahead to signal the advent to towns and villages scattered through the grayish-brown mountains of western China.

Every night along the way there were feasting and theatricals. Meetings of the Grand Council were held in provincial capitals to impress the outlanders. It was a happy reversal of the "defeated jackals" appearance the dowager empress and her retinue had presented on the outward journey a year earlier. Tzu Hsi wanted reports of the sumptuous and leisurely journey to get back to Peking and the foreigners. The foreign colony must understand that she was returning not in repentance but in triumph.

The first stages of the journey were along narrow mountain roads, and the Imperial Chariot, as the caravan was styled, was a spectacle of barbaric splendor imprinted, like the delicate brush-work of a Chinese watercolor, against the background of barren mountainsides. "Men looked like ants," as Wu Yung described the procession many years later. "A wooden bridge was built over the river. The water was white and clear; there were no waves, and the sky could be seen as in a mirror. The houses on the hillsides looked like stars. The Imperial outing was as pleasant as the hunting trips of the Han dynasty."

During the stopover in Kaifeng, Tzu Hsi's birthday was celebrated with nightlong fireworks, pageantry, and theatricals. The celebration was dampened for some when word was received of Li Hung-chang's death, upon which the dowager empress decreed that a shrine be erected to his memory in the capital. It was an unprecedented honor, never before conferred on any Chinese subject under the Manchu dynasty.

At the crossing of the Yellow River there were the usual propitiatory sacrifices to the river god. Local officials were waiting at the crossing with a magnificent barge constructed for that one trip across the wide river. According to a contemporary description:

> Tzu Hsi and the ladies of the court crossed the Yellow River in a barge expressly built for the occasion, shaped like a dragon and richly gilded and lacquered. Garlands of flowers floated on the surface of the river, and on the banks the imperial standards rose proudly against the autumn sky. Bonzes [priests] intoned litanies and burnt incense in honor of the Dragon who rules over the waters. On land, the roads were levelled and broadened to make travelling easier. The countryfolk came in crowds to witness the unaccustomed sight of the Old Buddha and the Son of Heaven moving in state across the empire.

The enthusiasm of her reception along the way, the bracing autumn air, and even more the knowledge that she was going home to her palaces, her remaining treasures, and her private shrines persuaded her to make one of the few quasi-democratic gestures of her long reign. Formerly foreigners were forbidden to watch her progress through the streets of the capital on the grounds that her personal splendor would be diminished if her image was reflected in the naked eyeball of a barbarian. That decree was rescinded. She announced that the foreign colony would be permitted to witness her arrival, further that, immediately afterward, the various ministers would be received by the emperor—but not by herself—in the main throne room. Few rulers have ever been more skillful than Tzu Hsi at what might be termed a controlled graciousness; she was grand mistress of the regal nuance.

The last stage of her homeward journey, by an irony which seems to have escaped her, was by railway. It was the construction of the railroads which had allowed the Boxers to focus a passionate resentment in Shantung and Chihli provinces, where so many bargemen had been thrown out of work by the railroads. Now she was about to travel by train for the first time in her life. Perhaps it could have been regarded as her obeisance to what an American poet called the Locomotive God.

Her railroad journey was divided into two parts, the first from Chengting to Fengtai on the Belgian-operated line, the second from Fengtai to the Peking city walls on a British train. The Imperial Chariot, now railborne, was itself divided into several sections. The first carried Tzu Hsi and her retinue in cars upholstered in yellow silk. They were attended by the grand councilors, eunuchs, and other servitors. The dowager empress' private coach contained a throne to assure the maintenance of the Sacred Mother's dignity. She was so pleased with the Belgian railway official who supervised those appointments that she presented him with the Order of the Double Dragon, Second Class.

Just after the whole Imperial Chariot was transferred to the British railway at Fengtai, she began worrying over whether she would arrive in Peking at the hour the court astrologers decided would be the most auspicious. Though the rail line had been brought into the city to a new terminus from Machiapu during the past year, the dowager empress insisted that she and her whole entourage must detrain outside the city walls and enter the capital in the traditional style; an empress stepping down from a railroad car somehow lacked the panache of an entrance on a palanquin, and Tzu Hsi was always acutely aware of the need to be impressive. The necessary awe of the populace could be secured only by expert staging, and David Belasco himself could have learned from her. So, in full panoply, heralded by yard-long trumpets, under a canopy of fluttering banners, the Imperial Chariot rolled through the Yung Ting Gate, then up the broad thoroughfare through the Chinese City and through the Chien Men. The tower over that gateway had been destroyed during the siege and had not yet been restored. On a sort of balcony extending over the Chien Men the more eminent members of the foreign colony had gathered as on a reviewing stand. The Imperial Chariot arrived exactly on the hour prescribed by the astrologers.

Most of the foreigners witnessing her arrival from their perch overlooking the Chien Men must have experienced strongly ambivalent feelings. They dutifully waved and cheered despite one of Peking's winter dust storms. But many knew her for a bloody-minded tyrant who only eighteen months earlier had tried to destroy them. Describing the scene for a daughter back home, Mrs. Conger, however, was inclined to take a more cheerful and forgiving view. To her it was a "wonderful" occasion:

> For months, there had been extensive preparations made by the Chinese to get everything in "proper" order for the return of the Court, and they surely did well. Paint, plaster and decorations upon the old and the new buildings made them smile a bright, cheery welcome to Their Majesties. As the massive gateway towers had been burned, in their place were improvised towers bedecked with royal emblematic decorations in the Imperial colorings. Between the lines of Chinese soldiers, who were kneeling with bowed heads, the Court passed with more than the usual display and ceremony.

To a watching Italian the pageantry of the imperial return was so impressive it erased the bitter and tragic memories of the siege, at least for the moment. Through the blowing dust, he watched the Manchu Bannermen trot up in column of fours on their small spirited horses, followed by a cavalcade of Chinese officials wearing their gorgeously brocaded official robes, and "finally the Imperial palanquins, which advanced at an almost incredible speed between two ranks of kneeling soldiers. The higher the rank of the person carried in the palanquin, the faster he should go. The Court chairs seemed to move as fast as the Tartar cavalry."

The procession halted at a shrine set in the Chien Men according to the ritual prescribed by the Book of Rites. Both the dowager empress and the emperor dismounted from their palanquins to burn incense and recite prayers in the tiny temple dedicated to the tutelary god of the Manchus.

As she stepped to the ground, Tzu Hsi looked up at the walls blackened by the fire which destroyed the gate towers, then at the foreign colony collected on the ramparts forty feet above her. Don Rodolfo, a young Italian midshipman, later described the scene:

> The eunuchs surrounding her appeared to be trying to get her to move on, as it was not seemly that she should remain there in full view of everybody. But the Empress was not to be hurried, and continued to stand between two of her ladies, who held her up under the arms on either side, not because she needed any support, but because such is the custom in China, when a great personage appears in public on a ceremonial occasion. The Emperor stood and waited a little distance away.
>
> At last she condescended to move, but before entering the temple where the bonzes were all ready to begin the ceremony, she stopped once more and, looking up at us, lifted her closed hands under her chin, and made a series of little bows.
>
> The effect of this gesture was astonishing. We had all gone up on the wall in the hopes of catching a glimpse, as she passed, of the terrible Empress whom the West considered almost an enemy of the human race. But we had been impressed by the magnificence of the swiftly moving pageant, and by the beauty of the picturesque group, in palanquins of yellow satin flashing with gold. Something told us that the return of the Court to Peking marked a turning point in history, and in our breathless interest we forgot our resentment against the woman who was responsible for so much evil.

The foreigners applauded what they took to be a gracious gesture, a hand reached out in reconciliation, but was actually a performance by one of the finest actresses of her time. "The Empress appeared pleased. She remained there for a few moments longer, looking up and smiling." She had held center stage for just the dramatically effective amount of time, a Bernhardt making her entrance in *L'Aiglon*; then disappearing from view, as though behind a swiftly falling curtain. How well she knew how to camouflage the humiliation of her defeated attempt to rid China of the foreign presence; she had returned in triumph, not in shame over the agony she had caused.

Once the ceremonies were out of the way, she hurried to the inner palace, according to the comptroller of her household, and "commanded the eunuchs to commence digging up the treasure which had been buried there at the time of her flight; she was gratified beyond measure to find that it had indeed remained untouched."

Three weeks later, on February 7, 1902, she made another gesture of reconciliation by inviting the ladies of the diplomatic corps to the Forbidden City. This time they were permitted to enter through the front gate and were received in the Pavilion of Tranquil Longevity. Sir Claude and Lady Macdonald having departed for their home island, Mrs. Conger was now Madame Dean of the envoys' ladies. The dowager empress was seated at a slightly higher level behind a table on which a coral scepter had been placed. After bowing three times, Mrs. Conger delivered her little speech and expressed the hope that the recent "painful events" would be forgotten and that "China will join the great sisterhood of nations in the grand march of international progress."

Tzu Hsi gave one of her better performances that day. In a tremulous voice she told Mrs. Conger through an interpreter, "I regret and grieve over the late troubles. It was a grave mistake, and China will hereafter be friends to the foreigners. No such affairs will happen again. China will protect the foreigner, and we hope to be friends in the future."

She granted a second audience on February 27 and presented Mrs. Conger with a jade statuette. Social intercourse between the palace and the Legation Quarter increased during the ensuing months. Globe-trotting Americans of high rank—notably Lieutenant General Nelson A. Miles, his wife, and a party of nine and Admiral "Fighting Bob" Evans and a party of equal size—made

Peking the first stopoff on their tours of the Orient. All the Americans, of course, insisted on being presented at court, having their photographs taken in the Forbidden City, and indulging themselves in the usual touristic pleasures. With some reason, the dowager empress began to feel that her hitherto-sacred privacy was being invaded by too many large, genial, well-meaning Americans. Peking was not Coney Island; the Forbidden City was not Niagara Falls; the dowager empress was not a sideshow attraction.

Privately Tzu Hsi expressed the opinion that Mrs. Conger was a little too demanding in her matiness. To her young lady-in-waiting, Princess Der Ling, she remarked that Mrs. Conger was "very nice" but didn't comprehend the "etiquette" of a superior civilization, that she didn't understand that "we are too polite to refuse anyone who asks favors in person." At the same time she was very conscious of the image she presented to the world. Before the Boxer Rebellion, she said, "I was just like a piece of pure jade; everyone admired me for what I had done for my country, but the jade has a flaw in it since this Boxer movement and it will remain there to the end of my life. . . . You need not feel sorry for me for what I have gone through, but you must feel sorry that my fair name has been ruined. . . ."

In that cause she suffered through what the rest of the world would experience later in the century: the bulldozer charm of Americans intent on creating goodwill, the overpowering geniality, the breezy equalitarianism, the crushing friendliness of the Yankee bridging gaps which it took centuries of effort to create. With heroic resignation she even allowed the princesses of the court to take "tiffin," as the increasingly sophisticated Mrs. Conger called it, at the American legation.

Despite the lacquered smile she presented foreigners, the dowager empress was not entirely regenerate in looking back on the Boxer Rebellion. To her it was more a terrible mistake than a terrible tragedy. On the palace grounds there was a magnificent marble boat which the allied troops had despoiled and which she would not permit to be renovated. "Look at those colored glasses in the windows and these beautiful paintings. They were all spoiled by the foreign troops in 1900. I don't intend to have it repaired as I don't want to forget the lesson I have learned and this is a good reminder."

Her hatred of Christianity and its works was never abated. She believed that the missionaries were stealing the spirits of her people, that they drugged the Chinese to convert them. "Missionaries," she affirmed, "also take the poor Chinese children and gouge their eyes out, and use them as a kind of medicine." The Princess Der Ling, having been reared and educated abroad, gently tried to argue the old lady out of her fantasies by relating how the missionaries fed and clothed the poor, educated their children, and provided medicine.

The dowager empress replied with asperity:

> That may be all right for them to help the poor and relieve their suffering. For instance, like our great Buddha Ju Lai, who fed the hungry birds with his own flesh. I would love them if they would leave my people alone. Let us believe our own religion. Do you know why the Boxer rising began? Why, the Chinese Christians were to blame. The Boxers were treated badly by them, and wanted revenge. Of course that is always the trouble, with the low class of people. They went too far, and at the same time thought to make themselves rich by setting fire to every house in Peking. . . .
>
> These Chinese Christians are the worst people in China. They rob the poor country people of their land and property, and the missionaries, of course, always protect them, in order to get a share themselves. Whenever a Chinese Christian is taken to the Magistrate's Yamen, he is not supposed to kneel down on the ground and obey the Chinese law as the others do, and is always rude to his own government officials. Then these missionaries do the best they can to protect him, whether he is wrong or not, and believe everything he says and make the magistrate set the prisoner free. . . .
>
> I know the common class of people become Christians, but I don't believe any of the high officials are Christians.

Evidently Tzu Hsi wasn't too certain about this because she lowered her voice almost to a whisper when she added, "Kang Yu-wai [the reform leader of 1898] tried to make the Emperor believe that religion. No one in my house shall believe as long as I live."

She had all the confidence of an absolute monarch that she

knew what was best for the Chinese people. The humiliations of 1900 were not so deeply imprinted that she lost her lofty self-esteem. She believed that she came out best in any comparison of her reign with that of the late empress of Britain and the realms beyond. "I have often thought that I am the most clever woman that ever lived and others cannot compare with me." She didn't think Queen Victoria's life was "half so interesting and eventful as mine." Few who had heard the mildest gossip of the Manchu court would dispute that claim. She added:

> My life is not finished yet and no one knows what is going to happen in the future. I may surprise the foreigners some day with something extraordinary and do something quite contrary to anything I have yet done. England is one of the great powers of the world, but this has not been brought about by Queen Victoria's absolute rule. She had the able men of parliament behind her at all times and of course they discussed everything until the best result was obtained, and she would sign the necessary documents and really had nothing to say about the policy of the country.
>
> Now look at me. I have 400,000,000 people all dependent on my judgment. Although I have the Grand Council to consult with, they only look after the different appointments, but anything of an important nature I must decide myself. . . .

During the eight years of life remaining to her after the Boxer Rebellion, Tzu Hsi to some extent redeemed herself in Western eyes. She allowed the Manchu princesses and other ladies of the court to mingle socially with Westerners outside the palace walls. Mrs. Conger wore down her resistance to the point that sending some of the younger princesses to visit the St. Louis Exposition was seriously considered. She and other Western women were particularly proud of having persuaded the ladies of the Manchu court to establish seventeen girls' schools in Peking, just one result of all those tiffins and teas at the American legation. By the time the Congers left Peking in 1905 Mrs. Conger prided herself on having established a "genuine friendship" with the dowager empress. Tzu Hsi never changed her mind about Christianity, however, and to the end of her life kept asking, "Why don't those missionaries stay in their own country and be useful to their own people?"

No doubt that question had been asked many times in China during the past centuries. It would not have occurred to those thousands of missionaries who cheerfully, for the most part, dedicated their lives to the cause of "saving" China. The China mission by all odds was the most extensive, the most costly, the most diligently pursued project ever assumed by organized religion. To the objective or agnostic observer, it may also have been the most futile. Like a hot wind from Mongolia, Mao withered Christ and all the works of His followers overnight. Christianity had been only an irritant in the eye of the great Buddha. From the Christian viewpoint, however, that wouldn't be true. The Chinese souls saved for Christ, whatever their number, justified the incalculable sacrifice.

Old China hands, a rather irreligious lot, generally claimed that the missionaries' flocks were composed of "rice Christians." The Boxer Rebellion, however, proved that many Chinese were dedicated to the faith into which they had been proselytized. They suffered far more by any standard than their Western preceptors. The defense of the Peitang Cathedral would have crumbled without them. About 250 missionaries, including 50 of their children, were killed during the Boxer risings; 3 of those were Catholic bishops and 31 were Catholic priests, the rest Protestants. Compare that to the approximately 30,000 Catholic converts and 2,000 Protestant ones killed by the Boxers and their partisans, and the casualty list alone attests to the price paid by Chinese Christians for their faith.

Martyrdom had always been one of the pillars of the Christian mission to China. Incredible as it may seem to the Christian world of the 1970's, there was always a sufficiency of young men and women eager to hazard their lives to spread the Christian faith. That spirit had endured for centuries, beginning, according to the early traditions of the church, with one of the Twelve Apostles. St. Thomas, it was recorded, traveled to China via India when the original Disciples left the Holy Land to spread the faith they had learned from Christ Himself. The legend that St. Thomas was the first missionary to China, however, rests on a narrow foundation. The principal authority was St. Francis Xavier, who made a pilgrimage to the supposed tomb of St. Thomas at Meliapur on the southeast coast of India, and wrote: "Many people say that Saint Thomas the Apostle went to China, that he made many Christians. . . ." The archives of the Armenian Church are also supposed to contain evidence of St. Thomas' journey to China. St. Thomas did travel widely through the Roman Empire, and it would have been possible for him to journey to India, then by junk from the Indian coast to China.

At any rate Christianity established a foothold in China very early in the first millennium after Christ; one Nestorian chronicler recorded that there was a metropolitan see in China in the eighth century, and the first members of the Society of Jesus reached Peking in 1601. Until the Jesuit presence was established, however, the missionary in China was more the figment of legend than verifiable fact. During the three centuries between the Jesuit arrival and the Boxer Rebellion, both the Catholic and Protestant missionaries often suffered privation and sometimes martyrdom. Saving the hundreds of millions of Chinese from Buddhism, from their countless domestic gods and the unseen spirits of land, air, and water, was one of the prime preoccupations of the Christian West except during the more intense periods of its own fratricidal struggles.

Despite indifferent success in trying to convert the masses, despite signs that many Chinese resented their proselytizing and that in many districts they were almost as unpopular as railway engineers or tax collectors, the China missions were caught by surprise—more than that, disbelief—when they came under attack. Even the more pessimistic believed that at least they were tolerated.

The worst incident occurred in Taiyüan, the capital of Shansi Province, where forty-five missionaries, Catholic and Protestant, plus a number of Chinese converts, were killed in one day. The provincial governor, Yu Hsien, personally supervised the executions at a chopping block in the courtyard of his palace. (Yu Hsien himself was decapitated as provided by the peace treaty. When the dowager empress and her retinue halted in Taiyüan on their flight to Sian, Yu Hsien boasted to her, "Your Majesty's slave caught them as in a net, and allowed neither chicken nor dog to escape." Tzu Hsi replied that he had done "splendidly.")

The atrocity at Taiyüan shocked the Western nations and

undoubtedly contributed to the severity of the peace terms they demanded. What may be taken as a fairly accurate account was supplied by a Chinese witness, a Baptist convert, who was swept along in a crowd of the townspeople rushing to Governor Yu Hsien's yamen to witness the executions on July 9. This was his recollection:

The first to be led forth was Mr. Farthing [an English Baptist missionary]. His wife clung to him, but he gently put her aside, and going in front of the soldiers knelt down without saying a word, and his head was struck off with one blow of the executioner's knife. He was quickly followed by Mr. Hoddle and Mr. Beynon, Drs. Lovitt and Wilson, each of whom was beheaded by one blow of the executioner's knife. Then the Governor, Yu Hsien, grew impatient and told his bodyguard, all of whom carried heavy swords with long handles, to help kill the others. Mr. Stokes, Mr. Simpson, and Mr. Whitehouse were next killed, the last by one blow, the other two by several.

When the men were finished the ladies were taken. Mrs. Farthing had hold of the hands of her children who clung to her, but the soldiers parted them, and with one blow beheaded their mother. The executioner beheaded all the children and did it skillfully, needing only one blow, but the soldiers were clumsy, and some of the ladies suffered several cuts before death. Mrs. Lovitt was wearing her spectacles and held the hand of her little boy, even when she was killed. She spoke to the people, saying, "We all came to China to bring you the good news of the salvation by Jesus Christ; we have done you no harm, only good. Why do you treat us so?" A soldier took off her spectacles before beheading her. . . .

When the Protestants had been killed, the Roman Catholics were led forward. The Bishop, an old man with a long white beard, asked the Governor why he was doing this wicked deed. I did not hear the Governor give him any answer, but he drew his sword and cut the Bishop across the face with one heavy stroke; blood poured down his white beard and he was beheaded.

The priests and nuns quickly followed him in death. Then Mr. Piggott and his party were led from the district jail which is close by. He was still handcuffed, and so was Mr. Robinson. He preached to the people to the very last, when he was beheaded with one blow. Mr. Robinson suffered death very calmly. Mrs. Piggott held the hand of her son, even when she was beheaded, and he was killed immediately after her. The ladies and two girls were also killed.

On that day forty-five foreigners were beheaded in all, thirty-three Protestants and twelve Roman Catholics. A number of the native Christians were also quickly killed. The bodies of all were left where they fell till the next morning, as it was evening before the work was finished. During the night they had been stripped of their clothing, rings and watches. The next day they were removed to a place inside the great South Gate, except some of the heads, which were placed in cages on the city wall. All were surprised at the firmness and quietness of the foreigners, none of whom except two or three of the children cried or made any noise.

That afternoon of butchery over which Yu Hsien so proudly and ruthlessly presided was paid for, not only with his own life but the blood money extracted from the Chinese people, most of them innocent of any participation in the Boxer outrages, under the title of the Boxer indemnity.

Militant Christianity triumphed temporarily over the ancient religions, not because great numbers of the Chinese were persuaded to accept the cross, but because they were converted to a belief in education. The mandarin class, contemptuous of all Westerners for their lack of subtlety and grace, failed to comprehend the insidious quality of that by-product of missionary work. Like most peoples trying to enter the orbit of scientific and technological progress, the Chinese would be selective about the offerings of the West; they would eventually reject Christ but accept John Dewey (and later Messrs. Marx and Lenin).

Almost en masse the Chinese read into the national humiliation they suffered as a result of the Boxer Rebellion the lesson that Western superiority was inherent in learning skills they could acquire themselves. One church historian has candidly analyzed the psychological effect of the Chinese defeat of 1900:

> The one thing they wanted was schools of the Western learning. They not only flocked to Christian schools, but the government itself set up a Ministry of Education in 1905. In the

same year the old examination system based entirely on the Confucian classics, which had been going on for two thousand years, was abolished. It was England which at the time stood out as the most flourishing nation. It was the British missionaries, none of whom were Catholic, who were prepared to provide the schools and the teachers. So English became the lingua franca, and the popular enthusiasm was for English political ideas. . . . The inevitable by-product of this sudden increase in the educated class was the creation of an intelligentsia. An intelligentsia has been described as a group of educated people in a country which cannot find them any other occupation than that of undermining the traditional institutions which keep that country from being in the front line of "progress." China certainly found herself with this irritant in the early years of the twentieth century.

The process of conversion plus westernization produced the man who led the republican revolution in 1911 which swept the Manchu dynasty into oblivion, both the dowager empress and the Emperor Kuang Hsü having died in 1908 and having left the throne to a boy emperor. That man was Sun Yat-sen, the founder and president of the Chinese Republic, who followed his older brother to Honolulu from their South China village. He attended the Anglican mission's Iolani School, was baptized, and became a lifelong Christian. His brother, angered by his conversion, sent him back to their native village. As proof of his Christian dedication, the youthful Sun Yat-sen smashed the idol in the local temple; this so outraged his fellow villagers that he was forced to flee to Hong Kong. From that British crown colony, from Japan and later in America he organized the revolutionary forces and raised the funds among the overseas Chinese which overthrew the Manchus.

Some who reflected on the lessons of the Boxer Rebellion as they pertained to the various attributes of the Western imperialisms saw the siege of the Peking legations as a sort of microcosm. Superficially it seemed to prove the moral superiority of Christendom. Hadn't the brave band defended the Legation Quarter against hordes of the heathen? The Christian West preferred to ignore the demonstrable fact that the Chinese commander in chief had restrained his own forces in the knowledge that their victory would be a worse disaster than their defeat and attributed the survival of the legations to the natural superiority of the Caucasian race and its official religion. The fact that, even with Jung Lu's benign refusal to use all the force and firepower at his command, the legations could not have been successfully defended without the Japanese, also could be explained away. The Japanese, by all odds the best and bravest of the contingents in Peking, had succumbed to the modern world and thus were sort of honorary Westerners, "plucky little fellows" who obviously had absorbed the teachings of G. A. Henty, Rudyard Kipling, and Horatio Alger.

For all the initial exhilaration over the relief of Peking and the humiliation of China, the victors were soon embroiled in recrimination and controversy, with so many of the survivors' accounts published in the several years following the event that a "battle of memoirs" broke out. Somewhat pointlessly, heroes and villains were nominated, and the "unity of the West" slogan which seemed to arch like a rainbow over the allied legions marching to the rescue of the legations soon sounded hollow indeed. The International Relief Force was an emergency device, not the forerunner of European unity.

Anglo-American propanganda claimed the credit for the "victory" and managed to ignore the fact that the bulk of the relief expedition was composed of Russians and Japanese. The Germans boasted of the ravages inflicted by the East Asiatic Corps. The French glossed over the abject failure of their colonial army.

One of those who flung himself into the controversy was the scholarly Dr. Arthur H. Smith, an American and the author of *China in Convulsion*, who was particularly taken by the theory that the siege proved the superior manhood of the Anglo-Saxon race. "From the first, there was a marked contrast between the Anglo-Saxons and many of the Continentals, who for the most part sat at ease on their shady verandahs, chatting, smoking cigarettes and sipping wine; while their more energetic comrades threw off their coats, plunging into the whirl of work and the tug of toil with the joy of battle inherited from ancestors who lived a millennium and a half ago." Those ancestors, of course, were the hairy Goths who emerged from the German forests to tear down the Roman civilization in somewhat the same spirit as that which animated the Society of Boxers. In any case, the casualty figures did not bear out Dr. Smith's conclusion. The British and the Americans together suffered fifty casualties in the defense of the legations, the continental Europeans almost three times that number.

The published recollections were notable more for acrimony than the tolerance and gratitude and generosity one might expect of people who had shared a terrible ordeal. Just before quitting Peking (with a warrant for his arrest issued by his own government spurring his departure), Bertram Simpson, as he recalled in his memoir, railed at Sir Robert Hart that "he and every other man of position had been tremulously fearing death at every turn for weeks, and had been unwilling to do anything when they might have really saved the situation, merely because they were so afraid; and that everything had been misstated in the reports. . . . I said that this petty life created by men without standards had ended by disgusting me, and that I had finished with it for good. . . ."

M. Pichon, the French minister, suffered heavily in the recollections of the besieged. Back in his homeland he was hailed as "the hero of Peking" and three times served as Foreign Minister, but he was variously termed a poltroon, an alarmist, and a scaremonger by his fellow survivors. Dr. Morrison of the *Times* called him a "craven-hearted cur." Undoubtedly M. Pichon would have found difficulty in finding corroboration of the statement in his memoir, *Dans la Bataille*, that he daily ventured to the French legation sector "under a hail of bullets." His real crime against his fellow diplomats, however, was that he had correctly estimated the danger of the Boxer movement while the others scoffed.

Those whom fate had cast together in Peking during the siege were not a microcosm of Western society but a rather special and exotic collection of diplomats, soldiers, adventurers, and cosmopolites. The ship-of-fools technique could not be applied to their ordeal. The generalizations so boldly drawn, the suggestion that their behavior under fire indicated the soundness of Western civilization, were largely invalid.

Nor were there any black-and-white conclusions to be adduced from studying the conduct of various figures under extreme stress. Some who conducted themselves with gallantry during the sieges of Peking and the Foreign Settlement in Tientsin or in the relief columns did achieve distinction in later life. Herbert Hoover attained the White House; General Chaffee and two young Army lieutenants, Malin Craig and Charles P. Summerall, became Chiefs of Staff. A young American infantryman named Tom Mix, who was shot in the chest during the fighting around Tientsin, was the top cowboy film star during the twenties. Three of the naval officers serving with the British contingent, Roger Keyes, David Beatty, and John Jellicoe, attained fame and high command in World War I.

On the other hand, equally instructive perhaps, there was the checkered history of the Chamots, who conducted themselves with so much vigor, dash, and courage during the siege, and of Bertram Simpson. All three, to the confounding of moralists, distinguished themselves as the most assiduous and expert looters once the moment for heroism and self-abnegation ended.

Auguste Chamot and his American wife won international renown for rescuing the outlying foreign communities trapped by Boxers before the siege began. During the siege, they held out in the Hôtel de Pekin, which served as a rest and rehabilitation center for the defenders of the Franco-Austrian sector of the defense line, and the Irish-American Mme. Chamot was said to have visited the barricades in a zouave uniform to help boost morale. Once the relief columns arrived, however, opportunism replaced self-sacrifice. With his knowledge of the city, Chamot was able to participate in the sack of Peking on a large scale and with an unequaled expertise. The Chamots sailed off to San Francisco with a fortune which enabled them to build two mansions and maintain a yacht. Then their luck ran out. Their houses were destroyed by the 1906 earthquake. Chamot divorced the woman who had shared so many adventures in China. He died a pauper in 1910, at the age of forty-three, after marrying his mistress, a manicurist named Betsy Dollar, on his deathbed.

Bertram Simpson's later career was even more harum-scarum. Sir Claude Macdonald had cited him in dispatches as one of a handful of civilian volunteers who deserved commendation for risking their lives repeatedly on the barricades. His participation in the looting—though not quite as reprehensible as several U.S. Army deserters who took up the leadership of Chinese bandit gangs—caused Sir Claude and General Gaselee to issue a warrant for his arrest. Simpson escaped arrest by staying out of any areas under British control. His vitriolic memoir, *Indiscreet Letters from Peking*, written under the pseudonym B. L. Putnam Weale, shocked readers in 1906 who still believed all they had been taught about the stiffness of the British upper lip, the old school tie, and never letting the side down. He stayed on in China as something of a black sheep, a Maughamesque figure, a participant in some of the more lurid episodes of the warlord years. A political adventurer, he was one of those shadowy advisers behind various freebooters who grasped for power in the twilight of Chinese anarchy. In 1930 he was assassinated in Tientsin by what were vaguely identified as "Chinese political agents."

And there was a curious *memento mori* from the dowager empress. She reputedly left a testament which could be read as a self-indictment or a reflection on the ability of women to govern wisely, which would be a little consolation to all-out admirers of Indira Gandhi or Golda Meir. On her deathbed in November, 1908, in accordance with the ancient custom, she was asked for a final statement, and replied, "Never again allow any woman to hold the supreme power in the state." Posterity would make of that what it would.

To China itself the Boxer Rebellion was of marked significance. It hurried along the modernization which in turn created the conditions that made a continuation of the Manchu dynasty an intolerable anachronism. It was the beginning of almost a half century of struggle, turmoil, and civil war. And a foreshadowing of certain episodes that would occur under Chairman Mao.

The Chinese genius for making something inspirational of the tragic past, for treating history as a creative exercise instead of an objective recital of dull and uninspiring events, was beautifully illumined in the case of the first article of the peace treaty of 1901. That article provided for the construction of a white marble arch in expiation of the murder of the German minister, which was enthusiastically torn down in 1917 when the Chinese Republic joined the Allies in the war against Germany.

"Even before it was taken down," Daniele Vare, a longtime Peking resident, observed, "the actual value of this monument as an object-lesson was doubtful."

The Chinese, in their creative way, made of the monument to

Baron von Ketteler's memory what they wanted it to be. Western tourists often asked their rickshaw coolie or guide who the archway honored. They were invariably told that it was built in honor of the Chinese soldier who killed Baron von Ketteler.

Notes on Sources

The complete listing of most of the sources indicated below under their authors' surnames may be found in the Bibliography, which follows.

Prelude

The dowager empress' edict of November 21, 1899, is quoted by Tan, *The Boxer Catastrophe*, p. 32.

Background of the Chinese secret societies from Bloodworth, *The Chinese Looking Glass*, pp. 150–55; Tan, pp. 43–46, and Steiger, *China and the Occident*, passim.

Li Ping-heng's memorial on the Boxer menace was quoted by Tan, p. 46.

Nathaniel Peffer's observations on the influence of the missionaries are from his *The Far East*, pp. 113–14.

The Boxer handbill issued by the "Lord of Wealth and Happiness" was quoted by Henry Savage Landor, the British correspondent, in *China and the Allies*, Vol. I, pp. 16–17.

Steiger on the origin of Boxers, *op. cit.*, p. 129; Tan's rebuttal, *op. cit.*, p. 38.

The dowager empress' edict calling for organization of a militia, quoted by Tan, p. 41.

The Reverend Mr. Brooks' death at the hands of the Boxers was reported in the *North China Herald*, March 31, 1900.

The dowager empress' edict of January 11, 1900, was cited by Tan, pp. 60–61.

Ridicule of the Boxers' "flummery" was published by the *North China Herald*, March 17, 1900.

1. Foreign Devils First Class

Mrs. Conger's account of her return to China was included in her memoir, *Letters from China*, pp. 85–90.

The development of the Open Door Policy is carefully traced by Peffer, pp. 182–85.

Professor John W. Davis was quoted by Lord, *The Good Years*, p. 7.

Bierce and London were quoted, respectively, in this author's *Jack London: A Biography*, p. 220, and *Ambrose Bierce: A Biography*, 239.

The *Atlantic Monthly* article quoted was "The Future of China," by D. L. Sheffield, January, 1900.

Reflections on pre-1900 Peking society by Bertram Simpson from his *Indiscreet Letters from Peking*, which he published under the pseudonym of B. L. Putnam Weale, pp. 4–5.

Mrs. Conger's account of the audience with the dowager empress is from her memoir, pp. 40–43.

Details of the dowager empress' early career from Charlotte Haldane's and Daniele Vare's biographies.

Observations on the strength of Tzu Hsi's willpower were made by Haldane, pp. 19–20.

Her eunuch's systematic overcharging of the dowager empress on household accounts was cited by Bloodworth, pp. 133–34.

The description of her life-style is included in the Princess Der Ling's *Two Years in the Forbidden City*, pp. 21–22, 65, 77.

The reform decrees of 1898 were quoted by Tan, pp. 20–22.

The Vermilion Rescript was quoted by Haldane, p. 133.

An account of the deposition of the emperor may be found in Tan, pp. 23–25.

2. The Dangerous Month of May

Sir Claude Macdonald's reports to the British Foreign Office were published as *Insurrectionary Movement in China*, H. M.'s Stationery Office, London, 1901.

Bishop Favier's letter asking for guards at the Peitang Cathedral was published in full by Landor, Vol. I, pp. 56–58.

Bertram Simpson's description of the queen's birthday dinner and reception, Weale, pp. 6–8.

Quotations from Mrs. Conger's diary were included in her *Letters from China*, p. 90.

The letter to the newspaper warning foreigners against the Boxer movement was published by the Peking and Tientsin *Times*, May 10, 1900.

Mrs. Conger's observations on foreign colony unit, *op. cit.*, pp. 90–91.

The account of the Squiers family rescue was provided by Polly Condit Smith, who wrote *Behind the Scenes in Peking*, under the pseudonym of Mary Hooker, passim. (Hereafter cited as Hooker.)

Foreign envoys' ultimatum to the Tsungli Yamen, Conger, pp. 91–92.

Simpson's description of the French minister's dinner party, Weale, pp. 12–14.

Simpson described his stroll around the Legation Quarter the night of May 31, *ibid.*, p. 14.

3. The Baron Brandishes a Mailed Fist

Sir Claude Macdonald's cable to the Foreign Office predicting the legations would be the "last place attacked," quoted by Peter Fleming, *The Siege at Peking*, p. 70.

The description of Count von Soden was provided by Weale, p. 1.

U.S. Minister Conger's refusal to part with any of the legation guard, Conger, p. 93.

Boxer attacks on the Peking-Tientsin railroad were recounted by Tan, p. 65.

Cynical Westerner on the subject of those attacks, quoted by Weale, p. 18.

The imperial edict of June 6 was quoted by Tan, p. 67.

Mrs. Conger's preparations for trouble were recalled in her memoir, p. 95.

First Secretary Squiers' comment on the "ill-informed" British legation was quoted by Weale, p. 29.

Sir Claude Macdonald's messages to the naval command at

Tientsin and the Foreign Office were published in *British Blue Books, China No. 4* (1900), Document No. 1.

The English diarist quoted on the Chinese colossus was Simpson; Weale, pp. 21, 23.

Classification of "foreign devils," *ibid.*, 22.

Baron von Ketteler's actions against the Boxers were described by Dr. George E. Morrison in his dispatches to the *Times* of London, which were published October 13 and 15, 1900.

4. The Other Side of the Wall

The imperial decrees of June 13 and 17 were published in the Peking *Gazette* and included in Tan, p. 71, and Steiger, pp. 226–27.

The account of the killing of General Yau by Boxers was translated from the Peking *Gazette* and published by the Shanghai *Mercury*, August 1, 1900.

Proceedings of the Grand Council were described piecemeal by Princess Der Ling in her memoirs (*Two Years in the Forbidden City, Old Buddha*, and *Imperial Incense*), which were secondhand accounts gathered from persons who had attended those urgent sessions; by Tan, pp. 72–75; Haldane, pp. 180–81; Steiger, pp. 226–29.

The Chinese diarist quoted on the Boxers' talisman was a functionary named Ching Shan; J. O. P. Bland and Edward Backhouse, *China Under the Empress Dowager*, p. 279. Hereafter cited as Bland.

Description of dowager empress' "great vehemence," *ibid.*, passim. "The Diary of His Excellency Ching Shan" was obtained by Bland and Backhouse and quoted at length in their own massive work. It was discovered in the ruins of Ching Shan's house and later deposited in the British Museum.

The dowager empress' speech to the Grand Council was quoted by Tan, p. 73.

Emperor Kuang Hsü's speech in opposition quoted by Haldane, p. 192.

Sir Claude's dispatch to the Foreign Office of June 18, *British Blue Books, China No. 4*, 22.

General Jung Lu's letter to the Viceroy of Fukien was included in Haldane, p. 179.

The dowager empress' edict of June 24 identifying the Boxers as "men of the people" was quoted by Steiger, pp. 236–37.

5. A Rush for Sanctuary

Scenes of terror in the Legation Quarter, June 13, were described in Simpson's diary, Weale, pp. 35–36.

Description of slaughter at South Cathedral from Morrison's dispatch in the London *Times*, October 13, 1900.

Ching Shan's description of the burning city from the vantage point of the Forbidden City, quoted by Bland, p. 263.

The flight of the refugees past the U.S. legation was described by Mrs. Conger, p. 103.

Quotations from Nigel Oliphant's diary are from his *A Diary of the Siege of the Legations in Peking*, pp. 17–18, 26–27.

Baron von Ketteler's sharpshooting essay was recalled by Weale, pp. 44–45; Conger, p. 104.

Bertram Simpson's recounting of the hunt for Boxers, Weale, pp. 44–45.

Polly Condit Smith puzzles over what to take with her on the flight from Peking, Hooker, p. 68.

Sir Claude Macdonald's recollection of Baron von Ketteler's decision to go to the Tsungli Yamen, quoted by Fleming, p. 106; Weale, p. 65.

The Boxers' assassination of the German minister, Weale, pp. 65–66; Cordes' account was included in Morrison's lengthy dispatch to the *Times*, October 13, 1900.

How the Foreign Settlement in Tientsin was defended was told by Herbert Hoover, *Memoirs*, Vol. I, pp. 48–50.

The anti-Boxer memorials submitted to the throne by the various viceroys are quoted by Tan, pp. 83–86.

Arthur Smith's recollection of the swarming of refugees to the British legation, *China in Convulsion*, Vol. 1, p. 78.

6. On the Barricades

The Austrian retreat from their sector of the barricades was related by Weale, p. 71.

The death of Professor Huberty James, *ibid.*, p. 77.

Conger quoted on impossibility of throwing themselves on the mercy of the Chinese, Ada Haven Mateer, *Siege Days*, p. 150.

Polly Condit Smith tries to keep peace between the French and German governesses, Hooker, pp. 32–33.

Formation of various committees, Ethel D. Hubbard, *Under Marching Orders*, pp. 164–65.

Admirer quoted on the Reverend Dr. Gamewell's organization of Legation Quarter's defenses, *ibid.*, 166–67.

Morrison's description of the "Carving Knife Brigade," London *Times*, October 13, 1900.

Bertram Simpson's praise of the Japanese contingent's military efficiency, Weale, p. 79.

His disgust with proliferating committees, *ibid.*, p. 82.

Polly Condit Smith's description of children playing Boxers, Hooker, pp. 55–56.

Young Fargo Squiers' feat of collecting rations from Imbeck's store, *ibid.*, pp. 58–60.

The panicky abandonment of much of the perimeter on June 22 was related by Weale, pp. 83–84, and by the Reverend Gilbert Reid in an article published by the Shanghai *Mercury* months later.

Collection of material for the sandbag-making industry was recounted by Hubbard, pp. 169–71.

Extinguishing fires set by torch-bearing Chinese infiltrators, Reid, *op. cit.*

The fire set in the Hanlin Library was described by Weale, pp. 95–97; Hooker, pp. 76–77.

U.S. diplomat's description of himself as "Major General of the Corpses" because of his burial detail, Hooker, p. 77.

Polly Smith's dialogue with Mrs. Conger, quoted in Hooker, p. 81.

Miss Evans' diary was quoted by Mateer, p. 150.

Discovery of General Gordon's report advising Chinese on night-fighting tactics was recorded by Oliphant, p. 72.

The Japanese devise a death trap for the Chinese attackers, Weale, p. 72.

7. *The Fish in the Stewpan*

Tientsin's ordeal under fire was described by Hoover, *op. cit.*, Vol. I, pp. 48–52.

Mrs. James Jones' account of her experiences in the siege of Tientsin was published by the Shanghai *Mercury*, July 19, 1900.

Washington's attitude toward the events in North China was recapitulated by Margaret Leech, *In the Days of McKinley*, pp. 519–20.

Smedley D. Butler's recollection of his regiment's sailing from Manila for Tientsin, Butler, *Old Gimlet Eye*, passim.

Herbert Hoover serves as guide for the U.S. force joining in the attack on the Native City, Hoover, Vol. I, p. 53.

Details of the attack on the Native City may be found in the Marine Corps archives, National Archives, and succinctly in Richard P. Weinert's "The Battle of Tientsin," *American History Illustrated*, November, 1966.

The sack of Tientsin's Native City was described in her article by Mrs. Jones and by Henry Savage Landor, who had accompanied the allied forces, Landor, Vol. I, pp. 190–91, 199, 202.

Joaquin Miller's stay as guest of the Herbert Hoovers, Hoover, Vol. I, p. 53.

8. *A Mysterious Cease-Fire*

Polly Condit Smith's description of the "Peking smell," Hooker, p. 91.

Simpson's description of the enemy soldiery "grouped together in one mass of color," Weale, p. 110.

An account of the palace intrigue which resulted in the cease-fire was given in "The Diary of Ching Shan," quoted by Bland, passim.

Sir Claude Macdonald's notes of June 24 were included in the government document, *Insurrectionary Movement in China*, pp. 25, 28.

Polly Smith's character sketches of various personalities is from Hooker, pp. 95–97.

Simpson's description of the hospital in the British legation, Weale, p. 124.

The recollections of the American missionary nurse of her hospital duty were quoted by Mateer, pp. 234–35.

Polly Smith recalls how they boiled rice water, Hooker, pp. 90–91.

Her recollection of what "giving up the Wall" meant to the besieged, *ibid.*, p. 94.

Nigel Oliphant's description of the counterattack to retake part of the Tatar Wall is from his memoir, pp. 78, 79.

9. The Shock Wave from Peking

The London *Daily Mail's* "Peking Massacre" story under a Shanghai dateline appeared July 16, 1900.

The London *Times* editorial on the subject was published July 17, 1900.

The *Times'* investigation into the "massacre" hoax was detailed in a letter from *Times* correspondent Morrison to Moberly Bell, general manager of the newspaper, dated October 20, 1900, and was quoted by Fleming, pp. 138–39.

The Kaiser's reaction to the supposed massacre and his invention of the Yellow Peril are recounted by Virginia Cowles, *The Kaiser*, pp. 148–49, 177–78.

The "ponderous calm" in Washington was detailed by Leech, pp. 520–22.

The exchange between the State Department and Minister Conger, *ibid.,* p. 522.

10. The Fabrication of "Old Betsy"

Norwegian missionary's nervous collapse and subsequent actions were recounted by Weale, p. 180, and Fleming, p. 151.

Typical menu offered those besieged in the British legation was provided by Mateer, pp. 196–97.

Polly Condit Smith's comments on the problem of arranging the food supply, Hooker, pp. 106–7.

The heroic labors of Dr. Gamewell in bolstering the fortifications were related by Hubbard, pp. 168–69.

Simpson's description of the ineffectiveness of the Italian one-pounder, Weale, p. 133.

His comments on the boring routine of manning the loopholes and on large numbers of shirkers in the British compound, *ibid.,* pp. 136, 146–47.

Polly Smith's remarks on the lackluster performance of the Italian contingent, Hooker, p. 95.

Correspondent Morrison's criticism of Captain Hall's effectiveness as a commander, quoted from his diary by Fleming, p. 142.

Dan Daly's exploit on the Tatar Wall is described by Stan Bair in "Fightingest Marine," *Above and Beyond the Call of Duty*, pp. 154–55.

The death of Captain Strouts and the wounding of Correspondent Morrison were related by Hooker, pp. 110–14.

11. Not Peace, Not War

The July 7 memorial to the throne from provincial viceroys was quoted by Fleming, p. 166.

Sightseer's surprise at the strength and complexity of the Chinese fortifications, quoted by Weale, pp. 156–57.

Description of fraternization with enemy soldiers, *ibid.*, pp. 157–59.

The exchanges between Sir Claude Macdonald and Prince Ching are included in *British Blue Book, China No. 4*, passim.

Strengthening of fortifications during truce was recounted by Weale, p. 162.

Domestic life in the besieged compound was sketched by Mateer, pp. 152, 237–38.

Neglect of Chinese Christians in Prince Su's palace was recorded by Weale, pp. 165–66, and Hooker, pp. 162–63. It is significant that the besieged diplomatic personnel and their guests failed to share the food supply with the Chinese, while at the Peitang Cathedral, under Bishop Favier's supervision, Caucasians and Chinese shared equally.

Morrison's comment on "British petulance" over being forced to admit the message from Tientsin was written by a British consul, quoted by Fleming, p. 175.

Simpson's list of the rumors which preoccupied the besieged, Weale, pp. 174–75.

Ching Shan's observations on family quarrels in the Forbidden City and among the dowager empress' advisers, quoted by Bland, pp. 281, 291, 293, 294.

The impact of General Li Ping-heng on morale at the Manchu court was conveyed by Tan, pp. 104–6.

Yuan Chang's memorial to the throne urging the suppression of the Boxers and its fatal consequences for its author, Bland, p. 309.

12. The International Relief Force

The march from Tientsin to Peking by the International Relief Force is described in detail in the memoir of one of its commanders, Colonel A. S. Daggett, *America in the China Relief*

Expedition. He commanded the Fourteenth Infantry. A more cogent essay on the subject is Richard P. Weinert's "The Capture of Peking," *American History Illustrated,* January, 1968.

A description of the Boxer activities in and around Newchang was published by the Shanghai *Mercury,* August 7, 1900.

The War Office report on logistical difficulties of the British contingent was cited by Fleming, p. 180.

Smedley D. Butler's recollection of the march to the capital, *op. cit.,* pp. 67, 69.

The battle of Yangtsun was detailed by Daggett, passim.

Roger Keyes' characterization of the French force, quoted by his biographer, Ceil Aspinall-Oglander, *Roger Keyes,* p. 48.

Butler's description of the sacking of Tungchow, *op. cit.,* p. 71.

General Li Ping-heng's report to Peking on the disasters suffered by the Chinese forces and their disorderly retreat, quoted by Tan, p. 110.

General Gaselle's refusal to commit arson, Fleming, p. 192.

13. The Ordeal Comes to an End

Polly Condit Smith's remarks on the message from the Tsungli Yamen, Hooker, p. 163.

Simpson's puzzlement at the Chinese attitude, Weale, p. 177.

His description of the Japanese success in buying Chinese ammunition, of the increase in the fighting, and the entry into Peking of the Chinese forces routed by the relief expedition, Weale, pp. 178, 186–90.

Mrs. Conger's "unearthly serenity" was noted by Polly Condit Smith in her diary, Hooker, p. 125.

The conciliatory note from the Tsungli Yamen and Sir Claude Macdonald's comment on its contents, Victor Purcell, *The Boxer Uprising,* p. 255.

The desperate effort to hold the Mongol Market sector was described by Weale, pp. 189–90.

Sir Claude's journal entry recording the sounds of the advancing relief columns was quoted by Purcell, p. 255.

14. The Footrace to Peking

The relief columns' approach to Peking, particularly the Americans' participation, is covered in Colonel Daggett's memoir and

W. H. Chalmers' biography of his superior, *The Life of Lieutenant General Chaffee*, passim.

Calvin Titus' wall-scaling feat, Daggett, p. 211.

British staff officer quoted as having feared the Legation Quarter had fallen to the Chinese, Fleming, p. 204.

Simpson recalls the "smell of India," Weale, p. 203.

General Gaselle's appearance at the British compound was related by Hooker, pp. 176–78.

General Chaffee's reception at the American quarters was recorded in Conger, p. 161.

Polly Smith pulls wires to get out of Peking on the first boat downriver, Hooker, pp. 180–81.

Assault on August 15 on Imperial City and comments on spectators who gathered to watch, Weale, p. 217.

General Chaffee's curt order to storm the Imperial City's ramparts, Daggett, p. 228.

American bitterness over having the assault called off, Weale, p. 219.

The tragic fate of Father Addosio was recorded in her diary by Polly Smith, Hooker, p. 177.

Description of Peitang Cathedral, Landor, Vol. II, pp. 218–19.

Bishop Favier's remarks on the siege of his cathedral, *ibid.,* pp. 240–41.

Reverend Gilbert Reid's reportage on the Peitang siege was published by the Shanghai *Mercury.*

Bishop Favier's account of the first attacks, Landor, Vol. II, pp. 228–29.

Sister Vincenza's story of rescuing Lieutenant Olivieri was recorded by Daniele Vare, *The Last Empress*, pp. 310–16.

Reverend Roland Allen's remarks on the "moral letdown" among those who survived the legations' siege are from his memoir, *The Siege of the Peking Legations*, p. 257.

15. The Flight of the Empress

Interview with Li Hung-chang in Shanghai appeared in the *Times* of London, July 23, 1900.

Li Hung-chang's memorial to the dowager empress was quoted by Bland, pp. 389–91.

The dowager empress' reflections on leaving Peking were quoted by the Princess Der Ling, pp. 180–82.

Mrs. Ker's recollection of Tzu Hsi's quarters, Vare, p. 225.

The imperial flight from the capital was recounted by Bland, pp. 340–51; Tan, pp. 116, 117, the latter from Chinese documents.

Description of the viceregal palace in Sian, Bland, p. 355.

Conspiracy for a *coup d'état* while the dowager empress was in Sian, Tan, pp. 88–89.

Viceroy Yu Lu's admission of error and suicide, *ibid.,* pp. 100–1.

Dr. Arthur H. Smith's meditations on why the Peking legations hadn't been attacked with greater force, *China in Convulsion,* Vol. II, p. 508. Simpson on the same subject, Weale, p. 242.

Sir Robert Hart's remarks on the "intervention" that may have spared the legations, *These from the Land of Sinim,* p. 40.

Account of how Tung Fu-hsiang had sought Jung Lu's impeachment is drawn from Vare, p. 221.

Sir Claude Macdonald on the curious restraints imposed on Jung Lu's troops, *British Blue Book, China No. 4,* p. 30.

Dowager empress recalls how Jung Lu condemned the Boxers, Princess Der Ling, pp. 359–62.

Jung Lu's withdrawal from the capital against orders from the dowager empress, Tan, p. 134.

16. The Sack of Peking

Beginning of looting recorded by a missionary, Allen, p. 231.

British correspondent observes feeble attempt to prevent looting, Landor, Vol. II, pp. 242–43.

Polly Smith on suicides among the Chinese, Hooker, p. 191.

Bertram Simpson recalls trading in stolen silks, Weale, p. 228.

"Very animated" generals' conference on looting, Hooker, p. 187.

Polly Smith describes her own temptations, Hooker, pp. 188–91.

An American captain's profitless ventures as a looter, Butler, pp. 76–78.

Simpson describes the search for gold under the Treasury, Weale, pp. 277–85.

Russian general makes off with ten trunks full of liberated valuables, Witte, *The Memoirs of Count Witte,* edited by Adam Yarmolinsky, p. 245.

U.S. minister allows himself to be conned out of possession of Prince Li's palace and its silver hoard, Hooker, p. 198; Reid's Shanghai *Mercury* article.

Quarrel of the French and Germans over the antique instruments in the Peking Observatory, Conger, p. 177.

Simpson's description of Russian convoy loaded with loot and "little fortunes" made by foreign envoys, Weale, pp. 241, 258, 260, 290, 293.

British officer quoted on Lady Macdonald "earnestly devoting herself to looting," Fleming, p. 243.

Simpson's stormy interview with his superior, Weale, p. 276.

Field Marshal Count von Waldersee recalls circumstances of his dispatch to China with the East Asiatic Corps, Waldersee, *A Field Marshal's Memoirs*, passim.

The British view of Waldersee's appearance on the Peking scene, Weale, pp. 301, 303.

His challenge to a German officer, *ibid.*, pp. 307–8.

General James H. Wilson described his participation in the occupation of Peking in his *Under the Old Flag*, Vol. II., pp. 521–35.

His description of the interview with Waldersee and his orders against looting, *ibid.*, pp. 525, 526.

His account of the Anglo-American operation against Patachow, *ibid.*, pp. 527–29, 531.

General Wilson's comment on the gulf between British and Indian officers, *ibid.*, p. 534.

British officer quoted on the effect of joint British and German operations in the countryside around Peking, Fleming, p. 253.

Russian Minister of War quoted on using Boxer Rebellion as excuse for seizing Manchurian provinces, Witte, p. 109.

Prince Radziwill's letter was quoted by Vare, pp. 242–43.

Russian minister to Tokyo's report on Japanese objectives, quoted by Tan, p. 181.

President McKinley's maneuver to withdraw from the Chinese imbroglio was recounted by Leech, p. 526.

The text of the Tseng Chi-Alexeiev agreement was published by the *Times* of London, January 3, 1901.

17. Peace, Indemnity, Decapitations

The victory parade in Peking was described by Landor, Vol. II, pp. 370–79.

U.S. State Department's distrust of Li Hung-chang, Leech, p. 522.

Li Hung-chang's interview with U.S. Minister, Conger, p. 187.

Mrs. Conger's reflections on the futility of continuing the partition of China, *ibid.,* pp. 188–89.

Attitude of Grand Council toward allied demands contained in their Joint Note, Tan, passim.

Li Hung-chang urges acceptance of allied terms, *ibid.,* p. 156.

Mrs. Conger's conviction that American soldiers were more humane than others, Conger, p. 194.

English historians quoted on the dowager empress' belief she could eventually return to Peking without being punished, Bland, p. 324.

Twelve men nominated by allies as "deserving death," *British Blue Books, China No. 6,* pp. 157, 158.

The enforced suicides of three Manchu officials were described by Bland, pp. 370–73.

The terms of the Boxer indemnity were contained in *Foreign Relations of the United States,* Washington, 1902, pp. 87, 127–29, 141–43, 145, 275–78.

Mark Twain's comments on "dollar civilization" and its emissaries were contained in an article he wrote for the New York *Herald,* December 30, 1900, and "To a Person Sitting in Darkness," *North American Review,* February, 1901.

18. Tzu Hsi Returns to the Dragon Throne

The dowager empress confided her worries over her possessions to Princess Der Ling, p. 184.

Her Penitential Decree was quoted by Bland, pp. 376–77.

Mrs. Conger's description of Li Hung-chang's funeral, Conger, pp. 212–15.

Wu Yung's description of the Imperial Chariot on its return to Peking, *The Flight of an Empress,* p. 245.

The poet who saluted the Locomotive God was William Ellery Leonard, a professor at the University of Wisconsin, who never left Madison because of his pathological fear of trains.

Mrs. Conger witnesses the arrival of the Imperial party, Conger, p. 216.

The young Italian who witnessed the welcoming ceremony, Don Rodolfo, was quoted by Vare, pp. 259–61.

Dowager empress' reception for the ladies of the diplomatic corps, Conger, pp. 220–25.

Her private resentment of American visitors' demands, Princess Der Ling, pp. 175, 362.

Her hatred of Christianity and its works, *ibid.,* pp. 76, 177–79, 356.

Death toll of missionaries and Chinese Christians during the Boxer Rebellion, Columba Cary-Elwes, *China and the Cross*, pp. 224–225.

The legend of St. Thomas' connection with China is explored by Cary-Elwes, *ibid.,* p. 10.

The Boxer massacre at Taiyüan is detailed by Smith, *China in Convulsion*, Vol. II, passim.

Church historian quoted on psychological effects of the Boxer Rebellion, Cary-Elwes, p. 227.

Correspondent Morrison's characterization of M. Pichon as a "Craven-hearted cur," quoted by Fleming, p. 147.

Cowboy star Tom Mix's participation in the Tientsin campaign is detailed in *The Fabulous Tom Mix*, by Olive Stokes Mix (with Eric Heath), passim.

The later career of the Chamots was traced by Dr. P. Campiche, "Notes on the Career of Auguste Chamot," *Revue Historique Vaudoise*, March, 1955.

The supposed last words of the dowager empress were quoted by Bland, p. 466.

The Chinese conversion of the purpose behind the monument to Baron von Ketteler was related by Vare, pp. 251–52.

Selected Bibliography

ALLEN, REVEREND ROLAND, *The Siege of the Peking Legations*. London, 1901.

ASPINALL-OGLANDER, CECIL, *Roger Keyes*. London, 1951.

BLAND, J. O. P., and BACKHOUSE, E., *China Under the Empress Dowager*. London, 1912.

BLOODWORTH, DENNIS, *The Chinese Looking Glass*. New York, 1967.

BROMHALL, MARSHALL, *Martyred Missionaries of the China Inland Missions*. Toronto, 1901.

BUTLER, SMEDLEY D., as told to Lowell Thomas, *Old Gimlet Eye*. New York, 1933.

CARTER, W. H., *The Life of Lieutenant General Chaffee*. Chicago, 1917.

CARY-ELWES, COLUMBA, *China and the Cross*. New York, 1957.

CHALMERS, W. S., *The Life of Beatty*. London, 1951.

CLEMENTS, PAUL HENRY, *The Boxer Rebellion*. New York, 1915.

CONGER, SARAH PIKE, *Letters from China*. Chicago, 1909.

COWLES, VIRGINIA, *The Kaiser*. New York, 1963.

DAGGET, A. S., *America in the China Relief Expedition*. Kansas City, 1903.

DER LING, PRINCESS, *Two Years in the Forbidden City*. New York, 1931.

FLEMING, PETER, *The Siege at Peking*. London, 1959.

FORSYTH, ROBERT C., *The China Martyrs of 1900*. Chicago, 1904.

HALDANE, CHARLOTTE, *The Last Great Empress of China*. Indianapolis, 1966.

HART, SIR ROBERT, *These from the Land of Sinim*. London, 1901.

HOOKER, MARY, *Behind the Scenes in Peking*. London, 1910.

HOOVER, HERBERT, *The Memoirs of Herbert Hoover*. New York, 1951. 2 vols.

HUBBARD, ETHEL D., *Under Marching Orders*. New York, 1909.

LANDOR, HENRY SAVAGE, *China and the Allies*. New York, 1901. 2 vols.

LEECH, MARGARET, *In the Days of McKinley*. New York, 1959.

LORD, WALTER, *The Good Days*. New York, 1960.

MATEER, ADA HAVEN, *Siege Days.* Chicago, 1903.

MIX, OLIVE STOKES, with ERIC HEATH, *The Fabulous Tom Mix.* New York, 1957.

O'CONNOR, RICHARD, *Pacific Destiny.* Boston, 1969.

OLIPHANT, NIGEL, *A Diary of the Siege of the Legations in Peking.* London, 1901.

PARKER, WILLIAM, ed., *Above and Beyond the Call of Duty.* New York, 1963.

PAYEN, CECILE, *Besieged in Peking.* New York, 1903.

PEFFER, NATHANIEL, *The Far East.* Ann Arbor, 1958.

PURCELL, VICTOR, *The Boxer Uprising.* Cambridge, England, 1963.

RANSOME, JESSIE, *The Story of the Siege Hospital.* London, 1901.

SMITH, ARTHUR H., *China in Convulsion.* Chicago, 1901. 2 vols.

STEIGER, GEORGE N., *China and the Occident.* New Haven, 1926.

TAN, CHESTER C., *The Boxer Catastrophe.* New York, 1955.

TUTTLE, A. H., *Mary Gamewell and Her Story of the Siege.* New York, 1907.

VARE, DANIELE, *The Last Empress.* London, 1936.

WALDERSEE, COUNT ALFRED VON, *A Field Marshal's Memoirs.* London, 1924.

WEALE, B. L. PUTNAM, *Indiscreet Letters from Peking.* London, 1906.

WILSON, JAMES H., *Under the Old Flag.* New York, 1912. 2 vols.

WITTE, COUNT, *The Memoirs of Count Witte,* edited by Adam Yarmolinsky. London, 1921.

WU YUNG, *The Flight of an Empress.* London, 1937.

Periodicals

Atlantic Monthly

North American Review

Revue Historique Vaudoise

American History Illustrated

North China Herald

Shanghai *Mercury*

New York *Times*

New York *Herald*

London *Times*

London *Daily Mail*

Acknowledgments

For assistance in research the author is indebted to the Public Records Office, Chancery Lane, for obtaining Royal Navy documents; to the National Archives in Washington; to the staffs of the Reading Room of the British Museum, the London Library, the library of Trinity College, Dublin, the newspaper library of the New York Public Library, the Atheneum of Boston, the Boston Public Library, the Hoover Library at Stanford University, the Bangor (Maine) Public Library and the western history department of the Denver Public Library.

INDEX

Index